818-06

Housing the Poor in Suburbia

Housing the Poor in Suburbia:

Public Policy at the Grass Roots

by
Charles M. Haar
Louis D. Brandeis Professor of Law
Harvard University

and
Demetrius S. Iatridis
Research Professor and
Professor of Social Planning
Boston College

Ballinger Publishing Company • Cambridge, Mass.
A Subsidiary of J.B. Lippincott Company

Copyright © 1974 by Ballinger Publishing Company. All rights reserved. No part of this publication may be reproduced, stored in a retrieval system, or transmitted in any form or by any means, electronic mechanical photocopy, recording or otherwise, without the prior written consent of the publisher.

International Standard Book Number: 73-11477

Library of Congress Catalog Card Number: 0-88410-405-2

Printed in the United States of America

Library of Congress Cataloging in Publication Data

Haar, Charles Monroe, 1921-
    Housing the poor in suburbia.

    1. Housing—United States—Case studies. 2. Poor—United States—Case studies. 3. Suburbs—United States—Case studies. I. Iatridis, Demetrius S., joint author. II. Title.
HD7290.H3   301.5'4   73-11477
ISBN 0-88410-405-2

For Mary and Nan

Contents

List of Figures	xx
List of Tables	xx
List of Maps	xx
Preface	xx
Introduction	1
Part One: Policy Perspectives on the Controversy	7
Chapter One **Suburbia: The Emerging Centerpiece of Urban America**	9
Chapter Two **Public Policy at the Grass Roots**	11
Chapter Three **Planned Social Change**	19
Part Two: Five Comunity Case Studies	23
Chapter Four **Newton: The Exceptional Suburb?**	25
The Exceptional Suburb	25

viii Contents

The Community	28
The N.C.D.F.: Its Strategy and Proposal	47
Public Reaction	77
An Ordinary Suburb?	109
A New Strategy: Toward 774	110
The State Looks at Newton	123
Reluctant, Paradoxical Partners	128

Chapter Five
Concord: The Freedom Suburb   133

The Community	133
Concord Home Owning Corporation: Its Strategy and Proposal	142
The Chapter 774 Proceedings	154

Chapter Six
Canton: The Suburb Encounters the Change Agent   159

The Community	161
The Change Agent	171
Controversy	176
Defeat	185

Chapter Seven
East Providence: The Atypical Suburb   189

The Community	189
The Press Reports	200
Riverside: Phase One	200
Riverside: Phase Two	211
Federal Pressure	219
Grass-Roots Response	228
The People Vote	235

Chapter Eight
Stoughton: The Successful Suburb   239

The Success Story	239
The Community	239
The Change Agents	248
The Great Trade-Off	252

Stoughton Revisited 255
 The Residents of Presidential Courts 256
 The Cooperative Way of Life 259
 Interaction with the Community 273
 Initial Arguments Reviewed 277

Part Three: A Discussion Framework: Policies, Programs, and Dilemmas 283

Chapter Nine
The Suburb as a Metropolitan Unit 285

Chapter Ten
Public Policy Options 319

Federal Policies and Equal Opportunities 319
Federal Housing Policy Alternatives 345
Federal Housing Programs: Sections 235 and 236 347
The Role of the State 353
Regional and Metropolitan Approaches 368

Chapter Eleven
Social, Judicial, and Institutional Change Strategies 373

Social Change 373
The Process of Change and Its Community Context 378
Planned Interventions 386
Judges as Change Agents 392

About the Authors 431

List of Figures

Newton 1.	Land Use Map Newton	26
Newton 2.	Income Distribution in Newton: A Comparison of 1960 and 1970 Census	30
Concord 1.	Land Use Map Concord	135
Concord 2.	Income Distribution in Concord	138
Concord 3.	Concord—the Proposed Site	144
Concord 4.	Problems of the Wheeler Site for High Density Development	145
Canton 1.	Land Use Map Canton	165
Canton 2.	Income Distribution in Canton (1960 and 1970 Compared)	167
East Providence 1.	Income Distribution in East Providence	190
East Providence 2.	New Residential Construction	198
East Providence 3.	Land Use Map East Providence	197
Stoughton 1.	Income Distribution in Stoughton	242
Stoughton 2.	Land Use Map Stoughton	245
1a.	White Attitudes Toward Residential Integration	289
1b.	Blacks in Neighborhoods	289
1c.	Blacks Next Door	290
2	Attitudes and Preferences of Low- and Moderate-Income Households	291
3	Attitudes of Suburban Residents	291

List of Tables

Newton 1.	Income Distribution in Newton 1960-1970; and Poverty Indicators	31
Newton 1a.	Population in Newton 1960-1970	31
Newton 1b.	Selected Demographic Characteristics 1970	31
Newton 2.	Employment and Payrolls—1970	34
Newton 3.	Labor Force Characteristics 1970—Newton	34
Newton 4.	Apartment Characteristics	38
Newton 5.	New Housing Units in Newton—1960-1969	39
Newton 6.	Apartment Zoned Land	40
Newton 7.	Tax Revenue Comparision: Apartment vs. Other Residential Use	40
Newton 8.	Land Use as Percentage of Total	40
Newton 9.	Tax Exempt and Taxable Land	42
Newton 10.	Selected Housing Characteristics 1970—Newton	42
Newton 11.	Size and Sex Characteristics of Apartment Residents	44
Newton 12.	Apartment Resident Characteristics Per Apartment	44
Newton 13.	Rental Structure	44
Newton 14.	Newton Community Development Foundation (NCDF) Proposals: Characteristics and Impact Indicators	68
Newton 15.	Newton Community Development Foundation (NCDF) Sites Analysis by The Newton Planning Department	87
Newton 16.	Site-by-Site Overview of the Planning Department's Professional Judgment	88
Newton 17.	Six NCDF Sites	118
Concord 1.	Income Distribution in Concord 1960-1970; and Poverty Indicators	137

Concord 2.	Population in Concord 1960-1970	137
Concord 3.	Selected Demographic Characteristics 1970	137
Concord 4.	Labor Force Characteristics 1970—Concord	139
Concord 5.	Selected Housing Characteristics 1970—Concord	140
Canton 1.	Income Distribution in Canton 1960-1970; and Poverty Indicators	162
Canton 2.	Population 1960-1970	162
Canton 3.	Selected Demographic Characteristics 1970	162
Canton 4.	Population 1950-1970 Canton Region	163
Canton 5.	Land Use Acreage Summary 1959-1971	166
Canton 6.	Area Requirements by Residential Zones	166
Canton 7.	Vacant Land (in Acres) by Zones	168
Canton 8.	Selected Housing Characteristics 1970—Canton	169
Canton 9.	Labor Force Characteristics 1970—Canton	170
East Providence 1.	Income Distribution in East Providence 1960-1970; and Poverty Indicators (1960)	191
East Providence 2.	Population 1960-1970	191
East Providence 3.	Selected Demographic Characteristics 1970	191
East Providence 4.	Ethnic Composition 1970	192
East Providence 5.	Labor Force Characteristics 1970—East Providence	192
East Providence 6.	Selected Housing Characteristics 1970—East Providence	196
Stoughton 1.	Income Distribution in Stoughton 1960-1970; and Poverty Indicators	240
Stoughton 2.	Population 1960-1970	240
Stoughton 3.	Selected Demographic Characteristics 1970	240
Stoughton 4.	Firms by Industry	243
Stoughton 5.	Labor Force Characteristics 1970—Stoughton	243

The Five Communities Compared

1A.	Population by Age—1960	292
1B.	Population by Age—1970	293
1C.	Changes in Population By Age Group—1960-1970	294
1D.	Median Population Age and Changes—1960-1970	295
2A.	Household Size—1960-1970	295
2B.	Families and Families with Children Under 18— 1960-1970	296
3.	Educational Indicators—1972	297
4.	Racial Composition 1960-1970	298
5A.	Family Income—1960	299
5B.	Family Income—1970	300
5C.	1960-1970 Changes in Family Income By Income Bracket	301
5D.	Median Family Income—1960-1970	302

5E.	Income Below Poverty Level—1970	303
6A.	Occupations of Residents—1970	304
6B.	Change in Occupations of Residents By Occupation—1960-190 (In Percent)	305
7A.	Employed Residents—1970 (In Percent)	306
7B.	Resident Labor Force Employed in County of Residence—1960-1970	307
7C.	Persons Employed Locally—By Industry	308
8.	Taxation	309
9.	Political Party Registration—1962-1972 (In Percent)	310
10A.	Housing Units—1970	311
10B.	Housing Units Change—1960-1970 (In Percent)	312
10C.	Characteristics of Housing Units—1970 (In Percent)	313
11.	Value of Specified Owner-Occupied Units—1970	314
12.	Characteristics of Vacant Year-Round Units Owner-Occupied	315
12a.	Densities of All Occupied Units (Onwer)	315
13.	Characteristics of Vacant Year-Round Units Renter-Occupied—1970	316
13a.	Densities of All Occupied Units (Renter)	316
14.	Gross Rents Specified Renter Occupied 1970	317
15.	Zoning-Percent of Total Land by Category	318

List of Maps

Eastern Massachusetts		24
Newton	Recreation—Conservation Plan	29
	Thoroughfare Plan	33
	School Plan	35
	Apartment Development 1960-1969	37
	Location of Proposed NCDF Sites in the City: The Scattered Site Strategy	57
	Proposed NCDF Site #1—Pine and River Streets	58
	Proposed NCDF Site #2—Jasset Street	59
	Proposed NCDF Site #3—Hunnewell Avenue	60
	Proposed NCDF Site #4—Stanton Avenue	61
	Proposed NCDF Site #5—Commonwealth Avenue	62
	Proposed NCDF Site #6—Beacon Street	63
	Proposed NCDF Site #7—Hamlet Street	64
	Proposed NCDF Site #8—Thurston Road	65
	Proposed NCDF Site #9—Goddard and Christina Streets	66
	Proposed NCDF Site #10—Dedham Street	67

Preface

This book could not have been brought to completion without valuable help from many individuals and sources who readily contributed time, effort, money, and inspiration. To all, we are deeply indebted.

Our students at Boston College and Harvard University, who have used versions of these case studies over the past few years, provided practical suggestions regarding the nature of the case studies, their usefulness in promoting learning, and the desirable structure for presenting them in a manner which enhances policy-oriented understanding and intellectual challenge. Several of our students have also contributed as workshop participants in data collection and interviews; this work proved invaluable in keeping up with developments in several communities simultaneously over a long period of time.

Various participants joined our seminar-workshops and provided unique insights of the intellectual and emotional conflicts and dilemmas generated in those caught in their community's conflict; some were able to go over parts of the manuscripts to ensure that facts or views presented in the five case studies were realistically objective and correct, particularly when viewpoints on specific issues were incomplete or unclear. We were painfully aware all along that our own ideological bias or the unconscious distortions of reality by those who provided information and insights could inadvertently penetrate the manuscript. That our professional inclination supports residential desegregation as a conscious national policy objective prompted us to check even more carefully the facts presented in order to prevent partiality and to present controversial views on an equal footing so that the reader can formulate his own judgment. If in spite of this effort for objectivity, inaccuracies occur in the description of the five case studies, we earnestly apologize in advance. Those concerned may rest assured that such possible errors were not deliberate.

We wish to express our thanks to the Harvard Interfaculty Seminar on Housing, financed by the Ford Foundation, which provided support to complete the last stages of the study.

Introduction

This book has grown out of a pair of connected convictions: first, one of substance, that racial integration of the nation's residential patterns, most particularly through the location of low-income housing in suburbia and the deep-rooted community conflict it has generated, is the most crucial domestic urban issue facing America in the 70s; and second, one of procedure, that grand generalizations about this have to be tested "in concrete," with a deep understanding emerging only out of the details of experience and the testing of theory in the crucible of community conflict and accommodation. The increasingly intense confrontation of low-cost housing and suburbia raises fundamental questions about the adequacy of the mechanisms of adaptation and integration to precipitate change in the urban system through rational, collaborative, and cooperative efforts.

Facts and feelings surrounding this major dilemma of postindustrial urban America are frequently confused. Little is known about what actually transpires when the suburbs are asked to introduce low-income housing in their midst. The few published accounts have been brief and fragmented; they frequently have presented one viewpoint only. Little has been discerned about the implications of the issue for other public policy concerns—jobs, social mobility, civil rights, metropolitan development, the quality of life itself.

Moreover, most accounts to date have not considered adequately the broader context of the suburb as a central component of the urban social system. They stand aloof, unrelated to an accepted body of knowledge about social behavior and public policy making and its implementation. In fact, much less is known about planned processes and methods to induce innovations at the suburban level than is known at the inner-city local level where most of the efforts at community organization have thus far been practiced.

This book is addressed to this deficiency. The five community studies presented—Newton, Concord, Canton, East Providence, and Stoughton—

represent an effort to place the conflict of societal values and geographic socioeconomic segregation generated by low-income housing in the suburbs within a broader social policy perspective. Selected from among several similar studies carried out by the authors during the last six years, the cases depict the very controversies now undergoing intense debate in America's legislative halls, courtrooms, municipalities, and town meetings. But, more than that, they highlight the sociopolitical processes within suburban America and its leadership, and community participation in decision making and its reaction and accommodation to federal and state policies concerning housing and urban development. Through the conflict—indeed, in some ways flowing from it—the fundamental community organization and planned change processes of the contemporary suburb spring into sharper focus.

The book may well be of interest to the general public, to urban planners and policy makers, to organizations and officials involved in housing or civil rights, and to social scientists concerned with planned social change, conflict resolution, or public policy formulation. But it is primarily designed for teaching and training purposes. The materials have been selected for in-depth analysis by students, and it is this purpose that has directed the way in which the cases have been presented. Part I provides a broad public policy perspective for the analysis of the five case studies which appear in detail in Part II. Part III focuses on conceptual issues underlying the cases; through selected topics, questions and discussion, it develops the housing issues in the context of urban planning and development, civil rights, mobility, and assimilation, as well as within judicial and legislative considerations, in order to facilitate understanding of the available options and the frontiers of institutional change.

The cases have not been selected to verify, disprove, or suggest a theory. The "state of art" in regard to this recent, explosive public policy question renders such a synthesis dogmatic or dubious. Rather, the histories, selected from the same broad geographical locale, provide a review of a wide spectrum of issues. Included are: 1) a variety of suburban community types, reactions, actions, and outcomes—in order to enhance the understanding of suburban dynamics; 2) differences in local acceptance, and implementation of national and state housing and urban development policies—in order to increase understanding of the application of general regulations and incentives at the grass-roots suburban level; and 3) varied planned-change strategies and community organization approaches—to enhance understanding not only of the selection of critical leverages, but also of the potential (including, necessarily, the limitations) for planners, political leaders, private financiers, civic groups, and other agencies in order to bring about change.

It is our hope that a systematic, in-depth analysis and discussion of the controversy in diverse suburban communities, under varied conditions and with varied outcomes, will lead to an understanding and, eventually, a resolution of the issues. It should permit students to scrutinize the conflicts—flexibly and individualistically—and to draw their own conclusions.

The Boston metropolitan region is ideally suited for such examination. The suburban communities in the area, which have actually made attempts to provide low-income housing, afford a desirable diversity; at the same time, the individual controversies can be placed within the broader context of regional needs, desires, and dilemmas.

The controversy in Newton—begun in 1968 and still continuing—is described at greater length than the others because it presents a well-rounded example of suburban dynamics and public policy implementation. Moreover, the situation there calls for a more detailed examination because of the diversity of elements contained within the proposal, and its plans and strategies, which have been evolving over a long period of time. In a way, Newton sets the stage for the other four cases.

Concord, a more conservative, less dense, but more historic Boston suburb than Newton, has been one of the first communities to test the unique Massachusetts "antisnob" legislation. Concord's strategy in support of a low- and moderate-income housing proposal has been based on that legislation; consequently, special emphasis has been placed on antisnob zoning, and the roles of state and local authorities in organizing and zoning space use. Concern over another public good, the environment, also has come into play.

The fight in Canton, unlike that of Newton and Concord, is already over. The short-lived, highly emotional community conflict produced no housing units at all. Paradoxically, the swift and decisive defeat of the proposed zoning changes involved exclusively moderate- not low-income housing. Why, then, the rejection of a proposal engineered by a coalition of "outsiders," the Interfaith Corporation of Boston, with other local church-related civic groups?

East Providence, unlike Canton, Concord, and Newton, is a lower-income city; it is less of a suburb in the conventional sense and has a considerable black population. The controversy there—continuing since 1966—has resulted so far in the building of only a modest number of low-income housing units. Partial success, to be sure—but at what costs and with what investment of community resources! The chief difficulty in East Providence is unique among the five cases: blacks have objected to the plan's designation of housing sites in their neighborhood. Does this suggest a paradox—that the conflict has been dominated by social class rather than racial considerations? In contrast to the Newton, Concord, and Canton cases, the agent for change in East Providence has not been a private, church-related or "outside" group but its own housing authority, which had been directed to build low- and moderate-income housing. The housing authority's efforts to fulfill this mandate have been repeatedly frustrated—sometimes by its own city council and sponsors.

Finally, success! Stoughton, alone of the five communities, has been able to implement its plan as originally conceived. Apparently a rather unusual "trade-off," whereby the city received a generous federal grant to improve its water system in exchange for building low- and moderate-income housing, was the cornerstone of the successful strategy. Stoughton presents a unique opportunity to assess the actual outcome of building a lower- and moderate-income housing project in suburbia. It is one of the few projects of this kind, the first in New England and, perhaps, in the nation, which has resulted in housing units that are administered by a co-op, and managed by the residents. Special emphasis is, therefore, placed upon Stoughton's reaction to the project two years after its completion, and upon the experience of project residents, both with their co-op and their new neighbors. Interviews with Stoughton residents and officials have also provided data for an unusual comparative analysis: predictions and admonitions made both by opponents and proponents during the hearings two years ago can be compared with experience since the inauguration of the project.

All of the cases have been studied systematically over a sustained period of time. For, it became apparent from the beginning that brief, snapshot examinations of low- and moderate-income housing controversies might well be inadequate, even misleading. Human behavior over periods of time is too unpredictable, and the social, legal, and technical aspects of the issue are too complex. Rather, a long-range, reiterative monitoring of the community conflict was felt to be necessary to place it in proper perspective, and to draw relatively reliable conclusions about its outcome and about the decision-making processes in the community. Consequently, research in each case continued over several years until the episode evolved sufficiently for its central parameters to be sketched realistically. In certain cases, general resolution of the controversy could be predicted almost from the beginning; in others, there were unexpected twists that changed much of the original nature of the objectives of the case.

Two kinds of complexities presented a challenge. One involved the multidimensional nature of the case, the mere existence of many variables: social, economic, legal, physical, or urban planning; construction, geological, engineering, service-delivery systems for public amenities; municipal financing; income redistribution; social justice, civil rights, and human welfare; public policy formulation and the authority of government at different political levels. Omission of one central variable could affect understanding of the controversy.

The other kind of complexity was dynamic, involving the way in which variables interact with each other and thus create new interdependencies, which, in turn, generate frequently unpredicted outcomes. For example, it is difficult to assess the direct and indirect impacts of a low- and moderate-income housing plan upon community cohesiveness and sociocultural growth, or upon the educational system. Moreover, property values are related to a host of factors—psychological, social, economic, locational, legal, technological—including municipal taxes, which affect municipal services, and are, in turn, affected by zoning, densities, and the specific financing of a housing project.

Diverse research approaches were therefore used for the collection, screening, classification, and analysis of data. For each case, these included one or more of the following: interviews with key protagonists, neighbors, developers, present and future consumers of lower-income housing, municipal officials;

site visits to public agencies and neighborhoods; observer participation in town meetings, hearings, community presentations and discussions; monitoring of local newspaper accounts and editorials which dealt with the controversy and the circumstances surrounding the arguments of supporters and opponents; reviews of official documents, reports, studies, master plans, zoning ordinances, federal and state programs of subsidized housing, minutes of proceedings and meetings, correspondence, and demographic, socioeconomic and technical analyses of data pertinent to the community and the problem at hand; reviews of legal decisions and administrative interpretations affecting these and other communities; and workshop analyses and class discussions in which parties to the controversy were invited to participate. In the case of Stoughton, the community was revisited to assess the performance of the low- and moderate-income housing project and to review, with the wisdom born of the event, the original arguments made by proponents and opponents.

Each of these cases presents certain unique features. Yet, collectively they combine to illustrate the intricate nature of public policy issues. They present empirical data to bolster or test certain assumptions and theories. They also provoke questions: What, in view of the inescapable interdependencies of blacks and whites in the United States, are the tolerable long-run solutions? What, for example, can be learned from the success in Stoughton and the defeat in Canton? Is the problem of low- and moderate-income housing solely a matter of unequal income distribution? Should "liberals" give up at the local level and concentrate their efforts on legislative programs at the state and national levels? What is the role of the Presidency in providing political and moral leadership to what seems, at first glance, so local an issue? Can courts, the least democratic branch of government, lend a hand in hammering out objectives of social justice in housing distribution? Will the issue be solved if the states take over control and responsibility for zoning? Or, rather, should new social institutions be established to provide an impetus for change through trade-off negotiations with the forces of the status quo?

While these and other options are explored, the puzzle and conflict remain: if suburbia does not want low- and moderate-income housing, and the central cities have neither the space nor the funds for it, then where do lower-income families go to live?

Part One

Policy Perspectives on the Controversy

The five community case studies described in this book, indeed the "low-income-family-in-the-suburbs" conflict itself, must be placed within a broader social policy context in order to be examined effectively. While several perspectives could provide effective avenues of analysis—and the student of this issue will hopefully keep a myriad of options open—we suggest one unifying approach, consisting of three interconnected strands.

First, the issue needs to be viewed within the wider setting in which it takes place: the suburb as it functions within the metropolitan system. Individual and group actions and reactions in the housing controversy, as well as the role of social class, status, and institutional values, can best be understood when the suburb is regarded as a component of the urban system.

Second, the controversy needs to be considered within the context of state and national housing and other related public policies as they are applied at the local level. What does a general formulation of public policy mean to specific individuals, population groups, and communities? How is it implemented and what are its implications for other public policy decisions—now and in the future—relating to such matters as poverty, transportation, municipal services, jobs, taxes, education, and income redistribution?

Third, the housing controversy is best explored in relation to planned change, decision-making processes and the various sociopolitical mechanisms of suburbia. Federal and state policies and local suburban values, interests, and politics produce a unique climate in which to grasp understanding of the levers of social development.

Chapter One

Suburbia: The Emerging Centerpiece of Urban America

We are no longer an urban, but a suburban nation. Efforts to develop low- and moderate-income housing in the suburban communities reflect the perception that it is in those suburbs, not the cities, where the action is today. Empirical evidence suggests that the deep crisis of the American city, publicly declared, is rapidly expanding and emerging as a crisis of the suburb. In the decade 1960-1970, the population of the metropolitan areas increased by 19.8 percent—yet the cities themselves grew by only 3.9 percent, whereas the areas outside central cities grew by 15.9 percent.

The pursuit of happiness continues to lure millions of Americans each year into pulling up stakes and resettling elsewhere. Each person, each family, makes the decision to move in response to individually felt needs and individually sensed opportunities; yet, the millions of freely made, particular decisions aggregate into marked patterns of migration. In our time, the significant movement has been, first, out of rural areas and into cities and, most recently and most intensively, out of the cities and into the suburbs.

The reasons underlying this vast migration mingle motives of individuals with public policy. Men come together to live in cities, Aristotle reminds us, in order to live the good life. All the benefits of city life arise from the interdependency of the citizens; unfortunately, many of the ills that offend city dwellers also arise from that same interrelationship and from the congestion that accompanies it. The automobile, the availability of land, new economic or technological functions and building forms, all have helped disperse populations from the central city. Increasingly, urban spread seems to be the future pattern of settlement in the United States.

Many Americans recently have come to interpret the essential condition of urban life as a distasteful and dangerous interdependency. They have come to regard the poor and the black as pollutants; they have moved to the suburbs to find a purer environment and higher social status. For many, the suburb has become not only an escape valve from the conditions of the central city, but also a real or imaginary life-style, with distinct values, attitudes, and interests.

Once ensconced in their suburban havens, members of the white middle class have erected walls and moats to keep out the unwelcome features of the central city and to protect their suburban turf. One obstacle has worked more or less automatically: the high price of suburban housing. But that has not been a sufficient barricade to exclude every alien element, so suburban residents have at various times turned to more complex methods. Some have been privately created, such as gentlemen's agreements and restrictive covenants; these have been held to be invalid and unconstitutional, however, and in the end have been rendered illegal by such statutes as the Fair Housing Act of 1968. Other barriers have superceded these, taking the form of public laws and official rules—particularly zoning and other land-use regulations designed with exclusionary results in mind.

The suburbs have become, for at least two major reasons, the focus of massive efforts to satisfy the nation's housing shortage. The first reason is that national policies have approached the problem chiefly through the private enterprise system, with mortgage guarantees, incentives for home ownership, and encouragement of the home-building industries. These policies have affected the patterns of residency, because, as a general rule, housing has been built primarily for those groups who can afford to pay enough to allow the developer a reasonable margin of profit. The second reason is that most central cities have had little remaining land suitable and realistically priced for housing; moreover, employment and population have been increasing faster in suburbia than in the inner city. Developers have naturally been attracted in that direction.

Chapter Two

Public Policy at the Grass Roots

Housing and urban development policies at the federal and state levels are designed to promote primarily national and regional collective interests, values, and objectives. At the grass-roots level, however, these goals are confronted by local values, interests, and objectives—either those of communities or of specific segments of the population—which are not necessarily identical to or reconcilable with each other or with the larger unit of decision making. In fact, the ways in which public policies are implemented at the local level, and their implications for parochial suburban interests and objectives, often generate consequences altogether unforeseen or unintended by their legislators.

Clearly, the potential for conflict among values when public policies and objectives are implemented at the local level is real and complex. Successful formulation and enactment of low-income housing policies, as well as those relating to land use and urban development, depend upon this fundamental reality. Like it or not, public policy must consider the suburban way of life; without feedback from the individual communities, edicts can be promulgated to no avail. At the same time, a change of suburban values and attitudes may prove necessary to promote national and regional needs, as well as development requirements. Let us highlight these assumptions briefly, as they relate to policies for housing, land uses, civil rights, and urban development.

Housing as a Social Good

Should shelter be treated in the same way as public education and employment, and, therefore, guaranteed as a fundamental right in American society, rather than be deemed a privilege obtainable only by economic strength? A primary aspiration of every American family, and one of the basic responsibilities of a democratic government, is a decent home in a suitable living environment. This explains why Congress has been centrally concerned with housing since 1949. If housing is accepted as a democratic right, then it could follow that the needs of low-income families require special aids, and that the accessibility of housing to jobs and recreational and cultural facilities should become a national goal, overriding contrary local objectives.

Public policy has also been concerned with the housing industry because its output is crucial in the stabilization of the economy. Americans spend about $50 billion a year to buy, rent, and maintain their dwellings, and an equal amount on utilities, furniture, and other housing expenses. Family expenditures for housing are second only to those for food. Housing is the single largest capital investment for any individual; he will be much concerned about the potential rise or fall in value of his property, and about his neighbors, whose very presence may affect his pocketbook. Residential land and structures represent about a third of our total national wealth. The types of housing produced, and their quantity, quality, location, and timing, are of national importance.

The suburban controversy raises questions about the success of national housing programs in helping the poor. By and large, private enterprise and the home construction industry have responded well to congressional expectations that they would satisfy the pressing housing shortage created by the Depression and World War II. FHA, and later, FNMA and GNMA, each proved to be a showcase of the mixed society. The annual rate of dwelling unit construction for sixteen years after World War II was double the rate at which new families were formed.

Yet the decision to let private enterprise satisfy the housing shortage without providing a public policy framework for urban growth has affected significantly the nation's geographic segregation of residences and the unequal satisfaction of housing demand by Americans. In spite of the high rate of dwelling unit construction by private enterprise, more than 12 percent of American families cannot now afford decent housing; at least 10 percent of the nation's existing units are in substandard condition. The movement of whites to the suburbs and their replacement by blacks in the central cities have been affected by, and have influenced, the creation of two separate and unequal markets: one for affluent, white middle-class homeowners of new dwellings in suburbia, and another for poor minority renters of old, usually substandard, dwellings in the inner city.

Recently the uneasy mixture of public and private in the housing sector has come under fresh analysis. Questions are now being raised about the adequacy of national housing policies and whether government expenditures are appropriate in terms of cost-benefit ratios and of location according to master plans. Even the form of subsidy is being reconsidered: which is more likely to lead to the building of low-income housing in suburbia, a producers' subsidy that reduces interest costs, or a housing allowance paid directly to the intended beneficiaries?

Note, too, another interesting trend in the opening up of suburbia. Builders—driven, it is true, by the profit motive rather than by any conception of the public interest—are moving on the legislative and judicial fronts to remove local zoning and building code barriers to low-income housing. The housing industry has welcomed to its ranks large and powerful corporations such as ITT and Westinghouse, and these corporations are seeking mass markets. Among the parties joining together to ask the Supreme Court to allow an amicus brief in the Valtierra case (infra, p. 406), which challenged California's requirement for local referenda on public housing decisions, were such improbable allies as the National Association of Building Manufacturers and the National Association of Home Builders. Increasingly, there are influential conservative forces in the industry that would welcome limitations on local land-use controls. Should not this be a major factor in formulating new housing dispersal policies?

Civil Rights, Segregation, and Antipoverty Programs

The suburban rejection of low- and moderate-income housing should also be studied within the context of civil rights, socioeconomic segregation, and strategies with which to combat poverty. Implementation of these policies at the grass-roots level in the suburbs inevitably collides with the values and demands of some individuals there.

First, it is instructive to glance at residential segregation. Two interrelated trends of population dispersion have greatly increased the spread of socioeconomic segregation in America's urban areas: the movement of whites to the suburbs and their replacement in the central cities by blacks. Practically all demographic analyses in the 1950s and 1960s, as well as congressional hearings and presidential commissions, emphasize that these phenomena have created two separate Americas: one black and poor in the inner city, and one white and affluent in suburbia. This socioeconomic racial dichotomy is directly related to suburban housing policies and practices, and it serves the purposes and needs of many people and interest groups.

The efforts of the white middle class to erect restrictive walls and keep out the unwelcome blacks and poor on the whole have succeeded all too well. The percentage of blacks in the United States population did not change between 1960 and 1970, remaining at 11 percent. Yet the central cities have experienced a sharp increase—from 16 percent to 21 percent. A black majority already exists in seven major cities: Atlanta and Augusta, Georgia; East Orange and Newark, New Jersey; East St. Louis, Missouri; Gary, Indiana; Washington, D.C. Meanwhile, the percentage of blacks in the suburbs has remained unchanged at 5 percent. In the suburbs of metropolitan areas with populations under 250,000 the proportion has decreased from 7 percent to 6 percent; in the suburbs of metropolitan areas with populations of 250,000 to 1 million, it has decreased from 5 percent to 4 percent. Only in suburbs of metropolitan areas with population of 2 million or more has the percentage of blacks increased—from 4 percent to 5 percent.

If present population trends continue, almost three-quarters of all urban whites will live in suburbs by 1986, while about three-quarters of all urban nonwhites will live in central cities. Nonwhites will constitute about 1 in 3 of all central city dwellers, but only about 1 in 30 of all suburbanites. The result is already, and will be increasingly, a core city where blacks represent a very large minority or even a majority, surrounded by a white noose. This amounts to de facto apartheid, which most Americans would not be willing to endorse or to deliberately bring about.

As a consequence, residents of the suburban communities are now almost exclusively white and relatively affluent—a product of land availability and speculation, of federal policies toward subsidized housing and the interstate highway system, of population growth and dispersion patterns, of the practices of the real estate, banking, and home-building industries. All the prevailing forces have tended to keep out low-income families, regardless of race or origin. Most black families have been economically incapable of purchasing a new home in suburbia; even when they could afford the move, often they were not allowed to make it. As a result, hierarchical differences in social standing and life-style have, in general, spread out horizontally in metropolitan areas.

Are neighborhoods better or worse off if the people in them all belong to the same general socioeconomic groups and have the same ethnic or racial origins? How do the virtues of socioeconomic homogeneity compare with the advantages of a population mix? We may not yet have all the answers, but at least the search has intensified. The dilemmas of residential segregation and housing patterns have been placed in sharper focus by society's efforts in the 1960s to combat poverty in the inner city, to increase intraurban geographic mobility and metropolitan-wide developments, and to create lower-income facilities in suburbia for younger families and the unskilled and semiskilled manpower necessary to sustain their economic base.

Geographic separation and the country's patterns of residency have profound socioeconomic and psychological effects upon human and social growth or development. School segregation is a key case in point. In its 1954 decision declaring unconstitutional segregation in public education, the Supreme Court held that racially segregated schools are still challenging individuals' rights in the North and South alike, and school busing has become a much-debated social policy issue. A major cause of segregated school systems is the population dispersion—a function, in turn, of low- and moderate-income housing dispersion. Civil rights measures to secure equality for minority groups in arenas other than in schools—in the job market, public facilities, and equipment—are also increasingly related to residence patterns. So long as geographic barriers keep citizens from their rights in education, employment, and public facilities, housing patterns can be seen to affect directly equality under the law and the national commitment to equal opportunity.

Moreover, it is almost impossible to deal effectively with the accumulated ill effects of deprivation and deep-rooted poverty when the victims are concentrated geographically. The resultant social and psychological demoralization often becomes self-reinforcing and produces a feedback reaction that hardly can be controlled, let alone eliminated.

Land-Use Policies and Exclusionary Zoning

Zoning ordinances and petitions for their change are invariably central to the controversies over subsidized housing; they are crucial in excluding families different from those already in residence, and they provide a key to the implementation of lower-income housing plans.

Land-use policies and zoning ordinances represent not merely decisions regarding land organization and physical planning, but also the issues of property rights, ecology, the public welfare, civil rights, and residential segregation. This has not always been recognized.

Direct public controls over land use are often truly employed as a means to insure that a community's land uses are properly situated in relation to one another, to stabilize and preserve property values, to enhance efficient municipal development, to exclude undesirable land uses and users—all, hopefully, contributing to the well-being of the inhabitants of the city, neighboring communities, and, indeed, the entire region. Yet nearly every land-use control entails some exclusion, even if indirectly, by raising the costs that the market would otherwise charge.

The potential for racial segregation to become a motive for legislative action was recognized (and put aside for consideration at some future, indeterminate time if the case could be established) by the first Supreme Court decision on the subject, which upheld the validity of comprehensive zoning in 1926. Fodder for sharp debate on both moral and constitutional grounds ever since that date, the exclusionary aspects of land-use controls have recently come to be recognized as a major roadblock to the implementation of national housing policies. Many believe that new zoning approaches to the use of suburban sites are among the most important changes that need to be made.

This underscores the crucial role of local-state relationships in the organization of space, over and above the traditional enabling legislation delegating to localities the power to control land uses. Several states, including Massachusetts and New York, have passed legislation or created agencies empowered to overturn local ordinances. What can the court say about legally enforced banning of economic classes and racial groups from the suburbs, and what can it say about states' rights overriding local ordinances? How directly can a judge probe into the motives of coordinate branches of government? And with what tools and expertise? Can the community's requirements for health, safety, and amenities be achieved without generating social and racial exclusion? Court orders and decisions are important. But how far can they move ahead of accepted mores and traditions?

Planning for Urban Growth

Public policies for regional and metropolitan development are not necessarily compatible with local grass-roots interests and values. This conflict is well-illustrated by several public issues, but it emerges with particular sharpness in the controversy over housing in the suburbs.

First, there is the question of where subsidized housing should be located. The inner city already has staggering concentrations of lower-income housing, high unemployment levels, and a scarcity of both land and quality services. It is in the interest of inner-city neighborhoods that low-income housing should be located elsewhere in the metropolis; this can provide an opportunity to upgrade the old neighborhoods and expand their socioeconomic structure. Meanwhile, the suburbs, where greater affluence prevails, reject lower-income housing and defy efforts to change their zoning ordinances. They want to control their socioeconomic environment and preserve the locally cherished values of low density, exclusiveness (racial and economic), reduced pollution, ample space, and pleasing aesthetics.

The second question to ask is how high density of low-income housing affects urban development policies. High concentrations of low-income housing in one location, particularly in the inner city, may cripple its capacity for absorption and its potential for development. The metropolitan area as a whole may also be affected. Will the central cities perhaps find themselves less and less able to cope with their problems? Reduced revenues due to the flight of the affluent to the suburbs, the increased cost and demand for municipal services for an inner-city population which has intense and special needs—these more recent difficulties increase the city's plight. By the same token, can the suburbs survive if the inner cities decline? Will suburban communities find themselves less and less able to cope with their own problems and destinies?

Third, both the central city and the suburbs stand to lose from the failure to adopt a metropolitan-wide approach. Revenues from property taxes have reached prohibitive heights in both places. Municipal expenses have increased rapidly merely to sustain levels of service delivery, and thus duplication and lack of coordination among metropolitan communities has become more wasteful and undesirable than ever. Public utilities throughout the metropolitan area face similar exigencies. Any attempt to exert significant public influence over the nature and location of metropolitan growth requires direct control of a significant part of the land, particularly at the peripheries. If most of the control over the metropolitan land area is left in private hands, with private ownership fragmented into thousands of small parcels, it becomes impossible to guide metropolitan or regional growth on any comprehensive basis. Transportation and sewer and water services, for instance, are directly dependent upon guided urban growth and location. A European example illustrates the possibilities. New growth areas in Stockholm are linked to downtown by subway, and feature high-density residential clusters around each station; huge shopping centers are built over each subway stop for the convenience of the pedestrian residents. In the United States, on the other hand, such developments evolve around the use of the automobile and near expressway interchanges. Whether the automobile or a fast mass-transportation system is to be the centerpiece of future urban trends, it is evident that rapid construction of new urban facilities to accommodate large-scale growth must be accomplished on what is initially vacant land, and it must take into account the metropolitan-wide development of transportation as well as other services.

There is a fourth consideration. Metropolitan-wide collaboration has never been easy. How should the scattering be arranged if the locus is to be the metropolitan area as a whole, and what criteria for the location of housing should be applied? Do metropolitan planning agencies and councils of governments have enough muscle to muster unified approaches?

Fifth, how should planners confront suburbia's life-style and its "American Dream?" And, conversely, how should they deal with the determination of certain minority groups to find local self-identity in the central-city neighborhoods? Social class consciousness, status, and race are so intricately interwoven that it is hard to separate them or ignore them in planning the growth of the metropolitan area, especially the siting of residences.

All these public policies, debated though they may be in the Congress and the state legislatures, cannot be grasped fully until they come to full view in the suburbs. The implications of the concrete elude us as we generalize. Yet, sharp and painful divisions also ensue. Realistically, individuals at the local level cannot be expected to make their decisions readily on the basis of abstract values or public objectives, even though such imperatives flow from their duties to provide equal treatment to all under the Fourteenth Amendment.

Surely the exclusion of certain groups from areas in which they would like to live is essentially unethical. Overcoming the new feudal view of suburban life, with its attendant enclaves and exclusionary moats, is the goal, based on a greater moral vision of society, that we have set out to find. But autonomous individuals remain unconvinced; and national policies must be unambiguous in order to be effective, because the problem is deeply embedded in the structure of our society and its social institutions.

Chapter Three

Planned Social Change

Perhaps the most difficult, yet essential, social context of low-income housing policies in the suburban scene is that of planned social change. For the public policy initiator, the decision maker, the political leader, the private citizen, the nonprofit organization chairman, the professional community organizer and the champion of planned social change, the low-income housing controversy takes the form of a special intrigue. The issue revolves around the appropriateness and effectiveness of strategies of change and of community planning processes.

Although planned change and community organization strategies are frequently ill-defined or inadequately tested, they form a wide spectrum of approaches and models. Inherent in the traditional American suburb is a barrier of complex ordinances, most notably zoning, which must be penetrated and lowered before social change can actually begin. In practical terms, political change must both precede and follow social change. At issue are the methods of applying social technology to facilitate residential, racial, and economic integration in suburban communities. Changing the residents' attitudes toward acceptance of socioeconomic differences and adaptations in life-style is one major area for consideration; further, it must be decided what should be changed in the suburbs, how, in what order and rate, by whom, at what costs, and with what consequences.

The social sciences have furnished some valid and usable knowledge and methods to guide certain types of planned change efforts in certain types of communities. At this stage of its evolution, however, social change theory is vulnerable: practitioners find it difficult to apply—for that matter, difficult to choose intelligently among diverse, often vague and untested, planned change methods.

In suburban communities, the change agents are often surrogates for those who cannot act effectively, given the exclusive nature of the community. In examining the case studies presented here, an important analytic focus is the

19

approach taken by the various change agents in their efforts to gain the approval of the community or the courts. The character of these change agents, their role in the community, their perceptions of class, their relationship to the decision makers, all are worthy of scrutiny by the student of the issue.

Two broad approaches to change are useful to recognize—those based on consensus and collaborative community efforts, and those based on competitive action, confrontation, real or suggestive coercion of opinion. These two strategies represent opposites. They depend, in part, on the number and status of those advocating change, their perceptions of the power structure, the community's perceptions of the change agents, and the possible ramifications of the change.

The tactics involved in the process of social change, as employed by both proponents and opponents of low-income housing, are essential parts of the central features of these case studies. Each presents a strategy in action, a counter-strategy, changes, feedback, retreats—all enacted by citizens who care deeply and who believe that they are right.

On the other hand, many champions of low-income housing emphasize a "rational," long-range planning approach, complete with technical studies and housing plans designed to serve the public interest and fulfill moral obligations. The sociopolitical processes involved in implementation are secondary. This contrasts with the suburban opponents of low-income housing, who emphasize the "irrationality" of the plan, the immediate problems raised by any influx, the hardship to specific residents, and the political process. Such opponents, while personifying the reluctance to change, understand the interest of the suburban decision-making process in maintaining the status quo.

How relevant to the suburban low-income housing problems are such approaches to planned change—particularly in view of suburban class consciousness and tendency to exclude low income groups? Would a reliance upon objective facts and rational planning—rather than on subjective personal or community values—be more relevant in suburbs? For that matter, how important is the actual choice of strategies for success? For example, would a longer range approach focused on modifying social institutions (or introducing new ones) be a more effective change strategy than short range efforts focused mainly on dissemination of information to increase understanding and produce acceptance of the issue?

Few suburban politicians perceive themselves as "change agents." More often, they act as solidifiers of the ratified suburban economic homogeneity. Who, then, is to advocate the interests of the frequently absent low-income families? What suburban political coalitions are both possible and effective to induce change? Should efforts be made to mobilize entire suburban communities, or even metropolitan communities, or should the focus be on a low-keyed approach aimed at local decision makers?

Does the situation suggest a need for alternative ways of blending the art of rational planning with the irrational political dynamics of decision

Planned Social Change 21

making? Can long-range, collective, metropolitan elements be combined with short-range, individually-oriented, local interests and values? Can the community development or urban planning processes be combined with those of social action?

A minority group leader, familiar with the efforts to house low-income people in the suburbs, commented that the activities reminded him of the following cartoon:

Is a primary reason for failure to establish low-income housing in the suburbs that too many toads have been attempting to teach frogs to be mice?

Part Two

Five Community Case Studies

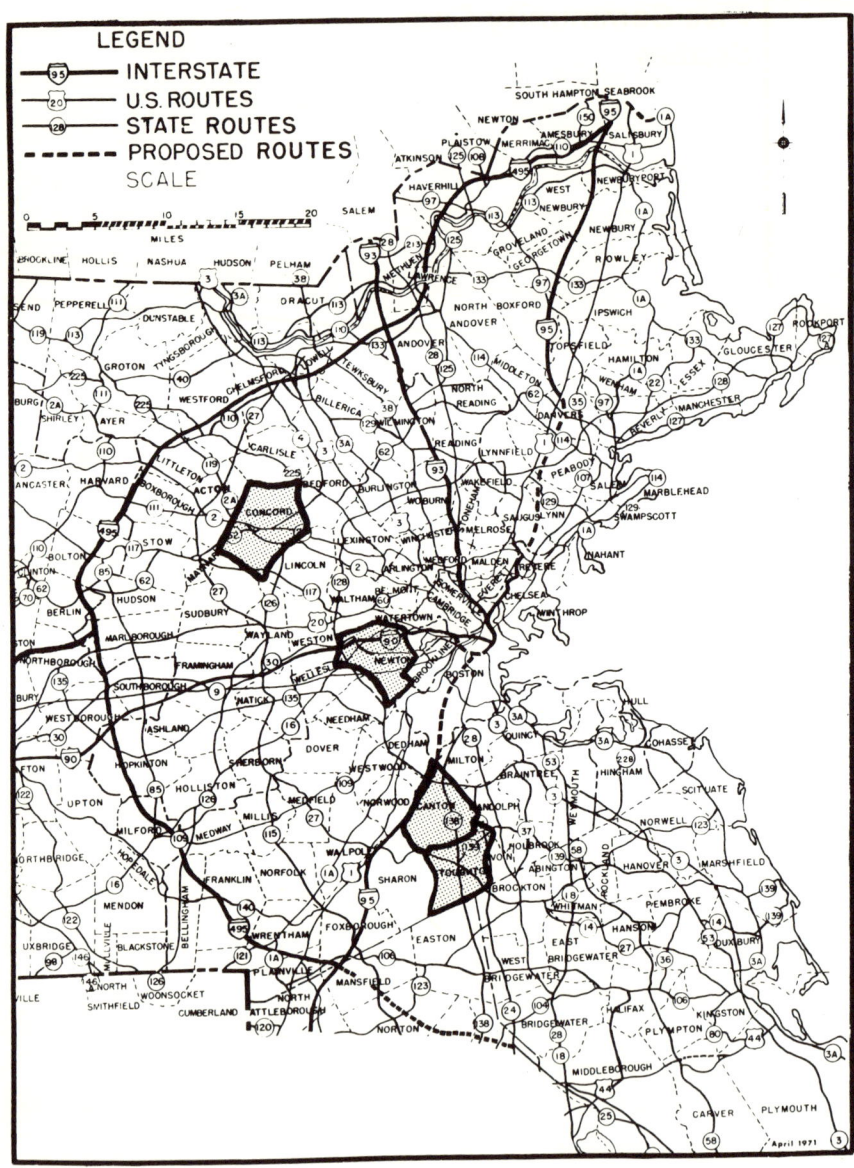

EASTERN MASSACHUSETTS

Chapter Four

Newton

---The Exceptional Suburb
--- An Ordinary Suburb ?

The fundamental reason for examining Newton in great detail is its liberal character and general reputation for innovation and change. Of all the Boston suburban communities, Newton best embodies the progressive tradition of America with a dedication to an open, pluralistic society.

Although the conflict is not yet resolved (appeal from the State's Housing Appeals Committee is still pending), its scope and intensity over a sustained period of time, as well as the wide range of carefully conceived arguments on both sides, present an almost classic example of the intricate social policy issues involved in introducing low-income housing in America's urban areas. In several important respects, the Newton arguments reflect the broader social dilemmas which face a free market economy of a pluralistic society committed both to individual liberty and to justice for all its social classes. For these reasons the Newton controversy and the social change processes involved are described comprehensively and documented in depth, setting the stage for the other four cases.

THE EXCEPTIONAL SUBURB

Newton, the "Garden City," is "No Ordinary Suburb," proclaimed the Newton Chamber of Commerce in 1969:

> Its people are committed to social betterment and change. It bears few traces of parochial self-centeredness, but extends its interests to the entire metropolitan region.

Or is it?
Newton's candidacy for the ground breaking role as innovator for accepting low- and moderate-income housing is fundamentally based on one

26 Housing the Poor in Suburbia

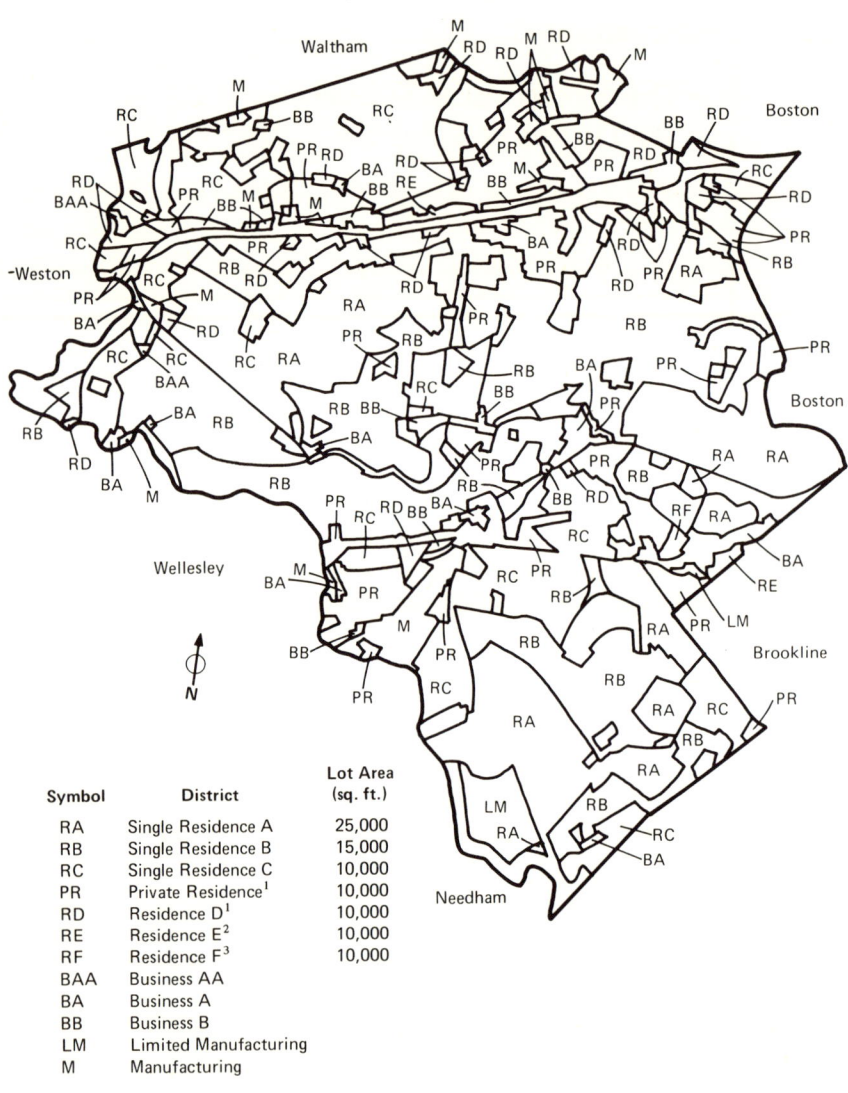

Symbol	District	Lot Area (sq. ft.)
RA	Single Residence A	25,000
RB	Single Residence B	15,000
RC	Single Residence C	10,000
PR	Private Residence[1]	10,000
RD	Residence D[1]	10,000
RE	Residence E[2]	10,000
RF	Residence F[3]	10,000
BAA	Business AA	
BA	Business A	
BB	Business B	
LM	Limited Manufacturing	
M	Manufacturing	

1. Two-family permitted.
2. Apartments by special permit.
3. Apartments by right.

Figure Newton 1. Land Use Map Newton

major assumption about its character: it is no ordinary suburb; if it cannot happen in Newton, it can't happen; a "liberal" community is most likely to accept LMIH. With this conventional wisdom in mind, Newton, it was assumed, could become a national model in the subsidized housing field. Now, five or so years later, Newton may well become a national model, but for the failure of "liberal" suburbia to implement its commitment to social betterment and change.

The effort of the Newton Community Development Foundation (NCDF) began when it was established in May 1968, but the controversy did not erupt until April 1969, when NCDF announced the 10 sites on which it planned to build 508 low- and moderate-income housing units. Throughout the debate, which centered first on the simplest rationale—the housing needs of current Newtonites—forces opposing and supporting the plan fought one another skillfully. But soon the rationale expanded and the entire community, together with its decision-making bodies, was intensely engulfed, the conflict becoming community-wide. The "Need Argument" was then buttressed by the "Heterogeneity Argument"—Newton will lose the cross-section of population which has added vitality to the city for years. As emotions and feelings rose and accusations multiplied, new concerns were introduced which ranged from strictly legal, technical, city planning considerations to socioeconomic issues, civil rights, and the fundamental right to choose one's neighbors.

As a nonprofit sponsor, NCDF was immune from slur of profit and materialism. Nor could it be attacked as an outside agent attempting to impose alien solutions upon Newton; NCDF was founded by Newton clergy, directed by a Board of Newton civic, political, and business leaders, and financially supported by a membership of 700 Newton residents. In brief, NCDF was a Newton solution to a Newton problem, designed by Newtonites who had the knowledge and background to pick their way through the social and political processes of the community. Unlike typical church groups, which often have difficulties establishing credibility within communities and in the housing field, the NCDF Board had expertise in design, construction, management, and financing. Its members, active in both political parties and in several civic organizations, had previous experience in government, subsidized housing programs, and other nonprofit housing organizations. NCDF's full-time Executive Director, an attorney, had real estate experience and had served as the executive assistant to the Massachusetts Commissioner of Community Affairs. The Chairman of the Board is credited with single-handedly persuading the Democratic Massachusetts Legislature to accept a Republican Governor's reorganization and modernization plan. All in all, NCDF did not lack expertise, credibility, political sophistication, ideological commitment, or enthusiasm. Was Newton, then, the "wrong" place? Was Newton's candidacy for innovator ill-conceived?

THE COMMUNITY

A Place to Live

Newton is neither virgin territory for (LMI) Low and Moderate Income families—white or black—nor a gathering ground for poor families. The city prides itself on its racial and economic heterogeneity—for a suburb. It is, in fact, a city of over 90,000 people, with 14 villages housing an ethnically, economically, and religiously heterogeneous population. Despite this reality, many people think of Newton as a strictly upper-income bedroom community of Boston, an impression gained, perhaps, by a drive from Boston College to Newton City Hall along the shaded streets of Commonwealth Avenue, lined with large, luxurious homes. Strict land-use controls have given Newton its image as a "Garden City." Yet, it is an "inner" suburb, a major suburban employment center, just 7 miles from downtown Boston, urban blight and racial conflict. Newton has a high percentage (36.0 percent) of households that earned over $15,000 in 1970. But, even so, 5 percent earned under $3,000, 11 percent between $3 and $6,000, and 18 percent of the households earned between $6,000 and $9,000 annually. The impression given by Commonwealth Avenue is not true for everyone: despite a $15,381 median family income in 1970, at least 2.8 percent of Newton's 22,694 families and 5 percent of its 91,066 population were below poverty level; 9 percent of the poor families received welfare. Whereas in most of Boston's affluent suburbs the percentage of lower-income families decreased during the 1960s while total population increased, Newton almost maintained its 1960 proportion of families earning less than $3,000 annually (losing only 1 percent), while its total population decreased by 1.4 percent—emigration exceeding immigration by 4,684 persons.

Politically, Newton operates under a Mayor-Council form of government. The Council is a Board consisting of 24 Aldermen, with 16 elected at-large and 8 elected by ward. The Aldermen serve without pay, for 2-year terms, and each serves on a minimum of 2 of 10 standing committees. A 7-member Planning Board is appointed by the Aldermen. The Mayor appoints 5 unpaid members of the Zoning Board of Appeals (5-year term).

Although once a conservative Republican town, Newton is now Democratic and has a "liberal" glow. In a recent election, Newton gave the liberal candidate, Father Drinan, 55 percent of its vote in a contest with a former Republican State Representative. Though elections for Mayor and Aldermen are supposedly nonpartisan, there is a distinct undertone of partisan politics; of the registered voters, in 1972 42.6 percent are Democrats and 22.6 percent are Republicans. Between 1962 and 1972 registered Democrats increased by 20.8 percent while Republicans decreased by 9.4 percent and Independents by 11.3 percent. Though the government was traditionally Republican, the Board of Aldermen in the summer of 1971 consisted of 11 Democrats, 11 Republicans, and 2 Independents. The Land-Use Committee, which makes recommendations on zoning petitions to the full Board, consisted of 4 Democrats, 2 Republicans, and 2 Independents. Its members are appointed by the President of the Board of Aldermen.

Newton 29

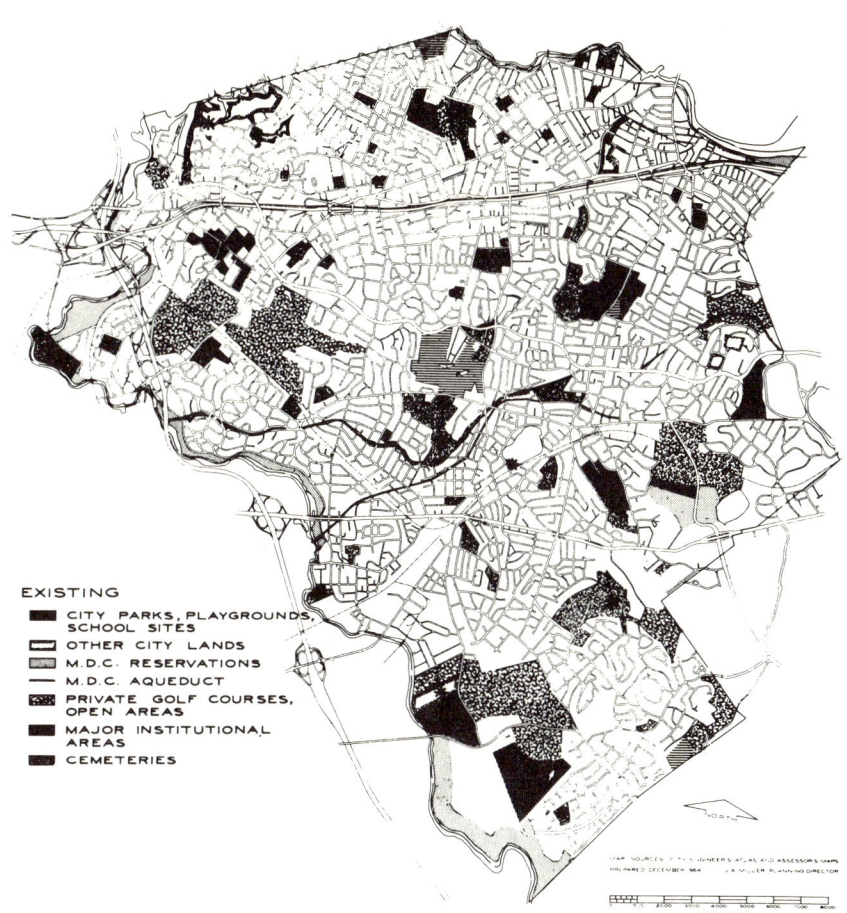

RECREATION—CONSERVATION PLAN

30 Housing the Poor in Suburbia

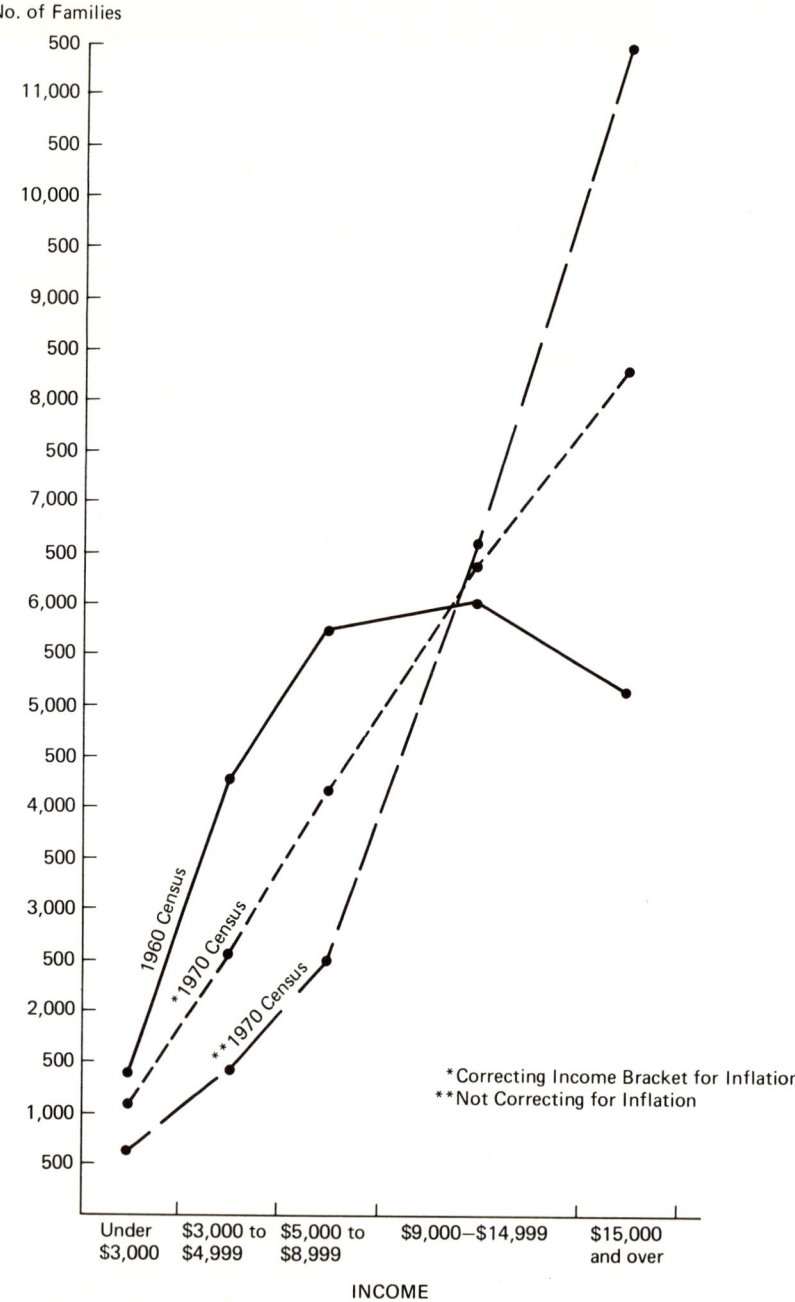

Figure Newton 2. Income Distribution in Newton: A Comparison of 1960 and 1970 Census

Table Newton 1. Income Distribution in Newton 1960-1970; and Poverty Indicators

					1970 # of Families	
1960 # Families	%	Income Brackets in $	*	% Change	**	% Change
1,391	6	Under $3,000	1,032	−1	645	− 3
4,376	19	3−5,999	2,564	−7	1,370	−13
5,759	25	6−8,999	4,247	−7	2,496	−14
6,085	26	9−14,999	6,460	+3	6,593	+3
5,465	24	15 and Over	8,392	+12	11,590	+28
23,076	100		22,694	−1.6	22,694	−1.6

*Correcting the income brackets for Inflation (CPI Index)
**Not correcting for inflation

	1960	1970	% Change
Median Family Income:	$9,008	$15,381	+70

Population in Poverty	1970
Families below Poverty Level	636(2.8%)
Persons below Poverty Level	4,371(5.0%)
Percent of poverty households lacking some or all plumbing	1.2%

Table Newton 1a. Population in Newton 1960-1970

	1960	1970	% Change	
Population	92,384	91,066	−1.4	−1,323
White	91,518	89,237	−2	−2,281
Black	672	1,092	+63	+226
Other Non-White	194	737	+279	+632

Table Newton 1b. Selected Demographic Characteristics 1970

Population		Yrs School Completed	
Count Of All Males	42,681	None−8 Years	5,571
Count of All Females	48,385	1−3 Years High School	5,450
Persons Age 5 And Under	7,067	High School Graduate	16,450
Persons Age 6 To 20	26,024	1−3 Years College	8,730
Persons Age 21 To 64	46,884	College Graduate Or More	16,381
Persons Age 65 And Over	11,091		
Count Of All Married Couples	20,171		

A Place to Work

With respect to the "jobs" argument, Newton is an advantageous location for young couples and low- and moderate-income families. Given its wide income distribution pattern and its status as a major suburban employment center, Newton can both absorb them and use them to its benefit. However, the median age of Newtonites, 32.9, is higher than the median age in Boston SMSA of 29.1 or Boston City's 28.1.

In suburban tradition, Newton is 98 percent white, 1.2 percent black, and 0.8 percent "other." The white population is divided almost equally by thirds between Catholics, Jews, and Protestants. Newcomers (11 percent of Newtonites are foreign-born, 10 percent for SMSA residents) have generally located their homes in accordance with their ethnic ties, resulting in clustering of different ethnic and religious groups around the city. Italians (the largest foreign-born group), Canadians (the second largest), Russians (the third largest), Irish, Polish, French, Asians, and Greeks provide wide ethnic heterogeneity which makes newcomers feel more at home. Divided into 14 villages, each having its own commercial center, library, civic organizations, and clubs, Newton provides, also, an organizational pattern suitable to encouragement of local neighborhood relationships at the grass-roots level.

At the same time, however, Newton's high-income families increased considerably, providing a more economically balanced population mix. Newton is located on the Massachusetts Turnpike and the suburban beltway—Route 128—that rings the Boston Metropolitan Area and gives access by automobile to both the core and suburban job markets, particularly the industrial plants and electronic industries. Its ties with the MBTA and commuter trains give access to Boston and the inner suburbs for those without cars. In 1970, 1820 firms in Newton reporting to the Massachusetts Employment Security employed 22,111 workers: See Table 2.

Newton's labor force of 38,937 in 1970 (16 years and older) is well-educated (median years of formal education completed: 14.0 years); the three largest categories are professionals (29 percent, compared to 20 percent for the SMSA) clerical (19 percent, compared to 23 percent for the SMSA) and managers (15 percent, compared to 9 percent for the SMSA).

In 1970, only one-half of incomes were earned within Newton itself—over one-half of the 38,937 regularly employed Newton residents worked outside of Middlesex County, where Newton is located, and two-thirds of them worked in Boston. On the other hand, of the people who worked inside Newton, several thousand lived elsewhere. Forty percent of these Newton employees are employed in manufacturing. Between 1965 and 1970, there was an increase of 2,390 people working in the retail and wholesale sector, and a 12 percent increase in the service sector. Newton's largest employer, Boston College, employs 1,755 people on its faculty, secretarial, and maintenance staffs.

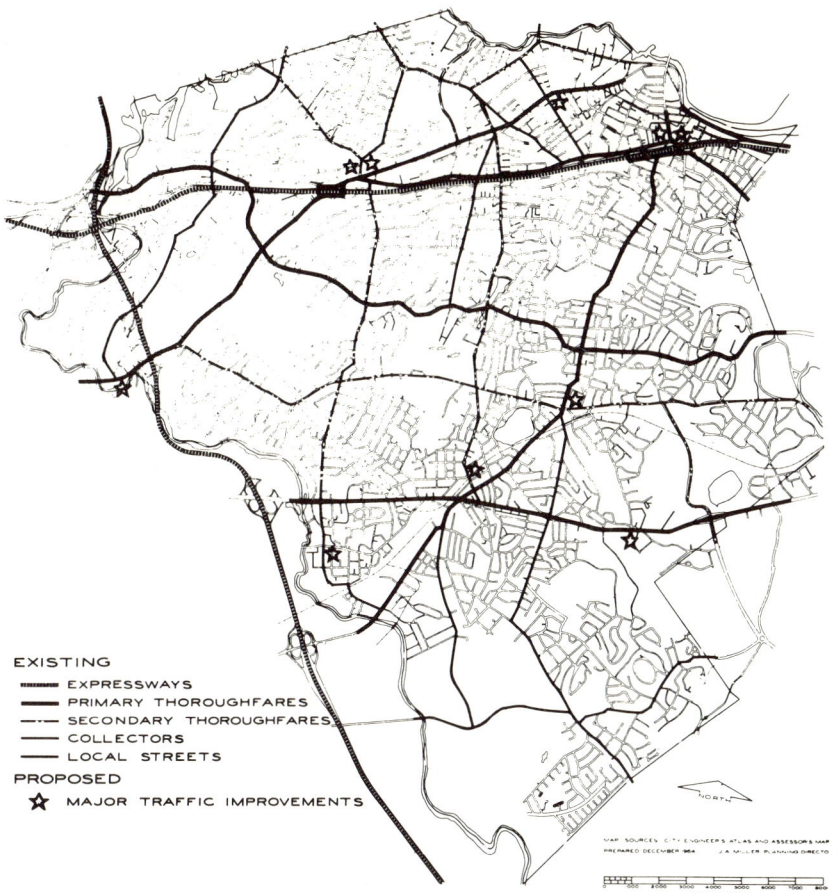

THOROUGHFARE PLAN

34 Housing the Poor in Suburbia

Table Newton 2. Employment and Payrolls—1970

Industry	No. of Firms	1970 Annual Payroll	Average 1970 Employees	Distribution by Employees
Agriculture & Mining	48	$ 755,406	161	percent
Construction	233	21,886,498	2,145	9.7
Manufacturing	89	33,592,515	3,791	17.1
Transportation, Commerce, & Utilities	46	3,906,191	583	2.6
Wholesale & Retail Trade	681	67,551,777	10,294	46.6
Finance, Insurance & Real Estate	196	7,090,300	1,028	4.7
Service	527	27,173,623	4,109	18.6
	1820		22,111	

Table Newton 3. Labor Force Characteristics—1970

A. General		
Total Employed (16 years old and over)		38,937

B. Occupation	Number	%
Professional, Tech.	11,334	29
Managers, Administrators	5,798	15
Clerical	7,247	19
Sales	3,692	9
Craftsmen, Foremen	2,928	8
Operatives	2,765	7
Private Household Workers	580	2
Service Workers	3,499	9
Laborers	1,001	3
Farm Workers	93	

C. Industrial Sector of Employment	
Agriculture and Mining	295
Construction	1,647
Manufacturing	6,352
Transportation, Comm., Util.	1,535
Wholesale	2,474
Retail	6,150
Finance, Insurance, Real Est.	2,428
Service	21,086
Public Adm.	1,657

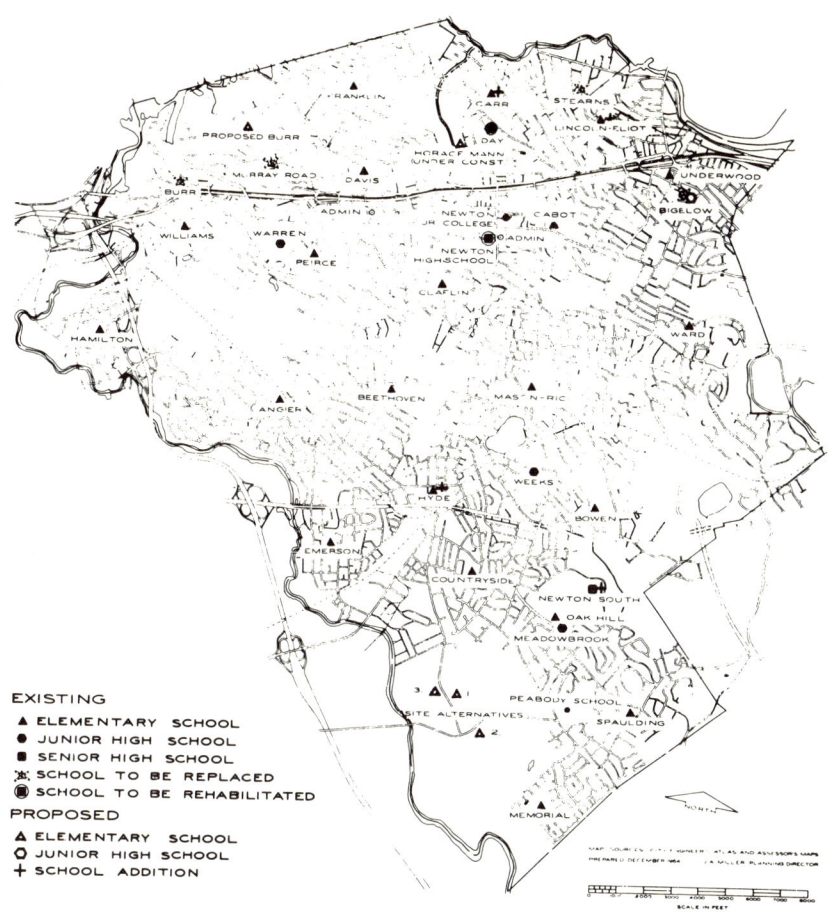

EXISTING
▲ ELEMENTARY SCHOOL
● JUNIOR HIGH SCHOOL
■ SENIOR HIGH SCHOOL
※ SCHOOL TO BE REPLACED
◉ SCHOOL TO BE REHABILITATED

PROPOSED
△ ELEMENTARY SCHOOL
○ JUNIOR HIGH SCHOOL
+ SCHOOL ADDITION

SCHOOL PLAN

A Place to Learn

Newton offers a school system with a national reputation for excellence and innovation. The city spent $1,233 per child in 1970-1971—among the highest five in the SMSA—and $25 million for building maintenance, facilities, and equipment. Newton schools are receptive to experimentation and diversity, collaborate with universities, receive Ford Foundation grants, and are geared both toward the college-bound and technically inclined—an important option for all children, particularly those of low-income families. Diversity and flexibility in meeting educational needs are well-imbedded in Newton's system. Newton participates in the METCO program, which allows inner-city black children to attend Newton schools. The City also supports a junior college offering both technical and terminal degrees and transferable programs in the liberal arts and business. All in all, Newton is an especially desirable place for young families with school-age children.

A Place for Apartments

Dwelling types, land use, density, and property taxes all converge at the center of the LMIH controversy. The fundamental question is one of impact: visual, economic, social. If Newton were to house LMI families in apartments—which is what the NCDF plan calls for—the structures (with 6 or more apartments per building) would not be unique. Newton has 53 apartment buildings or complexes containing 1,766 housing units or 6.8 percent of the city's 27,621 total housing units in 1971. Nor would the new apartments be a revival of a blighted past. Over half of the apartment units have been added in the past ten years; the production of housing in that period has been predominantly in the multi-family form—45.7 percent in apartments compared with 34.7 percent in single family detached residences. A large portion of the land in apartment zoned districts has been developed for other uses (364.7 acres or about 73 percent). Only 0.07 percent of the land in the City is available for apartment construction—vacant and properly zoned; even if all the City's remaining available land, essentially 42 sites, of 75.9 acres or 15.1 percent were put into apartment construction, the character of the City would not seem to be perceptibly altered. Furthermore, apartments have been a financial asset to Newton. They pay more taxes per person—$342 (based on the 1969 tax rate of $133, apartments provided approximately $766,874 in tax revenue) to $287. Of 2,245 residents, the apartments have only 40 school-age children.

Newton has low density (5,098 persons per square mile), as well as vacant land privately-owned (12.4 percent of its total area), public and semipublic land (11.1 percent), and golf courses of 641 acres (5.6 percent) —taxed, parenthetically, at a rate considerably lower than that of other privately-owned vacant land. Although the commercial and industrial areas are an important source of jobs and, to a considerable extent, of tax revenue, they occupy only 4.6 percent of the City's 18-square-mile land area:

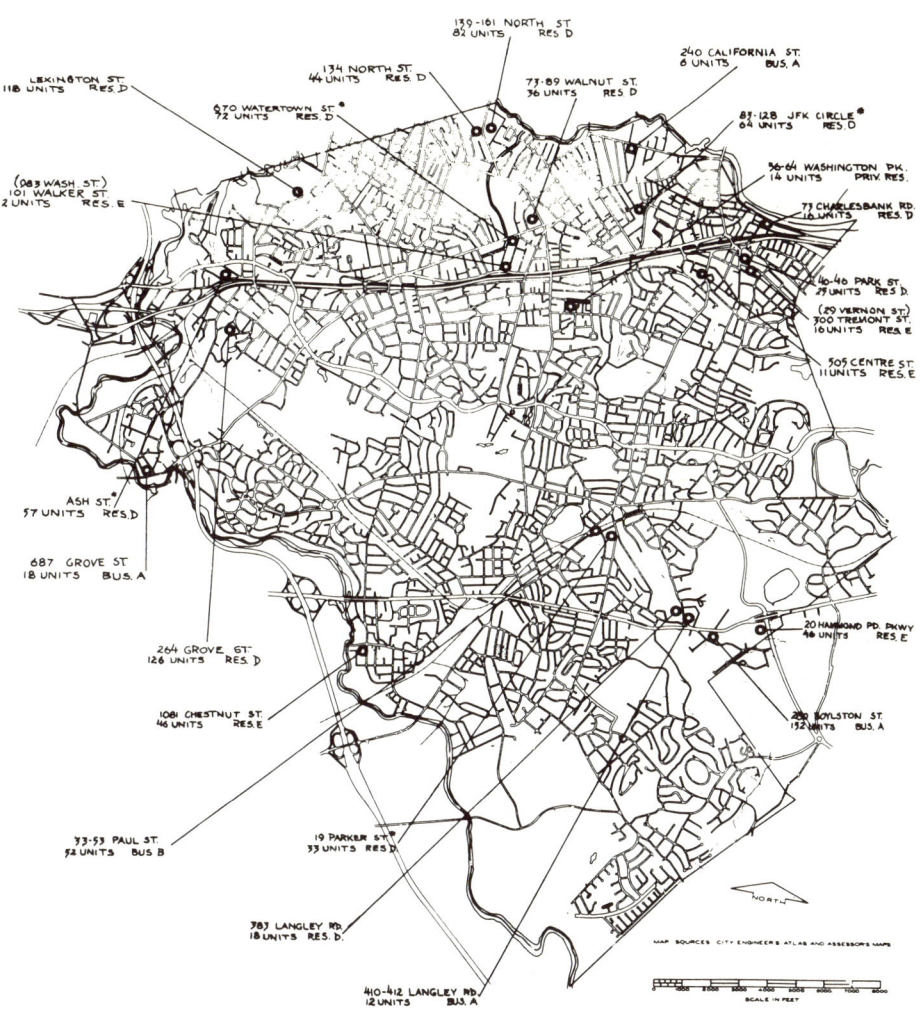

APARTMENT DEVELOPMENT 1960–1969

Table Newton 4. Apartment Characteristics

	Number of Units	Lot Area Sq. Ft.	Building Coverage Percent	Open Area Percent	Lot Area/ Apartment Unit
Units built 1960–1970	856	1,484,380	20.7	47.4	1,734
Units built before 1960	684	826,829	—	—	1,209
Housing for the elderly	226	389,799	23.3	60.3	1,725
Total	1,766	2,701,008	24.3	50.0	1,529

Apartment Buildings by Zone

Zone	Total	Percent
Residence D	27	51
Residence E	10	19
Residence F	0	0
Business A	10	19
Business B	1	2
Other	5	9
	53	100

Source: City of Newton, Planning Department, June 1970.

Table Newton 5. New Housing Units in Newton—1960-1969

Year	Single Family			Two-Family			Apartments/Elderly			Total DU*
	Permits	DU*	Percent	Permits	DU*	Percent	Permits	DU*	Percent	
1960	131	131	84.5	12	24	15.5	—	—	—	155
1961	83	83	57.3	8	16	11.0	1	46	31.7	145
1962	69	69	44.5	11	22	14.2	1	—	—	155
1963	78	78	65.5	12	24	20.2	2	17	14.3	119
1964	78	78	59.5	4	8	6.1	2	12	9.2	131
1965	76	76	19.1	9	18	4.5	3	232	58.3	398
1966	45	45	44.5	6	12	11.9	4	44	43.6	101
1967	32	32	8.5	1	2	0.5	6	344	91.0	378
1968	37	37	41.1	5	10	11.1	2	43	47.8	90
1969	20	20	10.1	2	4	2.0	2	118**	59.3	199
Total	649	649	34.7	70	140	7.5	23	856	45.7	1,871

*Dwelling Units
**Under Construction

Table Newton 6. Apartment Zoned Land

Zones Permitting Apartments	Total Area (acres)	In Apartments (acres)	Developed In Other Use (acres)	Undeveloped (acres)
Residence D	244.0	38.9	188.0	17.1
Residence E	25.4	11.5	12.0	1.9
Residence F	17.6	—	2.3	15.3
Business A	132.0	9.0	93.1	29.9
Business B	81.0	—	69.3	11.7
Total	500.0	59.4	364.7	75.9
Percent		11.9	72.9	15.1

11,406 acres = total land area of Newton
11,406 acres minus 1,700 acres (streets) = 9,706 acres
9,706 acres = net (usable) land

Table Newton 7. Tax Revenue Comparison: Apartment vs. Other Residential Use

	Apartments	All Other Residential Uses
Assessed value	$6,786,500	$219,612,950
Tax revenue @ $113/$1,000	$766,874	$24,816,263
Number of dwelling units	1,776	25,845
Tax revenue per dwelling unit	$434	$960
Number of persons	2,254[1]	86,328[1]
Tax revenue per person	$342	$287

[1] City Census, January 1970

Table Newton 8. Land Use as Percentage of Total

	In Acres	Percent of City Area
Residential	6,150	53.5
Commercial	267	2.3
Industrial	267	2.3
Institutional	400	3.5
Public/Semipublic	1,274	11.1
Vacant Land (privately-owned)	1,418	12.4
Streets (estimated)	1,710	14.9
Total	11,480	100.0

The most important source of income is the property tax. Business and industry pay only 14 percent of this total income, while private owners of vacant land supply 1.4 percent, and owners of residential property provide an overwhelming 84.6 percent, according to a 1967 Economic Base Study prepared by Newton's Planning Department. These monies go toward covering the growing annual expenditures which have risen from approximately $36,000,000 in 1967 to approximately $50,000,000 in 1970. To shoulder this growing burden, the City has increased the tax rate, per $1000 of assessed value, from $76.20 in 1967 to $113.00 in 1970, $121.60 in 1971, and $139.60 in 1972—almost three times higher a rate than those of the other communities studied. Yet 31 percent of Newton's land is tax exempt.

The Community's Awareness of Housing Need

Over 62 percent of Newton's housing stock (of 27,425 units) consists of 1-unit structures whose median value in 1970 was $33,600. In typical suburban traditions most units are owner-occupied (80 percent), vacancy and turnover rates are low while the overwhelming majority of the units are equipped with telephone, complete kitchen and plumbing. Due to land shortage and rising costs, only 17 single-family units were built in 1969. Concurrently, strict zoning laws and minimum-lot-size requirements prevented construction of many multi-family dwellings. Newton has the smallest percent (7.8) of units in structures built 1960-70 among the communities studied here (14.1 for Boston SMSA).

Newton apartments cater to older people, females, young adults, and those whose incomes are above the median. Average rent in Newton ran about $215 a month for a 1-bedroom unit, and about $230 for 2 bedrooms. Larger apartments were virtually unavailable. The median cost of rental in 1970 was $145. Of the smaller number of units available to low- and moderate-income people, 593 were substandard. It was anticipated (based on the mean rate of demolition for 1964-1969), that 150 of these 593 would be demolished by 1974. As of December 1971 Newton had 401 units of subsidized housing (1.5 percent of its housing stock).

What Newton Has Done

Since World War II, Newton has produced a new housing program every ten years.

In 1948 Newton responded to the national housing shortage in its fashion. Spurning public housing, the city constructed 400 single-family homes for the returning Newton veterans in the remote and undeveloped Oak Hill section. The City donated the land ($100 per lot) and sold the houses for $7,800, with no "buy back" provision, in order to keep the area for veterans. In 1970 these houses sold for about $30,000. Even with the patriotic spirit of the time, the single-family home concept, and the remote location, opposition to, and fear of, the kinds of people that would come into Newton was voiced.

42 Housing the Poor in Suburbia

Table Newton 9. Tax Exempt and Taxable Land

	Area in Acres	Percent of Total	Total Assessments in 1964	Percent of Total
Taxable Land	7,861	68.9	$303,156,650	79.5
Tax Exempt Land	3,545	31.1	77,869,950	20.5
Totals	11,406	100.0	381,026,600	100.0

Distribution of Assessed Valuations—1964

	Assessment Values	Percent of Total
Residential	$256,254,905	84.6
Commercial	36,985,113	12.2
Industrial	5,456,819	1.8
Vacant Land		
Golf Courses	2,868,900	0.9
Cemeteries (partial)	984,600	0.3
Other (not included in Residential)	606,313	0.2
Institutional	exempt	–
Public/Semipublic	exempt	–
Streets	exempt	–
Totals	$303,156,650	100.0

Table Newton 10. Selected Housing Characteristics 1970—Newton

A. Type, Condition, Density

Total Housing Units	27,425	
Housing Units Owner Occupied	19,101	
Housing Units Renter Occupied	7,857	
Vacant Housing Units	464	
Total 1 Unit structures	17,186	(62.7 Percent)
Housing Units with—		
1.01 to 1.50 persons/room	597	
1.51 or more persons/room	142	
Median number of persons per unit	2.9	
Density: 5,098 persons per square mile		
Units with telephone available	26,372	
Units with complete kitchen	27,212	
Units with complete plumbing	26,978	
Subsidized Housing (as of Dec. 31, 1971)	401	(1.5 percent of total)

B. Value

Median value of housing units	$33,600	
Median Contract Rental	$ 145	
Value of Owner-Occupied Units		
Less than $5,000		5
$ 5,000 to $ 9,999		112
$10,000 to $14,999		321
$15,000 to $19,999		1,048
$20,000 to $24,999		2,292

Table Newton 10. (cont.)

$25,000 to $34,999	4,808
$35,000 to $49,999	4,281
$50,000 or More	2,953
Total Reporting	15,820

Rental Contracts for Renter-Occupied units:

Less Than $60	404
$ 60 to $ 79	472
$ 80 to $ 99	711
$100 to $119	874
$120 to $149	1,511
$150 to $199	1,819
$200 to $299	1,301
$300 or More	356
No Cash Rent	385
Total Reported	7,448

C. Vacancy

Total vacant units	464
Homeowner vacant units (Sale)	50
Rental Vacant Units	213
Other Type Vacant	201
Home-Owner Vacancy Rate .3 Percent	
Median Value Home Owner Vacancy	$37,800
Rental Vacancy Rate 2.6 Percent	
Median Value Rental Vacancy	$176

D. Property Assessment

Rate per $1,000 assessed val. $121.00 (1971), $139.60 (1972), change 1971-72: + $18.00.

Assessed Valuation: $327.789,250
Tax Levy: $ 37,798,250

E. Year Moved into Present Units

1969-1970	13765
1968	8355
1967	5887
1965-1966	10026
1960-1964	15567
1950-1959	20958
1949 or earlier	10665
Always LVD Pres QT	5828

In 1958, Newton, recognizing the needs of the elderly—especially widows on fixed incomes—lobbied a housing authority for the elderly through a divided and reluctant Board of Aldermen, uncomfortable with "public housing." To date, 225 units, the total number authorized, have been constructed on four sites.

Table Newton 11. Size and Sex Characteristics of Apartment Residents

Age Group	Male	Female	Total	Percent
75+	57	142	199	8.9
71-75	66	118	184	8.2
66-70	102	178	280	12.5
56-65	145	291	436	19.3
46-55	74	138	212	9.5
36-45	65	74	139	6.2
26-35	211	186	397	17.7
19-25	135	180	315	14.0
7-18	15	17	32	1.4
0-6	25	26	51	2.3
	895	1,350	2,245	100.0

Source: 1970 City Census

Table Newton 12. Apartment Resident Characteristics Per Apartment

	Number	Percent
Total number residents	2,245	100
Male	895	39.9
Female	1,350	60.1
Total number of units	1,540	—
Average number of residents per unit	1.38	—
Average age		
Male	45.8	—
Female	50.8	—

Source: City Census, January 1970
Planning Department Survey, August 1970

Table Newton 13. Rental Structure

	Studio/Efficiency	One Bedroom	Two Bedroom	Three Bedroom
Number of Apartments	47	464	562	9
Percent	4	43	52	1
Rental Range				
Low	$145	$190	$210	Not available
High	$175	$300+	$400+	Not available
Median	$155	$215	$230	Not available

Source: City of Newton, Planning Department.

Ten years later the conservative reputation of the city had been replaced by a liberal image, and the concept of a scattered site, nonprofit sponsored LMIH constructed for needy Newton residents had been nurtured by civic, political, and professional groups. In November 1967, the Newton Board of Aldermen's subcommittee on low-income housing agreed unanimously that "there is a shortage of low-income housing in the City of Newton," and an immediate need of at least 200 units of low-income housing within the city. There was further need for moderate-income housing. The Committee recommended that no large-scale developments of low-income housing should be considered, to avoid creating ghettos for low-income residents.

Small projects of 20 to 50 families or units were favored by the Committee, which concluded that providing proper dwellings for low-income families was not only the problem of the urban communities but was and would become even more the problem of suburban communities. The Board of Aldermen, implementing the recommendations of the Subcommittee's report, struck the elderly limitation from the housing authority's power and directed it to apply for Section 23, leased housing funds, from the Department of Housing and Urban Development (HUD).

A conference, held on June 4, 1968, entitled, "Newton Looks at its Resources—Suburban Opportunity in the Crisis of Race and Poverty," set as its initial goal to define "accurately" and "clearly" the role of the suburb in regard to urban ills in America. The conference finally focused on what was perceived to be a manageable and attainable goal for Newton in the metropolitan housing market. One of the concrete suggestions which developed was to establish the Newton Community Development Foundation, to initiate planning and development in the following areas:

1. to develop a comprehensive housing program for moderate- and low-income families currently living in substandard housing. To provide additional housing for those young families and the elderly, who by reason of income restriction, need a greater range of choice;
2. to serve as a "community relations" resource, providing advocacy planning for the low- and moderate-income community in Newton;
3. to provide limited financial aid and professional assistance in cooperation with the Newton Housing Authority and other agencies in developing a comprehensive housing program for Newton;
4. to serve as a citizen's action-planning-resource to the city of Newton, in concert with government agencies, providing aid for constructive planning towards economic and cultural growth.

At the conference it was concluded that low- and moderate-income housing was needed for two groups predominantly:

1. young couples who were now forced to establish their first home in the outer suburbs. Census figures indicated that the average age of homeowners in Newton was rising substantially (25-35 age group down 10 percent from 1950 to 1960);
2. retired couples who were forced to move away from Newton because they could no longer afford to maintain a family-size home.

The proposal also contained suggestions for funding such an organization:

1. by initial grants, and seed money from sponsoring institutions such as churches, service organizations, business groups, banks, and industry;
2. by membership dues ranging from $10 for an associate membership to $5,000 for institutional membership and sponsorship;
3. by contributions solicited from private sources, above and beyond membership dues.

Responding to the conference, the Board of Aldermen passed an order in July 1968 requesting the Mayor to direct the Planning Department to undertake a study of low- and moderate-income housing needs in the City.

During the preparation of the report, the Board sold a parcel of land to an apartment developer. But pressure from aroused LMIH advocates made the Board require the developer to allot 3 units for the Newton Housing Authority to rent. It issued a strong resolution:

WHEREAS: An integrated society is desirable for the wholesome and full experience of life itself; and

WHEREAS: A genuine community is one in which all human beings have the opportunity to contribute to the welfare of others from their own experience, characteristics and talents; and

WHEREAS: In order to achieve community integration more fully, we must convey to black people our desire to have them buy homes and live in all Newton neighborhoods according to their own wants and means; therefore

BE IT RESOLVED: That the governing bodies of the City of Newton should continue their efforts to accomplish integration and that the Board of Aldermen endorse in principle the following statement submitted to it by homeowners in the City of Newton:

"We, the undersigned Newton home owners, express our hope and desire to be joined in our City by black people. We urge those of our friends who have decided to sell their homes to make special efforts to insure that these listings are known to potential buyers among black people by advertising in ways which are likely to be seen or heard by them, by dealing with real estate agents who will make the fact that Newton homes are for sale known to them, and by contacting associations likely to be able to encourage responses from the black community.

We feel that our City can benefit a great deal by having black people among us. Our children will benefit in and out of the classroom. Our local institutions will benefit by having the enthusiasm and talent of an emerging people in our midst. Our lives will be fuller as we come closer to understanding and loving all men as neighbors. We welcome our black brethren to share in the bounty and building of our City."

The Newton Democrats were the first political unit to issue a statement supporting LMIH, advocating:

1. the immediate construction in Newton of low- and moderate-income housing to help alleviate the present housing shortage;
2. the principle of economic integration in housing;
3. the reserving, as a guiding principle, of some units in all new apartment housing built in Newton, whether on public or private land, for families with low- and moderate-incomes.

The Planning Department's study, released in September 1968, gave professional approval to the earlier Aldermanic report and its conclusions that approximately 200 lower-income units were required, but considered the number a base figure which must be continually reevaluated.

Underscoring the need for housing for moderate-income families, the study recommended that the most productive combination of forces possible to assure the development of low- and moderate-income housing in the community would be private, nonprofit, cooperative or limited dividend corporations. They would acquire and develop recommended sites for construction of combination low-moderate-income units and rent-supplemented units. The study recommended that these developments be limited to 20 to 30 housing units in accordance with the "scattered, low density" units suggested by the Aldermanic Subcommittee.

Finally, the study evaluated over 200 sites and earmarked 42 as potentially favorable for location and construction of LMIH.

THE NCDF: ITS STRATEGY AND PROPOSAL

The consistent outpouring of community concern over housing from June 1967 to July 1968 convinced local religious leaders that an organization formed according to the criteria established at the housing conference would be viable. The publication in September 1968, of the Planning Department's *Low- and Moderate-Income Housing Study* added further legitimacy to the formation of

NCDF. Thus, in September 1968 NCDF was organized by 22 priests, rabbis, and ministers to act as a private developer in order "to provide significant quantities of low- and moderate-income housing in Newton." This group then appointed a Board of Directors. Although suggestions were made to include civil service employees and antipoverty group members on the Board of Directors, the Board was made up of businessmen, civic leaders, lawyers, architects, and professional people. The Chairman was Robert C. Casselman, a man prominent in community affairs. A former MIT faculty member, he was a member of the Newton Redevelopment Authority and Executive Secretary of Massachusetts State Government Modernization.

From September 1968 to the spring of 1969, NCDF solicited financial and official support and was successful in both endeavors. By June of 1969, almost half of the $100,000 fund raising goal had been reached. NCDF received verbal support from various official political sources; both the Republican and Democratic City Committees, for instance, issued supportive statements.

In March, 1969, the Mayor, Monte Basbas, appointed a Housing Coordinating Committee, chaired by the city planner and consisting of representatives from the Board of Aldermen, Redevelopment Authority, and Housing Authority, "to provide means for official coordination of the many public and private activities aimed at accomplishing the state's low-moderate-income housing goals of the City."

In April the Executive Committee of the Newton Republican City Committee issued a policy statement commending the Aldermanic report and the professional document of the Planning Department and assessing the actual need for both low- and moderate-income housing at more than 500 units. While the report emphasized single-family homeownership, it suggested that nonprofit corporations should be encouraged to investigate the opportunities under 236 and MHFA. But, since these innovative programs are discouraged in Newton by the high cost of land, it recommended that the City of Newton lease for a long term appropriate City-owned land to a nonprofit corporation for the express purpose of constructing low-moderate-income housing.

On May 5, 1969, the Board of Aldermen accepted the Planning Department's report of September 1968 and resolved that the City should not release any of the City-owned property named in the report for other purposes, unless the Board of Aldermen decided that the site is not suitable or available or required for low- or moderate-income housing. With respect to private property, the Board of Aldermen, when considering a site for any purpose, was to include in its consideration the suitability and availability of or need for the site for low- and moderate-income housing.

Also in May the League of Women Voters and the Newton Community Relations Commission sponsored an all-day conference on "Newton's Need for Low- and Moderate-income Housing." Almost 300 people—a surprisingly high number—appeared. Other sponsoring groups were the Housing Coordinating Committee of the City of Newton, the Newton Chamber of

Commerce, Newton Committee for Fair Housing and Equal Rights, Newton Community Council, and NCDF. Support was urged for NCDF—which took these proceedings to be an indication of general citizen approval of low- and moderate-income housing for the city.

The conference voted in favor of a resolution calling for the creation of at least 400 new housing units. Those attending agreed that such housing must be provided for those who live or work in Newton (especially young marrieds, the elderly, and city employees), and that a certain percentage should be reserved for residents of the core city. Many sites in different parts of the city should be developed at the same time to minimize protests by neighborhood groups. Developments should be small—not more than 50 units—to avoid creating new ghettos.

On the same day (May 7, 1969) the Newton Democratic City Committee commended the housing conference and the Republican City Committee and reminded the public of its support for LMIH the previous year. Noting that "The housing area is not, however, one in which partisanship should play a role," they confirmed that "The creation of housing opportunities for persons of low- and moderate-income is indeed 'Newton's critical need.' . . . Private groups, both nonprofit and profit making, can utilize existing federal and state programs to make inroads upon this need, and we encourage and support such efforts."

It was at this time, in June 1969, at the peak of its support, that the Foundation became operational and appointed Mark Slotnick as Executive Director.

In November, the Mayor wrote a letter to the president of NCDF in which he declared that:

> The City must do its share to help you succeed, and for my part, I will make every effort to make available City-owned land for the development of low- and moderate-income housing. . . .

And the following month, the Board of Aldermen unanimously passed a resolution supporting the NCDF concept and urging contributions.

For all this support, danger signals were not absent. The Planning Department in the September 1968 Low-Moderate Income Housing Study, indicated a dichotomy in Newton's attitudes on housing which could work against effective implementation of any comprehensive housing policy. While the community may exhibit an increasing awareness of its housing responsibilities, the practical and political realities of finding acceptable sites for low- and moderate-income housing developments generally run counter to what the protectors of the "Garden City" image consider to be sound land-use planning. Well-intentioned residents of the community find themselves on both sides of the issue—that is, in agreement with the basic philosophy, but diametrically opposed to the land-use decision required to create the project on a given site.

To meet truly its stated housing goals, the study concluded, the community must achieve a reconciliation of polarized community values.

From June to November 1969 the NCDF Board of Directors worked behind closed doors to develop its strategy. As one of the first nonprofit sponsors to attempt to build low- and moderate-income housing on scattered sites in a Boston suburb, they did not have the advantage of drawing upon the experience of many other groups.

The Board was in general agreement over which federal financial programs were feasible and should be investigated for their applicability to Newton. These were Sections 235, 236, and Turnkey III.

Under the 235 program the federal government pays a part of the interest portion of a homeowner's mortgage payment, thus allowing the home buyer to borrow from private lending institutions at market rates. The maximum federal subsidy runs between $40 and $70 a month and from $1000 to $3000 per unit for land. Land in Newton was selling for a minimum of $20,000 per acre. Minimum lot size varied for different zoning districts. The 235 program was attractive because single-family housing would fit in with existing neighborhoods, minimizing the risk of changing neighborhoods or lowering property values. No zoning laws would have to be appealed. The argument that low-income families neglect the care of rental units could be replaced with the likelihood that property maintenance would come with the pride of ownership.

Although the Board conceptually liked the 235 approach, it eventually rejected it because land shortage and high construction costs of single-family dwellings would have provided fewer housing units than the 500 units they had set as their goal. Also, an investigation showed that other attempts to build 235 housing in the Boston area had not been successful.

Another possibility considered was the Turnkey III program. Under this plan, a nonprofit sponsor such as NCDF would build single-family housing and then turn it over to the local Housing Authority, who would own the unit for a full 25 years while the homeowner paid 20 percent of his income on a modified lease-purchase plan. There would be an abatement of local taxes during the 25-year period, but, once the tenant became the owner, he would be responsible for taxes on his unit. NCDF rejected this plan for the same reasons it rejected Section 235; it thought land costs on a per-unit basis were too high, and the aggregate number of units was too low.

The third alternative was the 236 multiple-dwelling unit program. This program could accommodate the large number of units the Board wanted. Under Section 236 each tenant pays 25 percent of his income toward rent, and the federal government pays the difference between the tenant's payment and the market rent. With the maximum federal subsidy of $50 to $60 a month, it was expected that NCDF would have to charge each tenant between $120 and $170 a month. Only 20 to 25 percent of 236 housing units can be occupied by persons receiving Rent Supplement payments.

The major drawback to Section 236 was that as a multiple dwelling unit program it was necessary, in most cases, to obtain zoning changes before the program could be implemented. Approximately 965 acres of land were zoned for private residence in the city. About 500 of these were in zones which permitted apartment development. This amounted to 5.1 percent of the area of the city. Approximately 59.4 acres (or 11.9 percent) were already being utilized for apartments amounting to 0.66 percent, or two-thirds of 1 percent of the land in Newton. Additionally, 364.7 acres, or about 73 percent of the land in apartment-zoned districts had been developed for other uses, while 75.9 acres, or 15.1 percent remained vacant. The vacant apartment-zoned land amounted to 0.07 percent of the city's land area. This total of 75.9 acres was reduced by the fact that a number of parcels were below the minimum lot size requirements for apartments. A number of others were unsuitable because of soil conditions or locational problems. Thus, NCDF would have to acquire zoning changes in single-residence districts in order to build multiple-dwelling units. To obtain zoning changes, it was necessary for a special permit to be granted by the Board of Aldermen on recommendation of its Land-Use Committee. The NCDF board anticipated that obtaining these changes would be a problem because the 236 program, as a multi-unit, low-income housing program, was likely to muster opposition throughout Newton. Despite the drawbacks, the Board concluded that the multiple-unit 236 approach would be the best solution to Newton's low- and moderate-income housing need.

Political Strategy

During the months of Board meetings there was heated discussion about political strategy. Some members felt that the traditional route of presenting a petition to the Land-Use Committee for zoning changes and variances, and then proceeding to a vote by the full Board of Aldermen, was the most sensible approach. One of the Aldermen-to-be championed this approach because he felt that Newtonites would prefer the route that would eventually credit them with being the first open-housing community.

Other members of the Board, however, were not so certain that the majority of the community would be willing to accept low- and moderate-income housing on its own initiative. They, therefore, wanted to highlight eventual use of the "Anti-Snob Zoning" Law to force a favorable decision at the local level. Under that route, if the NCDF proposal were rejected by the Board of Aldermen, the NCDF could appeal the decision to the local zoning board of appeals, as specified in the State Zoning Enabling Act, Chapter 40A of the Massachusetts General Laws. Chapter 774 (the "Anti-Snob Zoning" Law—see p. 353) provides an additional means of appeal beyond the local zoning board of appeals to a Housing Appeals Committee in the State Department of Community Affairs. To go this route, the NCDF would have to give up City-owned sites because it could not file against the City and still use the City's land. In addition, the decision of the State Appeals Committee is limited to the issue of whether the decision rendered by the local appeals committee was "reasonable and consistent with local needs." Determination of whether local regulations and requirements are consistent with local needs is made by the use of the following planning criteria:

1. are they reasonable in view of regional needs for low- and moderate-income housing when the number of low-income residents is considered, along with the need to protect health and safety of occupants of proposed housing or residents of the city or town?
2. do they promote better site and building design in relation to the surroundings?
3. do they preserve open space?
4. are they applied as equally as possible to both subsidized and unsubsidized housing?

A decision by the State Zoning Board of Appeals overrides local zoning restrictions. NCDF knew there were at least two other communities, Hanover and Concord, where appeals had been filed with the State. There had been no decision as of the summer of 1969 on either petition to the State, but NCDF knew that community resentment ran high in both places. NCDF decided, however, that their case in Newton differed from that of Hanover and Concord, and that they could win their appeal to the local zoning board; they decided the threat of Chapter 774 should not be used. They recognized that there would be opposition, but they thought the excellence of their plans and the support shown by the community in 1968 and 1969 would override opposition before the Board of Aldermen.

The Plan

Selection of the Federal program and the local political route still left unanswered determination of the size of the entire housing package. The 1968 *Low- and Moderate-Income Housing Study* by the Planning Board pointed to the need for at least 200 low-income units, but did not even attempt to estimate the need for moderate-income units. NCDF was aiming to provide for the needs of both groups and felt that the moderate-income needs, based on the desire of people to live in Newton, were even greater.

NCDF had to decide whether to build on scattered sites or in one large project. Current professional planning practice suggested a scattered site approach with a small number of units on each site. But this strategy presented the dangers of opposition by many more abutters, with the possible outcome of no housing at all.

A decision also had to be reached as to whether the program implementation would be incremental or immediate. If zoning changes were sought on all sites at one time, construction could begin simultaneously, thus allowing economies of scale; if zoning changes were sought on one site at a time, NCDF might be able to minimize opposition and also have one site completed as an example of design, management, and maintenance.

Finally, NCDF was forced to consider the feasibility of working behind the scenes, quietly trying to gain Aldermen's support, or of using the community as its sounding board to generate pressure on the Aldermen to vote pro-NCDF. Some members of the Foundation knew that another nonprofit organization, sponsoring moderate-income housing developments, had come to the conclusion that the preferable strategy for developing housing with provocative social goals, especially in communities unreceptive to new multi-family housing, was to develop such projects with a minimum amount of public attention, but with a high degree of notice by other participants in the housing industry.

One result of NCDF's soliciting memberships, however, was the publication of a newsletter through which they informed members of plans and strategies. This information then became widespread and available to all interested—members and nonmembers alike. And, in the fall of 1969 the Foundation made its official strategy public in a pamphlet entitled "Newton ... No Ordinary Suburb":

> The initial NCDF plan is to construct not less than 500 units scattered throughout Newton's villages on as many sites as are economically feasible ... the initial plan will be presented as a city-wide package for city-wide study, review, and approval rather than a progression of discrete single-site proposals, any or all of which might otherwise have floundered because of some neighborhood opposition.... The immediate goal is to obtain zoning changes which will permit construction to begin. The decision was made to seek maximum publicity in the community and to request its support.

Site Selection

Consideration of various approaches to the development of the housing itself and selection of the political strategy to present this development consumed a large part of NCDF initial decision making, but the difficult job of selecting, bargaining for, and obtaining sites still remained. The problems involved in this process were immense. Foremost was the absence of vacant land in Newton: only 1,418 acres out of a total of 11,406, and not much of this land was suitable for housing.

Of the vacant land, there were parcels already zoned residence D, E, and F for town house and garden apartment construction, but the property owners wanted prices appropriate to luxury housing, not subsidized units. It was estimated that, based upon 15 units to the acre, the land needed for the entire plan of 540 units would be between 30 and 35 acres. Looking at alternative sites, NCDF felt they could acquire about 60 percent of their needs at prices of about $20,000 per acre. The private land would require zone changes. However, they hoped that the City would donate the remaining 40 percent of the land needed.

In May 1969 the Board of Aldermen had committed itself to the concept of making City land available for low- and moderate-income housing. Still, this didn't guarantee NCDF a choice of City-owned sites. The group would have to negotiate with the Board of Aldermen and other City departments for those individual sites.

There was competition for this land, whether owned publicly or privately. City agencies, such as the Recreation Department, were interested in acquiring sites for their own projects, and private developers were seeking desirable building sites.

Another constraint to site selection was the commitment to "scatteration," meaning that a desirable site in one village would have to be discarded for a less suitable site in another if the first caused clustering of low- and moderate-income units in the area.

Under all these constraints, the Board of Directors began its search. The most obvious starting point was those sites which had been examined and approved in the 1968 Planning Department Study. Yet, as these were the most desirable pieces of vacant land, they were in demand by many groups. Victory Field in Nonantum, a site marked with first order potential by the 1968 Planning Department Study, was a 150,000 square-foot playground declared surplus by the City Recreation Department. NCDF wanted the City to donate this piece of land, but the local American Legion Post 440 offered the Board of Aldermen $18,000 for the field, so that they could build a new headquarters. NCDF then received word that this site was no longer a possibility for their purposes.

Another desirable site of 90,000 square feet, near the Myrtle Baptist Church in West Newton, came to the attention of the Housing Authority which, prodded by NCDF's activity, now expressed the desire to build 125 units of low- and moderate-income housing for families on this site. When this site came up for discussion before the Board of Aldermen for transfer to the Housing Authority, Alderman Reidy, representing a ward known to be conservative, criticized this request as a political hoax: "It is time," he said, "we stopped degrading low-income families by giving them housing in areas where noone else will live." Under this premise, the Board voted against giving the land to the Authority, and this site remained unused.

Heated competition ensued for the Stearns and Pierce School sites, both designated by the planning study as having second order potential. Originally, the School Committee had agreed to release these two sites to the City upon completion of the New Day Junior High School. As these sites became the object of inquiries by NCDF, counter-pressure began to build up from the neighborhoods and the School Committee began to change its mind about releasing the sites to the City. Mayor Basbas showed his support for NCDF by urging the School Committee to release the land.

Mr. Casselman, attempting to cooperate with the School Committee, asked them to appoint a representative to work with his group in deciding upon possible housing sites. A compromise was finally worked out, enabling NCDF to acquire the Stearns School site.

Because of the requirement of obtaining City-owned land, NCDF was in close contact with City agencies and officials from November 1969, when NCDF met with the Mayor and Aldermen, until the following April when their plans and sites were announced. Throughout this period, they negotiated with representatives from the School and Recreation Committees while continually receiving verbal support from the Mayor and Aldermen.

Evaluation and negotiation for the 10 final sites took a total of 6 months, from November 1969 to April 1970. The 200 sites earmarked in the planning study were reviewed by the Board of Directors and narrowed down to 63, and, then again, to 45. These 45 sites were carefully analyzed according to Board-established priorities, which included land costs, availability of options, location, size, site conditions, and neighborhood impact.

The terms of the options, in both time and money, were crucial factors to the success of the NCDF plan. NCDF knew that as hopes to begin construction by the end of 1970 might not be fulfilled if the approval process hit any snags, it was crucial to obtain options for at least 2 years. The option costs, including tax payments, would have to be within the range of NCDF funds. It was difficult to obtain the terms they wanted, while still keeping down the price. NCDF then narrowed the field to 30 of the 200 original sites; 20 were privately owned and 10 City owned. To inform the community of its progress, NCDF invited the public to a special hearing to present these sites. At the meeting, it was emphasized that only 30 of the City's 1,000 acres of open space were being considered and that fears that NCDF was going to eat up the City's recreation grounds and parkland were unfounded. In anticipation of opposition to the general idea of multiple-family developments, Mr. Casselman presented figures to demonstrate that rising costs had made single-family dwelling units (SFDU's) unfeasible in Newton. Between 1960 and 1965, 439 SFDU's had been built; between 1965 and 1969, 187; and in 1969-1970, 17. He solicited moral and financial support at this meeting to sustain the Foundation's effort and to ensure realization of its program in the spring.

While NCDF was negotiating for sites, it was also interviewing architects. They wanted a firm that could begin work on each site as it was acquired. After reviewing the work done by several firms, the Board of Directors selected the Pard Team, Inc. as the project architects. Experienced in designing low- and moderate-income housing, the Pard Team had also done a large portion of the rehabilitation of Boston's South End.

In the last phase of site negotiations, NCDF sought options on 10 of the 20 private sites, and, also, told the City which sites it wanted. Final selection was left to the Board of Aldermen. By the end of March, when negotiations were complete with options signed and commitments made, NCDF had 6 private and 4 City sites on which to develop low- and moderate-income housing.

In April 1970, NCDF announced its 10 sites and its final proposal. Out of the total 40.7 acres, 24 were privately owned and 16.7 were owned by the City. The private sites, designed to contain 315 units, were located at Hunnewell Avenue, Stanton Avenue, Hamlet Street, Thurston Road, Goddard Street, and on Esty Farm. Two-year options were obtained at a cost of $15,000 per year, totaling a cost of $525,000 for all 6 sites by the end of the 2-year period. The City-owned sites, on which 193 units were planned, were located at Beacon Street, Commonwealth Avenue across from City Hall, Pine and River Streets, and the Stearns School.

The NCDF Proposal

The final proposal included 508 units, to be scattered almost equally among the 10 sites, which, in turn, were scattered among 13 of Newton's 14 villages. NCDF described it in this way:

Who Needs It?
Some of the groups obviously affected by the housing shortage are young couples (many of whom have grown up in Newton); parents, children, and relatives of Newton families; elderly couples now living in old, family residences, who were not eligible for Housing for the Elderly; city employees and service workers; many families who can contribute to the life and vitality of our city.

Why is this Type of Housing in Such Short Supply?
The cost of land and the cost of building has virtually stopped construction of single-family homes in Newton. (Only 17 were built in 1969). Apartments built since 1960 are almost exclusively one- or two-bedroom units, and average rentals are over $200 per month.

The Scattered Site Plan
Intensive study of available land in Newton proved that it is possible to plan 10 housing sites, scattered throughout the city, with one site in or near each village.

Housing would then be available in all areas of Newton. The obvious sociological, financial, and governmental problems of single-site, massive housing projects could be avoided.

LOCATION OF PROPOSED NCDF SITES IN THE CITY: THE SCATTERED SITE STRATEGY

58 Housing the Poor in Suburbia

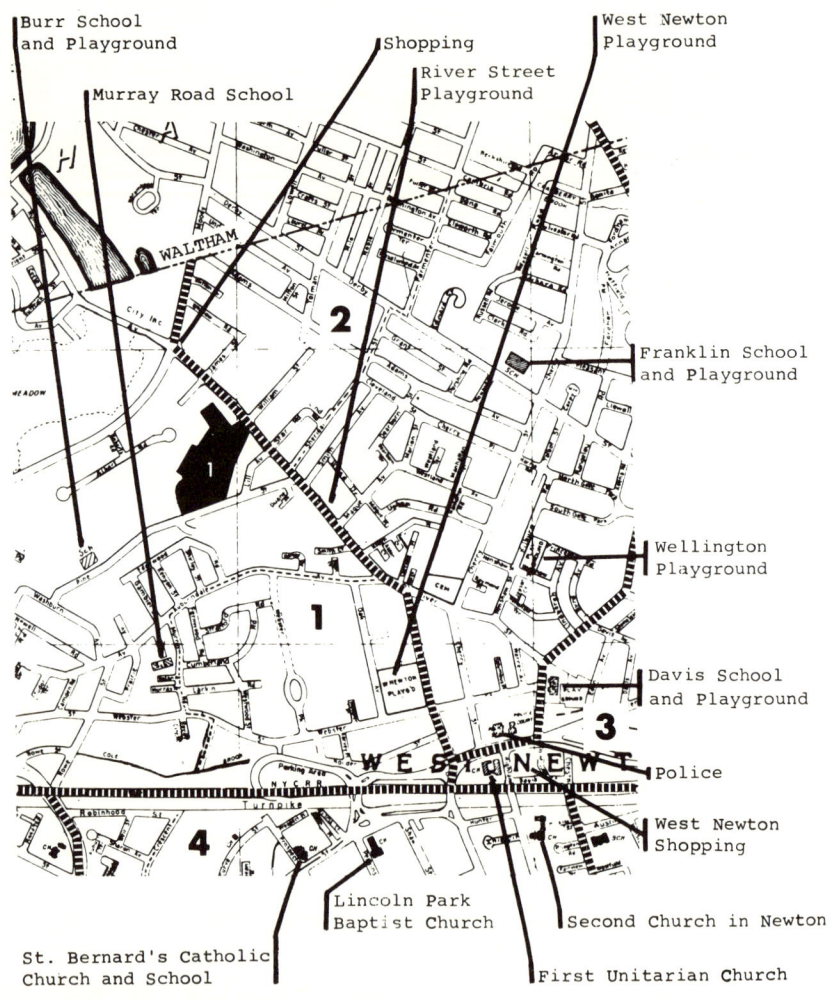

PROPOSED NCDF SITE #1—PINE AND RIVER STREETS

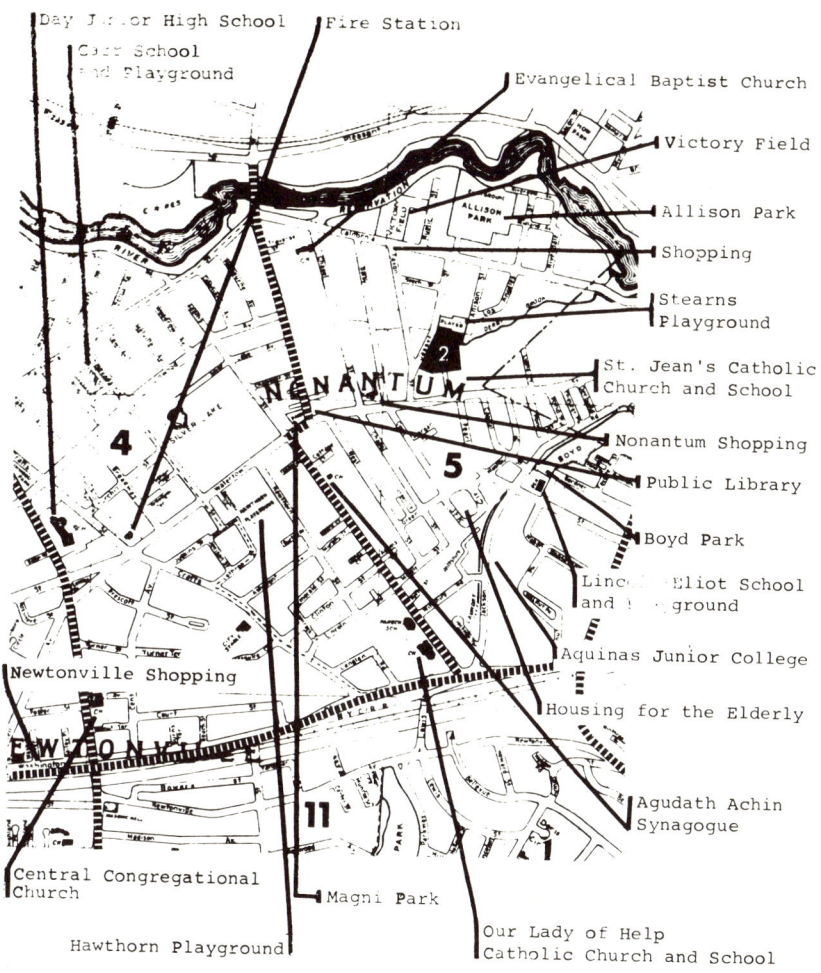

PROPOSED NCDF SITE #2—JASSET STREET

60 *Housing the Poor in Suburbia*

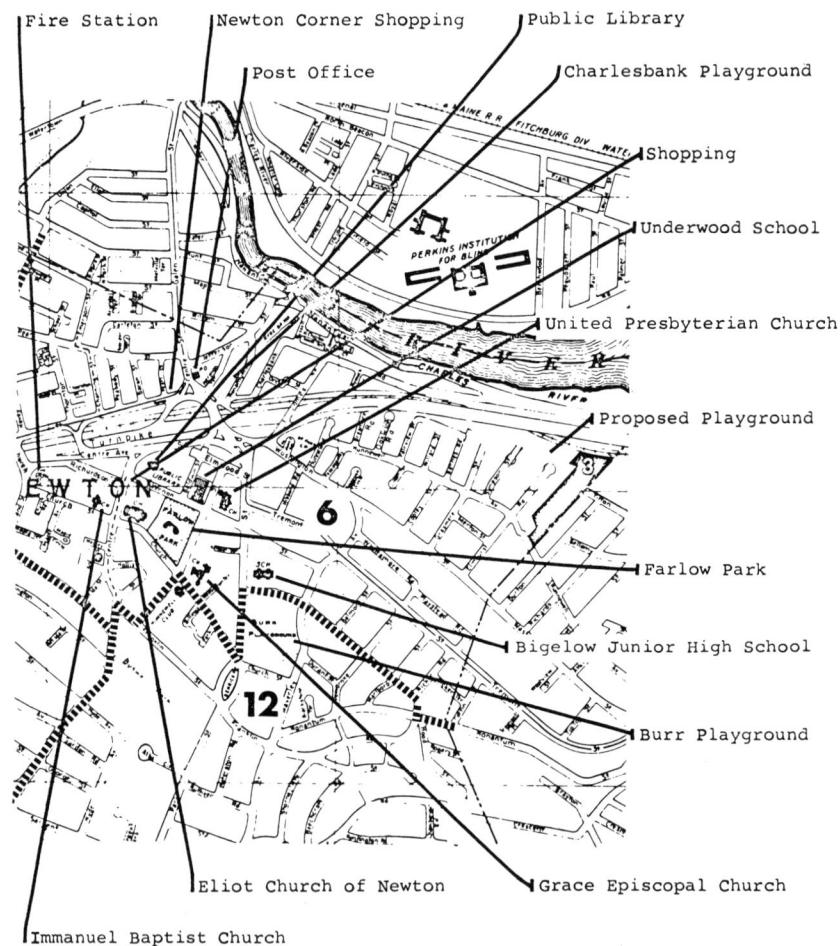

PROPOSED NCDF SITE #3—HUNNEWELL AVENUE

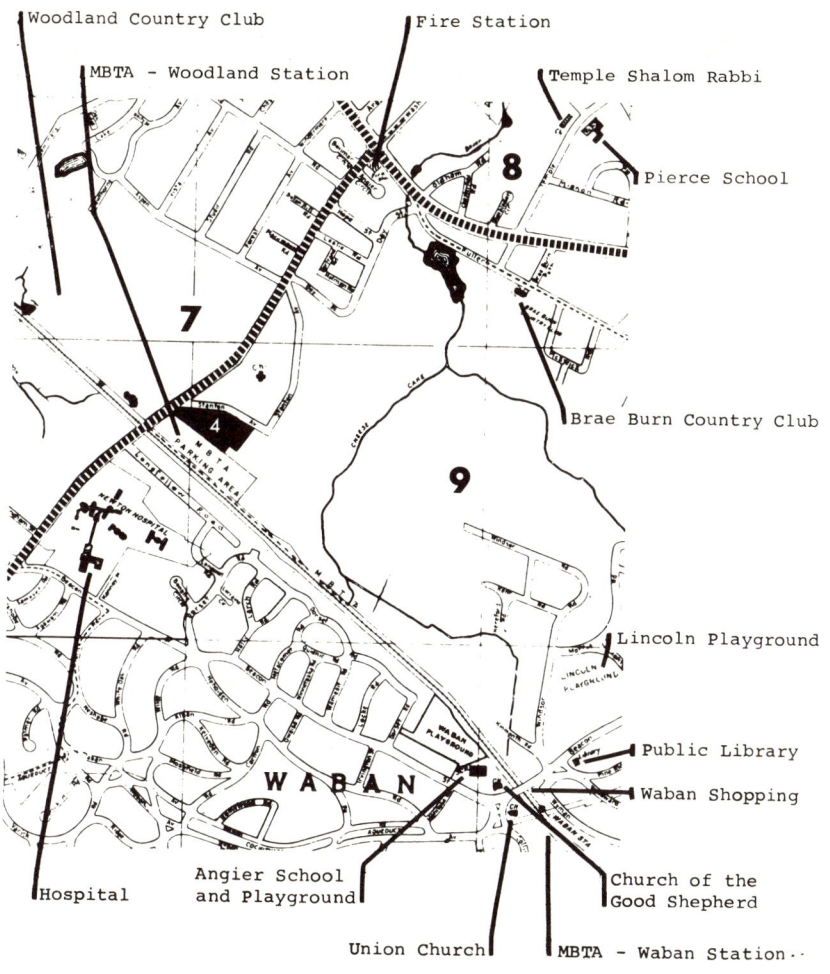

PROPOSED NCDF SITE #4—STANTON AVENUE

62 *Housing the Poor in Suburbia*

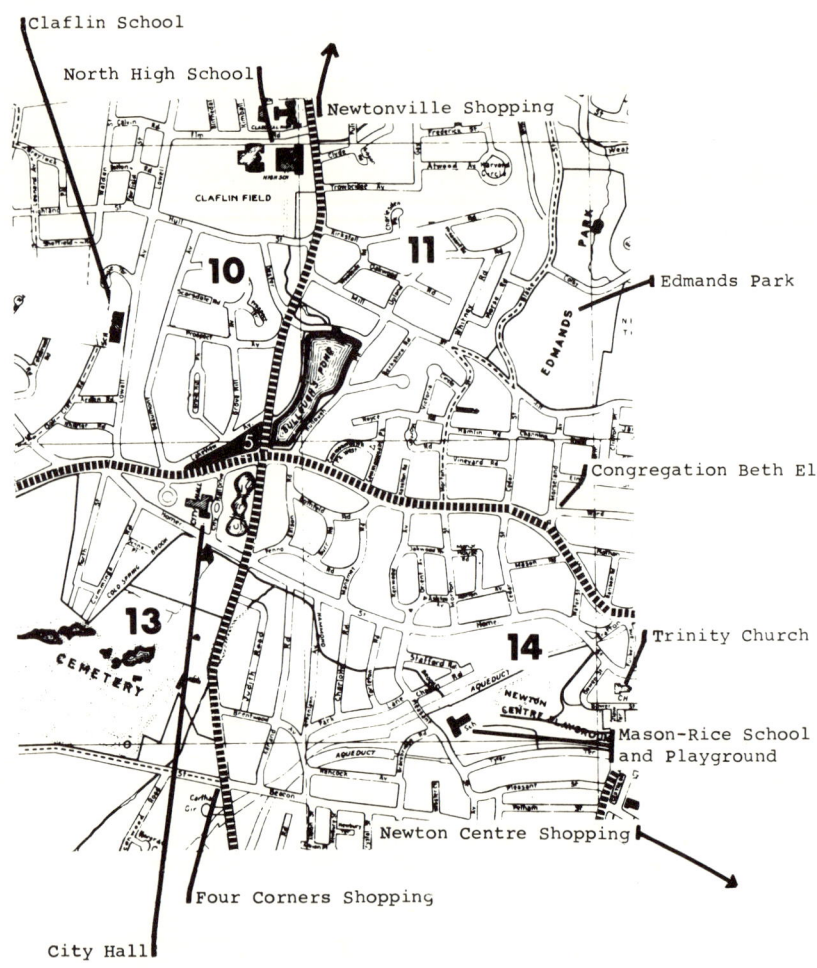

PROPOSED NCDF SITE #5—COMMONWEALTH AVENUE

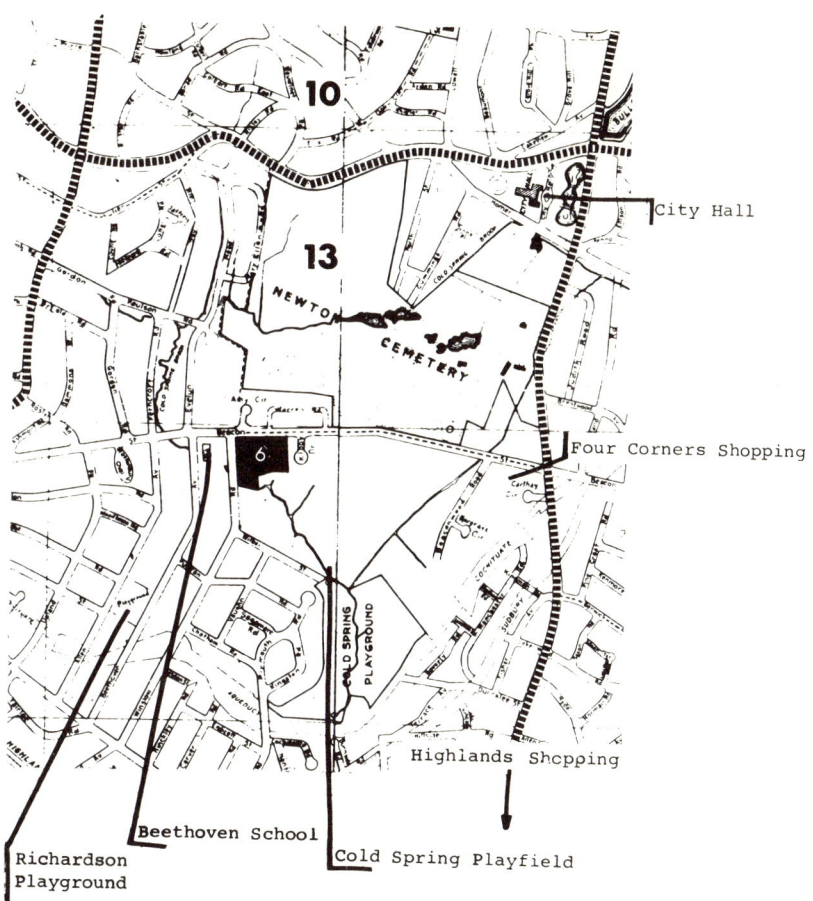

PROPOSED NCDF SITE #6—BEACON STREET

64 Housing the Poor in Suburbia

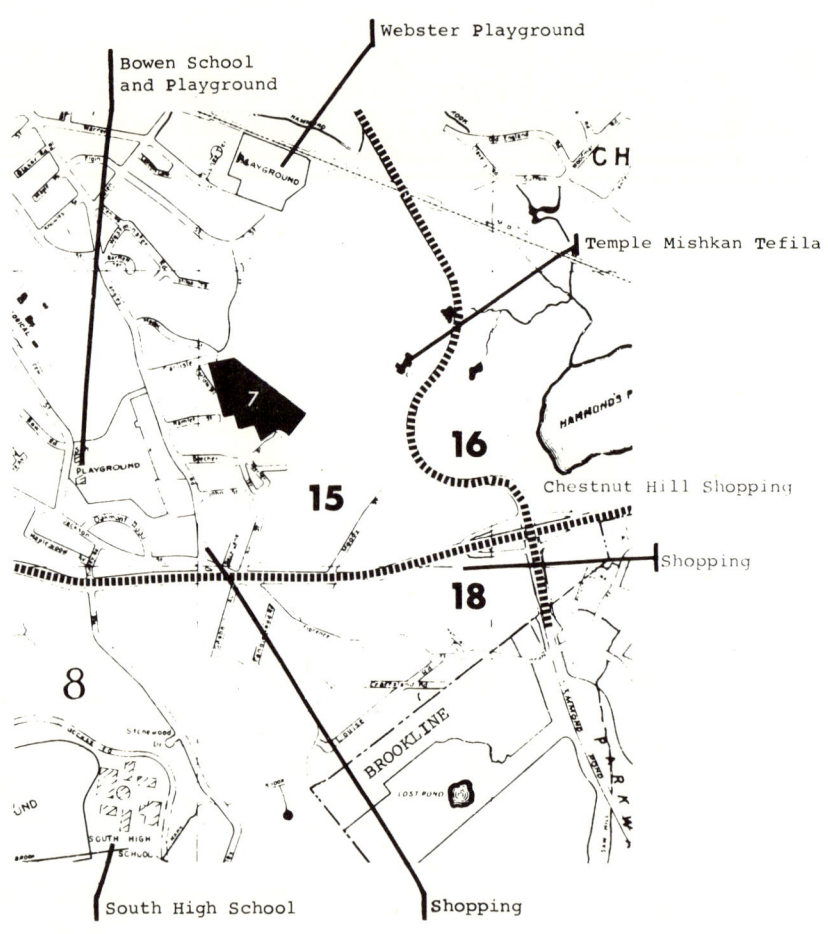

PROPOSED NCDF SITE #7—HAMLET STREET

Newton 65

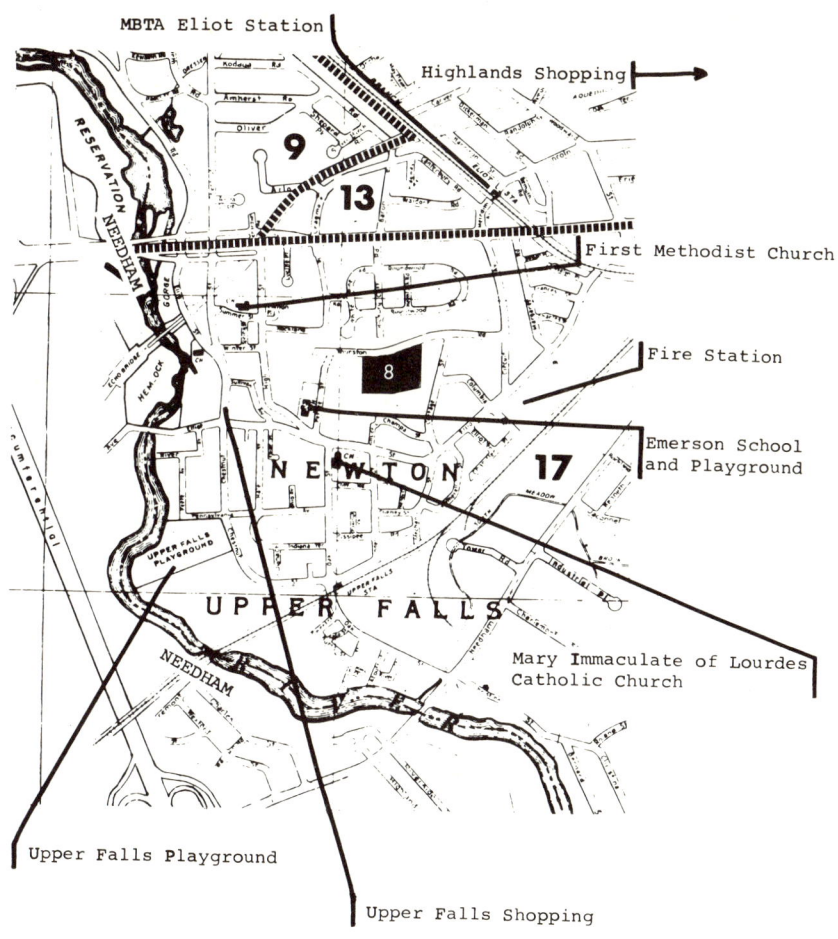

PROPOSED NCDF SITE #8—THURSTON ROAD

66 Housing the Poor in Suburbia

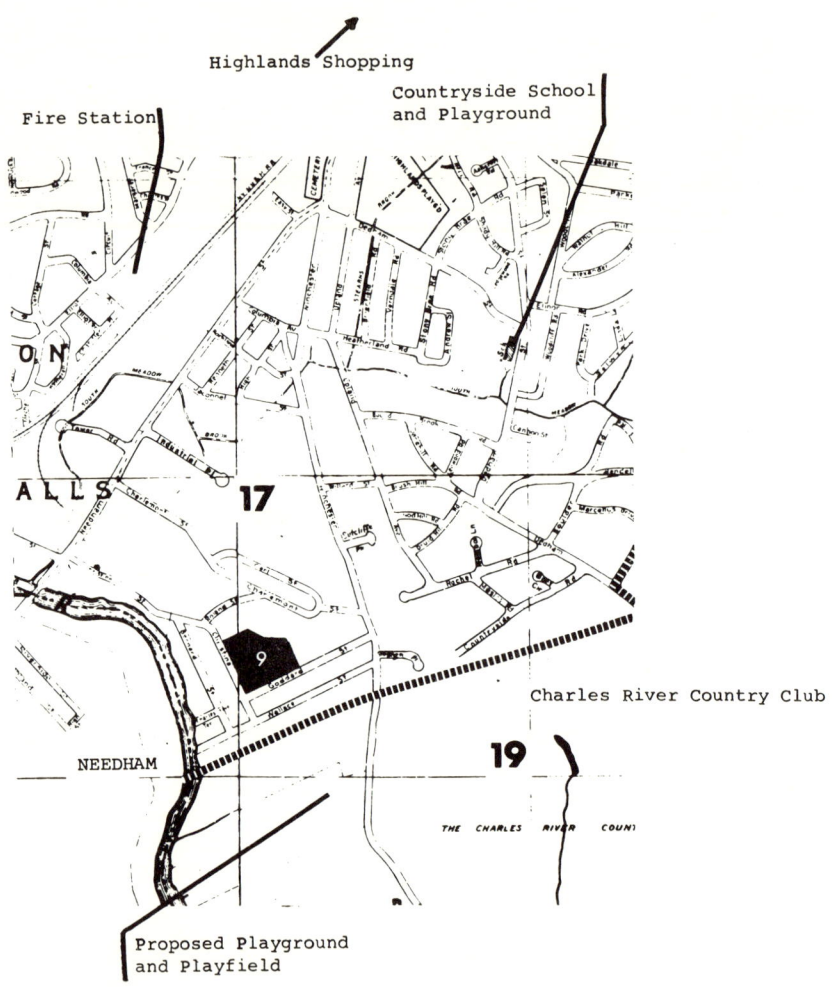

PROPOSED NCDF SITE #9—GODDARD AND CHRISTINA STREETS

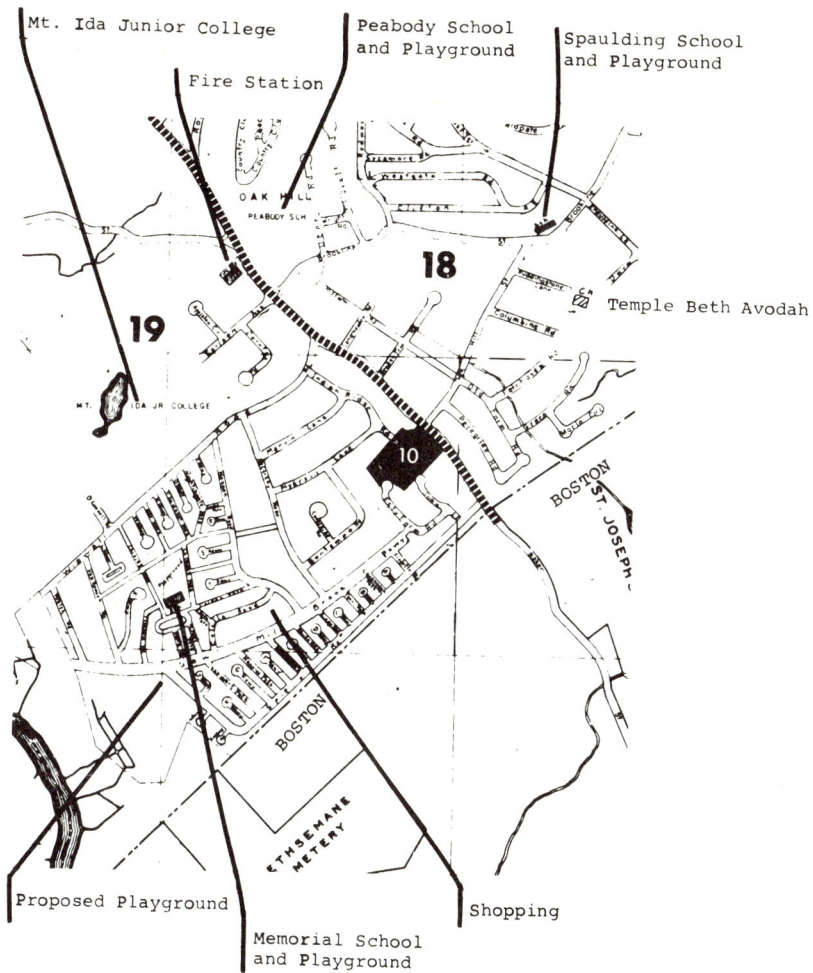

PROPOSED NCDF SITE #10—DEDHAM STREET

68 Housing the Poor in Suburbia

Table Newton 14. Newton Community Development Foundation (NCDF) Proposals: Characteristics and Impact Indicators

	Site #1 (River)	Site #2 (Stearns)	Site #3 (Hunnewell)	Site #4 (Stanton)
Proposal (as compared to zoning requirements)				
Size of parcel (min. size—24,000 s.f.)	221,360	122,800	160,050	152,727
Number of Units	59	43	51	52
Distribution of Bedrooms 1/2/3/4	14/14/16/15	18/16/5/4	20/20/6/5	17/15/10/10
Density (s. f./unit—1500/3000)	3,752	2,856	3,138	2,937
Maximum building coverage (35%)	14.8%	16.6%	15.0%	17.7%
Paved area (driveways, walkways, parking)	24.8%	21.2%	24.2%	22.3%
Open space (minimum—35%)	60.4%	62.2%	60.8%	60.8%
Number of parking spaces (required/provided)	74/74	54/54	64/65	65/65
Setback and side yard distances	OK	OK	OK	OK
Site Characteristics				
Existing use	vacant/	admin. off./	vacant/	vacant/
Existing zoning	Res. C	Unzoned	Res. C	Res. C
Soil characteristics	fill	hard	hard	gravel
Topography—existing	low, rolling	slopes gently 15'	slopes steeply 65'	slopes steeply 35'
Distance to shopping	1/4 m.	1/4 m.	1/2 m.	3/4 m.
Distance to elementary school	1/4 m.	1/4 m.	3/4 m.	3/4 m.
Distance to playground/park	1/4 m.	1/4 m.	1/2 m.	1/8 m.
Distance to churches/library/etc.	3/4 m.	1/4 m.	1/2-3/4 m.	3/4 m.
Distance to public transportation				
Local bus	abuts	200'	1/4 m.	abuts
MBTA trolley	1 1/2 m.	over 2 m.	over 2 m.	abuts
MBTA express bus	1 3/4 m.	3/4 m.	2/3 m.	3/4 m.
Penn Central train	1 m.	1 m.	2 m.	1 m.
Availability of utilities	OK	OK	OK	OK
Distance to major thoroughfares	1/8 m.	1/8 m.	1/8 m.	abuts
Natural amenities for housing	G	G	F-P	G-F
Neighborhood Characteristics				
Existing zoning	Res. C	Unzoned	Res. C	Res. A
Predominant land use	L D R	M D R	L D R	L D R
Density (persons/acre)				
Existing planning district	11	16	17	8
Immediate area	15	47	15	10
NCDF proposal	46	47	39	50
Planning district with NCDF	11	16	18	9

Newton 69

Site #5 (City Hall)	Site #6 (Beacon)	Site #7 (Hamlet)	Site #8 (Thurston)	Site #9 (Goddard)	Site #10 (Esty)
88,550	166,700	358,428	126,473	189,847	180,000
35	56	59	43	53	55
16/14/3/2	19/17/10/10	14/14/16/15	15/13/8/7	15/13/13/12	14/14/14/13
2,529	2,977	6,075	2,941	3,582	3,272
18.1%	17.2%	9.7%	17.4%	15.2%	17.6%
16.1%	22.7%	13.9%	22.4%	19.7%	22.6%
65.8%	60.1%	76.4%	60.2%	65.1%	59.8%
44/44	70/70	74/79	54/57	66/66	69/70
OK	OK	OK	OK	OK	OK
vacant/	vacant/	vacant/	vacant &	vacant/	vacant/
Unzoned	Unzoned	Priv. Res.	2 fam. hrs./	Unzoned &	Res. B
			Priv. Res.	Res. C	
hard	peat	rock	rock	wet	loam
slopes	low and	rolling	slopes	flat	gently
steeply 25'	flat		gently 10'		rolling
1/2 m.	1/2 m.	1/4 m.	1/4 m.	1/2-3/4 m.	1/4 m.
1/4 m.	adjacent	1/4 m.	1/8 m.	1/2-3/4 m.	1/2 m.
1/4 m.	adjacent	1/8 m.	1/8 m.	1/4 m.	1/2 m.
1/2-3/4 m.	3/4 m.	3/4 m.	1/4 m.	3/4 m.	1/2 m.
abuts	1/2 m.	1/10 m.	1/4 m.	2/3 m.	1/4 m.
1 1/4 m.	1 m.	3/4 m.	3/4 m.	1 1/2 m.	3 m.
1 3/4 m.	3 m.	2 3/4 m.	2 1/2 m.	4 m.	over 4 m.
3/4 m.	2 m.	3 1/2 m.	2 3/4 m.	3 1/2 m.	over 4 m.
OK	OK	OK	OK	OK	OK
abuts	abuts	1/4 m.	1/4 m.	1/4 m.	1/8 m.
G	G	G	G	G	G
Res. B	Res. C	Pr. Res.	Unzoned	Res. C	Res. C
L D R	L D R	L D R	M D R	L D R	L D R
9	10	12	12	8	5
15	22	23	16	19	12
45	48	27	48	44	50
9	10	12	13	8	5

Table Newton 14. (cont.)

	Site #1 (River)	Site #2 (Stearns)	Site #3 (Hunnewell)	Site #4 (Stanton)
Elementary Schools				
School district	Burr	Linc./Eliot	Underwood	Angier
Number of classrooms (1-6)	18	15	20	20
Enrollment (1-6)				
Current	414	337	480	472
*Projected–1972				
Without NCDF	387	378	474	456
With NCDF				
Minimum estimate[1]	417	391	490	481
NCDF estimate[2]	443	399	502	491
Maximum estimate[3]	478	416	521	531
Average classroom size (student/classroom)				
Current	23.0	22.4	24.0	23.6
*Projected–1972				
Without NCDF	21.5	25.2	23.7	22.8
With NCDF				
Minimum estimate[1]	23.1	26.0	24.5	24.1
NCDF estimate[2]	24.6	26.6	25.1	24.6
Maximum estimate[3]	26.6	27.7	26.0	26.6
Street Characteristics				
Nearest major thoroughfare	River	Watertown	Washington	Washington
Average daily volume	5,800	NA	NA	20,000+
Peak hour volume	800	NA	NA	2,700
Estimated peak hour capacity	1,745	2,000	1,880	2,140

*GLC School Study 1970
[1] Assumes 1.0 children age 9-18 in each extra bedroom

The NCDF Proposal. The plan is designed to fit the 236 program of subsidies which reduce mortgage interest charges to 1 percent. (This is the principal subsidy the housing will receive; taxes are paid to the City.)

Because the high cost of land in Newton would prohibit construction of low-moderate-income housing within FHA budget limits, NCDF has purchased 60 percent of the needed land, and asks the City to donate the remaining 40 percent. City land is also needed to provide scatteration. Because cost of construction is closely tied to volume, NCDF proposes simultaneous, multi-site construction of 508 units. Thus, NCDF can achieve the same economies that large developers get when building hundreds of units on one site—bulk purchasing of 500 bathtubs, 8,000 outlets, etc., and phasing of work crews from site to site.

Site #5 (City Hall)	Site #6 (Beacon)	Site #7 (Hamlet)	Site #8 (Thurston)	Site #9 (Goddard)	Site #10 (Esty)	Total
Claflin 13	Beethoven 12	Bowen 14	Emerson 14	Countryside 16	Memorial 12	154
317	274	333	246	299	229	3,401
349	271	313	268	301	188	3,385
358	293	343	285	326	215	3,599
363	313	369	296	343	258	3,777
375	338	404	318	376	269	4,026
24.4	22.8	23.8	17.6	18.7	19.1	22.1
26.8	22.6	22.4	19.1	18.8	15.7	22.0
27.5	24.4	24.5	20.4	20.4	17.9	23.4
27.9	26.1	26.4	21.1	21.4	21.5	24.5
28.8	28.2	28.9	22.7	23.5	22.4	26.1
Commonwealth (North Drive)	Beacon	Langley	Elliot	Winchester	Dedham	
1,200	9,400	7,708	4,600	10,003	9,800	
340	801	720	770	950	1,012	
1,015	1,670	1,745	1,415	1,670	2,140 NW 1,210 SE	

[2] Assumes 1.5 children age 0-18 in each extra bedroom
[3] Assumes 1.0 children in grades 1-6 in each extra bedroom

April 6, 1970. On this date NCDF completed the complicated work of site evaluations and acquisition, preliminary architectural and engineering studies. The final proposal included 508 units, scattered on 10 sites, in or near 13 villages. (The 14th village is Newton Lower Falls, where the Newton Redevelopment Authority is proposing 65 to 75 units.) Residents near each of the sites were invited to hear the story, first-hand, prior to issuance of information to the public.

Land

In all, 40.7 acres are involved on the 10 sites, of which 24.0 acres were privately owned, and 16.7 are in City ownership. Most of the City land is nondesignated. Only 1.26 acres of undeveloped, unused land are called for from land designated for the Recreation Department—one-half of 1 percent of the total of 250.2 acres of such land.

Designed for Newton

Two-Story Housing
The housing was designed by the Pard Team Inc., a Boston-based architectural firm that has designed middle-income housing in several cities. The units are 2 stories in height. They are grouped in differing cluster patterns, laid to blend with contours, trees, and individual neighborhood characteristics. Roof lines and setbacks are varied to provide the same atmosphere we find on all Newton streets. All units are treated wood stain, two-story wood frame-houses to blend with the kind of homes that are predominant in Newton.

Over 40 Percent Green Space
Densities are half that used for other garden apartments which have been built in Newton. NCDF's housing will average 3,510 square feet of land for each unit to be built. Private developers have allowed an average of only 1,200 to 1,800 square feet of land for each unit. All sites have over 40 percent of land reserved for open spaces.

Special Features. The designs contain 1- 2- 3- and 4-bedroom units, with the mix of units varying widely to match school facilities in each neighborhood and avoid overcrowding. All units have special play areas designed into them, and several of the sites provide 1/3- to 1-acre parks. All units have covered entryways, entrance foyers, private patios or balconies, and utility rooms. The larger units have family-room areas adjoining the kitchens and an extra half-bath. Plans call for each cluster to have a laundry facility and a community room for visiting nurses, meetings, nursery school, Boy Scout room, etc.

Who Will Live Here?

Who Can Qualify? Low- and moderate-income individuals and families qualify who meet the income eligibility limits based upon family size, which are established by the federal government. For example, a family of 4 with an annual income of under $8,000 today would be eligible. If the same family of 4 made less than $5,200 (low income), it would then pay a reduced rental (as low as $70-$90 per month) under the rent supplement program. NCDF expects that 20 percent to 25 percent of its units will be rented to low-income families under this program, though it will vary from year to year as family income rises. The income ceilings are expected to go up in the next 2 years; probably to about $10,000 for a family of 4.

Children
Federal regulations state that no more than 2 children may occupy 1 bedroom, and that children of opposite sex must have separate

bedrooms. Thus, a family with 3 boys and 1 girl would occupy a 4-bedroom town house. A family of 4 with 1 boy and 1 girl would need a 3-bedroom unit. (Two-bedroom units could also be occupied by sisters living together, mother and daughter, etc.) One-bedroom units could be occupied by young or elderly couples or single elderly persons.

How Will Tenants be Selected?
NCDF has proposed that a City-wide advisory committee be formed from sponsoring organizations. Six months prior to completion of construction this committee would (1) make available applications, (2) establish and publish guidelines for tenant selection (income maximum, room occupancy standards, school-age policies, legal requirements, Newton ties defined, etc.), (3) receive applications, screen each for: income eligibility, location preference, family size in relation to available units at preferred location, and remove the names—substituting a number code.

Ten neighborhood committees, at least half of the members of which must live in the immediate vicinity of the site, would then:

1. receive the unidentified (coded) applications, screen them (based on family size, Newton ties, income blend, etc.,) down to no more than twice the number of openings;
2. add names to the remaining applications and interview personally each applicant. Record all additional information resulting from the interview (reference checks, credit checks, personal needs, etc.);
3. make selections, return applications and all new information to the City-Wide Committee.

The City-Wide Committee has final review authority for fairness and reasonableness of the individual neighborhood selection packages, and, also, serves as a clearinghouse for rerouting applications from one location to another where preferences change or are not expressed, or where unit size availabilities require.

What is the Effect of Federal Policy upon this Process? The federal government requires only that tenant selection be fair and reasonable, and this process would meet that requirement. There is nothing in the federal regulations to prevent the committee from giving preference to relatives of Newton residents or to people who work in Newton. (For example, the Newton Housing Authority uses federal funds and has a 1-year residence requirement.)

What Will the Rentals Be? When the housing is built, rentals will be set at 25 percent of a family's income. It is expected rentals will range from $120 to $170 per month, including utilities (less than that for low-income families). . . . A family never has to move out as long as the apartment meets its needs; as its income increases, the rent increases correspondingly until the point is reached at which it is paying the same rent that it would pay if the housing were built without a subsidy. This gives stability to the family, enables them to become an integral part of the community, and provides for a stable, less transient community, as well. Of course, these rental aspects are all established by the federal government (Section 236 of the National Housing Act).

How Are Rents Kept Down? Nonprofit charitable foundations like NCDF are eligible for a 40-year mortgage for 100 percent of the construction, planning, engineering, and land costs. The federal government, under Section 236 of the Housing Act, pays a subsidy of each unit to reduce the mortgage interest rate from the present 8½ percent down to 1 percent. Such a subsidy on each unit reduces the rent on one unit by $90 to $160 per month.

What Will It Cost to Build? The housing NCDF proposes to build is quality housing. It has to be in order to meet the strict FHA construction standards. This is not low-cost housing, it is low-rent housing. The 3-bedroom house, for example, will cost, including site development and planning, over $25,000. NCDF estimates that the total cost, including planning and land costs, will be over $12,500,000.

Some Other Facts

Management and Maintenance. NCDF will hire professional managers and a complete staff to manage and maintain the housing. The only difference between NCDF and private housing is the federal subsidy to bring down the rents.

Will NCDF Pay Taxes to the City? Yes. NCDF will pay real estate taxes to the City, as would any other private housing. Assessment will be made in the usual manner when construction is completed. (Publicly built, low-income housing makes a nominal payment in lieu of taxes, but it meets a different need and operates under different set of federal laws.)

What Does "Nonprofit" Mean? What About Depreciation? None of the sponsors, Board members or officers of NCDF can make any income or profit from NCDF. FHA, the Massachusetts Attorney General, and the Internal Revenue Service supervise nonprofit foundations to enforce this rule. When the housing is in operation, any excess of income over expenses is returned to the federal government monthly to offset the subsidy.

Since NCDF is a charitable nonprofit corporation, it pays no income tax, and no depreciation deduction is available for its sponsors.

How Does this Plan Affect the Schools? Beyond the classrooms already required by present demands, NCDF's proposal will not necessitate the construction of a single new school or even a new classroom. The plan has been discussed with the School Committee, and NCDF will continue to work with it to plan the optimum distribution pattern.

Because of the flexibility in the design of the housing, the mix of unit sizes can be adjusted to meet the particular school's needs in the area. The final unit mix will reflect the capability of the various schools involved to handle any additional children.

Analysis of schools serving each site is on a separate fact sheet.

Traffic. One of the advantages of scattering construction of housing in clusters of 50 or so is that the impact on traffic is minimal or negligible. Actually, many of the sites have access from more than one street, thereby reducing the impact further.

"Antisnob" Zoning Bill. NCDF was formed prior to the passage by the Massachusetts Legislature of the so-called "Anti-Snob" Zoning Bill, which requires suburbs to devote 1.5 percent of the land area to low- and moderate-income housing. The bill permits private builders, as well as nonprofit foundations, under certain strict procedures, to appeal to the State to reverse a local rezoning denial. NCDF is proud that it represents Newton's own answer to the housing shortage, and we are confident that Newton will not need the antisnob zoning bill to find a solution. Reflecting that confidence, NCDF filed its applications under the traditional procedures provided for by the City, and that procedure does not provide for an appeal. NCDF did not file under the procedures outlined in the antisnob zoning bill.

Spot Zoning. Not a problem. NCDF's plan calls for a comprehensive rezoning of numerous large tracts in areas suitable for low- and moderate-income housing to meet a public need. Two- to four-acre tracts under such a plan would not be subject to "spot zoning" constraints.

The Hatch Act. (The Inland Wetlands Bill.) All requirements of the Hatch Act must be met before any construction can begin on any open land, and, where required, full hearings will be held to assure that proper drainage is provided. In addition, FHA has its own standards for drainage, and those requirements must be met as well, before construction can begin.

Can the Units be Sold to Tenants? NCDF could, if the community and the sponsoring organizations so desired, finance some or all of these units as cooperatives for sale to the tenants, with a nominal down payment. The same tenant selection process would prevail as with rentals. Each tenant would own a share of his cooperative cluster and participate in the management, though final management of the housing would still rest with the foundation itself. Tenants could sell their units only to the Cooperative, for resale to purchasers selected by the neighborhood committee.

How Will the Plan be Approved? NCDF has requested rezoning on 10 parcels, and hearings must be held before the Board of Aldermen before any approval can be given. Approval of the full Board of Aldermen is required before construction can begin on anything larger than a 2-family house in Newton. Further, the Board of Aldermen, in the drafting of its zoning ordinances, has retained the power to review complete construction drawings and see plans before giving final zoning approval.

NCDF does not have the power of eminent domain, is not a government agency, and its proposals follow the same procedures as any other rezoning.

When Will Construction be Completed? Construction can begin within 6 to 18 months from the time zoning approval is granted (the time it takes to complete construction drawings and obtain federal financing). Construction itself will take an additional 12 to 18 months, and could be completed some time in 1972 or 1973.

Can the Plan be Changed? Yes. There is nothing absolutely rigid in the plan, other than the scattered site, low density principle. NCDF is willing to work with interested groups to improve the plan in any way possible. The plan itself is a carefully considered, comprehensive plan for the construction of 508 units of low- and moderate-income housing, scattered on 10 sites, which has been in preparation for nearly 2 years. NCDF's Board, which insisted on review of nearly 200 sites in the City, feels that the sites selected are the 10 best suited to fulfill this principle, but it stands ready to consider alternative sites of similar size in the same areas.

Model Suburban Solution

In many ways NCDF is already a model. It is a coalition of nearly all of Newton's churches and temples, and has broad support in the business community as well. In addition, Newton itself is a community whose leaders, elected and otherwise, are strongly committed to the construction of low- and moderate-income housing—and, specifically, to the NCDF scattered site program. NCDF, in a very real sense, is becoming a demonstration program and will mark the beginning of a trend toward finding solutions to the nation's housing crisis.

NCDF's Program for Abutters

Though there was no concentrated attempt to gain citizen support during the period of site negotiations, there was communication through a fund raising drive, which resulted in the formation of committees with area captains who could talk with abutters once sites were announced. The first week in April, 1970, private meetings were held at sponsoring churches and synagogues with neighbors of the 10 proposed sites. NCDF hoped to counteract opposition, which might result from misinformation and hearsay, by meeting personally with abutters to the sites. Mr. Casselman felt that only the Oak Hill section showed outright hostility to the NCDF proposal for use of the Esty's Farm site.

The general NCDF plan called for a team of two people to visit personally the home of every direct abutter in the project neighborhoods. Each neighborhood chairman appointed a group of workers whose sole task was to make these individual visits. Workers chosen were primarily people who lived in the immediate vicinity of the project. The entire effort aimed to satisfy abutters' questions, concerns, fears; to marshall their support and thus influence Aldermen; and to improve grass-roots communication in general.

PUBLIC REACTION

Opposition Asserts Itself

From the moment the 10 sites were publicly announced on April 13, the phones of the Aldermen started ringing. One Alderman said he received 200 telephone calls in one week regarding the plans. Within two days, the Newton Civic and Land Association was formed to oppose the NCDF plans and began to proselytize its case. The law required a public hearing on each site before any vote could be taken by the Board of Aldermen. These sites were presented by NCDF as one package to be approved or disapproved as a totality. If no action on the NCDF rezoning petition was taken within 90 days of the hearings, the hearings were invalid and would have to be held again. The hearings were set to be held from May 26 to June 1, and both sides began to prepare their cases.

The outpouring of public opinion against the housing proposal during April and May was unexpected, as was the approach taken by the objectors. Perhaps the most important single opposing force in Newton was Robert Stiller, who organized the opposition most effectively into the Newton Land Use and Civic Association (NLUCA), becoming its first and only President. The following are excerpts from Mr. Stiller's interviews:

> I have been a lifelong resident of the City of Boston: I grew up in the Mattapan area of the City. After getting married I lived in Boston, Brighton, and finally bought a home in Newton 15 years ago....
>
> When I buy my home, I buy it with the stipulation that I cannot use my property for any other purpose than for a single-family home (if

that is the zoning at the time). As a result, I would expect our neighbor to be as limited in the use of his property as I am. . . . By the same token, if there is an existing school there and I move to that street, then I have made my decision based upon the existing adjacent structures and the existing public buildings that may be around. If I now live there and have public buildings brought into the area it becomes a different ball game. . . .

[margin note: pre-existent former right]

The reason why I moved to Newton was to get away from the apartment house concept; I lived in it all my life. . . . The concept of creating an opportunity for urban ghetto blacks to get out of the ghetto and follow industry on Route 128, I do not believe in; why must you live where your job is? . . . Boston today has the greatest concentration of manufacturing facilities far out-weighing that which is in the 128 belt. . . . I believe that when we hear the same thing said year after year we begin to accept it as doctrine: i.e., that the metropolitan communities owe a service to the City of Boston. I do not agree. I say that the City of Boston is a city unto itself and Newton owes nothing more to the City of Boston than it does to the City of Cambridge. . . . I believe that people want to live in their own environment, associate within their own economic groups, with persons of the same religious and ethnic background. People should have the freedom to choose their neighbor.

The opposition to the NCDF grew approximately three years after its founding, when 50 families received a brochure on the proposed development in our immediate neighborhood. An orientation session took place and an overwhelming number of neighbors participated. Mr. Casselman of NCDF said that the site and its proposed development was good for the total community. But he avoided my questions repeatedly and the crowd applauded when I insisted that he respond. Mr. Casselman finally pointed a finger at me and said "Let me tell you something; this is good for the community and good for the people; it is good for every one and it is going to be good for you." Twenty people arrived at my home later, after the meeting, asking for my help. Most of them were strangers to me. We all agreed that night to combine our efforts and fight the selection of the site in our neighborhood and against NCDF if other abutters in other parts of the city wanted to join us. I gave several months of my time (not going to my office from April to August), in order to establish and later be President of the Newton Civic and Land Use Association.

In the past the residents' problems in Newton had stemmed from high tax rates and the educational system. These problems would be enhanced through the higher densities of multi-story buildings.

Sites such as Esty Farm are zoned for single-family residences, so multi-unit residences would mean zoning changes affecting facilities as well as general appearance and ecological preservation. Esty's Farm is a watershed area and serves as a winter playground for our neighborhood children. It is flooded and children skate there.

The quality of the NCDF housing does not conform to the existing building codes and there is a question of materials for multiple housing within this area. Also the value of surrounding housing would decrease. Other sites, such as the Commonwealth Avenue site, were chosen without any notion of utility.

We owe no allegiance to other cities, such as Boston; we pay for too much of the facilities of the City of Boston as it is. People should live where their jobs are, and manufacturing facilities are still mostly in Boston.

We must start with the problems here in Newton first. Elderly housing is already being built on several sites and 40 new units are being considered for our low-income people. It is the lower middle-class people who are being driven out by the tax increases.

The sites could be zoned, as prior to 1958, for 7,500 square foot house lots rather than 15,000 square foot lots, and single-family housing built on these lots. This would help to keep down densities and still provide lower-cost housing for moderate-income families. Homeownership is preferable and the 235 program is best suited for Newton. If this plan is chosen, rather than 236, and for people who are already residents of Newton, then there would not be an increase in educational necessities—only a redistribution of Newton children. Town facilities would remain adequate. In some areas luxury apartments might be built to house the younger couples and older couples who do not require elderly housing. These would not drain the town facilities to any significant degree.

The concept of low- and moderate-income housing is a good one and I am not against it. But the NCDF and their plan approach is poor. The philosophy of splitting housing in 10 areas is fair; however, it is not easy to bring any plans to Newton areas, especially a plan which requires extensive zoning change.

The racism implication is mostly a red herring issue, but the toughest perhaps to deal with. Racial integration is opposed by some people. However, they are opposed more strongly to densities, the negative impact upon schools, the higher taxes.

The opposition, more vocal than the supporters of the Plan, grew rapidly, ranging from the grass roots, with abutters like Mr. Stiller, all the way to hard-hitting community-wide actions. One Alderman received a letter opposing the plan from a constituent who was in Rio de Janeiro. One group of abutters came out with a statement against the proposed site opposite City Hall. Opposition publications proved effective, as evidenced in one of their many pamphlets:

Eligibility of City Workers
NCDF's claim that its proposed housing projects will benefit city workers is a myth. Discounting increases pending under current wage negotiations, of a total of 462 police and fire department employees only 5 police cadets and 6 firefighters are earning under $8,000. Their wages are $7,775 and step increases will bring that figure to $8,400 within six months. These figures do not include overtime, special detail income, or any other family income.

Only six persons in the Engineering Department currently earn less than $8,000, and all six are eligible for step raises within six months.

A recap of all city employees' wages reveals that, except for a few custodians and sanitation workers, all full-time male employees earn more than the limits set by NCDF. Many of the sanitation workers will earn more than $8,000 when current wage negotiations are completed.

Only 130 women clerks earn less than $6,000, exclusive of overtime. Most of these persons are either single or are wives of working husbands.

Virtually all city workers are thus eliminated from eligibility.

Schools
One of the prime reasons a person chooses to live in Newton is its excellent school system. However, even now our schools are under strain. The School Department's March 30, 1970 issue of *Patterns* reports that approximately 13 percent to 15 percent of the Newton student population come to the school system with special needs and problems or acquire special problems by the time they reach junior high school. This group needs special attention, and small pupil-teacher and pupil-counselor ratios have become vital. *We cannot provide this counseling and maintain our high standards of schooling when classes become overcrowded.*

According to the presently completed demographic study 14 of the 23 elementary schools, 3 of the 5 junior high schools, and both senior high schools are rated by the school committee as being overcrowded. In fact, at the Underwood School the boys' lavatory has been converted into a classroom, as has the back of the stage of the Beethoven School. The Angier School auditorium has been converted into four classrooms.

NCDF's proposal would overload an already overcrowded school system which also faces the strong possibility of having to absorb 2,500 parochial school children. Newton's ability to maintain its excellent educational system, including its 25 to 1 child-teacher ratio is threatened by the NCDF proposal. Although NCDF talks about an added impact of only 2 or 3 children per classroom, they must all eventually get together at the junior and high schools where the impact will be in the hundreds.

Taxes

NCDF's proposal to add 500-700 new students to our school system will result in an additional outlay of $500,000 to almost $1,000,000 annually. To this we must add the cost of the increase in city services—trash collections, snow plowing, fire and police protection, etc.

Federal regulations (Chapter 236), require *absolute priority on tenancy be given to families displaced by urban renewal and low-income families.* There are virtually no displaced families in Newton. Therefore, the tenants will be from outside Newton, of low-income families who may or may not be nonresidents. When these two categories of tenants are exhausted, then, and only then, can moderate-income families from Newton be accommodated.

What does this mean to us as taxpayers? It means we will have to pay a subsidy four times for NCDF: (1) Our income taxes will pay the federal subsidy to support the project, (2) our state taxes will pay the welfare costs to low-income families residing within the projects, (3) our city taxes will pay for the tenants, (4) our city land purchased or taken by eminent domain is now requested to be given away to NCDF.

Wetlands

The Waban, Esty Farm, and Goddard Street sites are natural watersheds for the Charles River, and are subject to seasonal and periodic flooding. Even today homes in these areas have flooding problems. Combined with the marginal sewage systems in these areas, construction on these sites could create severe additional flooding. These sites fall under Hatch Act restrictions concerning natural "wetlands," and must be retained as a safety valve for the respective areas.

Traffic-Safety-Public Transportation

Any new housing development means more traffic. When developments are as dense as these proposed by NCDF, severe problems can result. On the Hunnewell, Esty Farm, and Thompsonville sites dead-end streets would be opened to heavy traffic to serve the projects. A different, but equally dangerous situation exists where a site fronts on a major highway with no protection for the children residing in the site, such as the Lakeview Avenue site fronting on

Commonwealth Avenue, the Stanton Avenue site fronting on Route 16, and the Beethoven School site fronting on Beacon Street. Upwards of 24,000 cars pass each of these sites daily. The Hunnewell site is also adjacent to the railroad and the Turnpike—a most dangerous situation, where a large concentration of children exists.

Many of the sites do not have adequate public transportation. Newton would have to provide additional bus service to the various sites, or else low-income families would be without transportation. Additional buses also greatly increase the traffic danger from large vehicles operating on residential streets.

The building of low- and moderate-income multi-unit housing on land zoned for single- or two-family dwellings must be prevented. Newton *can* house more low- and moderate-income families, and can do so without destroying our neighborhoods. Qualified builders and developers suggest there are better and more economical methods to provide this housing. They suggest, for instance, that before plunging into the construction of 503 units, a pilot project should be built to determine if this kind of housing actually could work in Newton.

Until a better plan is developed the NCDF proposals must be stopped.

Other organizations and individuals opposed the plan. Mrs. Babson, an abutter to the Goddard-Christina site, did not object to the NCDF plan, but objected to the site being in her neighborhood because of the existing "narrow streets" and "heavy traffic." She hired a lawyer to plead her case. Mr. Kennedy, head of the Auburndale Community Association, was wary because the plans were "so secretive." He criticized the Newton Chamber of Commerce for backing the plans, and said that it was not speaking for the "grass-roots people." Hearing rumors that inner city blacks were being recruited as prospective tenants, Mr. Kennedy said: "We haven't solved our own problems yet. People from the core city, the underprivileged, have always been welcome in Newton. But our first responsibility is to take care of our own family first."

The Newton Taxpayers Association wanted more information on costs. Some estimate "of this crucial cost to the City factor must be computed before the City can ... convert its land to a use other than that to which it is presently dedicated."

The accusation that NCDF's demands were too inflexible was heard many times. One abutter said, "You don't see any NCDF members upset, because they didn't put the sites next to their homes. They all live in big, expensive homes and are trying to run the neighborhoods of people like me, who have worked hard to be able to live in a moderate but comfortable home in Newton." Other community people said the NCDF leadership was "too snobbish," and "too uppity."

The Hearings

In the midst of this outpouring and as the hearings approached, Newton was the focus of much attention from outside experts and other communities where similar plans were underway. Yet attempts to get Senator Edward Brooke, a Newton resident, to attend the upcoming hearings failed.

From May 26 to June 1, the long awaited public hearings on each of the sites were held. These were widely attended. One thousand people attended one hearing in the high school auditorium that lasted until 3 a.m.; few left before the end. The booing, hissing, and catcalls at the meetings required the Aldermen to remind the audience that they were not at a baseball game.

Throughout the hearings, recurrent themes were heard from both sides. NCDF kept emphasizing Newton's need for housing its population, the City's position in the national spotlight, and the physical soundness of its site plans and unit design, worked out by the Pard Team. Mr. Casselman emphasized the moral commitment which must be met by passage of this proposal.

The hearings opened with a presentation by the architects, which was meant to counteract charges that low-income or subsidized housing meant "cheap housing." The Pard Team described the units as two stories in height, grouped in differing cluster patterns that blended with contours, trees, and individual neighborhood characteristics.

One of the largest issues centered around who would live in the housing. NCDF had taken the stand that the housing was for Newton's own residents and employees. Mr. Stiller stated that the Section 236 housing program stipulated that residents who had been displaced as a result of renewal had first priority. How then, the opposition wanted to know, could NCDF state in its literature that "There is nothing in the federal regulation to prevent the Committee from giving preference to relatives of Newton residents and to people who work in Newton"?

Another question regarding who would live in this housing was directed towards the income limits the federal government established for eligibility. The opposition maintained that most city employees had incomes above federal limits and, therefore, could not live in this housing as NCDF claimed. They felt that NCDF was pulling a hoax by constructing housing for which only a small percentage of Newton residents or employees would be eligible, even if given priority. The remainder of the units would be filled by inner-city blacks, they said.

Only after much confusion and many rumors did NCDF clarify its position. Tamara Bliss spoke for NCDF at the hearings on the issue of who would live in the housing. Mrs. Bliss was a social worker who had worked in the South End during renewal and was familiar with the relocation pattern of urban renewal dislocatees. She made it clear that NCDF existed because the local Public Housing Authority could construct or rehabilitate housing only for low-income people at rents of about $60 per month; any construction of moderate-income housing under Section 236 had to be accomplished by a nonprofit or limited dividend organization such as NCDF. Rents would average $125 per month. Then, within these moderate-income units, only 20 percent could be occupied by low-income people through an additional rent supplement program in conjunction with the local housing authority.

[Margin note: in this light / reply: what could happen,, the chance opened w/ it doesn't overbalance history.]

Mrs. Bliss did not negate the 236 stipulation that priority be given to persons "displaced by public action," but explained why at that time in Newton that requirement would have little effect. First, she stated that only if blighted buildings in Newton were condemned would tenants be "displaced by public action" from Newton itself. Secondly, displacees would not "swarm" into Newton from other areas. Drawing upon her experience in the South End, she pointed out that of 484 families displaced in the area in which she worked, only 12 had moved to the suburbs. Most preferred to remain in the South End. After contacting developers of moderate-income units throughout the Boston area, Mrs. Bliss concluded that of all applicants, not more than 2 percent were displacees, and not all these were eligible. She also indicated that renewal throughout the metropolitan area had practically ceased because of lack of funds, and, presently, there were not people being displaced in other areas.

With regard to the question of income limits, NCDF presented information to substantiate its claim that city employees would be eligible for the housing. The income limits allowed by 236 were matched against the salaries earned by various city employees. When the table was presented at the hearings, the Aldermen, as well as the opposition, accused NCDF of being evasive because the information was confusing. The table was supposed to show how many city employees had incomes within 236 requirements, but gave no indication of their family status and, therefore, their eligibility. NCDF admitted the table was difficult to understand, but emphasized that there was no intent to be evasive. Whether or not the table was accurate, NCDF made it clear that many city people were eligible for the housing.

NCDF also emphasized that the community would be responsible for selection of tenants. A city-wide Advisory Committee, formed from sponsoring organizations, would make applications available, establish and publish guidelines for tenant selection, and receive and screen applicants 6 months prior to completion of construction. Ten neighborhood committees, one for each site, would be responsible for reading the applications and interviewing applicants.

Increased taxes as a result of increased services needed by the housing was another anti-NCDF rallying point. NCDF prepared a statement which presented the revenue/cost figures for the entire plan. The increment to the tax rate of $113 per $1000 was small, but the opposition seemed to gain a lot of support from that point.

Opposition also used the argument of school crowding. Schools in the northern part of the city were experiencing increasing enrollments and would be burdened by yet an additional influx of children. NCDF realized the sensitivity of Newtonites to their school system, and had tried to plan with this in mind. NCDF told the community that their proposal would not necessitate the construction of a single new school or even a new classroom. The plan had been discussed with the School Committee, and NCDF had worked with it to plan an optimum distribution pattern. Because of the flexibility in the design of the housing, the mix of unit sizes could be adjusted to meet the particular school's needs in the area. The final unit mix was to reflect the capability of the various schools involved to handle any additional children. For example, the plan for the old Stearns School site in northern Newton leaned heavily toward small, bedroom units for young couples and the elderly because of the crowded conditions in this area's elementary school. The School Committee supported the NCDF plan by a 5 to 3 vote.

Though the great majority of those opposing the plans felt the housing should not be built at all, opposition was not entirely monolithic. At the hearings, one Newton resident indicated that the plans were too conservative. He stated:

> ... In response to those who oppose the plans on the grounds that too many black and low-income families will move to Newton, NCDF has accepted stricter and stricter tenant selection and income requirements. Of the 508 units proposed only 20 percent, or 100 units, are available for low-income families. Also, the largest unit proposed by NCDF has 4 bedrooms, and there are only 108 of these. Because of FHA regulations limiting 2 children to a room, a family could have 6 children at most. This excludes many low-income families who tend to have large numbers of children. So I oppose NCDF's plans because they will not accomplish the things for which the organization was chartered. Instead of providing housing for low-income people, NCDF will act to once again subsidize the middle class. ...

One of the hardest issues to deal with was the feasibility of sites which were questioned on physical grounds. Expert witnesses were available to support the contentions of both sides.

The Goddard-Christina Street site was close to the Charles River flood plain, and was said to present drainage problems for surrounding homes. Testimony given by a professor of resources and ecology at the Harvard Graduate School of Design indicated that drainage in the Goddard-Christina Street neighborhood would not be damaged by the development. He said that since the site sat well above the Charles River flood plain, it would play no discernible role in river flooding.

On the Pine Street-River Street site there was an existing underground gas problem which had already affected homes in the neighborhood. As with all the other sites, the civil engineering firm of Barnes Engineering Company, Inc. found this site technically feasible. It was suggested that any build-up of underground gases could be eliminated by using standard engineering techniques such as gas traps. NCDF assured doubters that detailed engineering plans had to be drawn up and approved by city engineers, as well as the FHA, before construction could begin. NCDF stated that the construction would not only not contribute to the problem, but might very well alleviate the present danger to adjacent homes.

Problems associated with the Hunnewell Avenue site were voiced by abutters before the hearing. To accommodate what was seemingly valid criticism about the proximity of railroad tracks, the NCDF architect revised the site plan so that all units were at least 135 feet from the tracks. These improvements required the elimination of one 4-bedroom unit. Fears of drainage problems arose from the experience of many homeowners, whose basements became flooded each spring. Here again, NCDF contended, proper engineering and drainage techniques would not only eliminate the problem in the housing, but might possibly alleviate the existing problem.

The Walnut Street site posed a different problem. Directly across the street from City Hall, this site had symbolic value for NCDF in that it, somehow, indicated the City's commitment to the reality of low- and moderate-income housing in the community. Yet, this land was also important to the City Planning Department because its preservation as a landscaped open space to offset the massive structure of City Hall had been initiated in the name of good planning. It exemplified the concept of Newton as a "Garden City." The housing would not be unsuitable to the site, but it would certainly change the character of its pastoral setting.

The Government Agencies

On June 19, after the public hearings, but two months before the actual Aldermanic vote was taken, the Planning Department recommended outright denial of the 2 sites at the City Hall and Beacon Street, but qualified approval of the other 8 sites. An alternative site in the area of City Hall was suggested for consideration. The Beacon Street site was rejected because it was part of a site that had been held in the planning stage for a major city-wide recreational facility for many years; an alternative site was proposed at a City-owned "snow dump" several hundred yards down the road.

The Planning Department questioned the legality of asking for a zoning change to Residence D (town house or garden apartment), on all 10 sites simultaneously. E. Michael Ferris, Planning Director, was also concerned that, in the event that NCDF was unsuccessful in financing or completing its program, the door would be open for "less sensitive" developers to build garden apartments on those sites not developed by NCDF. Ferris recommended that the zoning change should be made to a special Private Residence zone, which, with the Aldermen's approval, would permit the construction of town houses, but only by nonprofit or limited dividend sponsors. NCDF plans met the requirements of this zone in all but a few details. However, town house provisions meant that 1-bedroom units would use a far higher proportion of site open space.

Other less favorable opinions were also forthcoming. The City Planning Board voted 3 to 1 to recommend approval of only 4 sites. A minority report filed by one member recommended rejection of all sites. This Board

Table Newton 15. Newton Community Development Foundation (NCDF) Sites Analysis by The Newton Planning Department

Site	Change to Residence D	Site Plan Approval	Suitability for Housing	Impact Upon Community Facilities	Validity Residence D Zoning Change	Recommendation
1. Pine and River Streets	X		Good	Moderate	OK	Approval
2. Stearns School	X		Good	Significant	OK	Approval for 33 Units
3. Hunnewell Avenue	X		Fair-Poor	Significant	Questionable	Approve Private Residence Zone
4. Stanton Avenue	X	X	Fair	Significant	Questionable	Approve Private Residence for 43 Units with Site Plan Modification
5. City Hall	X		Fair-Poor	Significant	Questionable	Denial – Consider Alternate Site
6. Beacon Street	X		Good	Moderate	OK	Denial – Consider Alternate Site
7. Hamlet Street	X	X	Good	Moderate	Unnecessary	Approve Private Residence with Site Plan Modification
8. Thurston Road	X	X	Good	Minimal	OK	Approval with Minor Site Plan Modification
9. Goddard Street	X		Fair-Poor	Moderate	Questionable	Approve Private Residence Zone
10. Esty Farm	X	X	Good	Moderate	Questionable	Approve Private Residence Zone

played a lesser advisory role than did the Planning Department, but their report did increase doubt in the minds of the Aldermen as to the feasibility of the entire NCDF package.

During July, the Mayor held four sessions with the Aldermen, outsiders, and the NCDF to discuss issues surrounding the plan. In an attempt to allow the Aldermen to arrive at a decision based upon information rather than emotional community sentiment, the Mayor made his departments available to the Board.

The national media had picked up the issue by this time, and already were speculating as to its outcome. An article appeared in *Newsweek*, entitled "Liberalism Stops at Your Own Driveway."

The Land-Use Committee of the Board of Aldermen was charged with the responsibility of voting and making recommendations on petitions for zoning changes to the full Board. On July 30 the Committee took its first vote on the proposal and denied 2 sites outright, took no action on 6, and recommended zoning changes for 2. Though disappointed with the results, NCDF issued a statement asking for reappraisal by the Board.

It was apparent that outright approval was going to be impossible to obtain, but no one was sure what type of compromise or substitutions would be offered or accepted by the other side. Alderman Barkin, Chairman of the Land-Use Committee, recalled that Casselman was adamant about this being an all-or-nothing proposal. He thought, however, that some bargain could be reached which would be acceptable to both sides. He could not believe that Casselman would give up the opportunity to build less than the original 508 units, rather than build none at all. These issues were being raised in closed-door sessions by the Land-Use Committee in its attempt to arrive at a compromise solution which was acceptable to both groups.

Table Newton 16. A Site-by-Site Appraisal
___

The Planning Department's professional judgment was submitted in the following report:

Site #1—Pine and River Streets

Suitability of Site for Housing
The proposal is compatible with the neighborhood's single and two-family residential character. There is available open space in the neighborhood that will minimize the impact of the proposed relative high density of the development (46 persons per acre as compared to an average of 15 persons per acre in the immediate area). The site is reasonably well located with respect to shopping, services and public transportation and it is adjacent to a school and a playground/playfield. The additional population in the area will not overburden the recreational facilities which service this immediate neighborhood.

Impact on Community Facilities

This proposal will have a moderate impact on the Burr School as is shown on the accompanying table. Based upon current projections, Burr School's average classroom size will decrease from 23.0 to 21.5 by 1972. Newton Community Development Foundation housing would likely increase this to a minimum of 23.1 or a maximum of 26.6

The additional traffic generated on this site will have a minimum effect on traffic on River Street which is presently used to 85% of its capacity during peak hours. Traffic will increase on Pine Street but not in excess of the street's capacity.

Insufficient data is available regarding the adequacy of the soil for building. However, this is not pertinent to the change of zone as conditions may be attached to the subsequent granting of permissive use which would require conformance with standards of the City Engineer.

Analysis of Zoning Request

The creation of a Residence D district on the site would not be inconsistent with the established residential character of the neighborhood which is a mixture of single and two-family uses. Eighteen two-family residences, containing a total of 36 dwelling units, could be constructed on the land as a right in this zone. This compares favorably with the requested 59 units. However, in view of the low density of this proposal (3,752 sq. ft./unit) this plan might be approved under the less intensive Private Residence zone which allows town houses to be built at a minimum of 3,500 sq. ft./unit. Plan modifications may have to be made under this zone in regard to driveway improvements. A Building Board of Appeals ruling would be necessary for qualification of the design as town houses.

Site Plan Comments

The site plan is well designed with respect to open space and landscaping areas, parking arrangements and building locations and meets all of the technical requirements of the zoning ordinance. Because the site is reasonably flat, most of the open areas can be effectively used for play spaces. The proposed bedroom distribution on this site appears reasonable in view of the site's physical characteristics.

Recommendation

It is recommended that the change of zone to Residence D be granted, but only if it is determined that a change to Private Residence would not accomplish the same objectives.

Site #2—Stearns School

Suitability of Site for Housing

The proposal is compatible with the neighborhood's two-family and multifamily residential character. The proposed density of 47 persons per acre equals the existing average of 47 persons per acre in the immediate area. The site is reasonably close to shopping, services and public transportation and is adjacent to a neighborhood playground.

Impact on Community Facilities
The General Learning Corporation study shows a significantly increasing enrollment for the Lincoln-Eliot School in the future. With the increase resulting from NCDF housing, the student per classroom ratio can be expected to increase from 22.4 currently to a range of between 26.0 and 27.7.

The Stearns School playground will readily absorb the additional demand of the new housing without overburdening it.

The vehicular traffic generated on this site will have a minimum effect on traffic on Watertown Street which is presently used to an estimated 85% of its capacity during peak hours. Some traffic will also use California Street. Additional traffic will use Jasset Street, but not in excess of the street's capacity. The site has been mentioned as a possibility for future elementary school use although it does not exist within the published plans of the City.

Analysis of Zoning Request
The establishment of a Residence D district on the site would be a logical extension of the existing Residence D zoned land which completely surrounds it.

Site Plan Comments
The site plan complies with the technical requirements of the zoning ordinance. The plan provides a more esthetic housing environment than most of the existing neighborhood and hence may act as an upgrading influence. However, the plan contains certain limitations with respect to access and open space utilization. First, rather than orienting the units toward the existing playground, the arrangement instead creates a barrier to it. Further, four of the units are located on the playground site. While the plan replaces this lost play space within the area bounded by a circular drive, this is felt to be a poor substitute. Grouping the units to the rear results in complete loss of rear open space where more private activities can take place.

Additional access to the site could be considered from Watertown Street as one means to reduce the traffic impact upon Jasset Street.

Recommendation
It is recommended that a change of zone to Residence D be granted. It is recommended that the site plan be modified to remove the proposed units from the existing playground and, if necessary, reduce the number of units from this site to maintain the proposed density of 2,800 square feet of land area per dwelling unit.

Site #3—Hunnewell Avenue

Suitability of Site for Housing
The site is poorly located with respect to services, all of which are located one-half to three-fourths of a mile away. The only exception is a new neighborhood playground to be developed adjacent to the site.

The proposal is not incompatible with the single family residential character of the neighborhood although it represents a significant density increase (proposed density of 39 persons per acre compared with the existing average of 15 persons per acre in the immediate neighborhood on the Newton side).

The site's topography and nearness to the Turnpike subject it to environmental deficiencies which would have a detrimental influence on any housing located on the parcel. The steep slope of the site contributes to its orientation toward the Massachusetts Turnpike and Penn Central Railroad, subjecting it to their accompanying by-products—noise and fumes. In contrast, the abutting residential land is oriented toward Hunnewell Avenue since it is considerably above the grade of the City-owned land adjacent to the Turnpike.

Egress to the site is limited to only one point which is accessible only over narrow residential streets. No connection is available from Boston, thereby restricting convenient access and placing heavy demands upon existing neighborhood streets.

Due to topographic characteristics, existing environmental deficiencies, poor access and distance from community services, the site must be considered undesirable for housing, particularly for low-moderate income families.

Impact on Community Facilities
The General Learning Corporation study shows practically no change in enrollment for the Underwood School in the future. The increase resulting from NCDF housing can be expected to increase the student per classroom ratio from 24.0 currently to a range of between 24.5 and 26.0.

The proposed playground is of sufficient size to accommodate a greater demand.

The vehicular traffic generated on this site will have a minimum effect on nearby Washington Street and will have significant impact on Hunnewell Avenue and other residential streets in the neighborhood as traffic is, at present, minimal. However, the increased traffic will not exceed the capacity of any of the streets.

Analysis of Zoning Request
The establishment of a Residence D district on the site would represent a significant departure from the existing zoning of the area, Residence C.

However, it would appear to be a logical extension of the adjacent multifamily zone district in Boston thereby reducing the strength of a "spot zoning" challenge. Yet, the areas on both sides of the City line are completely isolated from one another by the lack of connecting streets or pathways and differences in topography. As a result, the Boston and Newton sides bear little relationship to each other.

Access to the site is over Hunnewell Avenue which presently terminates at the site. Minimal traffic movement occurs in this immediate area and on the streets servicing the neighborhood.

Approximately 13 two-family structures housing 26 families could be constructed on the total site in Residence D zoned land. This compares with the requested 51 units. A total of four single family residences would be erected on the privately owned portion only under the existing zoning. However, this would be a most expensive undertaking because of the topography requiring large amounts of fill, the removal of an existing structure and the construction of a street to City specifications.

In 1968 the Board of Aldermen denied a request to erect a 78-bed rest home on the privately owned portion of the site. The Planning Department recommended that the site was inappropriate for housing because of topography and environmental problems and could, in all probability, support the rest home use providing access is not gained from Hunnewell Avenue.

Site Plan Comments

The site plan complies with the technical requirements of the zoning ordinance and contains some desirable features including natural wooded buffers and an attempt to orient the housing away from the Turnpike. However, the proposed grade of 12.5% slope of the driveway and parking areas in the privately owned portion of the site exceeds the maximum desirable grade of 8%. The result is a definite potential for excessive water runoff and driving hazards during winter weather. The site plan locates the parking areas parallel to the excessive proposed slope rather than terracing them. Access to the units is over a long (900 feet) driveway which drops steeply over 55 feet in grade from top to bottom. This would be ideal for a bobsled run but questionable for autos. The lower end (City-owned) of the site is flat and wide and does not present the same design problems as the upper site but contains no access at this level. Also, as mentioned, this portion is in an area that has definite environmental problems caused by the Toll Road and the Penn Central Railroad tracks and the parking area of an industrial firm located in Boston at the same grade.

Recommendation

It is recommended that the requested change of zone to Residence D district be denied and that a change to Private Residence zone be explored as an alternative in order to restrict development to a lower density. It is recommended that the submitted site plan be redesigned in order to overcome the basic objection of excessive sloping grades in the parking and driveway areas. More attention should also be given to overcoming the environmental deficiencies in the area.

Site #4—Stanton Avenue

Suitability of Site for Housing
The site is poorly located with respect to community services, most of which are three-fourths of a mile or more distant and out of walking distance range. Its most favorable asset is the availability of public transportation. The Woodland station of the MBTA is adjacent to the parcel and Middlesex and Boston bus service is available on Washington Street.

Access to the site by automobile is convenient although major traffic problems exist at the entrance to the Woodland station. The MBTA has been petitioned to grant the City an easement in order that traffic signals may be constructed at the station's entrance. Traffic control at this location would also control traffic at Stanton Avenue.

The proposal is compatible with the present residential character of the area although the proposed density is somewhat higher (50 persons per acre compared to 10 persons per acre). However, the existence of abundant open space in the area offsets the potential impact of the higher density.

In 1967 the Board of Aldermen denied a petition to use this land for a "town house" development for 40 units. At that time the Planning Department indicated that medium density housing appeared to be an appropriate use for the site.

Impact on Community Facilities
The Angier School, which would serve this development, is projected by General Learning Corporation to decrease slightly in enrollment in the future. With the NCDF development, the current student per classroom ratio would increase from 23.6 to an estimated range of 24.1 to 26.6.

Washington Street is of sufficient capacity to absorb the additional traffic volumes generated by this housing development without any traffic signals at the Washington Street and Stanton Avenue intersection. However, turning movements onto the site from Washington Street would likely result in a significant interruption of traffic flow and a potential traffic hazard on Washington Street.

There are no neighborhood playground facilities in the area. The 1970 City census counted 515 persons residing in the neighborhood, defined as extending along Washington Street from Longfellow Road to Commonwealth Avenue, bounded by Brae Burn Country Club. A total of 111 children between the ages of 6 to 18 live in this area with an additional 32 between the ages minus 1 to 5 years. A one-acre portion of the subject site has been proposed in the 1969 Recreation/Open Space Plan to be acquired and developed as a neighborhood playground to provide recreational facilities for the residents of this area. The residents of the proposed development would also require recreational facilities. Since all of the subject site is proposed to be used for housing, there would appear to be no opportunity to provide presently needed recreational space as well as the additional need that would be demanded by new housing.

Analysis of Zoning Request
The proposed Residence D zone represents a significant departure from the existing low density Residence A district which predominates in the area. The Private Residence district would be a more logical zone to apply, although no similar district is within proximity. However, the heterogeneous land use pattern in the immediate area and the accessibility of this locus suggests that the continuance of a single family district on this land is not realistic and that a higher intensity development is more realistic. Only six single family structures could be constructed on the site under the present Single Residence A district and the development costs for same would be excessively high due to the site's steep topography.

Site Plan Comments
The site plan meets all of the technical requirements of the proposed Residence D districts, but suffers from several defects. The plan ignores the topography, minimizing the natural view potential and creating excessive slopes on the driveways and parking areas (10%). Slopes in excess of 8%, particularly in the New England area, present a potential pedestrian and vehicular hazard in the winter and cause too fast a water runoff for the existing drainage system to hold without creating temporary flooding conditions.

The site plan has extremely limited provisions for play areas for the site's potential 25 to 75 children. The proposed topography shows grades that will not allow enough reasonably flat areas for outdoor recreational activity.

Because of the topography, lack of recreational facilities, on-the-site traffic hazard on Washington Street and distance to elementary schools, it is felt that the bedroom distribution is inappropriate. Rather, the development should be predominantly one and two bedrooms with a minimum number of families with children.

Recommendation
It is recommended that the change of zone to Residence D be approved only after the suitability of changing the zone to Private Residence is fully explored. This district would necessitate changes in the site plan to comply with the provisions of attached dwellings. Further, approval should be conditional upon provision of adequate traffic control systems to serve turning traffic to this site and the MBTA parking lot.

The site plan should be modified to leave more open area to solve the recreational deficiencies which exist in the neighborhood as well as provide a solution to the excessive sloping grades of the parking and driveway areas and the open areas of the site. Further, the bedroom distribution should be changed solely to one and two bedroom units.

Site #5—City Hall

Suitability of Site for Housing
The site is inconvenient to most community facilities with the exception of public transportation and one elementary school.

The proposal is not inconsistent with the residential character of the neighborhood. However, the use of the site for residential purposes may infringe upon and potentially destroy an essential part of the open space which characterizes City Hall. The visual form of the City Hall setting is established by this heavily wooded land as well as the landscaped grounds of City Hall. Without this openness the bulk of the City Hall building would overwhelm the area and create an unwanted urban setting in this section of the City.

This site (which is the smallest of the ten sites) is irregularly shaped, its topography steeply sloping, orienting it toward Commonwealth Avenue and City Hall. To adequately design an appropriate plan to accept the proposed density is very difficult because of the parcel's size, shape and topography.

Access to the site is fair. Lakeview Avenue rises steeply from Walnut Street and also from Commonwealth Avenue. Commonwealth Avenue (north drive) is one way in a westerly direction.

Due to its topographic characteristics, site configuration, inconvenient access, distance from many community services and infringement on the City Hall setting, the site is undesirable for housing.

Impact on Community Facilities

The General Learning Corporation study shows an increase in enrollment for the Claflin School in the future of a little over 10%. With the increase resulting from NCDF housing, the student per classroom ratio can be expected to increase from 24.4 currently to a range of between 27.5 and 28.8.

The vehicular traffic generated on this site will have a minimum effect on traffic on Walnut Street or Commonwealth Avenue. The minimal traffic movements on Lakeview Avenue would be noticeably increased if access is off this street. However, it would not be in excess of capacity.

No neighborhood playgrounds exist within the area. The Recreation/Open Space Plan recommends that a one-acre tract of the Newton High School land be developed as a neighborhood playground. However, this is more than one-half mile away from the site.

The site is an important open space resource of the City.

Analysis of Zoning Request

The creation of a Residence D district on the site represents a significant departure from the existing Residence B district in the immediate area. It is doubtful that the challenge of "spot zoning" could be defended although a change to Private Residence might be justified as a logical extension of this zone from Lowell Avenue.

Access to the site could be gained by any of the three streets which form the site's boundaries. Minimal traffic movement occurs on Lakeview Avenue while traffic volumes on Walnut Street and Commonwealth Avenue are heavy.

96 *Housing the Poor in Suburbia*

Approximately 8 single family structures could be built on the site under Residence B zoned land. This is approximately one-fourth of the 35 units requested. The proposed district could produce a population density of 45 persons per acre, three times the existing area density of 15 persons per acre.

Site Plan Comments
Two site plans have been submitted and are identified as Plans 5 and 5A. These comments are directed to both since they are essentially similar in character with respect to number of units and land area uses. Plan 5 indicates the structures to be located on Commonwealth Avenue with access from Lakeview Avenue; 5A locates the buildings on Lakeview Avenue with access from Commonwealth Avenue. Neither plan offers substantial advantages over the other with respect to site design. However, only Plan 5 satisfies all the technical requirements of the zoning ordinance.

The configuration of the parcel which is long and narrow at the westerly end and progressively widens at the Walnut Street end, coupled with the steep sloping topography of the site, limits the site plan design to the two submitted. No other plan is feasible due to the site limitation and the requested density. As a result, the plans have few desirable features. The structures are strung out along the street lines and no opportunity is available to group them in identifiable clusters. There are no play areas available because of the proposed steep, sloping grades. The parking areas of both plans are forced to be located at the proposed locations because of the limitations of the site.

Recommendation
It is recommended that the zone change to Residence D district be denied. Because of the significance of the site as an open space resource and its important relationship to the City Hall grounds, it is further recommended that this site not be considered for development of any type, regardless of the social and/or humanitarian objectives.

An alternate site for the Newtonville area should be considered and among those which should be studied is Maguire Court.

Site #6—Beacon Street

Suitability of Site for Housing
The proposal is compatible with the immediate neighborhood two-family residential character although it represents a slightly higher density (48 persons per acre compared with the area's density of 22 persons per acre). The site is reasonably close to community services and is convenient to public transportation, the Beethoven School which abuts the site, and the remainder to the undeveloped Cold Spring park.

The site is relatively flat and is slightly below grade of Beacon Street. The subsoil consists of peat deposits of varying depths ranging from a reported 5 feet to 60 feet. The peat holds water and development of this site would necessitate extensive site preparation.

The site is part of a major City-wide recreational facility that has been in the planning stage for many years. The City is now taking by eminent domain a ten-acre tract of land to add to the present City holdings in order that enough land is available here to assure a park development of City-wide significance. The final plan for this facility has not yet been adopted. However, the removal of the proposed site from the present inventory would be inconsistent with the City's previous objectives of augmenting rather than reducing Cold Spring park.

Impact on Community Facilities
General Learning Corporation projections for Beethoven School show a relatively stable enrollment in the future. This NCDF site would likely raise present student/classroom ratio from 22.8 to a range of between 24.4 and 28.2.

The Richardson playground could easily absorb the additional demand that would be placed on it.

The vehicular traffic generated on the site would have a minimal impact on Beacon Street which is presently used to 75% of its capacity during peak hours.

The use of the land for housing would remove important open space from the City's inventory and would be inconsistent with the intention of creating a community-wide recreation area.

Analysis of Zoning Request
The creation of a Residence D district on the site or on the proposed snow dump site would be a logical extension of the abutting Private Residence zoned land.

Site Plan Comments
Since the site has been requested to be withdrawn by NCDF, it would be academic to comment on the plan which was designed for this site. No plans have been submitted for the alternate site which is the present snow dump off Beacon Street.

Recommendation
It is recommended that none of the Cold Spring land be used for housing.

Site #7—Hamlet Street

Suitability of Site for Housing
The site is well suited for housing of the type proposed. The proposal is compatible with the existing two-family and multifamily residential character of the neighborhood. The proposed density of 27 persons per acre compares favorably with the existing density of the neighborhood which is 23 persons per acre.

The site is large and abuts a large open space preserve of the Webster conservation land.

Many community services with the exception of churches are in close proximity of the site. Limiting factors of the site include access which is limited to Hamlet Street, a narrow, unpaved road and the existence of a large, illegal junk yard which abuts the property.

Impact on Community Facilities
The General Learning Corporation study shows a slightly decreasing enrollment for the Bowen School in the future, partially offsetting an increase resulting from NCDF housing. Students per classroom ratios can be expected to increase from 23.8 currently to a range of between 24.5 and 28.9.

The increased recreation demand on the Bowen playground could be easily handled by this facility.

The vehicular traffic generated on this site will have a minimal impact on Langley Road which is presently used at 75% of its capacity during peak hours.

Analysis of Zoning Request
The creation of a Residence D district on this site would be more desirable if a higher density use of the site were being requested. The change to Residence D could be defended since the land is now Private Residence district and it abuts the higher density zone of Residence F district. However, a density of more than 6,000 square feet of land area per unit is planned for this site. The existing Private Residence district could accept the proposed density with some changes to the submitted site plans in order to comply with the attached dwelling specifications.

Site Plan Comments
The plan complies with the technical requirements of the zoning ordinance under Residence D district.

The site seems to be well laid out with generous and well located open spaces and parking areas.

There is, however, only one access to the site on the southern side through Hamlet Street which terminates at the site. This presents a certain amount of risk in case of fire, a hazard to which the area is liable due to its densely wooded nature.

A secondary access to the site would be desirable from Carlisle Street along the western boundary of the site connecting this access to the Hamlet Street access.

Recommendation
It appears that the zone change to Residence D district is unnecessary in view of the low density of this proposal.

It is recommended, therefore, that the development of this site be under the present zoning district of Private Residence. This will require that the site plan comply with the attached dwelling provisions of the ordinance incorporating the suggestion that a second means of access be developed.

Site #8—Thurston Road

Suitability of Site for Housing
The site is within walking distance of virtually all community services which are within one-eighth to one-fourth of a mile away.

The proposal is compatible with the neighborhood two-family and multifamily residential character. The proposed density exceeds that of existing development within this two-family zone (48 persons per acre compared with 16 persons per acre for the neighborhood).

Access to the site is by residential streets of relatively steep grade.

The site's rocky terrain and hilltop location provide desirable natural amenities for housing although site preparation may be more difficult.

Impact of Community Facilities
The classroom size in the Emerson School is projected by General Learning Corporation without the proposed housing to increase from 17.6 currently to 19.1 in 1972. The average classroom size can be expected to range from a low of 20.4 to a high of 22.7, including this development.

The neighborhood playground could readily absorb the increased demand.

The vehicular traffic generated on this site will have a minimum impact on Elliot Street which is presently used to 80% of its capacity during peak hours. Traffic on Thurston Road will increase significantly, but not in excess of the street's capacity.

Analysis of Zoning Request
The creation of a Residence D district on this site would be consistent with the zoning in the area although the nearest Residence D district is one-fourth of a mile away. This site, as well as the surrounding areas, is presently zoned Private Residence.

Approximately 12 two-family structures housing 24 families could be constructed on this site under the present zoning provisions as compared with the requested 43 units.

Site Plan Comments
The site is well planned with respect to the arrangement of housing units. It is, however, felt that the parking area could be located more imaginatively, either by splitting it into two or more parts and/or locating it parallel to Thurston Road. This arrangement of the parking facilities would provide all of the residential units with a view of the green space rather than a sea of asphalt. The site plan complies with the technical requirements of the ordinance.

Recommendation
It is recommended that the change of zone to Residence D district be approved.

It is recommended that the proposed site plan be modified to incorporate the above suggestions prior to approval.

Site #9—Goddard Street

Suitability of Site for Housing
The site is poorly situated with respect to community services all of which are one-half to three-fourths of a mile away.

The proposal is not incompatible with the single family residential character of the neighborhood even though the proposed density is significantly greater. The proposed density of 44 persons per acre compares with the average density in the immediate area of 19 persons per acre.

Access to the site is over residential streets which presently experience minimal traffic movements.

The soil is wet and presently serves as a catch basin for water runoff in adjacent areas. The site does not appear to be part of the Charles River flood plain, however.

Impact on Community Facilities
The General Learning Corporation study shows a slightly increasing enrollment for the Countryside School in the future, partially offsetting an increase from the proposed housing. The student/classroom ratio can be expected to increase from the present 18.7 to a range of between 20.4 and 23.5.

There are no neighborhood playgrounds in the area; however, the site is within one-fourth of a mile of the proposed playground/playfield on the grounds of the former City Infirmary. The recreation facility could absorb the increased population in the neighborhood. The Goddard Street site was recommended in the Recreation/Open Space Plan to be developed as a neighborhood playground. However, it was felt that the proposed playground on the City Infirmary land would somewhat ameliorate the recreational needs of this neighborhood.

The traffic generated on this site will have a significant impact on Goddard and Christina Streets which presently experience minimal traffic movement. The effect on Winchester Street will be minor since it now carries only 54% of its capacity during peak hours.

Analysis of Zoning Request
The change of zone to Residence D district would be inconsistent with the surrounding Single Residence A zoning district. The physical character of this site is similar to the surrounding land which presently contains single family structures. Approximately 18 single family structures could be constructed on this site under the present Single Residence C district. This is significantly less than the requested 53 units. It is doubtful that a challenge of "spot zoning" could be resisted on this site.

A more logical change of zone here would be to Private Residence district which would not allow the potential of a significantly increased density which could be requested in Residence D district. A Private Residence district zone exists just to the north of the site on Winchester Street and, if extended, would allow the 53 town house units on this site by special permission.

Comments on Site Plan

The site plan complies with the technical requirements of the ordinance. The site plan contains very desirable features with respect to the arrangement of buidings, parking area treatment and reasonable concentration of landscaped areas. Natural wooded areas are planned to be retained to serve as a buffer between the structures and the abutting streets.

Recommendation

It is recommended that the zone change to Residence D district be denied as the proposal presently meets the 3,500 sq. ft./unit density requirement of the Private Residence zone, a more preferable zone for the area.

It is recommended that the change to Private Residence district be explored to allow the development under the provisions of the attached dwelling ordinance.

Site #10—Esty Farm

Suitability of Site for Housing

The site is reasonably close to most community facilities. The proposal is compatible with the single family residential character of the neighborhood. However, the proposed density of 50 persons per acre is significantly greater than the neighborhood's density of 12 persons per acre.

Access to the site is good from Dedham Street. Access to the site is also proposed over June Lane and Esty Farm Road, both of which terminate at the site.

Impact on Community Facilities

The average classroom size at the Memorial School has been projected by General Learning Corporation, without the proposed housing, to decrease from its present 19.1 ratio to 15.7. The ratio can be expected to increase to a range between 17.9 and 22.4 with the housing.

The proposed increase in population will have a significant impact on the inadequate playground at the Memorial School. The Recreation/Open Space study recommended that a new neighborhood playground to relieve the pressures on Memorial School playground be developed at the intersection of Spiers Road and Saw Mill Brook Parkway.

The vehicular traffic generated on this site will have a minimum impact on Dedham Street which is presently used at 60% of its capacity during peak hours. The impact on both June Lane and Esty Farm Road will be a significant increase in traffic since both streets now terminate at the site and presently experience minimal traffic volumes.

Analysis of Zoning Request
The Residence D district would not be consistent with the Single Residence zoned land which extends in all directions from the site for a mile or more. The potential increased density of residential uses that could occur within the requested Residence D zone would make it difficult to defend against a challenge of "spot zoning."

A less intensive zone that would bear a closer relationship to the existing zone is the Private Residence district. This district would allow the development of a density somewhat closer to that which is requested.

Site Plan Comments
The site complies with the technical requirements of the requested Residence D district. The site design contains some desirable features with respect to the separation of the parking areas which prevents vehicles from penetrating the site and ample usable open space for play areas. This feature will somewhat relieve the pressures on the overused neighborhood playground.

The rows of housing units are crowded too close to each other, particularly on the southern part of the site where the distances between rows are as low as 35 feet and 45 feet and in two cases the distances between the front of one row and the side of another are 18 feet and 20 feet respectively. These distances are considered as extremely low from the point of view of privacy of the residents. The recommended distance in such cases is about 70 feet.

This defect could be corrected by omitting two rows in the southern part of the site.

Recommendation
It is recommended that the change of zone to Residence D district be denied and that a change to Private Residence district be carefully explored. Revisions to the site plan would be necessary to make it comply with the district's requirements for attached dwellings.

In brief, the Planning Department's position reporting the NCDF plan, the sites and their impact on Newton is summarized as follows:

Overall Position
The Newton Community Development Foundation clearly provides an imaginative approach to the problems of housing Newton's less affluent families. In terms of density, unit design and residential amenity, it rates most favorably with any multifamily proposal on record in the City, private or public.

The "scattered site" package approach is a most desirable objective. It provides an opportunity to assimilate low and moderate income families within the City in a way which would result in the least impact upon the city and its residents from social, economic and political points of view.

Need in Newton
Precise estimates of the level of need for such housing are clearly unavailable. However, the following data tend to support the conclusion that there are sufficient numbers of current residents of the City with qualifying income to support several times the number of units proposed by NCDF:

Selected Data Re Low-Moderate Income Families—1970

Total persons receiving Welfare assistance*	− 1,005
Estimated total families earning less than $3,000*	− 700
Estimated total families earning $3,000 to $6,000*	− 2,500
Total number of full-time City employees earning $4,000 to $8,000 annually**—(820 male, 188 female)	− 1,008

*Estimates for 1970 Workable Program
**Computed from City payroll data

In terms of overall City needs, a more adequate range of housing choice remains high on the list of priorities. Despite certain limitations with regard to particular sites, NCDF's program appears to be a sound step toward reduction of that evergrowing need.

Impact on Schools
The impact upon schools has been estimated utilizing enrollment projections by the General Learning Corporation. Because the potential number of school children could vary so greatly depending upon tenancy requirements and selection policies, a range of minimum and maximum expected enrollments was produced for each school.

Overall a minimum of 214 and a maximum 641 school children are anticipated from all 10 sites. Of the 10 elementary schools affected, the average classroom size would likely increase from the current 22.1 students per classroom to a range of 23.4 to 26.1 students per classroom. Utilizing the NCDF estimate, the ratio would be 24.5 students per classroom.

It should be noted that the City-wide average is 30 elementary school children per 100 dwelling units (based upon approximately 27,000 dwelling units and 9,000 elementary school children) and this average has not changed appreciably in the last ten years. This is despite the fact that Newton is a school-oriented, essentially single family residential suburb. In contrast, the estimates for NCDF range from a low of 42 students per 100 dwelling units to a high of 127 students per 100 dwelling units.

Spot Zoning
Present petitions before the City concern zone changes to Residence D on 10 sites and site plan approval on 4 sites. Because the requested zone changes frequently occur in the middle of single family zones, the consistency of such action must be considered. The possibility of a legal challenge on the basis of "spot zoning" must also be faced.

Most cases of court overturned zoning have involved commercial development in residential zones. This case is clearly different. Yet the change of zone is not to the next intensive use on the scale (Private Residence) but in some cases represents a quantum jump (Residence A to Residence D).

The Newton Community Development Foundation is, in fact, proposing to build town houses (which may be permitted in Private Residence zones by Aldermanic action) which in all but certain details appear to meet the Private Residence zoning requirements on several sites.

Discussions with the Building Department reveal that the proposed design appears to meet neither the building code for garden apartments nor town houses and that a variance may be required from the Building Board of Appeals either way.

Thus it appears reasonable to suggest that if the proposals can be allowed a variance from the town house building code that a change of zone to Private Residence, rather than Residence D, would be advisable. A change to Private Residence zone would be more likely to stand up to legal challenge and, further, if NCDF is unsuccessful in its financing, the door has not been opened to other less sensitive developers for the construction of garden apartments.

It should be pointed out that a similar variance may be required from the Zoning Board of Appeals in regard to street frontage requirements under the Private Residence zone. This is admittedly a more complicated procedure than a Residence D zone change, but it is also felt to be a more preferable one.

Impact of Chapter 774
The issue of whether NCDF might choose to invoke the "Snob Zoning" appeal has often been raised. It appears that, should the Board fail to grant approval, this option would be available to NCDF. Under this law, Newton is obliged to build 23.7 acres of low-moderate income housing per year before public, nonprofit or limited dividend sponsors would become ineligible for appeals to the local Board of Appeals and State Department of Community Affairs. The package of NCDF represents 40 acres, more than would be required for one year. The City's overall obligation under this law is for 113.4 acres over five years (according to recent estimates). This is almost three times NCDF's proposal.

Whether or not an appeal under this Chapter 774 is successful depends upon the State Board's interpretation of whether or not the proposal is "consistent with local needs." The law is new and adequate precedence regarding this interpretation is not yet available.

Alternative Sites
Finally, the subject of alternative sites must be faced. When a proposal of this magnitude is submitted involving not one but ten sites, and where the financial feasibility of each site is predicated upon acceptance of all others, it is

incumbent upon the proposer to be ready to submit alternative sites for those which are unsuitable if his project is to be successful. Certainly this must be a partnership between the City and the nonprofit sponsor.

Where sites are rejected, several alternatives may be possible in order to salvage the project:

    a. Increase the number of units on good sites (such as Hamlet Street, Pine Street).
    b. Consider redevelopment sites. Urban renewal funds and the City's power of eminent domain make possible the assembly of small parcels of dilapidated housing at a low cost which could then be made available to nonprofit sponsors.

The latter may involve more time and effort in the short run, but in the long run may better serve City objectives.

The "Compromise" Plan

On August 19, 1970, the Land-Use Committee voted to endorse the NCDF concept and approved a largely prearranged compromise resolution accepted by NCDF, calling for 325-375 units on 7 sites. Of these sites, 4 were from the original privately owned portion of the package and 3 were new City-owned pieces of land. The resolution recommended that the NCDF sites at Stanton Avenue, Hamlet Street, Thurston Road, and Hunnewell Avenue be approved. A small portion of the Hunnewell Avenue site was City owned and had to be released by the Recreation Commission before it could be used for housing. The other 3 sites were identified in the resolution only as "one south of Route 9, one between Route 9 and Beacon Street, and one north of Beacon Street." Alderman Harrington said at the Committee meeting, however, that these sites were understood as being the City infirmary land in Oak Hill, the snow dump land off Beacon Street, and the corner of Homer and Walnut Streets across from City Hall. The resolution called for 25-60 units per site and contained a stipulation that two-thirds of the units would have residency requirements, hopefully quieting arguments that the housing would not go to present residents of Newton. The resolution also recommended that "the highest reasonable and practical proportion of the housing have provision for occupant-ownership." The resolution, as amended, is as follows:

> WHEREAS this Board of Aldermen reaffirms its recognition of the need for 200 units of low and a substantial number of moderate income housing units in the City of Newton in order to serve the needs of Newton residents and families with Newton ties; and
> WHEREAS a portion of this need has been and will continue to be satisfied by or through the Newton Housing Authority, and approxi-

mately 60-75 units of such housing will become available in Newton Lower Falls through the Newton Redevelopment Authority; and

WHEREAS a substantial number of Newton citizens presently live in substandard housing and there is an urgent need to provide sound housing for such citizens in order that those apartments may be vacated and condemned and made fit for occupancy; and

WHEREAS the Newton Community Development Foundation (NCDF), a charitable corporation, desires to erect several hundred units of low and moderate income housing on scattered sites located throughout Newton; and

WHEREAS the legal complexities involved in the NCDF petitions which have been filed with this Board make it essential that an overall plan be approved which will then be implemented with the cooperation of all the necessary governmental authorities and departments;

NOW, THEREFORE, BE IT RESOLVED that the Board of Aldermen does hereby approve the following general plan for the construction by the Newton Community Development Foundation of no less than 325 and no more than 375 units of low and moderate income housing in the manner described below, subject to the conditions hereafter specified:

That the units shall be located on not fewer than seven sites scattered throughout the city in such manner that no one site shall have less than 25 nor more than 60 units thereon;

To permit the construction of such housing and in accordance with the principle of scattering the housing throughout the city, at least three additional parcels of city land shall be made available and that the Executive Department is requested to declare surplus and release appropriate parcels;

That the transfer of city land to NCDF, and any other steps to be taken by any Newton governmental body to permit NCDF to construct said low and moderate income housing, shall be subject to the following conditions:

At least three-fourths of the units shall be subject to a priority for the following persons to the fullest extent permitted by law:

Persons residing in substandard housing in Newton. To implement this priority the Executive Department is requested to take whatever steps necessary, including requesting this Board to expand its Code Enforcement staff to assure that substandard apartments are identified prior to the completion of construction of the units by NCDF and that the units be declared unfit for occupancy and that the families be displaced into NCDF's housing, and that no further occupancy in such an apartment be permitted unless and until it meets all of the minimum standards.

Employees of the City of Newton.

Retired employees of the City of Newton and widows and widowers of deceased and retired employees of the City of Newton.

Persons who have been residents of Newton for at least one year at any time prior to application.

That the highest reasonable and practical proportion of such housing should have provisions for some form of ownership by the occupants, whether by cooperatives, condominium or outright ownership;

The foregoing is based upon the commitment of NCDF to cooperate in a further rezoning to the extent permitted by law to provide for the zoning of all parcels to a proposed public residence zone or permissive use or similar concept if such is adopted by this Board.

The foregoing is based on the assumption the entire project contemplated by NCDF is economically feasible and can be entirely constructed and operated as planned; and, without limiting the generality of the foregoing, that the operating budget will provide adequate funds for the maintenance of all units in good condition and repair and the payment of real estate taxes to the city.

The most important recommendation in the compromise, however, was that of placing all these sites in a new zoning category, to be known as the Public Residence Zone. The housing allowed in this zone must be built by the local Housing Authority or by nonprofit and limited dividend sponsors, with State and federal subsidies. The intent was to make land available for low-income, multiple-dwelling units without opening land to commercial apartment development. Under this proposal, the housing could be 1-family, 2-family, 1- or 2-family town house, attached, and garden apartments. The requirements for each type of unit were:

SFDU	5,000 square feet/unit
SFDU	4,000 square feet/unit
SFDU, town house	3,000 square feet/unit
SFDU, town house	2,500 square feet/unit

Frame or masonry construction: firewalls separating all units; no more than 12 attached together.

Setbacks were to be uniform:

15 feet from roadway
20 feet from back line
15 feet from sides
15 feet dividing each building

These requirements meant that there would have to be changes in some of NCDF's plans, but it was felt accommodations could be made.

The Newton Civic and Land Use Association continued to oppose the "Compromise Plan," claiming that "compromise" was a misleading term since the real opposition did not participate in any negotiations.

Vote by the Board of Aldermen

The energy and organization of the opposition made the Aldermen fully aware of the unpopularity of the housing proposal among segments of the community. Added to the fire of all the old protests were new ones regarding the compromise plan. One opponent to the plan complained: "All of a sudden, the Aldermen will be voting on a plan that we knew nothing about. We demand that new hearings be held so we can give opinions on the new sites."

The apparent strength of the opposition made it appear that endorsement of the plan would be political suicide, but the Aldermanic elections were over a year away. By that time, things might have quieted down, with eventual acceptance of the housing. The Aldermen were also aware of their opportunity to make a precedent-setting decision. Still, each Alderman feared voting for a site in his own ward without a guarantee that the other sites would also be approved. This led to constant postponement of a vote on the NCDF petition until the idea of an endorsement vote emerged. The vote endorsing the concept of NCDF was to be taken by the full Board before it voted on the zoning changes requested for each individual site. Essentially, it was a moral commitment by those who voted in favor of the concept of voting for zoning changes on all sites which were deemed feasible for housing. As *The News-Tribune* of August 20, 1970, described the situation,

> two formidable hurdles remain. The first one will be faced when the full board considers adopting the resolution. A total of 18 affirmative votes out of 23 aldermen will be required for passage. The reason is that a sufficient number of legal abutters have indicated their opposition to the necessary zone changes so that a state law requiring a three-quarters vote goes into effect.
>
> Then, if approval of the zoning changes on the seven sites is gained, each site plan must receive aldermanic approval, which would require an additional seven public hearings.

On August 23, 1970, under increasing pressure from the opposition, the Aldermen met to vote on the endorsement resolution and zoning changes. A majority vote was normally needed to pass the resolution, but, because abutters to the site opposed the zoning, a three-fourths affirmative vote of the Board—18 out of 23 Aldermen—was needed to approve each site. One seat was vacant, pending a coming election.

The first vote for the resolution passed 17 to 6, indicating that the 18 votes needed for three-fourths approval might not be forthcoming. In a tumultuous session, the Aldermen defeated all but 1 site for rezoning. All 7 sites received a majority in favor of the rezoning, but only 1 got the necessary 18. Thus, the 1 site passed was vetoed by the Mayor, on the grounds that it was not feasible, considering the original plans of NCDF.

Despite the rejection of zoning changes, NCDF viewed the 17 to 6 vote on the compromise concept as a victory. They believed that the 1 or 2 extra votes could be obtained if some site modifications were made, and if the Public Residence Zone (PRZ) were passed before the 90-day limit expired, invalidating the June 3 hearings. If the PRZ were passed by the Board within the next 2 weeks, NCDF could resubmit its plans for a new vote. But, by September 3, no action was taken by the Board on the PRZ and the hearings became invalid.

The NCDF Board of Directors met on September 8 to determine what strategy and plan of action they should take next. Despite all the setbacks, general feeling was optimistic for adoption of the PRZ. Hopeful of quick passage, the NCDF Board decided to lobby for support of this measure as a compromise zoning alternative, and to revise their plan to comply with the new requirements once the bill passed.

On September 21, the Land-Use Committee held hearings on the PRZ and deferred a decision until a completed draft was prepared. A meeting was tentatively scheduled for October 27, but again, the PRZ was not acted upon, and there was no decision as to when it would be brought up again.

On top of this disappointment came the results in the election for the Ward 5 Alderman-at-large seat. In one of the most heated Aldermanic election campaigns in the City's history, no less than 8 candidates were vying for the seat. NCDF's housing plans became the key issue for the candidates. In a conference held so the community could put questions to the candidates, 4 of the men running favored the 7-site compromise proposal, 3 were opposed to it, and 1 had no opinion.

NCDF could see that votes by those who sympathized with its plan would be split among the liberal candidates, but it never thought that the candidate most strongly opposed to the plan would receive a vote surpassing the total received by the 7 other candidates.

Not only did the landslide election support the opposition's contention that NCDF was attempting to force something on an unwilling community, but also it presented an additional obstacle to local resolution of the problem. With Antonellis on the Board of Aldermen, NCDF wondered if there were any hope for obtaining acceptance of the NCDF plan, and, if not, what they should do.

AN ORDINARY SUBURB?

In September 1971, over 4 years after its formation, the Newton Community Development Foundation had not succeeded in constructing a single unit of low- and moderate-income housing. Its original hopes of breaking ground for over 500 units on 10 scattered sites had been thwarted by community opposition to the plan and subsequent denial of necessary zoning changes by the Board of Aldermen. A compromise housing plan of 325-375 units on 7 sites was also defeated, and a bill proposing creation of a public residence zone for low- and moderate-income housing was killed after months of postponed action.

Since its inception through April 30, 1971, NCDF had invested $107,732 in this effort—land costs, $18,436; architectural-engineering and legal fees, $24,325; salaries of staff and office expenses, $64,971. For the same period, gifts to NCDF amounted to $111,788, of which $34,977 came from individual givers (700 persons), $43,095 from foundations, and $33,716 from business and churches.

The two-year options NCDF held on their 6 sites were in their final year. NCDF knew that once the options expired, there was little hope of implementing their plans. Community pressure would most likely prevent the owners of the 6 parcels from renewing the options, and, even if new sites could be obtained, the need for new plans and new rezoning petitions would require at least another year and would greatly tax NCDF's financial resources.

Some thought it might be more hopeful if federal support for nonprofit and limited dividend sponsors attempting to build low- and moderate-income housing in the suburbs were forthcoming. Yet, statements made by President Nixon in December 1970 indicated that he would not "force" the suburbs to zone for subsidized housing. Noting his hands-off policy, many persons thought the NCDF's objective might be accepted at some future date, but that its ideas could not now be implemented. NCDF attempted to assess the situation and to determine what to do.

A NEW STRATEGY: TOWARD 774

Mr. Casselman called a meeting of the NCDF Board of Directors for January 18, 1971, to discuss the options available to the organization. All members felt, at that time, that there were four alternatives to consider.

The first was to refile the petition for zoning changes on a 7-site package, similar to the one proposed in August 1970, but with substitution of the Pierce School for the Homer and Walnut Streets site. This would leave the plans for Stanton Avenue, Hamlet Street, Thurston Road, Hunnewell Avenue, the site at Oak Hill, and the snow dump off Beacon Street, intact. After investigating this possibility, the Board decided that the time needed to obtain zoning changes under any ordinance (even the Public Residence Zone, if passed), release of City-held land by various departments, permissive use approval on specific site plans, and FHA financing would probably exceed the remaining land-control time. The Board, also, was not confident that the plan would finally be approved. They now realized the strength of the opposition. With these factors in mind, the Board voted not to adopt this option.

A second option was to revise the original plan to include some 1-family dwelling units, and thus quell some fire of the opposition. The plan was to provide these units under a combination of the Federal 235 and Turnkey III programs. To assess the feasibility of this approach, Board members reviewed design and cost possibilities with their architects and HUD. They analyzed other parcels of land as new sources for what would be needed under this program. All findings pointed to the economic unfeasibility of this approach, especially because of land costs in excess of FHA limits. The Board had no choice but to reject this alternative, too.

Mr. Slotnick raised the third possibility of abandoning the effort and conceding that NCDF had gone through a process of self-immolation. He stated, "It is very possible that we have served our function. Perhaps we have burned ourselves out in the heat of the rhetoric surrounding the proposals, but the controversy begun here will spread and continue in other communities until it is resolved." The rest of the Board felt that they had gone too far to give up, as long as any route was open for action.

The fourth option, to appeal the previous rejection to the local Zoning Board of Appeal, was the one route which NCDF had refused to consider until now. In fact, NCDF had publicly told the community it would not use this approach. There was an additional problem in using this approach: NCDF could not file against the City and still use the City's land. Also, as chances for the success of a zoning appeal were minimal, this approach was valuable only if followed by a petition for a comprehensive zoning permit, on the privately-owned sites, to the state under Chapter 774. Under this law, a qualified developer might submit a single application for zoning changes to the local Zoning Board of Appeals, instead of the usual separate applications to a plethora of City offices. The local Board would be given 30 days in which to hold a hearing, and 40 days thereafter in which to make a decision. If these deadlines were not met, permits were automatically issued.

In addition, the local Zoning Board of Appeals was not required to abide by the community's zoning and building ordinances unless they were "consistent with local needs"; this was determined by balancing the regional need for low- and moderate-income housing with the "need to protect the health or safety of the occupants of the proposed housing of the city or town, to promote better site and building design in relation to the surroundings, or to preserve open spaces." The Act did not define regional need, nor did it indicate in what manner this need obliged particular towns to accept a proposed housing project. But it did specify maximum percentages which automatically exempted a town from having its ordinances waived. A town's ordinances would never be found unreasonable if it met any of the maximum percentages; even if it did not, the town could still show special circumstances that could excuse it from shouldering any regional need.

Mr. Casselman realized that the local Zoning Board and Chapter 774 presented the only feasible route for continuing NCDF efforts. There were some positive aspects to this approach. Chapter 774 established mandatory deadlines for action which could considerably shorten the time period to bring the project to fruition. The switch from financing under the Federal Housing Administration to the Massachusetts Housing Finance Agency also shortened the time process.

The Massachusetts Housing Finance Agency (MHFA), created in 1966, is a State agency in, but not subject to the supervision or control of, the Department of Community Affairs. Its purpose is to provide both construction and permanent mortgage loans to profit and nonprofit developers involved in the development or rehabilitation of housing designed for low- and moderate-income persons and families. It raises funds by issuing its own bonds and has an unofficial priority on a certain percentage of the Boston area's share of federal 236 money. The advantage of using MHFA, rather than straight FHA financing, is that MHFA will accept a preliminary application for funding for a program involving land which may not yet be zoned for the proposed use. FHA, on the other hand, requires that land be zoned for the use in question before application for financing, a requirement that NCDF could not fulfill.

However, there were a number of disadvantages associated with this option. Without City land, the housing would have to be denser than in the original proposal if NCDF still wanted to build at least 325-375 units. That these units would now be located on only 6, rather than the original 10 sites, also meant there would be less scatteration throughout the city.

The most serious drawback was the impression that Chapter 774 would force this housing on an unwilling community. The possible repercussions were many: a divided, bitter community; possible animosity towards those who would eventually occupy the housing; a rejection of other proposals; and, a lessening of support by public officials who, by losing any chance for credit if the housing were eventually to be built, could now safely oppose the NCDF plan.

Even if the Chapter 774 appeal proved successful, there still was the possibility of further appeals to higher courts by the City of Newton. In addition, the various town departments could be overly technical in their requirements. Although the long-range prognosis would then be favorable, there could be many short-term delays.

The NCDF Board examined the applicability of their situation in Newton to the stipulations necessary for filing under 774. They found that Newton complied with the technical criteria in all three cases, as follows:

1. 774 applies if subsidized housing does not exceed 10 percent of the existing housing stock in the community:

In Newton	Units
1970 units	27,425
Housing guidelines of 10 percent	2,743
Existing subsidized units	377
Current housing deficit	2,366

2. 774 applies if total area occupied by subsidized housing is less than 1.5 percent of the community's total land area, minus its publicly-owned land

In Newton	Acres
Total zoned land	11,406
Public lands	3,158
Total zoned land, less public land	8,248
Chapter 774 guideline of 1.5 percent	123.7
Existing area of subsidized-housing	10.3

3. 774 applies if the program does not seek to construct on more than 0.3 percent in one calendar year

NCDF Proposal	Acres
Hunnewell	1.95
Thurston	2.90
Stanton	3.51
Hamlet	8.23
Goddard	3.22
Esty	4.13
TOTAL	23.94

Chapter 774 Guideline: 8,248 acres × 0.3 percent = 24.74 acres. In each case, the technical criteria were met.

No decision had been handed down in either the Hanover or Concord case. But the local and State appeals process established in Chapter 774 provided the only means for NCDF to be actively, rather than passively, waiting for moves which might never come from the Aldermen or executives on the local level. Thus, the Board voted unanimously to instruct the Pard Team to redesign plans for submission to the Newton Zoning Board of Appeals under Chapter 774.

NCDF Announces Its Decision

On January 22, 1971, Mr. Casselman sent a letter to the Mayor and the Aldermen explaining the action that had been taken. He explained that the decision had not been made public in any other way, and that he and NCDF would be happy to meet with any of them if they wanted to discuss the implications of the decision. He made it clear that the doors were still open to another solution if the Aldermen made any advances in that direction.

Though there was no public announcement of the decision, NCDF did not expect that it would remain a secret very long. Within a few days, the entire community learned of the decision and was again in an uproar. NCLA, still in high gear from the elections, began to organize and prepare leaflets against this new NCDF move.

The Association told its constituents that it questioned the constitutionality of the "antisnob zoning" law, but that it was on the books and could be a viable instrument for NCDF to force proposals on the City. One flyer stated: "Time after time, we heard Casselman and Slotnick tell us they had no intention of filing under 'antisnob'. Once again, NCDF's credibility gap widens." The activities of NCLA were expanding into the politcal arena and their leaflets urged sympathizers to take out papers to run for Mayor and Aldermen in the November 1971 elections.

The local hearings, scheduled for May 1971, were a new phenomenon, and neither side was exactly sure what to expect from the local Zoning Board of Appeals or from the State, if the process went one step further. Petitions for zoning changes before the Land-Use Committee of the Board of Aldermen were common, and both sides in such cases normally knew what was expected of them by the Board. In this case, all participants were groping toward the kind of legal record that might influence the State Board. Was this really going to provide a mechanism for overriding local zoning authority? Would every "do gooder," nonprofit, and limited dividend sponsor be able to build subsidized housing against the wishes of the community? Or was Chapter 774 to be a paper tiger? Also, there was the question of its constitutionality. Did the State have the power to override a local zoning ordinance under its present constitution? The New York State Urban Development Corporation had such power granted to it, but since it had never utilized it, its legality had not yet been tested. Both sides in Newton were determined to see the issue through the courts, and, even, had visions of it reaching the Supreme Judicial Court of Massachusetts, because of the constitutional separation-of-powers issue involved.

The uncertainty put great pressure upon both NCDF and its opponents to present well-prepared statements and documents before the local Zoning Board of Appeals. Both sides spent several months on their efforts.

Community Reaction

What had begun as a seemingly simple attempt to provide a needed supply of low- and moderate-income housing now had far-reaching effects on the entire political, as well as social, structure of Newton. Every officeholder was either noticeably silent or vocal on the housing issue. Most opposed NCDF's current efforts.

Even after he announced that he would not seek reelection, the Mayor was silent on the NCDF decision to follow the antisnob zoning route. Opponents took this silence as being in their favor, commenting: "Mayor Basbas has finally seen the light. He knows we don't want the housing even though he favored it before. He won't contradict himself now, but instead just stays silent." NCDF realized this was a blow, especially when other efforts to obtain official support were unsuccessful.

The pressure of the housing issue was felt by more than the elected officials, however. Many City departments felt a mandate to action because of requests by the opposition that housing be provided by official bodies, rather than by nonprofit or private organizations.

The Redevelopment Authority was already involved in a project to provide 70-80 subsidized units on a single site. This was part of a State and federal project in the Lower Falls section which had been approved by HUD, and which was now awaiting zoning changes by the Board of Aldermen, where a conflict between Board members and the head of the Authority had created a delay.

The Newton Housing Authority, despite the power it had held since 1968 to build low- and moderate-income housing for families, had only 4 projects for the elderly, plus a few contracts for leased housing units on its record. Therefore, in early May, the Authority, feeling the pressure, said it was "impatient to build housing," and undertook a plan to build on 4 parcels of City-owned land. The possibilities for sites and turnover of City-owned land were to be debated by the Board of Aldermen.

The Planning Department took on the role of providing information, and gave a data base against which comments made by both sides could be guaged and measured. Its *Apartment Study*, published in April 1971, provided valuable information to be used at the hearings. Its findings, in effect, supported the efforts of NCDF. The report corroborated the belief that, if new housing were to be built in Newton, it would have to be multiple-family units, because of the high cost of land. It also invalidated the attacks against the increased density of NCDF's new plans; the report listed approved project densities greater than those proposed in the 1971 NCDF plans.

The path was also opened for other private developers and nonprofit groups who were interested in building low- and moderate-income housing. These people felt NCDF had laid the groundwork, and if NCDF were granted a permit, their own efforts almost surely would succeed. With the possibility that it was NCDF's proposal and tactics, which were the object of opposition rather than low- and moderate-income housing itself, some developers believed they could pull off a zoning change where NCDF had failed. However, even before the hearings took place in front of the Zoning Board of Appeals, several attempts by other developers were denied. It soon became apparent that the prime target was not NCDF, but low- and moderate-income housing itself. Still, some developers claimed that if NCDF had not totally bungled its initial plan and presentation through inflexibility and lack of professionalism there would have been a real chance for success in Newton.

The New Plan

Preparations began for the hearings before the local Zoning Board of Appeals which were to be held on the evenings of May 17, 19, and 20, 1971, with proposals for 2 of the 6 sites presented each night. An attempt was made to avoid the hysteria and histrionics that characterized the hearings of a year before. Names of speakers had to be submitted before the hearing, and only those persons listed would be allowed to speak. Discussion of each proposed site was to be limited to two hours, with each side given an hour to present its case and views.

Mr. Casselman knew that the only way his organization could gain the approval of the Board of Appeals was to present a full plan of action with detailed information on every area questioned by the opposition. They knew that attacks would arise over issues of density, unit mixes which would create school crowding, unit design, tenant selection, traffic problems, and the cost of providing municipal services compared with the revenue returned. Detailed information was prepared for the scrutiny of not only the Zoning Board of Appeals, but the public as well.

The new plan was necessarily confined to privately-controlled sites—the same 6 included in the proposal of the previous year: Hunnewell Avenue, Stanton Avenue, Hamlet Street, Thurston Road, Goddard Street, Esty Farm. Because of the exclusion of City-owned land, an increase in density was required over the original proposal to make the plans economically feasible. The actual number of units on these sites, compared with the number for the same sites in the original plan, showed an increase of 48. The opposition jumped on this fact and used it to discredit the new plan. Its flyer asked: "Who Shall Rule Our Destiny? The Citizens of Newton have overwhelmingly turned back NCDF 'low density' housing. NCDF now tells us they will *force* 'higher density' housing on us."

Thus, the NCLUA opposed the new plan, declaring that:

> **NCDF Files Again**
> The Newton Community Development Foundation has filed an application with the Newton Zoning Board of Appeals for a comprehensive permit to construct 367 units on 6 sites: Hunnewell Avenue, Stanton Avenue, Hamlet Street, Thurston Road, Goddard Street, and Esty Farm. They have increased the densities of their original proposals on all project sites, supposedly to make their program financially feasible. This is NCDF's first step in filing under

the so-called "antisnob" zoning law. We are prepared to contest any of their threatened actions and are fully prepared to use all legal means available to prevent the encroachment of NCDF in the City of Newton. Were they genuinely interested in housing people of low income, as well as moderate income in the City of Newton, we would have expected them to have supported the plans of the Newton Housing Authority and to have made some effort to work closely with this authority.

In three separate polls taken throughout the city, and in a special election in which NCDF was made the paramount issue as well as at public hearings, almost 63% of the voters rejected NCDF. It is with this mandate we intend to respond to any of the challenges offered by NCDF.

Proposed Zoning Changes

The various zoning changes suggested by Alderman William Carmen and drawn up by the Planning Department would lower the zoning requirements for low- and moderate-income housing, and would set up a double standard of zoning for the city....

The Newton Civic and Land Association has taken the position that whatever requirements are fair for a developer building low- and moderate-income housing should be the same as those for building conventional dwellings.

Under Alderman Carmen's plan, the zoning and building requirements would regress to those in effect before 1952. We are opposed to taking a step backward to 1952 standards. Properties once built for families of low- and moderate-income housing can later pass into private ownership, creating a double standard of regulations: one for low-income housing and one for conventional housing. These new zoning proposals, if passed, would be detrimental to the growth of Newton, negating changes that were made in 1952 to upgrade the entire city. We urge all of you to contact your Alderman.

Newton Housing Authority

At this time, the Newton Housing Authority is requesting permission to build approximately 120 units of elderly- and low-income housing on various properties throughout the city....

The executive board of the Newton Civic and Land Association is convinced that the NHA, an established agency within our city, is the most qualified to solve our elderly- and low-income housing requirements. They are under no stringent limitations as to the costs of construction. The housing must be for Newton residents, having resided here for at least one year. This naturally means little or no impact upon our already overcrowded schools.

Given half a chance and cooperation, the Newton Housing Authority can be effective.

Table Newton 17. Six NCDF Sites

Site	One BR	Two BR	Three BR	Four BR	Total Site	Total Acreage	Land Area Per Unit
Hunnewell Avenue	4	20	3	3	30	1.95	2,835 sq. ft.
Stanton Avenue	6	38	10	10	64	3.51	2,386 sq. ft.
Hamlet Street	24	44	17	17	102	8.23	3,514 sq. ft.
Thurston Road	6	30	8	7	51	2.90	2,479 sq. ft.
Goddard Street	4	18	13	12	47	3.22	2,983 sq. ft.
Esty Farm	6	40	14	13	73	4.13	2,465 sq. ft.
Total:	50	190	65	62	367	23.94	[Average] 2,841 sq. ft.

I CARE

Enclosed is my check for the Newton Civic and Land Association Legal Fund.

I want to join the Newton Civic and Land Association. Enclosed are my $2.00 family dues for 1971-1972.

Name _____

Address _____

Tel. No._____

The opposition could not negate, however, the statement made by the City Planning Department in its *Apartment Study*—that NCDF's housing was less dense than most projects already existing in Newton.

The new NCDF plan called for 367 dwelling units, compared with 313 on the same sites in previous plans. Of the units, 50 were 1-bedroom, 190 were 2-bedroom, 65 were 3-bedroom and 62 were 4-bedroom. The plans provided for more than 70 percent of the total acreage to remain open, with over 55 percent of all land landscaped and planted, and the balance to be used for roadways and parking areas.

The new structures were varied in design. There were some 3-bedroom town houses, and a few 4-bedroom town houses. This arrangement assured that elderly people living in a downstairs 1-bedroom would not be bothered by a larger family living above them. Each unit had its own living room, dining-room area, and kitchen (over 90 percent of the units, excluding only the first floor 1-bedroom units, had an eat-in kitchen, as well as a dining area), separate storage area, individually controlled heat, reserved parking, and a sliding door which opened onto a terrace or balcony from the living room.

All of the units were of fixed width (24 feet) and had the same framing pattern to facilitate construction. The town houses or modules were of varying lengths, creating an attractive pattern of setback and varying roof lines. This design provided an atmosphere similar to most Newton streets.

The impact on schools was examined with cooperation and information gained from the School Committee. Armed with data on the present situation and future expectations once the school building program was completed, NCDF carefully designed its housing mixes for each site. Three controls were used to minimize the impact on schools: scatteration, unit mix, and tenant selection. By varying these factors, the overall unit mixes were chosen to minimize the impact upon the schools involved.

One of the most important issues—cost to the City versus revenue received—was also faced. Previously, Mr. Casselman had not realized the seriousness of this argument, and felt people would willingly pay higher taxes to allow their community to be mixed. He had stated: "Taxes are a specious argument. These units will pay fairly significant taxes. Anybody that feels housing is such a remote need that it is not worth a 2 percent tax increase is not looking at the problem rationally." The detailed study of the housing costs put out by NCDF this time testified to Mr. Casselman's loss of faith in the "rationality of men"—at least when pocketbooks are affected. The study included the annual and capital costs of its proposal, compared with those costs which would be incurred if construction took place on each site according to the use for which it was presently zoned. Exhibits were submitted by NCDF to the local Zoning Board of Appeals and to the public to illustrate the revenue/cost ratio of the housing to the City.

Evidence was presented to show the total revenue received from all 6 sites under NCDF or its zoned use. For all private homes, taxes were calculated at the then present rate of $103.60 per $1000 of assessed valuation. For NCDF housing and other rental units, taxes were based on the annual rent roll for the structure. The going tax rate is 25 percent of the annual rent roll, but NCDF hoped to negotiate with the City for a reduction to 18 percent under the aegis of 121(a) of the Massachusetts General Laws. The figures Mr. Slotnick presented gave the revenue at each rate. The excise tax is an average charge of $61.84 on every automobile registered in the City, and adds to the revenue contributed by use of the sites under either plan. The figures presented showed clearly that the revenue received from NCDF housing at 18 percent was almost that received from the other uses at the normal rate. NCDF knew that this was only half the story, however, and almost meaningless until compared with the costs incurred by each plan.

The determination of how much each new pupil would represent in some resulting future need for more schools was no easy task. And the opposition was not satisfied with the NCDF results. Mr. Stiller made it known that he was displeased: "How can you possibly say that the capital costs of 5 children who might crowd an existing school would be $15,000 (estimated at $3,000 per child)? Does that mean that you will build a school for that amount of money, or, maybe, some floating classrooms? Do we take the total figure to mean that we must allocate $308,000 of our already tight tax dollars to build new mini-schools to accommodate 88 new children? I admit these costs are difficult to estimate, but your figures are ridiculous."

Though these comments shed some doubt on the credibility of NCDF's estimates, the more important information covering annual costs was not argued. The opposition, in fact, was pleased to see these figures. Again, Mr. Stiller saw himself as vindicated: "There should be no doubt now that NCDF housing will be very expensive to the community, as the chart just presented substantiates. Essentially, the costs are much greater, because of the larger number of school children, than those costs for use of the sites as they are presently zoned. Elderly housing does not force the town to incur these extra costs, or to risk a possible lowering of school standards. In total, the cost of

NCDF housing is $515,606 greater than the revenues it provides at the 18 percent tax rate. That means, once again, higher taxes for something that no one of us even wants."

The more important issue of who would live in this housing was dealt with more easily this time because of the constraints imposed by the financing NCDF was seeking. MHFA requires submission of a tenant selection plan with its application for financing, and so this was fully worked out. The funds available through MHFA also changed the composition of the tenant income mix. Under MHFA financing, 25 percent of the housing (91 units) would be available to families with incomes higher than those specified under the Federal 236 limits, which go up as high as $16,000 for a family of 4. These 91 units would be financed at the maximum MHFA rate of 7 percent interest. The remaining units would be financed as under the previous plan: 50 percent (182 units) under the 236 program which subsidizes the interest rate down to 1 percent, and the remaining 25 percent (92 units) would be either leased to the Housing Authority or receive federal rent supplement assistance to reduce rents to 25 percent of a family's income.

The last issue that NCDF explored had not been debated the year before. Casselman and Slotnick began to consider the possibility of making NCDF a limited dividend corporation. As a nonprofit organization, it could obtain 100 percent mortgage financing, an advantage not possible as a limited dividend sponsor. However, rents are established so the sponsor makes no profit, and all the seed money is provided by the sponsor, though some of it is reimbursed later. Because NCDF was facing an economic squeeze, the financial advantages of a limited dividend corporation looked attractive. Since a limited dividend corporation is not tax exempt (as is a nonprofit sponsor), it can make use of accelerated tax depreciation provisions; NCDF, as the general partner, could sell its tax losses to acquire funds which could be used to provide more amenities, reduce rents, or help finance the project.

All of this information was compiled for the benefit of the local Zoning Board of Appeals, and was included in the application for a comprehensive permit.

Hearings and Opposition

On the night of May 17, no one knew less of what to expect than the Zoning Board of Appeals. Should the Board see the hearings as a means to solve the problem by acting favorably on the petition, or should they assume this hearing was a step in the process that would necessarily move to a higher jurisdiction? And what of the opposition? Did it see positive action a real possibility, or did it, too, view the hearings simply as a formality in a process that would inevitably be resolved in the courts?

The answers to these questions were apparent as the hearings opened. NCDF reiterated all the information it had submitted to the Board. Its attempt to present expert witnesses on all questionable issues indicated its attempt to win over the votes of the Board and resolve the issue at the local level. Mr. Casselman emphasized that he did not want these hearings to be a "social, emotional forum," but that he regarded them as a quasi-judicial process.

As clear as were the intentions of NCDF towards these hearings, so were those of the opposition. Knowing that NCDF defeat here only moved the process to the state level for deliberation, the opposition wanted to establish a route of recourse for itself. For that reason, it opened its testimony with Mr. Cohen, a lawyer representing abutters to all sites, who immediately put the legality of the hearings into question by asking if there were meant to be 3, 6, or only 1 hearing. Since only 2 sites were to be discussed in each of the 3 evenings, his question confused the Board. Mr. Cohen also challenged the right of some members of the Board to deliberate this issue because they had contributed money to NCDF. It seemed that the opposition was not viewing these hearings as anything that would resolve the issue. This impression was substantiated by a comment of a member of the opposition: "Nothing is going to be resolved by these hearings. We just want to get all our objections into the record so we have material for a court case on at least procedural grounds."

Though the fervor of the hearings of a year before was gone, there was still much laughter and applauding by anti-NCDF spectators. Opponents presented very much the same arguments as the year before, some relating to specific site characteristics, others to general feelings against what was expressed as "foreign elements from other parts of the country." Basically, as one Alderman testified, the feeling was that, "NCDF had its chance to sell its program and it failed to do so."

Again, the issue that NCDF's plan was too conservative came up. One speaker attacked the new plan on the grounds that NCDF would be providing 25 percent of the housing conventionally and would be violating its purpose of incorporation as a nonprofit sponsor to provide housing only for low- and moderate-income people. He said, "Here we go again, subsidizing the middle class. Conventional builders should construct housing for people with incomes of $15,000 and $16,000, not organizations like NCDF." Others took the opposite approach, condemning the 25 percent of the units going to tenants who qualified for public housing.

The Board of Appeals had 40 days from the last hearing on May 20 to render a decision, and it announced that it would hold deliberations on the petition in public at City Hall. On June 1, in response to opponents' accusations of partisanship, 4 Appeals Board members disqualified themselves from the deliberations, leaving only 1 member of the regular Board. Three associate members were obliged to sit on the Board. As a result, 4 men sat as the Board and a favorable decision by a majority, or 3 out of 4, was necessary to approve the petition.

Though the plan submitted to the Appeals Board differed from the one reviewed by the Board of Aldermen a year before, the present 6 sites had been in the old package, and the validity of their reaction by the Aldermen could now be deliberated. These deliberations were open to the public. Throughout the open meetings, the Board was interested in obtaining more detailed information upon which to base a decision. On June 14 the final vote was taken. By a 3 to 1 vote the Board decided to deny NCDF's petition for a comprehensive permit. The decision formally issued by the Board did not detail reasons for denial, but NCDF knew that these reasons would have to be presented in the appeal before the State Board of Appeals.

THE STATE LOOKS AT NEWTON

By the time NCDF's petition was to go to the State, the State Zoning Board of Appeals had reversed the lower Board opinion in the Hanover case. The decision upheld the constitutionality of Chapter 774 and said there was a need for elderly housing in Hanover. Sensitive to the site problems involved, the Board made its ruling subject to the developer's provision of proper sewerage and drainage facilities. The town immediately appealed the case to a higher court and there was no indication when it would come up on the court docket.

The Concord hearings before the State Zoning Board of Appeals had not been completed at this time in mid-June, but the hearings were much friendlier and cordial than had been the confrontation with the Hanover litigants.

With this evidence, most members of the NCDF had no second thoughts about proceeding with an appeal to the State. They knew they had 20 days from the date of notification by the local Board of its decision to file an appeal, and were ready to proceed. Mr. Slotnick was more reluctant than the other members, however: "I think we may be too optimistic. The State ruled in favor of Hanover, but what good has it done. They haven't built any housing and have no idea how long the litigation process will be. I think we all agree that the opposition will appeal a favorable decision by the State to a higher court. Some people even have visions of carrying this to the Supreme Court. Considering the limited options on our land, I want to submit these thoughts for discussion before we decide to proceed."

Though the Board listened to Mr. Slotnick's remarks, no one seriously considered halting efforts. The prevailing feeling was to file the petition as soon as possible, so hearings could begin. From the date the appeal was filed, the local Board had 10 days to transmit a copy of and reasons for its decision to the State Committee. Chapter 774 stipulates that the Board would hear the appeal within 20 days of receipt of such notice.

These time specifications were one reason NCDF had decided to use the 774 appeal process. Time was the most important factor for the organization; undue delays could mean the loss of its land options and demise of its plan. However, it appeared that things would not go as smoothly as had been hoped. The first hearing on August 3 was stalled by procedural problems. The meeting 2 days later was cancelled because there was not a quorum, and attempts to schedule the next meeting were thwarted by conflicting summer vacation plans of the participants. Finally, the meeting was set for August 11.

At that meeting, the opposition declared that it expected to see the hearings drag on for at least 7 months; it requested that the State Board of Appeals schedule 4 more meetings for August on the NCDF issue, and another for September. The State felt these demands were unreasonable, but they were obliged to comply with the requests to be heard from abutters. It was clear that the opposition knew that time was running out for NCDF—they realized that the best chance of stopping the housing plan was to stall the developers in court until land options expired or NCDF was out of money.

This strategy had so far been effective. Since August 1971, 42 hearings had been held—and no end seemed in sight. Marc Slotnick, the lawyer for NCDF, made his case for the comprehensive permit within the first 2 hearings. Robert Cohen had used 40 public hearings to show that the NCDF proposal was "unreasonable" and, therefore, Newton should reject it; he had attacked NCDF's credibility, suggesting it was an irresponsible developer. Other issues had been traffic problems, accessibility to the sites by fire equipment, poor drainage and catch-basin locations, and NCDF's failure to meet existing building codes. As pointed out in an article in the *Wall Street Journal*, Mr. Cohen's list of witnesses for the public hearings was endless. "There was Joe Fitzsimmons, a Newton fireman; Al Schianone, the City engineer, was asked to give his views. So was Janice Cadwell, a housewife, and Alfonso Mascia, a police captain, and Henry Murphy, the assistant fire chief, and James Hinkle, former assistant school superintendent, and Helene Ryan, another housewife, and many more." Mr. Cohen denied that he was stalling; he was "merely trying to make sure the law is interpreted correctly."

A NEW IMAGE IN THE MAKING

Although the legality of NCDF's plan will continue to be considered at the 774 hearings, the scattered 6-site plan is dead. Financial pressures forced NCDF in the Fall of 1972 to give up 5 of the 6 sites, partly because of lack of funds and partly because they were no longer available. NCDF bought the Hamlet Street site in March 1972 for the low price of $20,000 (8.22 acres) obtaining a 100 percent financing.

Thus NCDF's leadership took a hard look at itself, its strategy, its options. The most recent statement by President Nixon, in June 1971, emphasized that he would not act against discrimination in housing unless it was shown to be a cover-up for racial discrimination. He mentioned that patterns of racial segregation create employment problems, as "minority Americans are unable to find housing near the suburban jobs for which they could qualify." Yet, he left the solution to this nationwide problem to local option. NCDF did not believe the Governor was likely to intervene before a decision by the Board of Appeals, while at the local action level, NCDF could not count upon organizing the consumers successfully (that is, the lower-income families) to articulate their needs and to request satisfaction.

Several Board members wondered whether NCDF had not already done more than its share in raising the issues of the debate and whether it should disband. Even under Chapter 774, the litigation processes could be a long haul. If the courts finally approved NCDF's approach, people would still fight the decision on the local level, as had been the case with the school desegregation issue. The decision would stir up even more resentment and antagonism by Newton residents than had NCDF's initial actions.

Moreover, the NCDF plan really proposed only a few hundred units to be occupied by moderate-income families, basically. Perhaps NCDF was only encouraging tokenism in Newton, as some suggested, because of the conservative nature of its plan.

It may be that no court decision would really work until a consensus for change occurred at the local level itself, and that might not occur until another generation could "buy its way" into the suburbs. Given their experience in Newton, they wondered whether it was now worth continuing the fight. Although emotionally they did not want to give up, they questioned the practical advantages of continuing.

NCDF's decision was to carry through the Chapter 774 process to the end in spite of these prospects. While proceedings continued, NCDF attempted to establish a "new image" before the community. They brought "new blood" to the Board, changed leadership, introduced committee work for developing new community action methods, and decided to concentrate upon only one site—the Hamlet Street site. Accordingly, NCDF changed 50 percent of its Board and elected Reverend Gil Avery, a Protestant minister, as its Chairman. Casselman and Slotnick remained Board members—having resigned their posts—and have assumed a "low profile" in NCDF's external affairs, but they continue to be active in internal deliberations.

Considering that the opposition made a strong point of questioning NCDF's ability to develop its plan, the new NCDF Board decided to engage a professional developer, Ed Abrams, who committed himself to NCDF's purpose and agreed to the special contract conditions set up by NCDF—that NCDF maintain its right to determine tenant policy selection, to approve design and population mix, and to be responsible for political strategy. NCDF would share 50 percent of the tax shelter profits (estimated at approximately $100,000), while the developer would bear all costs incurred while awaiting approval to proceed.

While the developer and the architect were busy on the drawing board, considering several options for the Hamlet Street site, NCDF Board committees had begun to explore ways to (1) secure more community support for the new plan, (2) decrease opposition (they feel Mr. Stiller would support the 1-site idea as the Esty Farm site was dropped), and (3) elicit State and federal support of other Newton projects (as, for example, the Newton Corner redevelopment, the Lower Falls redevelopment, or other municipal needs requiring outside support) in exchange for acceptance of NCDF's present plan. A committee was to study approaches to abutters. Another committee was appointed to explore strategies in negotiating with the Mayor and Aldermen. Finally, a committee was to study approaches to City officials and municipal agencies.

The plan for the Hamlet Street site, which had been purchased by NCDF, called for a minimum of 70-90 units in 70-90 separate buildings, of which:

> 15-20 units would be 4-bedroom apartments,
> 15-20 units would be 2-bedroom apartments (50 percent for the elderly), and
> the balance of units would be 3-bedroom apartments.

This plan called for no 1-bedroom apartments and required a request for a variance, not rezoning, for town houses (for which a two-thirds Aldermanic vote was required). A vertical partition between each party wall was required, and, consequently, 1-bedroom apartments were excluded; this presented a problem for the elderly, who will then have to be placed in 2-bedroom apartments at a higher cost. The cost is estimated at approximately $22 per square foot, or $25,000 per unit—a total of $2 million. MHFA seemed the most likely way of financing, as well as 236. The new NCDF image and one-site plan was announced by the October 10, 1972 letter of President Avery III:

> Dear Friend of NCDF:
>
> To build quality housing in Newton for persons of low and moderate income has been and continues to be the goal of NCDF. This letter brings you news of changes in NCDF and of progress toward the achievement of this important goal as well as an earnest appeal for financial support from you now.
>
> A change in the Foundation's leadership was made this summer when Bob Casselman, who has led the Foundation since its inception, stepped down. As your new president, I shall do my best to complete the work he has so ably begun.
>
> Of major importance is the fact that NCDF has selected a developer with whom we expect to build housing on the Hamlet Street site, purchased last March. The firm is Edwin D. Abrams, Inc., experienced in building housing in the Boston area, and highly respected in the field. We believe this relationship will enable NCDF to fulfill its purposes and is most unusual in that it makes possible the channeling of substantial additional funds into the housing itself.

We have been working hard at both the state and local level. At the state level, the appeals proceedings are still dragging on, but our goal remains unchanged. At the local level, Newton's political leadership is encouraging.

Financially, NCDF is at a critical point. We have old debts which must be honored. We have mortgage payments, taxes and options on land we own and control. The church where our headquarters have been was sold recently and we must find new office space and the income to cover this expense. The Foundation needs funds and it needs them desperately.

I write to ask you to renew your association with NCDF—to renew the basic commitment to low income housing which originally brought us together. We still face obstacles, but I believe we have reason to be encouraged. The day when we shall see housing being built in Newton may not be too distant.

We need your continued, generous support. A gift of $100 or more will help enormously, but any amount will be appreciated. I ask you to do whatever you can.

Sincerely yours,

Gilbert S. Avery III, Pres.

The financing prospects, however, became problematic when Secretary Romney announced on January 7, 1973 that the Nixon Administration had halted new commitments to subsidize low- and moderate-income housing construction. The Administration placed a hold on applications for a variety of other federal programs, including water and sewer grants, open space grants, and public facility loans. On January 8, after the announcement of a "moratorium" on funding 236 projects, Abrams met with the NCDF development committee and reported that no work was being done on the drawings for the site, and that he was unwilling to invest more money in the drawings.

On January 12, 1973, the committee met and decided to recommend to the Board the following:

1. that the informal relationship which NCDF had with Ed Abrams (kept informal at his request) be terminated, without prejudice to any future decisions about a developer;
2. that NCDF be prepared to "ride out" the moratorium by holding on to the Hamlet Street site and seeking development at a more appropriate time;
3. that the costs of retaining the land be reduced as far as possible, by

a. seeking cooperation of the Board of Assessors in deferring tax payments for up to two years,
b. seeking the cooperation of the Unitarian Society in deferring interest payments for the same period.
4. that there be a concerted effort to sell the Esty Farm option (on sale since December 1972), to realize funds to keep the organization alive and to provide a base for action after the moratorium.

In arriving at this recommendation, the committee tried to think of all options open to it, and found them to be as follows:

1. proceed immediately and face down the obstacles, both political and administrative, and fight the issue out;
2. sell the land for a profit, bank the money, and wait for another chance, in the hope that NCDF could be kept together;
3. wait out the moratorium and try again, if NCDF can continue to exist.

RELUCTANT, PARADOXICAL PARTNERS

In spite of 42 hearings of the Housing Appeals Committee, no end seemed in sight at the end of summer, 1973.

While formally NCDF awaited the official transcripts of the hearings held so far in order to determine future action, informally the Foundation admitted that it was running out of the patience and resources required to pursue effectively further judicial action. The opposition's strategy was working all too well. For example, Mr. Slotnick, NCDF's lawyer at the hearings, had invested more than six months work without pay.

Interesting developments have taken place sealing the destiny of the 5 sites formerly optioned by NCDF. *Esty Farms*: After NCDF tried unsuccessfully to sell its option (exclusively through newspaper advertising) the site was sold in early summer 1973; the new owner's plan for 12 subsidized single dwelling family houses has already been approved by the Planning Board. *Stanton Ave.*: its new owner has already submitted an application for a nursing home facility—still pending. *Thurston Road*: The Housing Authority has already approved the construction of 50 units for the elderly and four family units. *Christine Street*: the site has been zoned into flood plain zone, permitting no construction. *Hunnewell Avenue*: The Conservation Commission recommended the inclusion of this site into the Capital Improvement Program, along with the Christine Street site; both will probably be bought by the city eventually for this purpose.

A dramatic turn of events occurred in September 1973. An improbable "marriage of convenience" between luxury condominium developers and low- and moderate-income NCDF appears now to be the key to continuation of the $42 million Chestnut Hill Towers project.

Chestnut Hill Towers is a proposed 28-apartment, 16-story, two-tower condominium project at Hammond Pond Parkway and Route 9. Apartments will be selling in the $70,000 to $200,000 range.

All work was halted on the site early in September when Ward 7 aldermanic candidate Mark White announced publicly that the special permit for the development had expired. The original permit, granted by the aldermen in 1966, was to run for a five-year time span, but for reasons unexplained and unclear, notice was not taken of that fact. By November, 1972, site work underway since 1966, had cost $426,582, and a building permit had been renewed every six months since 1966.

Approval of the permit extension requires a two-thirds vote of the Board of Aldermen. Many sources within and outside the Board expressed skepticism about its chances—in spite of the sizable tax revenues coming to the city from the development, estimated at over $1 million annually. Two major reasons seem responsible for the Board's reluctance. One is the aldermanic, mayoral, and public pressure building for years that Mr. DiCarlo, the owner of the land, resign his seat on the Redevelopment Authority, due to potential conflict of interests. The other reason is the conviction some aldermen have that the scope of the project should be limited and, further, that a percentage of low-income family housing should be required in the development.

The question of the Towers' involvement in low-income housing is especially pertinent, since a proposed amendment to the zoning ordinance would require developers to set aside a certain number of apartment units to the Housing Authority for its leased-housing program. It also requires builders to offer condominiums for sale to the Housing Authority. But in the developers' opinion, the "10% rule" should not apply, and it "would be totally unfeasible." Among the proponents of the Towers project is former alderman Adelaide Ball, who is quoted as saying that "We've heard about the needs of the less affluent. The affluent also need some place to go. There's very little available for them." Ms. Beram, representing the Newton Committee for Fair Housing and Equal Rights, urged the Land Use Committee to deny the request for extension and to address itself to the real housing needs of the city.

Faced with the apparent reluctance of a majority of the committee to extend the Towers' permit without a commitment to low-income housing, Towers senior attorney, Richard H. Lovell (who is also Vice President of the NCDF) suggested a four-point program to link the Towers with the NCDF Hamlet St. site. The plan calls for installation of utilities for the Hamlet St. NCDF land through the Towers site.

The Land Use Committee adjourned its meeting on October 1 in order to let the Towers and NDCF discuss further their arrangements. The developers claimed that an end-of-the-month deadline exists on the $29 million mortgage.

The October 4 *Newton Graphic* reported as follows:

The possibility of some housing units arising from the ashes of NCDF brought out several familiar Foundation adversaries, including Robert Stiller and Robert Cohen.

Stiller argued before the committee that no plans for NCDF could be approved without a separate proposal and public hearing. The Towers should be separate and considered "on its own merits," he said.

Ward 7 Alderman Harry Crosby said, "The Towers are making a big mistake if they feel that way."

Just the day before the October 23 meeting of the Committee, a "behind closed doors" agreement between NCDF and the Towers was concluded:

> This letter will outline the terms on which we believe that Chestnut Hill Towers Trust and Newton Community Development Foundation have reached agreement with reference to construction of housing on the Hamlet St. property, owned by the Foundation, and which adjoins the property of the Trust.
>
> 1. We will join forces in a combined program to build on the Hamlet Street site the maximum number of housing units which could legally be constructed, as two-family houses, under the present zoning of that parcel. From the Subdivision Plan layout we have studied, it appears that twenty-five (25) houses or a total of fifty (50) units could be built under the present zoning.
>
> 2. We both agree that construction of two-family houses, spread out over separate lots with much of the area necessarily devoted to streets and utility extensions, etc., would be wasteful, inefficient, poorly adapted to the very difficult ledge and site conditions, and would produce an undesirable result. We have, therefore, jointly determined that we do not wish to construct two-family houses, as such, on this site, but will jointly seek permissive use, within the existing zoning of this parcel, to construct as attached dwelling units, the same number of housing units which could legally be placed on the property in a two-family house subdivision. A proposed Site Plan will, therefore, be submitted for consideration by the Aldermen as soon as possible, showing the location of the proposed units, together with the open space obtained by clustering the dwellings, and providing recreational facilities on part of the parcel not needed for buildings, parking or roads.
>
> 3. We agree that the proposals for vehicular access from this parcel to Hammond Pond Parkway are not feasible. Therefore, the Site Plan to be presented will show a division of access over Carlisle and Hamlet Streets, where this property has legal frontage.
>
> 4. Forty (40%) per cent of the dwelling units—which we estimate at twenty (20) units—will be offered to the Newton Housing Authority for lease under its leased housing program for low-income families. The remaining units will be planned for lease as moderate income and market income rental units.

5. Utility services for the site will be extended, at the expense of this Trust, across our property to the joint boundary line of this site, and suitable arrangements will be made to handle surface drainage from the site for which existing drainage facilities may be inadequate.

We will jointly seek financing of this construction through the Massachusetts Housing Finance Agency, and will meet all its requirements to qualify for such financing. . . .

7. Since we both recognize that the feasibility of this project depends, in turn, upon approval of the pending petition of the Trust to extend the time for exercise of its Permissive Use and, thus, qualify for its financing, we have agreed that this understanding will be terminated on October 24, 1973 if the Board of Aldermen has not, prior to that date, favorably acted on the pending Extension Petition.

On October 24, 1973, the developer announced that, being out of the country, he was unaware of the NCDF agreement and unilaterally negated it on the grounds that "it is not proper to deal with private groups." Instead, he offered the city $150,000 cash payments, or to sponsor a low-income development elsewhere. Aldermen continued to encourage Goodman to work out an agreement with NCDF, reminding the developers of the aldermanic condition put on the extension that no more than 350 units of the condominium could be occupied until 20 units of low-income housing were up.

The Land Use Committee was scheduled to meet on November 5, 1973 for a final decision. Just before this meeting a new agreement was reached between the Towers and NCDF. Consequently, the Committee approved unanimously the lifting of the eight-week-old cease-and-desist order against the luxury condominium development. According to the agreement reached in repeated sessions, the Towers will aid NCDF build 50 units of mixed low-and-moderate income housing at the Hamlet St. site.

Mr. Goodman agreed to devote $162,500 toward the construction of the 50 NCDF units and gave NCDF a $37,500 check as a first installment towards engineering costs—borings and other tests—for the site. The agreement took effect when the aldermen extended the permit on November 5, 1973. The $37,500 is held in escrow until the Tower's revised site plan is also approved.

Naturally, construction of the 50 townhouse NCDF units must still await full hearings and an approval by the full Board of Aldermen.

QUESTIONS

1. Was it NCDF's proposal and tactics which were the object of the opposition or, rather, the idea of low-income housing per se? Do you think such class considerations, rather than racial prejudice, dominated the opposition's drive?

2. Where did NCDF go wrong? What aspects of the community and of the housing problem did the members underestimate or overestimate? Why did the original support and community-wide endorsement diminish? What would you advise NCDF to do now? Or if it were to start another project in a suburb like Newton?

3. NCDF advocated initially the "scattered site" approach, proposing 10 sites to more equitably distribute low-income housing throughout Newton. The current "alternative" plan calls for only one site. What are the advantages and disadvantages of the "scattered site" approach? In retrospect should NCDF have taken the one site approach? Relate your arguments to (a) resistance-acceptance by abutters, (b) development costs, (c) preferences of families likely to reside in units proposed, (d) Federal housing policies.

4. The supporters of the plan favored Section 236 for financing; the opponents, including the Newton Civic Land Use Association, favored Section 235. Given the nature of the two proposals and the objectives, explain the reason. Which of the two programs would you propose and why? What is the likely impact of each upon Newton?

5. Discuss critically the advantages and disadvantages of the Towers–NCDF agreement as well as its implications for low-income housing in suburbs.

Chapter Five

Concord: The Freedom Suburb

Although the immortalized "embattled farmers" fired their "shot heard 'round the world" from the village green in Lexington, Massachusetts, it was in nearby Concord that the first significant armed resistance to British domination took place, marking the outbreak of the American Revolution. The battle at Concord Bridge took place nearly two hundred years ago. But its flavor is kept alive for thousands of visitors each year who stream to the historic spot and are treated to guided tours, lectures, and quite unprofessional displays of musket shooting by groups of local citizens clad in tricornered hats and colonial costumes. Concord has done much to preserve its image as the birthplace of American independence. Indeed, one cannot be blamed for concluding, after a view of the rolling green acreage and huge white frame houses with black shutters, that things haven't changed very much in Concord in the last two centuries.

THE COMMUNITY

But, outward appearance to the contrary, things have changed. The urbanization and metropolitanization that have characterized America in the twentieth century have turned the town into a well-to-do and exclusive Boston bedroom suburb. The 1970 median income of Concord families is $16,460 and the average is much higher. One thing that hasn't changed very much, though, is Concord's racial composition. The Town was all white in 1775 and it was 98 percent white in 1970; of 16,148 people, 208 or 1.3 percent are black and .6 percent other nonwhite. Owner occupied units comprise 77 percent of dwelling units. As of December 31, 1971, only 32 units (or 0.7 percent) of subsidized housing were in existence—most for the elderly. Eighty-seven percent of all housing are single family dwellings—detached.

The People's Image of the Town

Concord's attractiveness as a residential suburb has not been fortuitous. Though it remained a small farming community well into the present century, the Town felt the pressures of the postwar suburban explosion and made a conscious effort to keep its growth under control. In 1958, the Comprehensive Town Plans Committee made a "sense and opinion" survey of the Town. It revealed that the residents wanted to preserve the appearance of the Town, to provide a public school system of the highest quality, to emphasize conservation and outdoor recreation, to enlarge industrial zoning only when the need was clear and the candidate desirable, and to plan commercial zoning to serve the Town, rather than a larger area. A firm of planning consultants was engaged to prepare a long-range plan for the Town's development, consonant with these wishes. Their report was presented in 1959.

Residential controls such as density, floodplain, and historic districts zoning, all recommended by this report, have since been put into effect. Two-acre zoning was legislated for most of the Town's undeveloped land in 1961. The report also recommended enlarging the areas in which garden apartments are permitted, but this has not been done. On the other hand, the recommendation that more open areas be brought into public ownership for conservation and recreational purposes has been followed.

In September of 1969, at the request of the Planning Board, the Selectmen appointed a new Comprehensive Town Planning Committee for the purpose of updating the long-range plans of the Town. A new consultant was engaged, and in the spring and summer of 1971 a questionnaire was circulated throughout the Town. The results are summarized in a League of Women Voters publication as follows:

> According to the survey, the people of Concord valued as highly as ever the rural and open character of the town. They indicated approval of the town's acquisition of or control over agricultural land, floodplain areas, open space along rivers and brooks, high land, green belts, areas not in floodplains, but too wet for housing and recreational areas.
>
> The only method which the people of Concord did not favor was the use of eminent domain.
>
> Continued interest in and support for recreation was expressed in the 1971 survey. . . .
>
> The 1971 survey indicated that Concord residents saw no need to bring in more industrial plants or to enlarge the area zoned for industry.
>
> The survey also showed that people still wanted stores to be primarily for the use of Concord residents. Some support was indicated for a few specialty shops and for a few neighborhood stores, but there was definite opposition to department stores, community shopping centers, or a large regional shopping center.

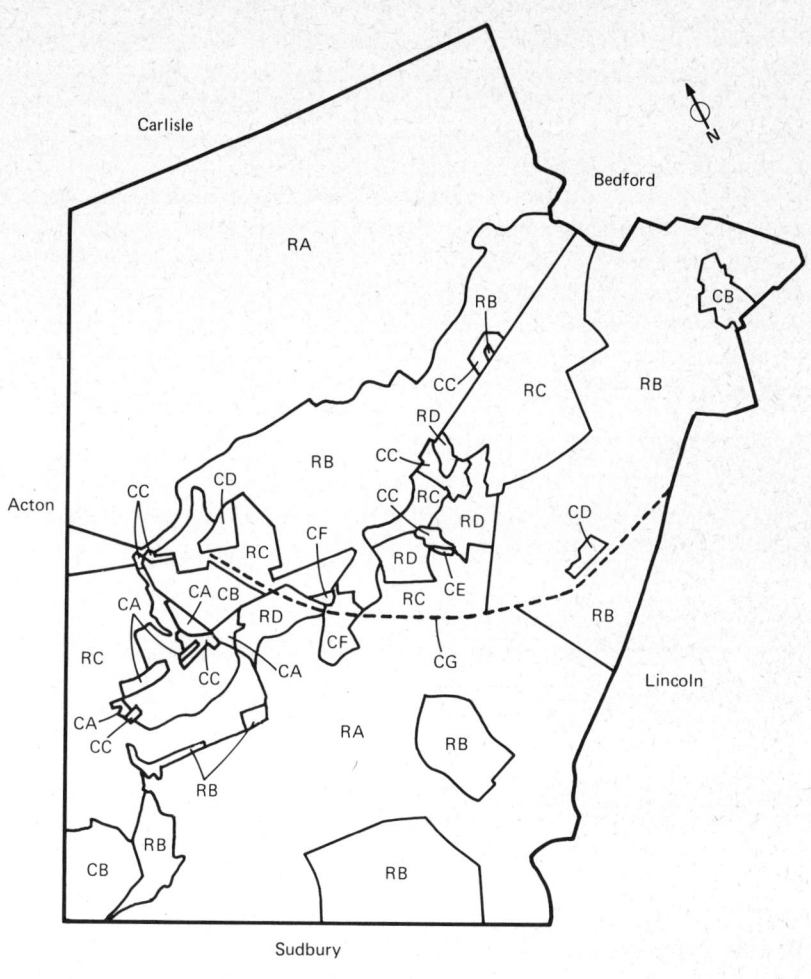

Figure Concord 1. Land Use Map Concord

For tourists, the people favored more restaurants, more picnic areas, more parking facilities and rest rooms, but did not want motels or hotels, trailer campsites or tent campsites.

Most people in Concord did not wish the town to grow any faster than it had in the last ten years (a 28 percent increase). They indicated that they would like any new housing in Concord to meet the needs of Concord residents, primarily, and for families with yearly incomes of $6,000 to $10,000 or over. Should state law require the building of low- or moderate-income housing in Concord, a clear preference was expressed, first, for garden-type apartments and then for subsidized single-family or two-family homes scattered throughout the town.

Land-use planning in Concord has conformed basically to these stated preferences. More than 10,000 acres—of a total of about 11,000 zoned for residential, commercial, or industrial uses—are zoned residential. And the bulk of this land is in large-lot categories. Only 73 acres are zoned for business use, 138 acres for industrial use, and 400 acres for industrial parks. These latter uses have been confined to a few well-defined areas so as not to detract from the primarily rural-residential character of the Town. Meanwhile, fully one-third of the Town consists of exempt property, almost all of which is undeveloped and/or being held for conservation and open space purposes.

Residential development has been "controlled" to the extent of reducing the rate of population growth from 45 percent in the 1950s, to 33 percent between 1955 and 1965, to 28 percent in the 1960s. The average number of building permits issued yearly over the past 7 years for dwellings has been about 90. This compares with an average of 120 in the 1950s and a projection of 150 per year for the 1960s and beyond. These controls, plus the affluence of new residents, have affected the composition of Concord's population. In 1950 the people of Concord were a well-balanced mixture of different age, income, and social groupings. Median family income at that time was only slightly higher in Concord than in the metropolitan area as a whole—$3,250 compared to $3,042. By 1960, however, median income in Concord had jumped to $8,538, compared to $6,687 for the entire Boston metropolitan area. By 1970 it was $16,460 (92 percent 1960-1970 increase) compared to $10,845 for the state and $11,445 for the Boston SMSA. Almost 38 percent of Concord families had in 1970 an income level above $15,000—a 19.8 percent increase since 1960. At the same time Concord's $6,000-and under income level families decreased by almost fifteen percent.

Current selling prices for homes being built in Concord start at about $50,000—the median value of housing units in 1970 being $33,100. Added to the cost of homeownership is a rising real estate tax, which increased 34 percent between 1965 and 1970—reaching a rate of $44.40 in 1972.

As compared to the 4,444 housing units in town, there are only 15 apartment buildings. Most rentals are now in the $250-$300 range—the median

Table Concord 1. Income Distribution in Concord 1960-1970; and Poverty Indicators

1960 No. Families	%	Income Brackets in $	*	1970 % Change No. Families	**	% Change
215	7.2	Under $3,000	134	−3.2	80	−5.2
572	19.2	$ 3 − 5,999	289	−11.2	176	−14.2
823	28	6 − 8,999	752	−8	294	−20
815	27.4	9 − 14,999	1,152	+2.6	1,157	+4.6
550	18.2	15 and Over	1,430	+19.8	2,050	+34.8
2,975	100.0		3,757	+26	3,757	+26

*Correcting the income brackets for Inflation (CPI Index)
**Not correcting for Inflation

	1960	1970	% Change
Median Family Income:	$8,538	$16,460	+92

Population in Poverty	1970
Families Below Poverty level	89 (2.4%)
Persons Below Poverty level	517 (3.4%)
Percent of poverty households lacking some or all plumbing	4.0%

Table Concord 2. Population in Concord 1960-1970

	1960	1970	% Change	
Population	12,517	16,148	+ 29	+3,631
White	12,436	15,845	+ 27	+3,409
Black	72	208	+188	+ 136
Other Non-White	9	95	+955	+ 86

Table Concord 3. Selected Demographic Characteristics 1970

Count of all Males	8,022	Count of all Married Couples	3,500
Count of all Females	8,126	Years School Completed	
Persons Age 5 and Under	1,457	None−8 Yrs	814
Persons Age 6 to 20	5,474	1-3 Yrs High School	852
Persons Age 21 to 64	7,819	High School Graduate	2,306
Persons Age 65 and Over	1,398	1-3 Yrs College	1,450
		College Graduate or More	3,040

rental in 1970 being $137. The 32 units of subsidized housing, reserved for persons 65 or older, with incomes of no more than $2,500 for an individual or $3,000 for a couple, are filled.

The most noticeable characteristic of the new Concordites is their affluence. The striking difference in Concord income levels in 1960 and 1970 is apparent from the chart below.

The changed economic structure of the town was reflected by the types of people coming to Concord in the last ten years. The 1970 census recorded an increase of 1,211 professionals over the 1960 census figures (more than 200 percent); also increasing was the number of managers (by 397), of clerical and kindred workers (1,093), and of sales workers (338).

The number of black Concordites increased from 72 to 208 (188 percent) and other nonwhites increased from 9 to 95 (955 percent) during the 10-year period of 1960-70. However, few of the black and other nonwhite families are in the lower-income levels because their breadwinners are mainly professionals.

There is relatively little poverty in Concord. In 1970, during a serious regional recession, only 3.7 percent of Concord's labor force was unemployed. In 1969, 517 persons (3.4 percent of the population) were below the defined poverty level. In 1970, 2.4 percent of the families and 3.4 percent of

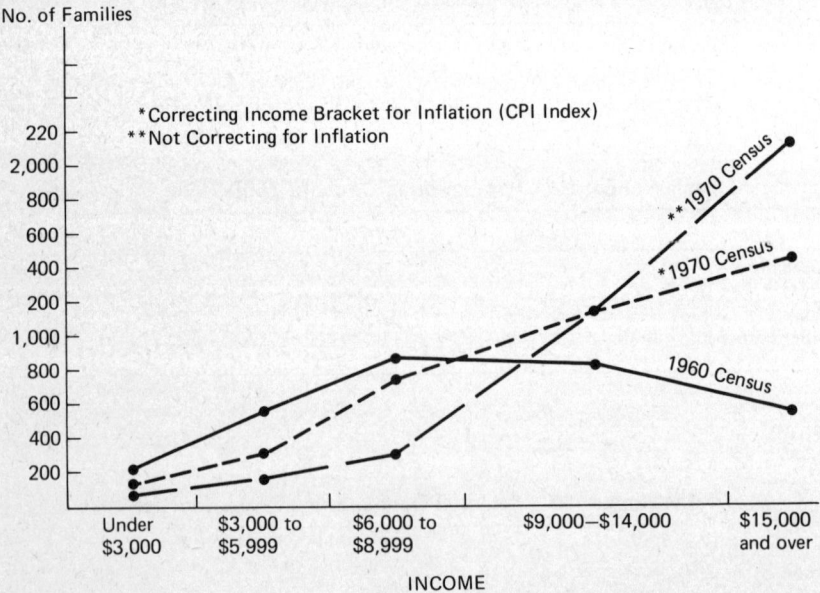

Figure Concord 2. Income Distribution in Concord

the population were below poverty level. Many of these were elderly or disabled persons on social security (58 percent) or were living with their parents (34.5 percent, presumably students). As usual, social status follows income. Nearly three-fourths of Concord's 1970 population were in white-collar occupations.

Although primarily a residential community for the Boston area, Concord also contains an economic base. There are approximately 25 industries in the town, most of which are small. Manufacturing is the leading source of employment (36.7 percent), followed by wholesale and retail trade (22 percent), insurance, construction, printing, and woodworking. The Concord public schools and the Concord-Carlisle Regional High School recruit new staff members each year. And, in 1971, the Concord Reformatory employed 290 people to care for the 675 inmates. Finally, the Town itself employs 144 permanent full-time workers and 80 part-time, temporary, or special workers in its various operating departments. Minority employment in Concord is virtually nonexistent.

There is a limited number of unskilled and low-skill jobs in the area, but no substantial number goes unfilled. The only exception in this regard is the instance of the Emerson Hospital, which reports a persistent shortage of low-skilled workers. Poor public transportation has been cited as an important obstacle to filling these hospital jobs. Workers at this income level generally cannot afford to live in Concord or nearby, and hence must rely on some means of transportation in order to get these jobs.

Table Concord 4. Labor Force Characteristics 1970—Concord

A. General	
Total Employed (16 years old and over)	5,851
B. Occupation	
Professional, Tech.	1,821
Managers, Administrators	922
Clerical	1,016
Sales	481
Craftsmen, Foremen	404
Operatives	249
Private Household Workers	124
Service Workers	597
Laborers	109
C. Industrial Sector of Employment	
Agriculture and Mining	85
Construction	189
Manufacturing	1,344
Transportation, Comm., Utilities	258
Wholesale	140
Retail	716
Finance, Insurance, Real Estate	449
Service	2,350
Public Administration	320

Municipal Finance and Administration

Concord's real estate tax increased 34 percent over the 1965-70 period. The tax payment in 1970 on a house assessed at $30,000 (1968 median selling price) was about $1,175. The annual tax levy is devoted mostly to education (82 percent), the balance being spent for water (10.4 percent) and sewers (6.5 percent).

Government is by Town Meeting and Town Manager. There are also Boards of Selectmen, Assessors, Planning and Zoning Appeals officials, as well as a Housing Authority and a Redevelopment Commission; there is also an Engineering Department doing the day-to-day work of the part-time Planning Board. Citizen participation in the work of the various part-time Boards has been both successful and impressive, in terms of the calibre of those willing to serve.

Concord established its Housing Authority in 1960. It was created to provide housing for the elderly. Its one project has 32 units. Concord residents are given priority over outsiders. In 1969 there were about 12 people on the waiting list for these units, but there were only 3 changes of tenants that year.

Politically, in 1972 Concord has more registered Republicans (33.7 percent) than Democrats (32.3 percent). Yet this is a distinct change favoring registered Democrats—in the 1960-70 period registered Democrats increased by 19.9 percent, while Republicans decreased by 5.8 percent.

Table Concord 5. Selected Housing Characteristics 1970—Concord

A. *Type, Condition, Density*

Total Housing Units	4,444	
Housing Units Owner Occupied	3,428	
Housing Units Renter Occupied	911	
Vacant Housing Units	105	
Total 1 Unit structures	3,647	(82 Percent)
Housing units with—		
1.01 to 1.50 persons per room	59	102
1.51 or more persons per room		19
Median number of persons per unit		3.4
Density: 626 persons per square mile		
Units with telephone available	4,225	
Units with complete kitchen	4,410	
Units with complete plumbing	4,394	
Subsidized housing units (as of Dec. 31, 1971)	32 (0.7 percent of total)	

B. *Value*

Median value of housing units	$33,100
Median Contract Rental	$ 137
Value of Owner-occupied units	
Less than $5,000	2
$ 5,000 to $ 9,999	16

Table Concord 5. (cont.)

	$10,000 to $14,999	53
	$15,000 to $19,999	223
	$20,000 to $24,999	491
	$25,000 to $34,999	942
	$35,000 to $49,999	670
	$50,000 or more	707
	Total Reporting	3,104

Rental Contracts for Rented-Occupied Units
	Less than $60	88
	$60 to $79	51
	$80 to $99	44
	$100 to $119	97
	$120 to $149	191
	$150 to $199	180
	$200 to $299	81
	$300 or more	49
	No Cash Rent	97
	Total Reported	781

C. Vacancy

Total vacant units	101	
Homeowner vacant units (Sale)	35	
Rental Vacant Units	9	
Other Type Vacant	57	
Homeowner Vacancy Rate 1 Percent		
Median Value Home Owner Vacancy	$44,000	
Rental Vacancy Rate 1 Percent		
Median Value Rental Vacancy	$128	

D. Property Assessment

Rate per $1,000 assessed value $43.30 (1971), $48.00 (1972), change 1971-1972: + $4.70

Assessed Valuation	$162,777,232
Tax Levy	$6,300,867

E. Year Moved into Present Unit

1969-1970	2683
1968	1508
1967	1301
1965-1966	2296
1960-1964	2999
1950-1959	2935
1949 or Earlier	1369
Always LVD Pres QT	1057

F. Transportation from Residence to Work

Private Car, Driver	4145
Private Car, Passgr	615
Bus, Streetcar	45
Subway, Elevated	
Railroad	287
Walk	555
Other	235

CONCORD HOME OWNING CORPORATION: ITS STRATEGY AND PROPOSAL

In striving for solutions to urban problems, some have advocated that part of the housing burden borne by urban core areas should be redistributed among the various adjacent suburbs, including Concord. Spurred to action in the aftermath of the tragic killing of Martin Luther King in 1968, a group of Concord citizens formed the Concord Moderate-Income Housing Committee to provide a modest amount of housing in town for blacks and low-income whites.

The first order of business was to make a thorough survey of available land in Concord to see if a suitable site on which to develop apartments could be located. The survey was made, but it produced nothing. Two-acre zoning had been legislated for most of the town's undeveloped land in 1961. Apartment construction had been restricted to districts zoned "Residence C" or "Business." Of a total of 11,438.76 acres in Concord zoned for commercial, industrial, or residential uses, only 513.70 acres were within Residence C or Business districts. (This can be compared with the 8,740.33 acres zoned "Residence AA" (80,000 square-foot minimum lots) and "Residence A" (40,000 square-foot minimum lots). Of the 513.70 acres where apartments might be built legally, only 29 acres were composed of undeveloped parcels of 5 acres or more, about the minimum size required to render a multiple-unit development financially feasible. Thus, under the existing zoning law only 29 acres—or 4 parcels—or 0.25 percent of the zoned land in Concord, was available. In reality, water problems, and the fact that some owners were unwilling to sell their property, made the paltry 29 acres unavailable.

Due to the apparently insuperable zoning barrier, the group decided to shift its approach. Instead of concentrating upon new construction, the Committee felt that it would best be able to produce tangible results by locating available, existing homes in Concord, buying them, and then selling them at no profit to black or poor white families from the city. To carry out this plan the Committee formed the Concord Homeowning Corporation. Using money donated by supporters and personal notes taken out by officers of the corporation, the group did manage to acquire two houses. The first, purchased by CHOC for $15,000, was rather quickly resold to a black family from Roxbury that already had an interest in the Town; the husband had been commuting each day to Concord, where he worked, and a child of the family was attending a Concord school under the METCO program, through which suburban towns provide schools for a limited number of black children from Boston.

Shortly thereafter, in July 1969, the Committee made its second purchase—this time for $25,000. But by December of that year, they were still unable to find a purchaser. The attendant drain on CHOC resources threatened to drive the organization out of existence. The group decided that it was time to review its overall objectives with respect to low-income housing in Concord. This reevaluation led to the conclusion that the program of buying and selling existing houses had serious defects. Among these defects were:

1. no "new" housing was being created. Housing was merely being transferred from white residents to new black residents, and this, in fact, was causing competition with local needs for low-cost housing;
2. finding prospective buyers at the prices asked was difficult, and promised to become an even more exasperating task with the passage of time;
3. the buy-sell approach, at least with the slim resources available, was an extremely slow method of creating housing in Concord for black or low-income white families.

Disillusionment with its present programs, plus two other developments, led CHOC in late 1969 to abandon the buy-sell approach and concentrate again on the original idea of new construction. The first of these developments was the passage of Chapter 774 of the Acts of 1969 by the Massachusetts Legislature. Chapter 774 had been passed in August, but even by December little was known about it other than that it had been dubbed "The Antisnob Zoning Law."

In December 1969, with the Housing Appeals Committee still unappointed, and nobody certain how that Committee would function, the statute nevertheless created optimism on the part of community groups interested in developing low-income housing which had been heretofore blocked by restrictive zoning measures. The Concord Homeowning Corporation was no exception. "At that early stage we were very naive about the statute. Even though it was untested and vague, we decided to rely on it. Our only reluctance came, not over the statute itself, but over the fact that using it meant going around the Town Meeting which always had to approve any zoning change under Concord's bylaws. For us, at that time, this was the biggest consideration."

The other significant development was the addition to CHOC's ranks of a group of new members who had professional backgrounds in real estate, including a vice president of the Hotel Corporation of America.

The Site

Although its search was no longer limited to properly zoned land, the Corporation faced another significant problem in locating a site. It had no money to purchase an option on a parcel of land or to maintain the option through the period consumed by the necessary hearings. CHOC was thus limited in its choice to sites whose owners, for one reason or another, were willing to cooperate by not demanding any cash either as a down payment or as the price of an option. This was a severe limitation, and, perhaps, it forced CHOC to be satisfied with a site it might otherwise have rejected. From the time the decision was made to build housing units, the possible availability of one parcel in particular had been of prime interest to CHOC. This was the Wheeler property, located on Sudbury Road adjacent to a Stop and Shop supermarket, not far from the center of town. (See Figure 4.) The site seemed ideal because of its proximity to shopping, transportation, school, and other facilities. Also, its size (approximately 5-1/2 acres) made it suitable for a low density development of townhouse-type garden apartments. In addition, the Board had noted the reduced impact upon the surrounding neighborhood by reason of the Boston and Maine Railroad right-of-way and the adjacent Stop and Shop parking lot.

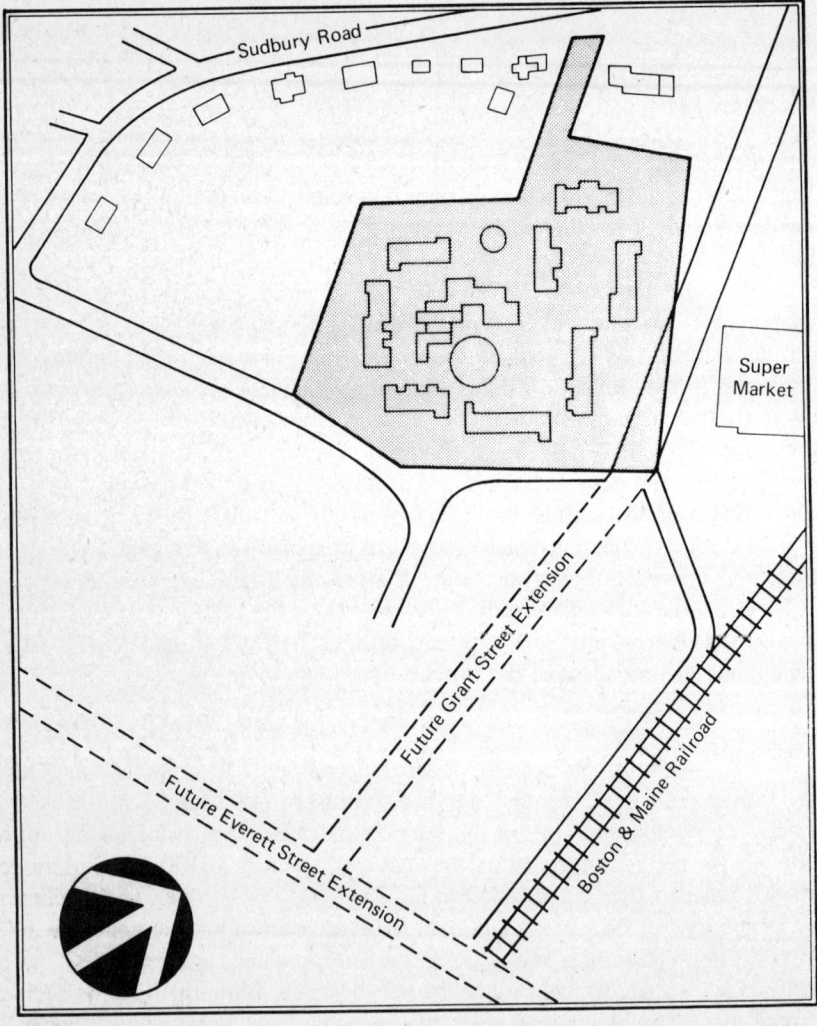

Figure Concord 3. Concord—The Proposed Site

But CHOC was also aware that a proposed rezoning of the land (Residence B Zone) for an apartment development had been overwhelmingly rejected at the Town Meeting in 1969, largely because the land was considered unsuitable for building, due to adverse water and soil conditions. The area had a history of high groundwater and drainage problems, with periodic flooding of basements, extensive use of sump pumps, and marginal operations of septic disposal systems. In addition, the site itself is part of a 90-acre watershed, and many in the town believed that the delicate ecological balance of this area could be adversely affected by development of this parcel.

The 5.4 acre site is part of a 90 acre watershed. This watershed is relatively flat and is drained by Swamp Brook which flows to the Sudbury River. The site itself is mostly surrounded by water: Swamp Brook, Arena Pond and connecting drainage ditches. Should a permit to build be issued, a hearing would be held under the Hatch Act.

An agreement was reached with Wheeler whereby the site was made available to CHOC for feasibility studies. It was at this point that the advantages

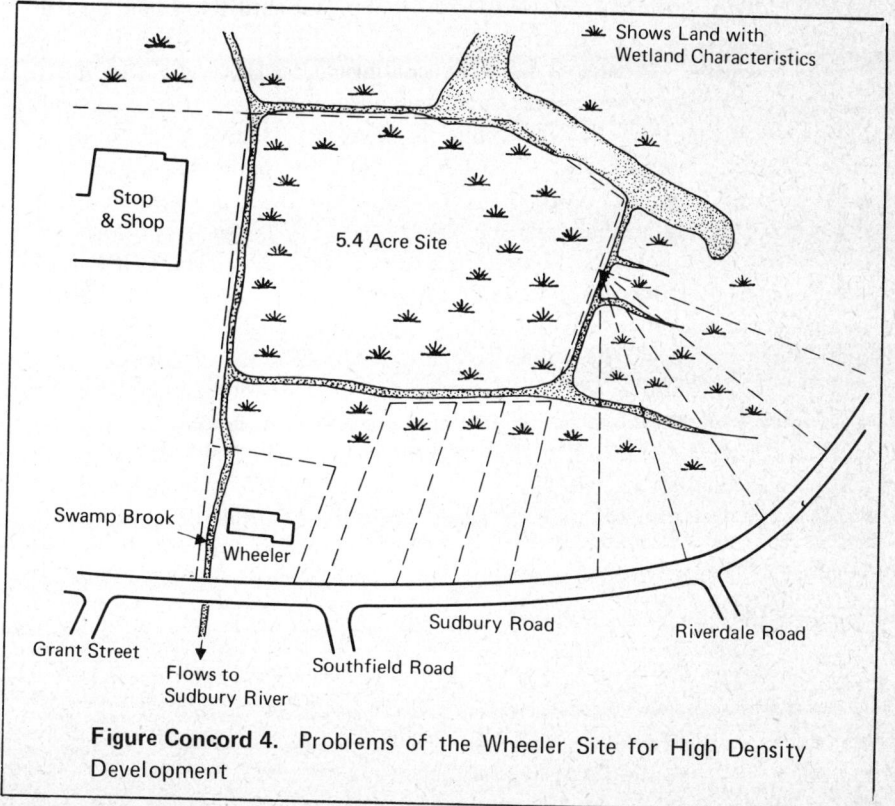

Figure Concord 4. Problems of the Wheeler Site for High Density Development

of a community like Concord—with its many sophisticated and professional residents—made themselves felt. "We enlisted former officials of the town, expert in these matters, to tell us if the project was feasible." From late spring to midsummer a number of engineering studies and architectural plans were developed. It was determined that the soil conditions on the site were, indeed, suitable for building and that the water and drainage problems could be handled without deleterious effects on the surrounding area.

Based on these results, CHOC entered into serious negotiations with the owners, and concluded a purchase and sale agreement in October of 1970. The agreement gave the Corporation an option on the land, with CHOC paying real estate taxes on the property, as consideration. The sale price was to be $32,000.

Government Applications

The next step was to submit a Section 236 feasibility application to FHA in order to obtain a reservation of funds necessary to finance the development. CHOC needed FHA approval to apply for a comprehensive permit under Chapter 774 because, without governmental subsidization, the Corporation could not possibly come under the statute's definition of a qualified developer. FHA, however, refused to give its approval until the zoning on the site was changed.

Unable to satisfy the FHA contingency, CHOC was forced to abandon its proposal for 60 moderate-income units under the 236 program and to seek financing from the Massachusetts Housing Finance Administration (MHFA). Under MHFA there are no interest reduction payments as there are under 236. That agency, however, does lend at low rates, provided that the developer set aside a minimum of 25 percent of its units for low- or moderate-income occupants. Thanks to FHA's circular reasoning, CHOC was now down to proposing only 15 units of low- or moderate-income housing. CHOC hoped that the Concord Housing Authority might lease the entire low-income portion, and the Authority's initial reactions to this were positive. In addition, the Authority and the Massachusetts Department of Community Affairs thought it might be possible to lease an additional 25 percent of the units under the Commonwealth Rental Assistance Program. In May, MHFA, after examining the site for a close-up inspection of its supposed problems, approved the proposal. CHOC was now a qualified developer under the terms of Chapter 774.

Seeking Local Approval

By the end of May, CHOC could have submitted its application for a comprehensive permit to the Zoning Board of Appeals. But it chose not to do so. It decided instead to confer with all the Town bodies concerned with the development, just as it would have been required to do had Chapter 774 never been available. Thus, meetings were scheduled between representatives of CHOC and the following organizations: Department of Public Health, Department of Public Works, Traffic Safety Committee, Natural Resources Board, Planning Board, Board of Selectmen, Building Department, and School Committee.

The statements below, prepared by CHOC, explain how the group attempted to assess and establish the need for moderate-income housing in Concord:

> We spoke to builders, homeowners, real estate brokers, shopkeepers, bankers, lawyers, town employees, including firemen, policemen, teachers, and municipal personnel. We asked the older citizens—newly married folk, single people, families with children—what their housing desires were. We visited local and neighboring and Route 128 industries and businesses to determine the employment picture. We contacted town agencies, the Family Service Bureau, Emerson Hospital, Concord Housing Authority, Concord Redevelopment Authority, Board of Assessors, Fair Housing, Inc., the League of Women Voters, Welfare Department, METCO, and the Metropolitan Area Planning Council.
>
> The following is a summary of our questions and collective findings:
>
> 1. *What is low- and moderate-income, and are there those in Concord who are in these categories?*
>
> We conclude that there are, indeed, people living in Concord who are in the two categories.
>
> 2. *What is the character and makeup of the town?*
>
> There are approximately 3,875 houses in town and 15 apartment buildings. Apartment rentals range from a low of $115 to a high of $400. The bulk of rentals is in the $250 to $300 range. Young married couples, unable to find housing in Concord, are moving to neighboring towns. The demand for housing and apartments outweighs the supply.
>
> 3. *What is the tax picture?*
>
> Of particular concern to the homeowner with a fixed income is the increase in the Concord Real Estate Tax.
>
> 4. *What has Concord done for the veterans in years past?*
>
> In 1946 the town built 20 homes in different parts of Concord for returning World War II veterans. The homes rented for $45 per month and now sell, privately for $12,000 to $25,000, with appropriate additions and modifications.
>
> 5. *What has Concord done to meet the needs of the elderly?*
>
> There are 32 units for tenants 65 or older, who are capable of caring for themselves. Maximum income for a single person is $2,500 and for a couple, $3,000. There is a substantial waiting list for Everett Gardens now, and few vacancies exist.

6. *What is the labor market in Concord, and in neighboring towns?*

There is a limited number of unskilled and low-skill jobs available in Concord. Employment is available in neighboring towns and public transportation is available. Looking at Concord alone, there is obviously a large number of households requiring moderately priced housing. It is generally assumed that a low- or moderate-income family can spend 20-25 percent of its monthly income on housing, without sacrificing necessities. The Bureau of Labor Statistics allows $1,633 annually for total housing expense, without sacrificing necessities. This amount will not even cover the interest and taxes on a $20,000 house in Concord on which there is an 80 percent mortgage at 7-1/2 percent, let alone be sufficient for heat, light, repairs, or principal repayments, all of which are meant to be included in the $1,633 figure. A survey of local real estate brokers indicates that there are almost no rentals available in Concord for less than $165.00 a month, and almost no properties with rents at this price appear on the market; vacancies are filled from the waiting lists.

The Proposal

An information brochure, model, slides, and poster-size plans and renderings were prepared to present the planned development to interested town boards and residents in the neighborhood. The project was to consist of the following elements: The developer would be a limited dividend partnership, with CHOC as the sponsor and general partner. Limited partnership interests were to be sold to residents of Concord and local contractors were to be encouraged to bid on the construction contract. In organizing the partnership, CHOC hoped to raise between $100,000 and $120,000, which would be used as equity in the project. Added to the arrangements with the CHA and DCA, respecting the low-income units and rental assistance, it was expected to result in the following breakdown of units: 25 percent low income, 50 percent moderate income, and 25 percent market level (with skewed rents).

Tenant selection would be handled by a committee whose membership would include the manager and representatives of the tenants, the partnership, and residents of the Town. Policies for selection would be flexible, but would allow for priority treatment of certain groups, such as persons displaced by highways or urban renewal projects, Town employees, young people, and the elderly.

The project was designed as a low-density development to maintain the character of the neighborhood. Apartments would be grouped in 8 buildings, 6 containing 8 units, 2 containing 6. Except for the fact that the development would be within a "B" zone, and would lack the required minimum frontage of 80 feet on an existing public way, the project was designed to meet all requirements (side yard, front yard, rear yard, height, parking, and density) of the Concord Zoning Bylaws for the construction of garden apartments within a Residence C zone.

CHOC's original schedule called for application to the Concord Board of Appeals in November (after the information sessions), for a hearing in December. However, the residents in the immediate neighborhood, with whom CHOC was meeting, requested that the hearing be delayed to enable more discussion of the engineering aspects of the proposed development.

Opponents of the plan were concerned about its possible effects upon the already bad water and drainage situation in the neighborhood to the west and south of the site. Residents remembered how past developers of the area had assured the Town of their intentions to handle drainage satisfactorily, and how conditions had only become worse—presumably because of the development. They now wanted stronger guarantees in the form of more extensive testing of the site. Many argued that an in-depth study of the entire drainage situation should be undertaken by the Town, in cooperation with neighbors of the area before any further development was permitted.

An organized opposition had by this time been mobilized. Preparations were made to present materials at the hearing before the Board of Appeals, opposing CHOC's application. An attorney was engaged to represent the group, and studies were initiated to point out the adverse water and drainage conditions of the area.

Meanwhile, CHOC had been hit by another bombshell in early November, immediately prior to its scheduled application for a hearing. The Concord Public Works Department advised the group by letter that CHOC's plans to connect to the Town sewer system were now invalid. The reason was that the Water Pollution Control Board of the State Division of Natural Resources had just banned further additions to the Concord sewer system until improvements were made. New connections leading into the existing collection system were considered "additions" by the State Board. This presented CHOC with a real dilemma. It was not clear that either the local Board of Appeals or the State Housing Appeals Committee had the right to issue a building permit for a proposed development which had no means of disposing of its sewage. And the Division of Environmental Health requirements precluded the use of an on-site sewage disposal system on this parcel. Efforts to gain more information as to just what this ban on Concord's system meant, and/or how long it would last met with little success. CHOC finally submitted an amended application for a comprehensive permit to the Board of Appeals in December 1970, making it conditional upon an authorized tie-in with the sewer system, once that system became upgraded according to law. They were granted a hearing date for January 27, 1971.

The Hearings

The first session of this public hearing was not held under ideal conditions. A local newspaper described the scene as follows:

The presentations and discussion were very warm, compared to the temperature of the auditorium. Unfortunately the heating system had failed during the day, leaving only cold air blowing through the air-flow grill in the wall. Although the majority kept their coats on, and fur hats if they had them, the hearing went on according to schedule and the only thing that was cut off by the lack of heat was possibly the customary multitude of questions.

The meeting began with a brief introduction by the Board Chairman, who then turned the floor over to CHOC's representatives for a presentation by the Corporation. James Craig, CHOC's President, began by advising the public that although they were requesting a comprehensive permit by law they realized that the project could not tie into the Town sewer while the State ban was in effect. However, the Corporation would like to have everything approved, pending a tie-in with the sewer system once it became upgraded as required. Craig then pointed out that representatives of the group had discussed the project with all the Town Boards and with residents of the neighboring (South Meadows) area. He emphasized that CHOC was an indigenous organization of concerned Concord citizens and not a group of outsiders who would come into Town, build a project, and then leave.

The next two speakers discussed the background and purposes of the sponsoring group and the need for low- and moderate-cost housing in the Concord area. They were followed by Dr. Karl Aldrich of Concord, one of CHOC's consultants, who specialized in soil mechanics. He advised that the group was fully aware of ground water problems in the area and stated his view that the water level could be lowered, so as not to affect any flooding of Swamp Brook. This could be done by dredging ditches on the site and cleaning up the Brook to increase its potential flow. It was his opinion that ground water conditions could thus be improved, not only on the Wheeler land, but in the surrounding area as well. The next speaker was David Perley, engineer for the Corporation and former Town Engineer, who outlined the proposed storm drainage system, which included a storage pond and a number of leaching manholes.

Next to speak was CHOC's architect, Frederick Day (also of Concord), associated with Karl Koch, Architects. He advised that the buildings were designed to be in keeping with the architectural character of the Town. With the exception of four units, construction would be at ground level, consisting of 1-, 2-, 3- and 4-bedroom combinations. The units would have pitched roofs with outside frames of clapboards or brick veneers. Each unit would have a terrace or a patio, while the 2-story units would be equipped with balconies.

At this point, a member of the Board asked if the Corporation would be willing to assist it in determining its role and its authority, under Chapter 774. Craig replied that a memorandum outlining the Corporation's interpretation of Chapter 774 would be submitted. He was then asked what the range of rentals in the project would be. His answer was that the 15 units of low-cost housing would average 25 percent of the tenant's income, plus a subsidy under the Commonwealth Rental Assistance Program, bringing this lowest range of rentals received by CHOC to a level of $165 a month for a 1-bedroom, $185 for a 2-bedroom, $200 for a 3-bedroom, and $215 for a 4-bedroom unit. At the other end of the scale, "market" level rents could be as high as $325 for a 3-bedroom unit, though most would have only 2 bedrooms and would rent for about $275. With this CHOC's presentation came to a close.

The Chairman next called for statements of the various Town Boards present. The Planning Board, the Board of Health, Public Works Department, and the Board of Selectmen all indicated that they would submit reports after further study. Finally, a representative of the Town's Natural Resources Commission advised that his department felt that the Swamp Brook watershed was a very critical water area. Members of the department believed that the peat soil and high-water level made the land unsuitable for any building purposes, and they would go on record as opposing the project unless improved plans were submitted for better runoffs.

At this point, the Board recognized various speakers from the audience. A representative of the League of Women Voters requested favorable action on the proposal, provided the Town sewer system could be used. This recommendation was based upon the results of the survey of housing in Concord published by the League in 1970.

The League representative was followed by various members of the organized opposition, who evidently had come well prepared to state the opposing view. First to speak was Joseph Hannon, an attorney representing residents of the adjacent area. He argued for Board disapproval of CHOC's application on three basic grounds: (1) Chapter 774 did not provide the Board with authority to override local zoning in granting a comprehensive permit, (2) the application itself lacked sufficient information regarding financing and treatment of the drainage situation, and (3) the project as presently planned would cause substantial health and safety problems (i.e., sewage disposal, traffic problems, police and fire considerations).

Next spoke Mr. Carlton Gray, a resident of the neighborhood, who summarized a report prepared by himself and two other residents of the water problems in the area. He stated that 62 neighbors in the Southfield-Riverdale Road area pumped more than a million gallons of surface drainage water per day during peak high-water level periods, and that a number of homeowners' septic systems conformed only to State Department of Health regulations during very dry periods. Another resident, Charles Holt, who had aided in the preparation of Gray's report, stated his view that CHOC had the right idea in wanting to construct low- to moderate-income housing in Concord, but that they had picked the wrong site, due to these drainage problems.

Another speaker, also a resident of the area, had been a realtor in Concord for many years, as well as a member of the Concord Planning Board. He noted a large demand for all types of rental housing in Concord. But, in his opinion, it was time for the Town to stop increasing water problems and to cease further construction in such problem areas. He questioned whether putting 15 units of low-income housing in the area could justify imposing further undue hardship on neighboring families. A resident followed with the statement that this was clearly a wetland area and should not be used for development. She mentioned the probable applicability of the Hatch Act (the State wetlands law) to the proposal if digging and filling were to be carried out, and noted that this could result in many changes to the site plans.

CHOC's President Craig tried to counter these objections by reiterating that the Corporation was aware of all the problems raised, that professional engineers had studied them, and concluded that the site could be rendered suitable for building. He pointed out that the Corporation intended to follow the Hatch Act procedure.

The final thrust of the opposition was delivered by George Ames, another resident of the neighborhood. He opposed the project as a departure from the type of planning that Concord had pursued over the years. This development promised to be nothing more than an island surrounded by drainage ditches, with one access road, located next to industrially zoned property. He did not think Concord really needed such low- to moderate-income housing, but noted a desire on the part of "certain groups" to locate such housing in the Town. He felt that CHOC represented only a "very small select group" of residents. He wondered how such a project, if constructed, would look in five or ten years, questioned the soundness of the idea of mixing persons of different income levels, and asked who would assume responsibility if the project failed. He also questioned the constitutionality of Chapter 774 and noted that no housing had yet been built under the new law. Finally, he predicted that approval of CHOC's project would downgrade the zoning regulations, depreciate property values in the adjacent area, and increase drainage problems.

One of CHOC's members made a brief rejoinder, stating that the basic question was one of land use in the Town. He warned that, unless suitable provisions were made, families in the lower-income brackets would not be able to reside in Concord. By this time the meeting had run for 2-1/2 hours. It was adjourned until February 10.

Some attempt had been made by CHOC to encourage a turnout on its behalf, but, on the whole, the Corporation shied away from such political tactics. "We felt that to get our own people to fill the auditorium would be antithetical to the kind of procedure we felt should take place before the Board of Appeals." Consequently, the neighbors not only turned out in greater numbers than the supporters, but they also had a preponderance of speakers. Craig later speculated that the decision not to fill the audience with supporters was "poor judgment. As it turned out, the Board of Appeals probably was very much influenced by the gallery."

When the January 27 meeting of the Board of Appeals was adjourned, the CHOC hearing was far from complete. The Board submitted a four-page list of questions to CHOC, to be answered by February 10. Although there were many queries contained in the four-page list, the Board had begun to zero in on two main areas. First, on what basis and authority could the Board overcome the prohibition of the zoning bylaws? And second, what steps was CHOC taking to ensure against an aggravation of the surface drainage problem?

On February 10, as scheduled, the hearing resumed. It was much like the earlier session, with CHOC's forces greatly outnumbered by the South Meadows residents and their supporters. CHOC's opposition again made a convincing show of strength, but matters remain unresolved, and an unprecedented third session was scheduled for February 24.

The final session of the public hearing was attended by about 100 persons. It featured the opposition's live presentation of three long reports (by their own experts) bolstering the case for denial of CHOC's petition. Craig again took the floor on behalf of CHOC and repeated his earlier arguments. Studies by people who were the "best in their field" showed that the development would not aggravate drainage problems. He pointed out that the project might be modified to include only 2 levels of rents, meaning that substantially 50 percent of the units would be moderate-income level. And, finally, he promised that the points raised in the opposition's paper would be fully investigated.

With this the hearing came to a close. In all, 10 individuals had spoken on behalf of the CHOC proposal, all but 1 a member of the Corporation. Fourteen people spoke out against the project, and a petition containing 392 signatures—opposed—was presented to the Board. Nevertheless Craig felt optimistic at the conclusion of the hearings: "We felt that the hearings were conducted fairly and that we had a good chance of getting the permit."

The Board of Appeals requested opinions from the various local boards prior to making its decision. It was during the period when these opinions were coming in that the optimism within CHOC began to fade. Craig related that "as it came time for a decision and we saw the recommendations of the individual boards, we realized that it would be awfully difficult for the Board of Appeals to rule in our favor." Some of the boards, such as the Board of Health, had continuously opposed the CHOC proposal. But the others, such as the Department of Natural Resources and the Planning Board, that had earlier, in the informal meetings prior to the hearing, reacted positively, withdrew their support. Asked what had caused the unfortunate turnabout, Craig responded that "pressure was brought on them." Sensitive town officials could not help but sense which way the wind was blowing at the three public hearings and around Concord. Not one board submitted a favorable recommendation.

The Board's Authority and Decision

Thus, it was not surprising when, on April 6, 1971, the Board announced its decision to deny a permit to CHOC. The Board concluded that it was not empowered by Chapter 774 to "ignore or override the restrictions contained in the Town's Zoning Bylaw." And second, even if empowered to ignore the zoning regulation, the Board held that granting a permit "would not be consistent with local needs, as it could be detrimental to the health and safety of the residents of the Town in the vicinity of the proposed project."

The Board found it significant that "[t]he statute contains no specific and unequivocal language granting the Board such authority (to override zoning regulations)." Since "no other board or official has such authority ... (in Concord only the Town meeting—not mentioned in Chapter 774—has that power) the Board is led to the conclusion that it lacks the authority to issue the requested permit." In view of Chapter 774's ambiguity and the certainty that their denial would be appealed, the Board apparently felt that it was wisest to abstain from asserting such authority, that it should let the decision be made at a higher level.

The decision, with respect to the drainage problem, indicated that the residents of South Meadows had made a strong impression. "We believe the ground water and drainage problems in the neighborhood are of sufficient severity that it is essential for any further development in this area to offer a high degree of certainty that these problems will not be aggravated. The proposal under consideration does not offer that certainty and, therefore, ought not be permitted...."

THE CHAPTER 774 PROCEEDINGS

There was never any doubt that CHOC would appeal an adverse decision to the State Housing Appeals Committee (HAC). A substantial amount of time, money, and effort had already been invested in the project, and the group was determined to see the case through. It was also important that Chapter 774 be tested in the courts, and this case seemed a good one to carry out that test, since the Board had adopted CHOC's suggested findings that the Corporation was a qualified developer proposing to build low- and moderate-income housing and that there was both regional need for such housing and local need in Concord.

The appeal would mean further expenses, however. By this time, it had been necessary to procure an extension of the purchase and sale agreement. CHOC anticipated that an additional $15,000 to $16,000 would be needed to cover the costs of delay and legal proceedings, that were expected to last about a year. Obtaining such new funds would not be easy. In addition, financial support the Corporation was receiving from its members came without the benefit of tax deductibility. Though organized as a nonprofit corporation under Chapter 180 of the Massachusetts General Laws, CHOC failed to qualify for tax-exempt status as a charitable organization under section 501(c)(3) of the Internal Revenue Code.

At the end of April, application was made to the Permanent Charity Fund of Boston for financial assistance to meet anticipated costs, but this request was eventually denied. The search for other sources of charity funds thus became a crucial CHOC activity in the weeks and months following the Board of Appeals decision.

Some delay was encountered in scheduling a public hearing of the case, in part because of difficulties in obtaining a quorum of Housing Appeals Committee members for specific days and times. Prior to the actual hearing, conferences were held at which the parties agreed to certain stipulations and consented to intervention by certain landowners and homeowners near the proposed site. A hearing was finally scheduled for July 28, at the DCA office in Boston.

The main focus at this hearing was the water problem, since the Housing Appeals Committee had ruled in a recent case (the Hanover case) that a Board of Appeals did have the authority to override local zoning ordinances. Testimony by experts from both sides at the hearing tended to reiterate (and clarify, given the opportunity for cross-examination) arguments that had already been made at the local level regarding the water and drainage situation. There was some disagreement as to what burden of proof CHOC should be required to sustain with respecto to possible hazards arising from the project.

A second session of the hearing was held at CHOC's request at the site in Concord in early August. The purpose was to show the Committee "more clearly than the strongest oral testimony ever could that we are not attempting to build apartments on a swamp." Final arguments were made at a public meeting place in Concord following inspection of the site, and the hearing was then declared closed.

Housing Appeals Committee Decision

In November, the Committee finally handed down its finding that the decision of the Concord Board of Appeals was unreasonable and not consistent with local needs. The decision revolved around the issue of the burden of proof. HAC decided that the "severity of the water problem and the understandable fear of the neighbors" justified the Board's requiring that CHOC's proposal offer a high degree of certainty that these problems would not be aggravated. But the Committee felt that the Board had, in effect, demanded a "guarantee that the abutters to the site downstream would not be adversely affected"—a degree of certainty which "goes far beyond the statutory requirement of reasonableness."

HAC proceeded to find that the measures designed by CHOC's engineers would not worsen the drainage problems, and, in fact, might improve the conditions. CHOC had sustained its burden of proof that its proposals comply with the statutory requirement of "the need to protect the health and safety of the occupants of the proposed housing or of the residents of the City or Town."

The Committee directed the Board to issue a comprehensive permit, with certain conditions, agreed to by CHOC. Such conditions included securing approval of the plan by the State agencies concerned with sewer systems and wetlands, making additions to the plan suggested by the police and fire chief, meeting all the standards of the MHFA, and conforming to Concord's Housing Code. If disagreement were to arise between local officials and the builder as to whether the buildings complied with local requirements, the Department of Community Affairs, if asked, would certify proof of compliance.

The Case Goes to Court

Shortly after the HAC decision was announced (amid considerable publicity), the Concord Board of Selectmen voted unanimously to appeal the decision to Superior Court. In order to expedite matters and avoid undue expense, CHOC and the Town agreed not to litigate issues of fact any further. They would simply ask the judge to set a date for oral argument, argue the issues of law (i.e., the constitutionality of Chapter 774, the powers given the local board, and the burden of proof on the applicant), and then request that these issues be taken under advisement pending the outcome of the Hanover litigation. The Hanover case by this time was on its way to the Supreme Judicial Court.

At this stage of the case, CHOC's officers and representatives still expressed optimism about the eventual success of their own proposal and about Chapter 774 in general. The law, they felt, was basically sound in its approach. It left a good deal to local initiative and control, yet announced a clear State policy that persons in urban-suburban regions, regardless of their income, be given a chance to choose their habitat from a greater diversity of housing. Court approval would provide "teeth" to this statute, and that would compel communities to take the initiative and begin to plan sensibly with respect to low- and moderate-income housing needs throughout the region.

Others were more pessimistic about the effect of Chapter 774 (even if the Supreme Judicial Court declared it constitutional and interpreted it liberally). Unless the costs in time, effort, and capital of using the 774 procedure could be significantly reduced, its net effect might be negligible. In the Hanover case, for example, the year-and-a-half fight for a permit, plus the later court fight, had left the developer corporation on the verge of financial disaster. Even in Concord, where it had been possible to defer most costs and where the town had cooperated in achieving an expeditious resolution, CHOC had been hard-pressed for funds.

One member of the Concord Board of Appeals, William D. Andrews, a Professor at Harvard Law School, suggested that Chapter 774 was of limited value because the real problem was not with the zoning bylaws. He pointed out that CHOC, according to its interpretation of Chapter 774, had its pick of all the land in Concord; that it had decided upon a parcel with all the potential problems of the Wheeler land suggested to Andrews that developable land was even scarcer than had originally been assumed or, more likely, that nonproblem sites, regardless of zoning, are unattainable by nonwealthy organizations. Thus, relaxation of zoning might not have its expected dramatic consequences and would not begin to solve other problems (such as the lack of public transportation), which are closely related to low-income housing.

In fact, Craig agreed with Andrews that the only real solution of the low-income housing problem would be a "massive income redistribution," to enable presently low-income families to afford truly decent housing.

But lacking that ultimate solution, CHOC was not prepared to give up the fight. For the present, the main task would be to carry through on the current development (if the court decision were favorable) and to demonstrate to other suburban communities that quality housing for low- and moderate-income persons could be provided in a suburb such as Concord.

The State Supreme Court Decision

The decision came down, at long last, on March 22, 1973. In upholding the Committee's determinations and its reversal of the local Concord board, the Supreme Judicial Court ruled that the statute's grant of power does not violate the Home Rule Amendment, that there is no merit to the claim that the standards set forth are impermissibly vague, and that Chapter 774 "represents the Legislature's attempt to satisfy the regional need for housing without stripping municipalities of their power to zone."

The Court concluded that "[b]y creating a 'consistent with local needs' criterion which expands the scope of relevant local needs, considered by the local boards to include the regional need for low- and moderate-income housing, the Legislature has given the boards the power to override local exclusionary zoning practices in order to encourage the construction of such housing in the suburbs. By fixing a ceiling on the extent to which a board must override local zoning regulations, the Legislature has clearly delineated that point at which local interests must yield to the general public need for housing. This ceiling establishes the minimum share of responsibility that each community must shoulder in order to alleviate the housing crisis that confronts the Commonwealth."

In light of this latest directive from the Court, will the housing picture change in Concord? Will a historic "shot" be heard once again from Concord, this time signaling a new era for low-income housing in the suburbs?

QUESTIONS

1. Explain the difficulties in securing a proper site for the project; do you agree with Mr. Andrews that the barrier is not the zoning ordinance?

2. Opposition at hearings is habitually vocal, and the job of the change agent to prove the positive effect of his position is a difficult burden to sustain; it is always easier to pick holes in an argument and to find its negative implications. Is this a fair argument?

3. How do you evaluate the effectiveness of the antisnob zoning law as an instrument for change, as a tool to achieve support for socioeconomic integration in the suburbs? Was the Town acting out of a superabundance of caution in bringing judicial proceedings to test the validity of the law?

Chapter Six

Canton: The Suburb Encounters the Change Agent

Canton's short-lived, emotionally charged controversy, which produced no housing or zoning changes, is both unique and familiar.

It is partly unique because the unsuccessful effort was aimed at serving the housing needs exclusively of moderate-income families, those earning $6,000-$11,000 annually. Thus, the sponsors assumed from the outset that Canton would not accept any proposal involving low-income housing.

Further, it is partly unique because the change agents—those who felt the responsibility to introduce moderate-income housing in Canton—were church-related and highly idealistic in their motivations. The group's name alone reflects this fundamental orientation: the Canton Human Concerns Association was the main instrument of change. It was established by the Canton Clergy Association and it promoted the plan in conjunction with the Interfaith Housing Corporation, a Boston-based, nonprofit organization. This dominant orientation is reflected in the very first letter by the Clergy Association inviting citizens to an open meeting in the Town Hall, February 28, 1971:

> ... The need for housing is especially brought home to us as we notice newly married couples who, due to the high cost of new and used homes and the lack of available apartments, are mostly unable to remain in Canton. If these trends continue, Canton will lose one of its most important assets—its character as a community where families of all ages and income levels live together.
>
> We feel that those fortunate enough to live here have the responsibility to provide for their own youth, as well as others eligible for moderate-income housing. These include elderly persons whose income is above the level needed for public housing and persons now living in crowded or unsuitable housing in Canton and other towns. The Human Concerns Association already has a list of sixty such persons who live in Canton.

As clergymen, may we point out that our Judeo-Christian tradition teaches us that, first we are all basically prophetic. This tradition is at all times sensitive to the dignity of man. It is the dignity of the person that is outraged and sinned against when a fundamental human need such as housing is denied.

Secondly, we are sensitive to the needs and welfare of the family. And it is the welfare of the family that is threatened by bad housing. The family, and not the street, should be the teacher of the child.

Thirdly, we are alive to the dimension and demands of the community. And the problem of housing is also a community problem. Man cannot live in the streets. He must have a home.

Our Judeo-Christian tradition can raise a cry for justice and decent human living standards for fellow human beings. We not only shout justice, but also sweat it into being. We now have a chance to provide homes for 165 families in need, through this moderate-income housing plan.

> Rev. Philip Conroy, St. Gerard Majella Church
> Rev. Arthur H. Doherty, St. John the Evangelist Church
> Rev. Robert A. Navien, St. John the Evangelist Church
> Dr. Edward W.W. Lewis, The United Church of Christ
> Rev. James Babcock, Trinity Episcopal Church
> Rev. Stephen Theil, St. James Lutheran Church
> Rev. John Hay Nichols, First Parish Unitarian Church
> Rabbi Daniel Polish, Temple Beth David of the South Shore

On the other hand, the Canton effort is partly familiar because:

1. it did not succeed;
2. proposed zoning changes were denied by the town;
3. the opposition challenged the need for moderate housing in Canton and underlined the project's impact upon municipal taxes, services, and facilities;
4. the initial negative reaction of site-neighbors was swift and strong.

The project's impact upon the neighborhood, particularly upon its congestion, was central to the early, determined reaction of the neighbors-to-be, as illustrated in their letter to the editor of the local newspaper:

> ...We were STUNNED to see the 'letter to the editor' from the members of the clergy endorsing the rezoning of fifty-seven acres of land off High Street for moderate housing at the March Town Meeting.
> To the best of our knowledge, NOT ONE of these men inquired of, or met with, the people most affected—the residents of High, Norfolk, Tolman, and Highland Streets, nor have they evaluated the proposal against the effects such a concentration of families will have on the very congested area.

WE ASKED TO BE HEARD and have received an appointment to present our side to them.

The residents of the High Street area will certainly attend the open meeting at the Town Hall at 8:00 PM, Sunday, February 28th.

We urge all voters, especially taxpayers, to come. You, too, are involved.

> Alfred A. Citrano, Thomas F. Finn,
> Martha A. Reeves, Sam Swardlick,
> David P. Leary, Virginia Leary,
> Susan O'Neill, Mary O'Brien,
> Helen F. McEnaney, Francis X. McEnaney,
> William J. Owirka, Jordan L. Shatz,
> Marion Maxim, Lillian Owirka

The Community

Canton, Massachusetts, is located south of Boston on an extension of Blue Hill Avenue, which runs through one of Boston's major ghetto areas. Canton center is in close proximity to downtown Boston—within approximately 16 miles. The working force of the town is composed of white- and blue-collar workers. Of the 17,100 population in 1970, only 66 (.4 percent) were black. Like the Boston SMSA, of which it is a part, Canton has been experiencing rapid population growth—125 percent between 1950 and 1970, and 33.9 percent in the past decade, mainly through immigration (probably from Boston). While families with income over $15,000 increased by 20 percent during the 1960s, those earning less than $3,000 declined by 3 percent, and those earning between $3,000 and $6,000 declined by 16 percent. Yet 2.3 percent of Canton's families and 5.2 percent of its households were still below poverty level in 1970.

The increase in absolute numbers of Canton's more affluent population is attributable to an influx of professionals and managers. In the 1960s the number of professionals increased considerably; the number of managers increased by 350, clerical workers by 1,100, and skilled workers by 200, while the number of operatives decreased by nearly 300. The 1970 Census indicates the number of operatives decreased by nearly 300. The 1970 census indicates a 77 percent increase in managers, 57 percent increase in professional personnel and a 95 percent increase in service workers—while farm workers decreased by 85 percent. Generally, the 1970 Canton population is slightly younger than 1960 (28), with a median age of 26.3, compared to 28.1 in Boston and 29.1 in the Boston SMSA. In the 1962-1972 period Canton experienced a 6.7 percent increase of registered Democrats and an 11.2 percent of Independents—Republicans decreased by 17.9 percent. Yet the 1972 Democratic plurality over Republicans in Canton (38 percent Democrats, 11.3 Republicans, 50.7 percent Independents) should be also seen in a broader state context; Canton's Democratic percentage is 4 points below the State's (8.3 less for Republicans) and the Independents' percentage exceeds the State's by 12.4 points.

Table Canton 1. Income Distribution in Canton 1960-1970; and Poverty Indicators

1960 No. Families	%	Income Brackets in $	*	1970 No. of Families % Change	**	% Change
233	8	Under $3,000	168	− 3	103	− 4
885	28	$ 3 − 5,999	486	−16	227	−22
1,096	34	6 − 8,999	980	−16	589	−20
773	24	9 − 14,999	1,354	+ 9	1,411	+10
178	6	15 and Over	1,100	+20	1,758	+37
3,165	100		4,088	+29	4,088	+29

*Correcting the income brackets for Inflation (CPI Index)
**Not correcting for Inflation

	1960	1970	% Change
Median Family Income:	$7,241	$13,752	+89

Population in Poverty	1970
Families Below Poverty level	96 (2.3%)
Persons Below Poverty level	523 (3.1%)
Percent of poverty households lacking some or all plumbing	6.3%

Table Canton 2. Population 1960-1970

	1960	1970	% Change	
Population	12,771	17,100	+33.9	+4,329
White	12,756	16,991	+33	+4,235
Black	8	66	+725	+ 58
Other Non-White	7	43	+514	+ 36

Table Canton 3. Selected Demographic Characteristics 1970

Count of all Males	8,382	Count of all Married Couples	3,759
Count of all Females	8,718	Yrs School Completed − None−8 Yrs	1,079
Persons Age 5 and Under	2,070	1-3 Yrs High School	1,128
Persons Age 6 to 20	5,434	High School Graduate	3,746
Persons Age 21 to 64	8,339	1-3 Yrs College	1,320
Persons Age 65 and Over	1,257	College Graduate or More	1,532

Table Canton 4. Population 1950-1970 Canton Region

	1950	1960	1970	Percent Increase 1950-60	1960-70
Canton	7,465	12,771	17,100	71.1	33.9
Dedham	18,487	23,869	26,938	29.1	12.9
Milton *	22,395	26,375	27,190	17.8	3.1
Norwood	16,636	24,898	30,815	49.6	23.8
Randolph	9,982	18,900	27,035	89.3	43.0
Sharon	4,847	10,070	12,367	107.8	22.8
Stoughton	11,146	16,328	23,459	46.4	43.7
Westwood	5,837	10.354	12,750	77.4	23.1

Canton's growth has been rapid, even compared to its neighbors. Projections by the Metropolitan Area Planning Council indicate that in 1990 Canton's population will range between a low of 32,200 and a high of 33,400 (almost doubling its 1970 peak). This dynamic growth must be absorbed within Canton's 19.01 square mile area. (The present density of population is only 900 persons per square mile.)

Due to its accessibility to water power, Canton initially developed as a manufacturing center. Even today the town retains a strong, light industrial base (providing much of the $153,783,596 tax base). But while manufacturing still supplies over 50 percent of all jobs in Canton, the character of the community has changed; Canton is now a predominantly Catholic, upper-middle-class bedroom suburb of Boston with a 1970 median family income of $13,752 (89 percent increase since 1960)—far more prosperous than the rest of Norfolk County. The highways of the region encourage commutation to Boston and to satellite suburban areas. Such renowned recreation facilities as Blue Hills Reservation, MDC winter skiing, and two golf courses enhance the attractiveness of Canton as a place to live.

Land Features, Master Plan, Zoning

The organization of land, space, and housing frequently reflects dominant value orientations of the people who reside in a human settlement. Canton is no exception. The restrictive 1-acre zoning (AA district), which passed at the 1963 Town Meeting, reflected the distinct dislike of many upper-income persons, and of the Republicans in charge in Canton, for the smaller $8,000 houses built during the late 1950s in the Cedarcrest Highland section of the Town. This dislike was intensified by the fact that the real estate taxes from these homes did not pay for the increased cost in services—homeowners paid about $300 in taxes, while it cost the Town $432 to educate one child. The approval of the AA District zoning effectively stopped the influx of less affluent people into Canton, since nearly all the good land not rezoned AA had already been built up.

Since the adoption of the first Master Plan in 1959, total developed land increased 25 percent from 5,081 to 6,874 acres. About 25 percent of this difference must be credited to the inclusion of land uses unaccounted for in 1959. By 1971 developed acreage had climbed, as a percent of total land area, from 42 percent to 56.6 percent. Two characteristics of this overall change are particularly worth noting:

1. growth has taken place in every part of the Town;
2. recent growth has been predominantly denser than that of the past, with typical house lots smaller, although expansion allowances have been made on many new industrial sites.

These two points are salient because they apply mostly to the largest and most active segment of the new development—residential expansion.

The categories of developed uses and undeveloped land, their areas for 1959 and 1971, new development by category, and net shifts made between established uses are shown in Table 5.

The types of districts, minimum areas, and frontages required in the Town's bylaw, amended in 1972, are shown in Table 6.

The lack of apartments, as well as the existence of ample undeveloped land, is evidenced by the following:

Land-use acreage for Apartments: 0.4 percent of developed land
                                  0.2 percent of town
Total Undeveloped Land: 43 percent of total area.

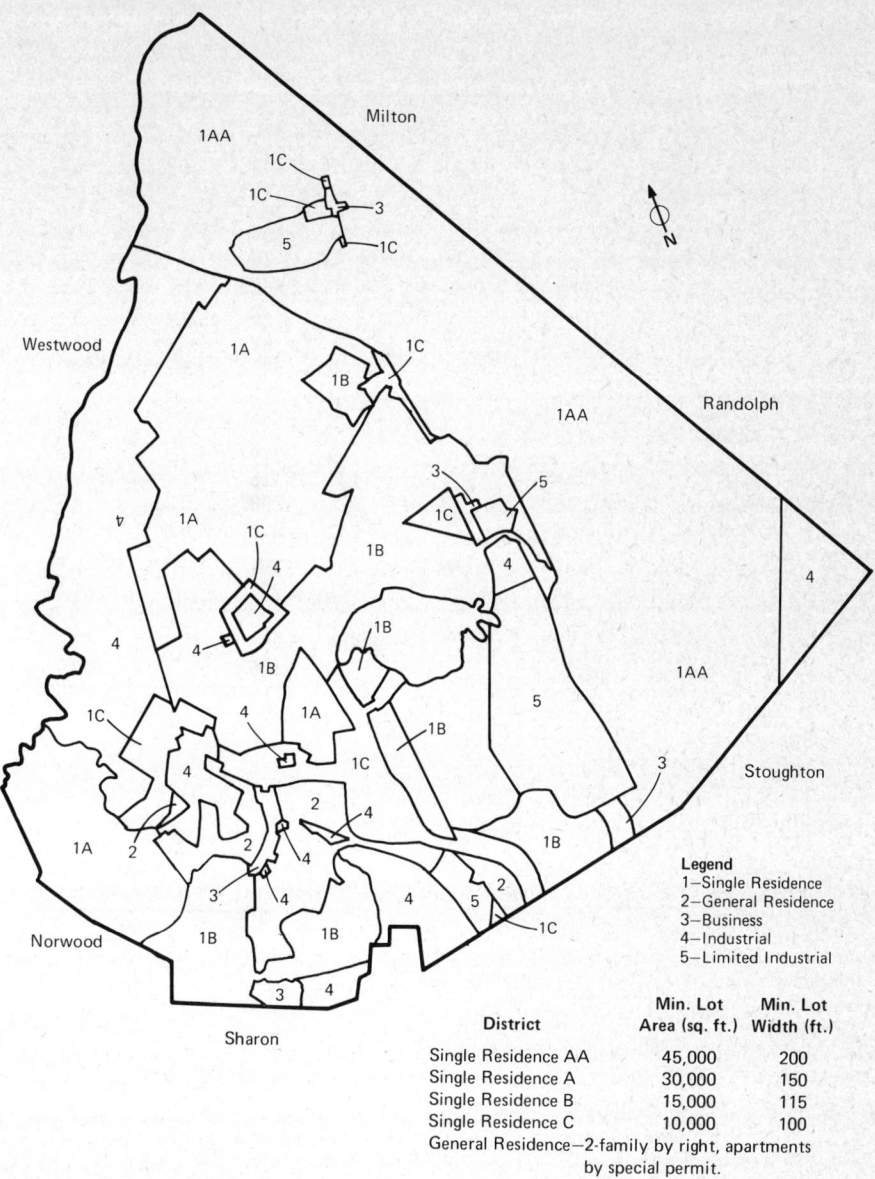

Figure Canton 1. Land Use Map Canton

Table Canton 5. Land Use Acreage Summary 1959-1971

	1959 Uses	New Development	Net Internal Change	1971 Uses	1971 Distribution Percent of Developed Area	Percent of Town Area
Residential						
Open and Scattered Development	940	183	−234	889	12.9	7.3
Medium-Low Medium Development	562	624	207	1,393	20.3	11.4
High-Medium Development	575	10	−26	559	8.1	4.6
Apartment Development	−	21	5	26	0.4	0.2
Residential Subtotal	2,077	838	− 48	2,867	41.7	23.5
Retail Business	15	0	5	20	0.3	0.2
General Business	63	27	− 1	89	1.3	0.7
Industrial	211	184	0	395	5.7	3.2
Sand & Gravel	−	154	15	169	2.5	1.4
Industrial Subtotal	211	338	15	564	8.2	4.6
Agriculture	−	190	29	219	3.2	1.8
Public/Semipublic	2,165	128	123	2,416	35.1	19.9
Streets and Highways	550	30	120	700	10.2	5.8
Total Developed Land	5,081	1,551	243	6,875	100.0	56.5
Lowland/Swamp	2,443	46	−195	2,294		18.9
Vacant	4,642	26	−2,671	2,997		24.6
Total Undeveloped Land	7,085	72	−3,866	5,291		43.5
Total Land Area	12,166			12,166		100.0

Table Canton 6. Area Requirements by Residential Zones

District	Minimum Area (Square Feet)	Lot Width (Feet)
Single Residence AA	45,000	200
Single Residence A	30,000	150
Single Residence B	15,000	115
Single Residence C	10,000	100
General Residence	−	−
Business	−	−
Industrial	−	−
Limited Industrial	−	−

Housing Market

In typical suburban tradition 75 percent of Canton's 1970 housing is owner-occupied—94 percent of its housing stock consisting of single-family

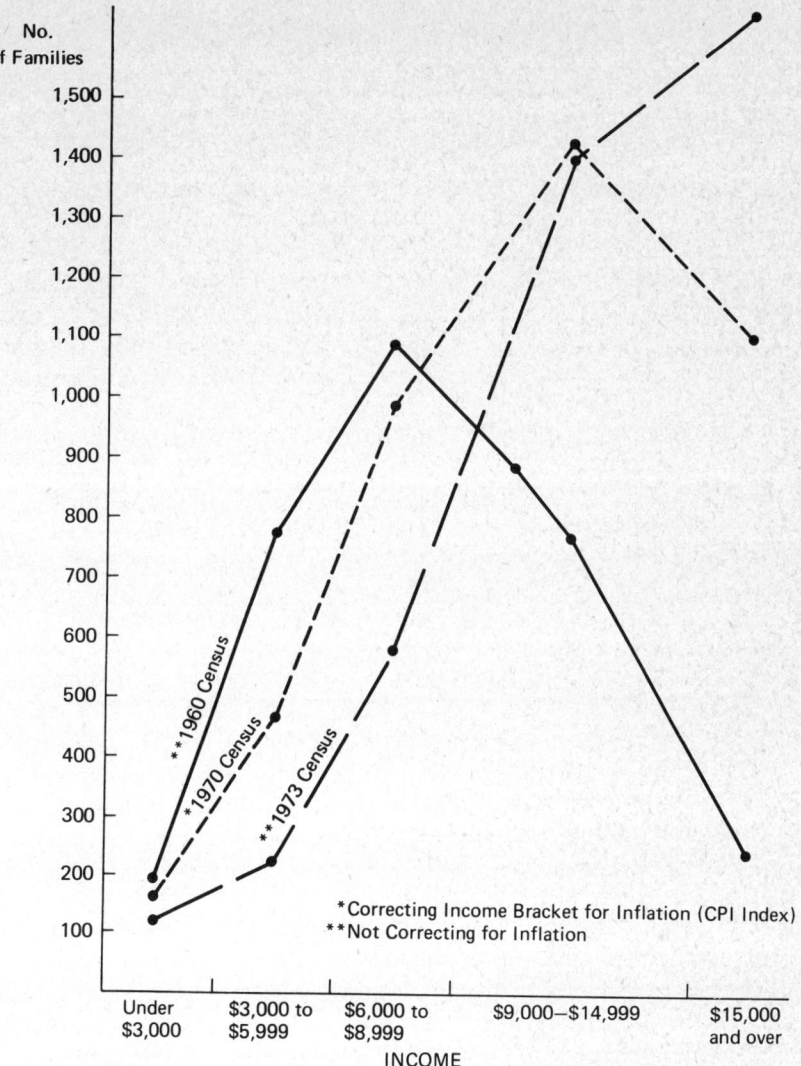

Figure Canton 2. Income Distribution in Canton (1960 and 1970 Compared)

dwellings (detached). A considerable number of its families would be immediately eligible for low- and moderate-income housing. At least 6.3 percent of Canton's households below poverty level lack some or all plumbing facilities—8.6 percent in Boston.

Canton's housing of 4.673 units consists primarily of 1-unit structures (80.9 percent)—a 13.3 percent decrease since 1960 when Canton had 3,544

Table Canton 7. Vacant Land (in Acres) by Zones

Zoning Districts	Potentially Developable	Suitable for Homes/ Unsuitable for Industrial	Physically Unsuitable	Total Unsuitable	Percent Suitable	Percent Unsuitable
AA	624	53	556	609	35.15	49.84
A	417	4	318	322	23.50	26.35
B	225	19	104	123	12.67	10.06
C	54	–	40	40	3.06	3.28
GR	52	–	9	9	2.92	0.73
BUS	6	–	–	–	0.33	–
LI	204	–	33	33	11.50	2.70
I	193	5	81	86	10.87	7.04
Totals	1,775	81	1,141	1,222		

Total Vacant Land 2,997 Acres
Percent Total Land Area 24.6 Percent

units (90.2 percent sound, 7.6 percent deteriorating, and 2.2 percent dilapidated).

Due to an increasing scarcity of land, high taxes, and a tight mortgage situation, single family housing construction has diminished considerably from a high of 182 units in 1965 to a current rate of approximately 75 units per year. New home prices are averaging $35,000, well out of the range of the old Canton residents, as the median family income of Canton went from $7,241 in 1960 to $13.752 in 1970. Older homes cost somewhat less, but $22,000 is almost an absolute minimum. The median value of housing units was $24,700 in 1970 and the median rental $98.00.

Canton has a small number of public housing units and apartment houses. There are 72 units for elderly housing on Cobbs Corner and 26 units of Veterans' housing on Pequit Street, both under the jurisdiction of the Canton Housing Authority. A total of approximately 200 private apartment units are available in five different apartment complexes—Chancellor, Althea, Will Drive, Center Street, and Revere Street. As of December 31, 1971 Canton had 98 subsidized housing units or 2.1 percent of its total housing—3.1 percent less than its neighbor Stoughton.

According to a 1969 *FHA Analysis of the Boston, Massachusetts Housing Market*, rents in Canton are assumed to vary between $115 and $190 per month, depending on the number of bedrooms. However, this range seems too low. According to the census, the median rent per unit in 1970 was $132, including utilities. Rents at the Chancellor apartments range from $135 to $185 per month, while rents at the Will Drive apartments range from $180 to $210 per month. Further, one Canton realtor reports that he never receives an apartment listing for less than $200 per month. According to federal guidelines, not over 25 percent of an individual's net income should be spent on housing. Thus, using this guideline figure, an individual must earn approximately $9,000 or more per year in order to afford an average apartment in Canton.

Table Canton 8. Selected Housing Characteristics 1970—Canton

A. Type, Condition, Density

Total Housing Units	4,673	
Housing Units Owner Occupied	3,647	
Housing Units Renter Occupied	919	
Vacant Housing Units	107	
Total 1 Unit structures	3,772	(80.9 Percent)

Housing units with—
1.01 to 1.50 persons per room	211
1.51 or more persons per room	25
Median number of persons per unit	3.5

Density: 900 persons per square mile

Units with telephone available	4,464
Units with complete kitchen	4,622
Units with complete plumbing	4,601
Subsidized Housing Units (as of Dec. 31, 1971)	98 (2.1 percent of total)

B. Value

Median value of housing units	$24,700
Median Contract Rental	$ 98

Value of Owner-Occupied Units
Less than $5,000	18
$5,000 to $9,999	67
$10,000 to $14,999	219
$15,000 to $19,999	628
$20,000 to $24,999	802
$25,000 to $34,999	985
$35,000 to $49,999	493
$50,000 or More	171
Total Reporting	3,383

Rental Contracts for Rented-Occupied Units
Less than $60	86
$60 to $79	184
$80 to $99	166
$100 to $119	106
$120 to $149	116
$150 to $199	151
$200 to $299	23
$300 or More	6
No Cash Rent	53
Total Reported	838

C. Vacancy

Total vacant units	96
Homeowner vacant units (Sale)	30
Rental Vacant Units	22
Other type vacant	44
Homeowner Vacancy Rate .8 Percent	
Median Value Homeowner Vacancy	$38,500
Rental Vacancy Rate 2.3 Percent	
Median Value Rental Vacancy	$103

D. Property Assessment

Rate per $1,000 Assessed Val.: $38.00 (1971), $40.50 (1972), change 1971-72: + $2.50

Table Canton 8. (cont.)

Assessed Valuation:	$160,319,219	
Tax Levy:	$ 6,092,133	
E. Year Moved into Present Unit		
	1969-1970	2092
	1968	1795
	1967	971
	1965-1966	2144
	1960-1964	3882
	1950-1959	3805
	1949 or Earlier	989
	Always LVD Pres QT	1422
F. Transportation from Residence to Work		
	Private Car, Driver	4620
	Private Car, Passenger	809
	Bus, Streetcar	112
	Subway, Elevated	42
	Railroad	355
	Walk	310
	Other	290

Table Canton 9. Labor Force Characteristics 1970 — Canton

A. General	
Total Employed (16 years old and over)	6,699
B. Occupation	
Professional, Tech.	1,324
Managers, Administrators	857
Clerical	1,466
Sales	508
Craftsmen, Foremen	826
Operatives	562
Private Household Workers	37
Service Workers	684
Laborers	238
C. Industrial Sector of Employment	
Agriculture and Mining	25
Construction	540
Manufacturing	1,678
Transportation, Comm., Utilities	426
Wholesale	405
Retail	947
Finance, Insurance, Real Estate	408
Service	1,854
Public Administration	348

THE CHANGE AGENT

The Canton Human Concerns Association (CHCA) and the Interfaith Housing Corporation of Boston initiated and guided the effort.

The Human Concerns Association was born in November 1968 with the help of the Canton Clergy Association and perished through apathy in mid-1969. However, its Subcommittee on Moderate-Income Housing, having more concrete goals than the parent organization, survived. Both the Subcommittee and the CHCA were firmly rooted in the civil rights movements and were organized by its supporters in Canton. CHCA met until May 12, 1969 with diminishing attendance each time. At the last two meetings lack of leadership was apparent, as well as the lack of a long-range commitment of the members to the goals of the organization. The President of CHCA, Dr. Gualtieri, admitted that he had allowed the group to lapse when he could find no one else willing to take over his position as President.

The MIH Subcommittee of approximately 18 members early became the focus of activity for most of the members of the parent CHCA. Housing was a concrete issue and the leadership of the group under Mr. Zlochiver and Mrs. Cunha was more committed to the achievement of specific results.

The MIH Subcommittee invited several guest speakers for advice, both before and after being formally organized. The speaker who apparently had greatest effect on the development of the group at both stages was Robert McKay of Citizens Housing and Planning in Boston, who addressed the CHCA in January 1969. He urged the group toward practical action; the MIH Subcommittee first met formally in February 1969, only one month later. Mr. McKay was again a catalytic agent in October 1969, when he advised the Subcommittee members that if they wanted to build low-income housing, they would have to establish a good working relationship with the Canton Housing Authority. However, given the opposition of the Chairman of the Housing Authority to low-income housing, except for that built for the elderly, this seemed an impossible task. McKay further advised that to construct any housing, the group needed the services of an outside sponsor/developer who would have the time, money, and expertise necessary to see the project through completion. He suggested Interfaith Housing Corporation of Boston, a nonprofit developer of low- and moderate-income housing.

Another individual consulted by the MIH Subcommittee was James Heggie, Planning Board member and former Chairman of the Zoning Board of Appeals. Mr. Heggie traced for the Subcommittee the historical reasons for the passage of restrictive 1-acre zoning (AA District) at the 1963 Town Meeting. Although he favored maintaining Canton's residential character, he expressed the fear that unless the town allowed more apartments, the State would step in to force housing of blacks. He noted that an updated Master Plan would recognize that the 1963 zoning ordinance was economically discriminatory.

A month later, in November 1969, Mr. Zlochiver, of the MIH Subcommittee, met with Marvin Fannin of Interfaith Housing. A coalition of MIH Subcommittee forces, the Canton Clergy Association, and Interfaith Housing of Boston seemed mutually beneficial and a decision to seek a suitable site was reached, as follows:

Letter of Agreement

Interfaith Housing Corporation of Boston and the Moderate Income Housing Sub-Committee of the Canton Human Concerns Assoc. agree to the following as of February 8, 1971:

1. That it is the desire and intent of Interfaith Housing to construct 165 units, providing site improvement costs and required amenities proposed by potential residents and other Canton citizens, and any unusual financial requirements of local approving bodies permit this development to be financially feasible. Should additional units be required to assure such financial feasibility, we can in no event forsee any possibility of building more than 250 units. The moderate income monthly cooperative charges will be the chief determining factor in maximum project costs and number of units.

2. That Interfaith Housing explore the feasibility that the construction be of Colonial design with brick veneer. That a committee made up of members of the Canton Human Concerns Committee and potential residents shall meet as an advisory group with the architect and builder as appropriate to help in planning and design of the project and individual units.

3. That the COMMITTEE TO SELECT RESIDENTS OF THE COOPERATIVE prior to initial occupancy and for the approximately one year before the resident Board of Directors assumes control, consist of three voting members, one from Interfaith Housing and two from the Canton community as follows: (This committee will assure a selection policy guaranteed to meet the housing needs of qualified Canton residents and will be responsible for initiating a cohesive social environment.)

The first voting member shall be the director of management for Interfaith Housing. The second voting member shall be appointed from the Canton Human Concerns Committee. The third voting member shall be appointed from the Canton community and approved by the Canton Human Concerns Committee and Interfaith Housing Corp.

That this selection committee shall have developed and reviewed a list of applicants for residency six months prior to completion of construction.

That after the resident Board of Directors assumes control they will determine tenant selection, continuing a previous policy of meeting the needs of qualified Canton residents and assuring that all are qualified and aware of their responsibilities as members of a cooperative.

4. That a minimum of trees be removed from the land—just what is necessary for construction and recreational use—and that there be trees between the cooperative and the abutters where these already exist.

However, that Interfaith Housing Corporation intended to build moderate-income housing in conjunction with the Subcommittee was only announced to the community at large in November 1970. By then, Interfaith had already obtained a free option on John Trayer's 57-acre tract bordering on High Street and filed a warrant to rezone the land, but the actual site was not disclosed to the public.

The origins of the MIH Subcommittee do not appear to have tainted it in the eyes of the general population. Its members were known to be liberal, civil rights supporters, but only as individuals. Their collective image appeared more that of "do-gooders," since they were white, middle-class church-goers. If they started out to help blacks, this fact was either not known or forgotten, as evidenced by the relatively peripheral role of racial prejudice in most of the open meetings. Or was it? Interfaith, on the other hand, was known to be distinctly committed to religious, economic, and racial integration in housing and had received such publicity in nearby Stoughton.

The Interfaith Housing Corporation was first chartered in 1965 by a group of Protestant, Catholic, and Jewish religious leaders who felt action was required to improve housing conditions in Greater Boston through increased government housing subsidies. Interfaith has a large staff and several departments headed by professional and technical experts. There is an unpaid Board of 17 Directors, among them a leading realtor and a builder. They have overseen the construction of $7 million worth of housing in Massachusetts and $4 million worth of housing for the elderly in Ohio. Interfaith's completed projects include a 104-unit apartment complex in Stoughton and a 160-unit development in Framingham. The Executive Director at the time of the Canton controversy, Sam Larsen, who withdrew from active ministry in the early 1960s, stated that Interfaith's central thrust in housing was toward creating cooperative management companies.

Marvin Fannin, Head of the Division of Suburban Development, was the primary IHC staff member on the Canton project and worked closely with the MIH Subcommittee from late 1969 until the Town Meeting in March 1971.

The Sponsors Present the Plan

The Canton Human Concerns Committee sponsored a series of meetings, discussions, and neighborhood coffees. These were organized well before the zoning change needed for the construction of the project was discussed by the Planning Board at the Town Meeting in March 1971. A final presentation in

Upper Memorial Hall on February 28, moderated by Reverend Philip Conroy of the Canton Clergy Association, topped these efforts by the sponsors. Close to 200 townspeople jammed into Memorial Hall to hear the sponsors and their presentation of the case for building 165 moderate-income apartment units on a 57-acre parcel of land off High Street. Mr. Larsen, of the Interfaith Housing Corporation of Boston, outlined the proposal.

The Plan

The project was to be a 2- and 3-story town house and garden apartment complex with 165 units: 40 1-bedroom apartments, 65 2-bedroom units, 40 3-bedroom apartments and 20 4-bedroom apartments. A community building, maintenance and repair garage, playgrounds, and 248 parking spaces were included in the plans, as were ranges, refrigerators, disposals, and laundry facilities. The buildings were planned to be wood frame with exterior finishes of masonry and shingle and of Colonial design.

The Site

It had been difficult for the Housing Subcommittee of CHCA to find a suitable location for a moderate-income housing project, particularly one which the owner was willing to sell.

In their search for land, members of the MIH Subcommittee found that there were no parcels of more than 10 acres within the General Residence or Apartment zoned area. A further constraint was placed upon the location of the land, since FHA requirements stipulated that the housing had to be convenient to public transportation and near public sewers. With this in mind, committee members contacted every owner of a large parcel of land along Washington Street and Route 138. In all, 11 owners were contacted—1 church, 6 private owners, 2 corporations, 1 real estate agent, and the Metropolitan District Commission.

One of the private owners recognized the need for moderate-income housing and agreed to give Interfaith a free option to buy his land. The 57-acre tract owned by John P. Trayers of 200 High Street was located in South Canton, directly in back of Mr. Trayer's home. It was near public transportation, had quick access to Route 195 and was within walking distance of shopping areas.

Site Organization

The project was to be cluster zoned, with a special court for the elderly. Four-bedroom apartments would be scattered throughout, to be sure that the larger families were not all in one area. Cluster zoning would allow for recreation and park development; Interfaith guaranteed that at least 20 acres of conservation and recreation land would be available for town use. Sam Larsen told the Planning Board that this would be accomplished by granting an easement for town residents to use the park. The Planning Board reportedly "expressed interest" at the proposal.

The land chosen had two rights-of-way, but had little frontage, so the development probably would not have been visible from High Street.

Zoning Changes

The tract was zoned for single-family residences on lots of a minimum of 15,500 square feet. Approximately 109 such residences could be built on the tract. The Zoning Board of Appeals would have to approve a variance to allow multi-family dwellings. Further, the Planning Board would have to approve the cluster development concept. In the event this Board decided it was not within its jurisdiction to make a ruling, the subject would be referred to the Town Meeting (as it, in fact, was). However, in Canton, a cluster development requires site zoning approval.

Financing of the Development

Financing is still unclear, as it was at the time the plan was defeated. Federal aids (under 221(d)(3) or more likely 236) were to be requested. It was possible that the Massachusetts Housing Finance Administration would be involved. There is no information available on projected costs for the development. Interfaith officials used the Stoughton experience as a rule of thumb.

Cost to the Town

The sponsors claimed that their proposal would not cost the town money.

The following portion of a newspaper article espouses this view:

> The project would be taxed at 100 percent valuation. The proposal is to build 40 1-bedroom units, 65 2-bedroom units, 40 3-bedroom units, and 20 4-bedroom units. If single family homes were built on this land they would all be built with 3 and 4 bedrooms. The apartments are designed to attract all age groups—the 50-plus group who are not eligible for senior citizen housing, as they are not yet 65, or whose income is above the very minimal limit; the 30-50 group and the young marrieds.
>
> By design, with the number of bedrooms planned, these units will not bring in nearly as many children as single-family homes. What the town cannot afford is to buy up all the vacant land in town. The town is not being asked to give anybody anything. It is being asked to rezone a piece of land to allow people of moderate income to have decent housing in Canton.

Ownership-Maintenance

The project was to be a cooperative, with each family buying a share in the cooperative as they made monthly payments and accumulated equity. It was hoped that this approach would promote a feeling of pride in the premises. The residents would elect a Board of Directors on a one family-one vote basis. Interfaith Housing Corporation was to manage the housing for about three years to see that it was properly started; the tenants could then, through their Board, continue to retain IHC as managing agent or choose another (subject to HUD approval). The managing agent would contract for rubbish and snow removal services, and hire a manager to care for the grounds; the cooperative would pay for these services, and would be 100 percent assessable for tax purposes.

Tenant Selection

A three-member tenant selection committee, consisting of two Canton residents and one Interfaith representative, was to screen prospective tenants. Every effort was to be made to meet the needs of Canton residents first. Selection of tenants was to be based upon their ability to get along in a cooperative and on income in relation to sliding limits set by FHA.

Rentals

Rentals would range from about $117 to $165 per month, including heat, hot water, and utilities, and depending on the number of bedrooms. Persons with income from $6,000 to $11,000, depending on the number of children, would be eligible. The Canton Housing Authority could lease up to 20 percent of the units for low-income Canton residents, such as the elderly and families presently living in poor housing.

Controversy

A fundamental prerequisite to a successful LMIH effort is that the need must be demonstrated.

At the time of the controversy, there was no formal study of housing needs in Canton. A land-use study was being undertaken by John Brown Associates, a Boston firm hired by the Planning Board. This was not completed until July 1971, well after the plan was defeated. In the absence of any housing study or census, the MIH Subcommittee (1) surveyed local factories in an effort to estimate the number of workers living outside the community, (2) questioned teachers and other school system employees, and (3) asked the League of Women Voters to undertake a survey of housing needs.

The survey indicated a housing shortage, with only 154 apartments and 98 units of public housing (all for elderly and veterans). Other than these facts, the proponents of the Interfaith plan relied on a newspaper article about the plight of newlyweds who could not find any suitable housing in Canton and upon the fact that 10 percent of the residents of Interfaith's development in Stoughton worked in Canton. "Will Canton take care of its own?" became the theme.

In March of 1971, just before the annual Town Meeting, the MIH proponents attempted to defend the need for the proposed housing also, on the basis of 77 persons who indicated that they would like to live in the apartments planned:

Canton residents;	48
young married couples from Canton who have been forced to move elsewhere, but would like to come back;	10
families who work in Canton;	14
elderly and others with friends or relatives in Canton.	5
	77

No effort was made to relate Canton's housing needs to those of the SMSA, particularly of Boston, apparently because this approach was likely to strengthen the opposition's claims that Canton would become the "gathering ground of Boston's slum dwellers."

In a predominantly Catholic community like Canton, the support of the Boston Archdiocese and its assessment of need is an important factor which was not ignored by the supporters. In a Letter to the Editor of *The Reporter*, Reverend Michael F. Groden stated:

> One fact that is only slowly coming to the public awareness is the inability of many Americans of moderate income, as well as lower income, to find a safe and standard house in which to live. Though this has been recognized in our older city areas, little attention has been paid to the needs of our suburban middle-income families, firemen, teachers, policemen, city or town workers, or of any young married couples who would like to stay in a community, but cannot because of costs.
>
> The citizens of Canton are now in a position to do something within their own community about the housing crisis. The proposed development of 165 housing units on a large 57-acre site is an excellent opportunity to help themselves and be an example for other communities to follow. This proposal, in my judgment, is a well-designed and developed housing program by a reputable firm, Interfaith Housing Corporation. A 57-acre site provides an extremely low density complex, providing and safeguarding a substantial amount of green and open space. Canton residents should welcome, encourage, and work to see new housing built that well serves their own citizens.

The position of another religious group regarding the need is stated with equal force in a letter to members of the Temple Beth David:

As you probably already know, a program has been undertaken to bring medium-income housing to the City of Canton. I enthusiastically support this program, and will be actively working in its behalf. I shall not here elaborate on the specifics of the project; you will be reading about it in your newspapers. I would, instead, like to tell you why I support it.

The American dream states that everybody is entitled to the fruits of whatever they earn. The American reality, however, is sadly at odds with this. The area of housing is one of the most glaring examples of this. The fact is that a person earning a moderate amount of money can find precious few places to live. We just are not building accommodations for these people. It is society's responsibility to insure the availability of decent living units to everyone.

I support the Canton Project because it is a step—albeit an extremely modest one in this direction. Naturally, Canton is only one of many communities, not only in this area, but around the country undertaking to meet its responsibility in this area. Perhaps when we see the validity of such undertakings, we could then be able to set about creating proper environments for low-income families as well. Only by producing decent and healthy environments for all people—when we integrate economically as well as racially—will we be able to break the cycle of resentment and antagonism that poisons the festering atmosphere of our overcrowded, ill-maintained, and dispiriting inner cities.

But a religious issue? Why is this a religious issue? Because a man cannot pray, cannot love God, cannot love the world, cannot love his fellow man, or trust his fellow man decently when his soul is oppressed. The rabbis who understood life and the human psyche, said that 'a beautiful home puts man in a cheerful frame of mind.' Only thus can he see his life as worthwhile or meaningful. Who is not entitled to as much?

We do live in blessedly pleasant surroundings. They will be no less peaceful and no less blessed if we share them with others.

Perhaps the most vital, central, and frequent concern is the assessment of the positive and negative impacts a project has upon the social and physical environment of a community.

The sponsors of the project in Canton made the following claims:

Land-Use Impact

Item	Comparative Development Under:	
	Present Zoning: Single-Family 109 units 15,000 square foot lots	*Proposed Zoning:* Multi-Family 165 units
No. of units	109	165
No. of bedrooms	367	370
No. of occupants	550	550

No. of automobiles	163		163	
No. of children	403		297	
Additional children to Canton schools	103		67	
Tax yield	$96,226		$70,950	
Real Estate	$89,380		$64,020	
Excise Tax	$ 6,846		$ 6,930	
Total Tax	$95,974		$62,639	
Educational		$73,954		$48,106
Municipal		$22,020		$14,533
Amount of open space	none		20 acres	

Arguments Aired at Memorial Hall

The presentations of the proposal were followed by discussion.

The opposition among town residents centered on the lack of a specific site plan, the possibility that more than the requested 165 units would be built on the acreage, and the effect on the town's tax rate of increased municipal services. Proponents described the project as being "100 percent taxable," pledged themselves to a written agreement limiting the number of units to be built, and emphasized their view that a real need for such housing exists in Canton.

Frequent references were made to Interfaith's project in Stoughton and to rumors regarding its negative effects—aesthetic, as well as organizational. In commenting on the architecture of Presidential Courts (the moderate-income apartments built by Interfaith in Stoughton), Mr. Larsen stated, "Design is purely a matter of taste," and concerning Stoughton "We've nothing to apologize for." In responding to the allegation that federal influence was used to change the building code, Mr. Larsen explained that this misconception arose because Presidential Courts was the first unit to be constructed under Stoughton's new building code. (This is the BOCA performance building code, a national code which allows for more flexibility in the choice of materials and design.)

One indignant member of the audience noted that the clergy are "transients; they come and make trouble and then leave."

Many residents wanted to know why this particular site had been selected and why this type of housing could not be scattered throughout the town. Philip Zlochiver, Chairman of the Canton Human Concerns Association, replied that many sites had been explored, but this one had been chosen because it would allow for construction of "low density housing." Mr. Larsen explained that it is not "economically feasible" to have scattered sites.

George Bertoletti of Norfolk Street, and a sergeant in the Canton Police Department, stated that he had inquired and found that "no Canton police officer intends to move into that housing." James Houghton of Marilyn Drive, and a member of the personnel board, asked how it had been established that there was a need in Canton for these apartments. He noted that the members of the Fire Department and municipal workers would not qualify for moderate-income housing because they make more money than the guidelines allow.

Attorney Joseph Malloy, representing the neighbors, commented that under the existing Canton zoning, 1,197 units of apartment housing could be built on the site and asked why so much land was needed "if they don't intend to build more than 165 units." He charged that the project could create a "gross, modern slum in Canton." Mr. Malloy also questioned a letter of endorsement for the project from the Canton clergy.

Proponents and Opponents

Although there were both opponents and proponents, the former were frequently more numerous, more vocal, more organized, and, apparently, in a more central position to influence decision makers. Abutters and neighbors who feared that the project would depress land values were the most active and earliest organized opponents. But before examining this opposition, a look at two public decision-making organizations is appropriate.

The Canton Housing Authority. The 5-member Canton Housing Authority is empowered to promote organizations which will help clear slums and to furnish low-income housing in case of need. The Chairman of the Authority at the time of the controversy, Joseph Kessler, was generally opposed to the Interfaith proposal and thought that the other members of the Authority felt the same way, with the exception of George Jenkins, a member of the MIH Subcommittee and an active proponent of the proposal. Mr. Kessler expressed the opinion that low-income people needed the housing more than moderate-income people, who could probably afford market rents without a federal subsidy. The CHAC had conducted a survey of the need for low-income housing by circulating a questionnaire through the public schools to parents of school age children; the group was criticized for this approach, however, since not all needy families would have children of school age. Mr. Kessler admitted that there was "a lot of confusion concerning the survey and that only 109 replies were filed."

The Planning Board. The proponents believed that 2 of the 5-member Planning Board favored the proposal: James Heggie and Michael Burke. The final vote was 3 to 1 against the proposal; Heggie did not participate in the voting for this one Article, although he did participate in most of the other decisions of the Planning Board announced on March 6, 1971. That year, Heggie was up for reelection to the Board; he was in fact reelected at the same Town Meeting that rejected the Interfaith proposal. Michael Burke dissented, issuing a minority report to the Town Meeting.

The following are excerpts from a pamphlet circulated by the proponents:

> The Choice is Yours!
>
> The Benefits to Canton are *not* subtle.
>
> At least 20 acres of valuable conservation and recreation land for town use, without the usual price tag.
>
> A chance for hometown families to upgrade their housing standards... especially elderly and younger couples.
>
> A controlled limited increase in school children to Canton public schools.
>
> Binding, long-range control over the impending specter of urban sprawl.
>
> A chance for Canton to fulfill a local housing requirement without coercion from higher official bodies. Canton's own elected officials would participate to protect your interests.
>
> These benefits are not possible today with new, single-family homes.
>
> Vote "Yes" on Article 25

In brief, the arguments most frequently used by proponents are as follows:

1. there is a local need for more moderate-income housing, especially for newlyweds, persons living in substandard Canton units, and workers forced to commute to Canton;
2. any development of the site under present zoning would have a more negative impact on taxes than would the Interfaith proposal described as being "100 percent taxable" and limited to the number of units proposed;
3. the Interfaith proposal would result in more open space than would the construction of single-family residences.

The proposal had several proponents other than the MIH Subcommittee:

League of Women Voters. Nearly all of the fourteen female members of the MIH Subcommittee were members of the League of Women Voters. The League supported the proposal from its birth; they reported in favor of the proposal to the Planning Board and the Town Meeting, and attempted to get the Board of Selectmen to take a stand on the question as early as January 1970.

The Clergy. The support of the Catholic Church was crucial in a community where nearly 70 percent of the population is Catholic. Monsignor Jacobbe initially favored the moderate-income housing idea, but later declared that the Church should not take a stand. However another local priest, Father Conroy, was insistent that the Church should intervene. Since the new Archbishop of Boston was coming to Canton late in January of 1971, the MIH Subcommittee members attempted to get him to speak out in favor of the plan during his visit. They were unsuccessful at first, but Father Groden of the Archdiocesan Planning Office intervened on their behalf. The statement of the Archbishop on January 26, 1971 was a general one in regard to housing: " . . . housing—any program to improve the living conditions of our brothers and sisters—is patriotic and religious, and we are all brothers and thus we have responsibilities to our brothers. . . . Every progress is change; if we all want to (make) progress, we must change."

In general, while strong in the beginning, the clergy's support later became "conditional" and then even less vigorous when community conflict mounted.

Prominent Citizens. Several prominent Canton residents had endorsed the proposal, including John Morgan, George Jenkins of CHAC, Attorney Joseph Galligan, Mr. and Mrs. John Rushworth of the Democratic Town Committee, Michael Burke of the Planning Board, and the St. Jude Nurses Association, which sent a petition to the Selectmen supporting the project.

Opponents to the Interfaith plan were numerous; over 500 residents signed a petition against it. They contended that multi-family zoning in this area would open the way for "deterioration of public and private property, human conflict, and monumental municipal crises." They cited increased taxes, overburdened school facilities, lack of adequate water and sewerage facilities, additional traffic congestion, and the density of building which might be allowed.

Early and determined objections came mostly from 14 abutters of the High Street area, who provided core leadership of the opposition. Stunned by the fact that none of the clergy members who endorsed the proposal had talked to them beforehand, they collected funds to hire a lawyer and distributed leaflets in opposition. They contended that the project would cause them the greatest injury, while the Town would bear the brunt of providing services. They also objected to the tenant selection procedure used by Interfaith in the Stoughton development and distributed a dismal poster that depicted a back-alley view of the Interfaith apartments in Stoughton. The poster read: "This is what Interfaith Housing Corporation created in Stoughton! Can Canton afford this? Vote 'No' on Article 25."

Interfaith attempted to meet these objections by demonstrating that development according to the present zoning would require more town services, add more children to the schools, and yield less tax money. Interfaith also assured the town of Canton that the development would house only a few poor people and blacks, and that property values would not be endangered.

Active opposition from outside the affected area came generally from two groups: first, friends or relatives of neighbors; second, newer residents who were "pushed out" of an urban area by blacks. Opponents held organizational meetings to coordinate their action. Although they did not establish a formal organization, as had Newton residents, they urged civic organizations, like the "Town Club," to oppose the plan.

The fundamental arguments of the opposition centered around the following issues:

The lack of a specific site-plan, specific construction cost analysis, and maintenance estimates. For example: members of Canton Industrial Development Commission expressed criticism of the proposed plan because "it showed a lack of preparation," and noted only that the plan might aid the town in obtaining federal funds for sewers (as in Stoughton). Others pointed out: "They do not know how much it costs them to build a single unit."

Concerns that more than the requested 165 units would be built on the site. For example: Attorney Joseph Malloy's query at the Memorial Hall as to why so much land was needed if only 165 units were to be built.

The negative effect on the town's tax rate of increased municipal services; the influx of "undesirables." Examples: Mrs. Harold Fitzgerald, Selectwoman and area resident, commented:

> "I'm not trying to deprive people in dire need of a place to live. I believe in apartments, I believe that people should have low-cost housing and I don't deny more housing is needed, but there is no sense making a squatter's village out of a tract of land and leaving the town to pick up the tab later.... Areas of town with far more elbow room, such as Route 128, Route 138, and Dedham Street would be far more appropriate sites for such construction...."

A seriously concerned group of area residents met at the Canton Town Club and began to organize an ad hoc committee to oppose the proposal on the grounds of traffic congestion, lack of sufficient water and sewer lines to the area, and the high cost of providing school space for children living in the apartments. Close to 70 people attended the meeting.

The opposition's literature focused on the "triple-instant" argument: Mrs. Owirka seemed to express the opinions of the entire group when she commented that "instant housing brings instant problems." To illustrate her statement, she aired some pertinent facts: With 165 additional families in the area, there would be problems with trash collections and road maintenance; it would be the Town's responsibility to provide these services. Since the Canton development would contain 20 4-bedroom apartments, the units could house over 400 children; carried further, she reasoned, this could mean as much as $171,000 in additional school expenses.

There were persistent rumors that "undesirables" had come into Stoughton through the Interfaith development. (The Stoughton project has 13 black families and 9 women receiving Aid to Dependent Children.)

The credibility of Interfaith as a developer. The feeling of distrust toward Interfaith, based on the experience of Stoughton and Interfaith's reluctance (as perceived by the opposition) to present all details of the proposal to all concerned, is best exemplified by the headline in the newspaper story, "We Have No Faith in Interfaith." The opposition pointed out that Interfaith's name was at best a misnomer and possibly a lie, as there were no "members of the cloth" employed by Interfaith. In predominantly Catholic Canton, this may have been a potent argument.

The role of racial prejudice. While racial arguments were notably absent in public discussions, there were several incidents with racial overtones, particularly toward the end of the controversy. Proponents seemed to think that racial prejudice was a major motivating force of the opposition. Interfaith held the same belief. But to say that the opposition to the Interfaith plan was only a reflection of racial prejudice would be an oversimplification. Rather, opposition was the result of several factors, of which race was only one. And the race issue was generally kept in the background by both proponents and the opposition. Yet motive is hard to decipher. When promoderate income housing speakers at the Town Meeting attempted to raise the question of race, they were shouted down. Even the local attorney, Joseph Galligan, who represented Interfaith in the controversy, denied that race was a factor in discussions and debates.

This was not the case, however, in several activities against the plan. A group of teen-agers at a Canton school took an informal poll of their classmates, asking the question, "Do you want the niggers to come in?" When site neighbors took up a collection to retain a lawyer, they reportedly went from door to door through the town asking for contributions "to stop the niggers moving in."

Finally, external conditions influenced the course of events. For example, the March 1971 statement of President Nixon that federal pressure would not be exerted to integrate the suburbs weakened the proponents' position. Earlier, some people had thought that acquiescence to the Interfaith proposal might be the only way to enable Canton to obtain federal money for sewers; now they could have the money for sewers even if they rejected the moderate-income housing proposal.

Defeat

The atmosphere in the Canton High School auditorium on the night of the Annual Town Meeting, March 15, 1971, was tense. Thirteen hundred people jammed the auditorium and each one knew that Article 25 was the Interfaith proposal. If passed, it would rezone the 57 acres off High Street for moderate-income housing. Members of the MIH Subcommittee, who had worked with dedication on this project for more than two years, were particularly anxious.

Moderator MacLaren MacGregor set ground rules before the discussion opened on the article, noting, "This is not a site plan hearing. The issue is solely whether to vote on a zoning change or not." He added, "We are not here to discuss the merits of any future use of any land." A subsequent attempt by Planning Board member, Michael Burke, to present a "minority report" in favor of the issue was stopped by the moderator when Mr. Burke began by saying, "I am convinced of the need for moderate-income housing."

Stating that presentations on either side could be made relating to density, traffic, and other zoning related matters, Mr. MacGregor ruled out of order any references to "specific development plans." Attorney Joseph Galligan, representing Interfaith, described the zoning change as "beneficial and salutary." He added that 20 acres of the parcel "can be made available to the town for conservation and recreation, on a permanent basis." He appealed for "faith and trust in the time-tested governmental bodies" such as the Appeal and Planning Boards and building inspectors.

Attorney Joseph Malloy, who represented High Street residents in opposition to the item, charged that the change would constitute "spot zoning." The neighborhood's character is "changing in the exact opposite direction" from the zoning request, he said, "and moving from General Residence to Single Residence." Mr. Malloy asked that the town "consider the long-range impact on town services," citing "an adverse" effect on the school system, drainage, and sewage. An objection raised from the floor by Mrs. Kay Rushworth of Ponkapoag, that Mr. Malloy was exceeding the guidelines laid down for the item, led to the comment by a proponent of the article, to the effect that "it appears obvious only a lawyer can speak under your rules."

Further objections from the floor halted a vote on the item to allow Jerome Hoffman of Algonquin Road to say, "The problems brought up in connection with this article—schools, taxes, and the rest, face the town whether this is passed or nor. We've always told our children to love each other and not to give up on the country. This article offers us a chance to show we are not giving up."

The entire proceedings were punctuated by cries of "sit down!", "Move the question!" and boos from the audience. Finally, Article 25 was resoundingly defeated by a voice vote. A motion to reconsider was also decisively defeated. Mrs. Rushworth described the reconsideration attempt as a "travesty against representative democratic government," while Mr. MacGregor said, "Some aspects of this town meeting may not have been the best example of a town meeting for foreign visitors," but disagreed strongly that there had been a "travesty," adding that there had previously been advocates of the winning side of an issue who had asked for reconsideration. The arguments on the moderate-income housing continued in the halls and corridors of the high school during the intermission that followed the vote.

There was no consolation in the fact that this article was one of 6 zoning changes defeated at the meeting. Article 26, the largest single zoning proposal which would have extended a limited industrial district off Route 138 into 253 residential areas, was disposed of with little comment.

A further zoning request in Article 27 requested a change on 9 acres in the Kirby Drive area from Limited Industrial to General Residence. Pasquale Russo, developer, had distributed sheets describing the tax benefits of the proposal to meeting members as they entered the high school, and Richard Driscoll, his attorney, told the audience that "in the present zone you could have a very fine electrical plant or truck terminal." Attorney Malloy, representing area residents, said the abutters "have no quarrel with Mr. Russo's right to develop the property as Limited Industrial, but feel the property will be devalued if apartments are built there." The article was rejected.

Approved by the meeting was the transfer of $13,000 for a professional updating of the 1959 Town master plan, which the Planning Board had indicated would concentrate heavily on a zoning updating.

According to several participants in favor of the Interfaith proposal, the speakers were interrupted and a general state of confusion appeared to exist. The voters were often unsure of just what issues they were voting on because of the many distractions from the floor.

Although the reason given for defeat of Article 25 was that major zoning changes had to be delayed until the Town's Master Plan could be updated, the underlying reason for the defeat may have been that the predominantly white middle-aged audience did not wish to face the issue of economic and racial discrimination. They did their best to avoid the subject throughout any of the previous discussions. Yet their resistance could be based on the fear of a massive influx of blacks and poor from Boston, as well as the impact they felt it would have on property values. Many townspeople, suspicious of different life-styles, were also upset by some of the long-haired conscientious objectors on the staff of Interfaith. Thus, it may be that taxes and congestion diverted attention from the emotionally explosive subjects of life-style and racial socioeconomic prejudice.

Interfaith Leaves Canton

By April 22, 1971, Interfaith Housing was still considering its future plans for the 57-acre site on which it was holding an option. In the meantime, no definite decision to drop its interest in the site was made. *The Reporter* published an interview with Mr. Trayers. He confirmed that Interfaith still held first option on the site and that another developer had expressed interest. Mr. Trayers stated that he was still interested in cooperating with Interfaith, despite the fact that the proposed plan experienced a poor start.

In May 1971, Mr. Larsen announced that Interfaith would continue its efforts to ensure ways to work out neighborhood and regional incentives for the project. It would maintain its search for the financial and professional resources to help organize the abutters, who could then participate in working out the proposal. But soon thereafter even Interfaith admitted formally that the project was dead.

John Keith, a local developer, has since acquired Mr. Trayer's site, and plans to build 100 single-family homes thereon.

The Moderate-Income Housing Subcommittee ceased to exist after the Annual Town Meeting of March 1971, but most of its members remain active through the League of Women Voters Unit on Human Resources.

Sam Larsen, Marvin Fannin, Norman Thompson, and Norma Banish—the persons primarily connected with the plan—have all left Interfaith.

QUESTIONS

1. Canton turned down several proposals for zoning changes at the Town Meeting. Discuss the following aspects of this phenomenon:

Are you satisfied with the procedure of determining zoning changes in Canton? What are the disadvantages you observed? How can they be eliminated? What are the advantages? How can they be preserved?

Zoning is essential for planning and guiding municipal growth. Yet zoning ordinances should also be flexible to allow for a changing technology and new conditions stemming from urban developments. How can both principles be observed?

2. Some residents expressed their approval eloquently and with deep sincerity. Most citizens of Canton, with no less sincerity, pondered the question with the added dimension of personal and community economics. How do you respond? The question of race was kept in the background most of the time during the conflict. The "gentlemen's agreement" not to bring in any questions which were overtly racial was apparently adopted by Interfaith. Discuss the advantages and disadvantages of this approach. Did it influence the outcome? What is your position regarding the role of racism and social class life-style in opposing low- and moderate-income housing in middle-class affluent suburbs?

3. Local clergy supported the principle of low- and moderate-income housing and the values it embodies. Yet the support seemed to decline or even vanish when community conflict intensified. Why? Some suggest that community consensus requires that religion should not be involved in daily political or

economic decision making. What do you think? How do you assess the role of this social institution in intervention for social change?

4. On February 8, 1971, Canton Human Concerns and Interfaith signed a letter of Agreement which among other things commits Interfaith to study the possibility of selling or donating part of its property as conservation land to the Town. Included in the agreement were such points as consideration of colonial architecture, appointment of a clerk of the works to ensure quality construction, and landscaping that would leave a screen of trees between the cooperative and abutters. What are the merits of this policy? At a time when environmental quality and control is so important for the nation, why did these environmental policies associated with housing construction receive relatively little or no attention in the conflict?

5. Time and again opponents pointed to the fact that "Interfaith is an outsider" and could not be trusted to protect the interest of Canton. How does a developer gain acceptance and social legitimacy? What do you think of Interfaith's coalition with the Human Concerns group? Would a different political coalition have been more effective?

Chapter Seven

East Providence: The Atypical Suburb

Unlike most suburban communities, East Providence is not a bastion of white, middle class exclusiveness. The racially integrated residents, though mainly middle class, include such a substantial number of lower income families that the Public Housing Authority of East Providence objectively perceived a need for LMIH. Seemingly receptive and with few serious limitations, such as zoning problems or lack of site, blocking the way of such housing, East Providence gave every indication of being a promising place in which to introduce LMIH. But, in April, 1966, when plans and sites for the housing were confidently proposed by the Housing Authority there was violent public reaction which touched off a five and one-half year controversy.

The original plan called for the building of a 100-unit apartment complex for low income, nonelderly families. Four other plans were proposed, ranging from apartment complexes to duplex housing to single family units—all were confronted by various combinations of arguments and fears, some based on facts, others on misunderstandings, emotional prejudices, and social discrimination. There was public confusion, and neither the proponents nor the opposition had a clear strategy or line of argumentation. The advantages and disadvantages of the plans themselves, as well as the actual sites, repeatedly were topics of heated debate. The end result was a drastically modified version of the original, optimistic plan.

THE COMMUNITY

The People

The population of East Providence has grown 14.8 percent in the 1960-1970 period. Of the 48,151 residents in 1970, 1,343 (2.7 percent) were blacks and 339 (.7 percent) other non-white. The city has a higher percent of blacks than the Providence SMSA (2.3) or the other communities studied.

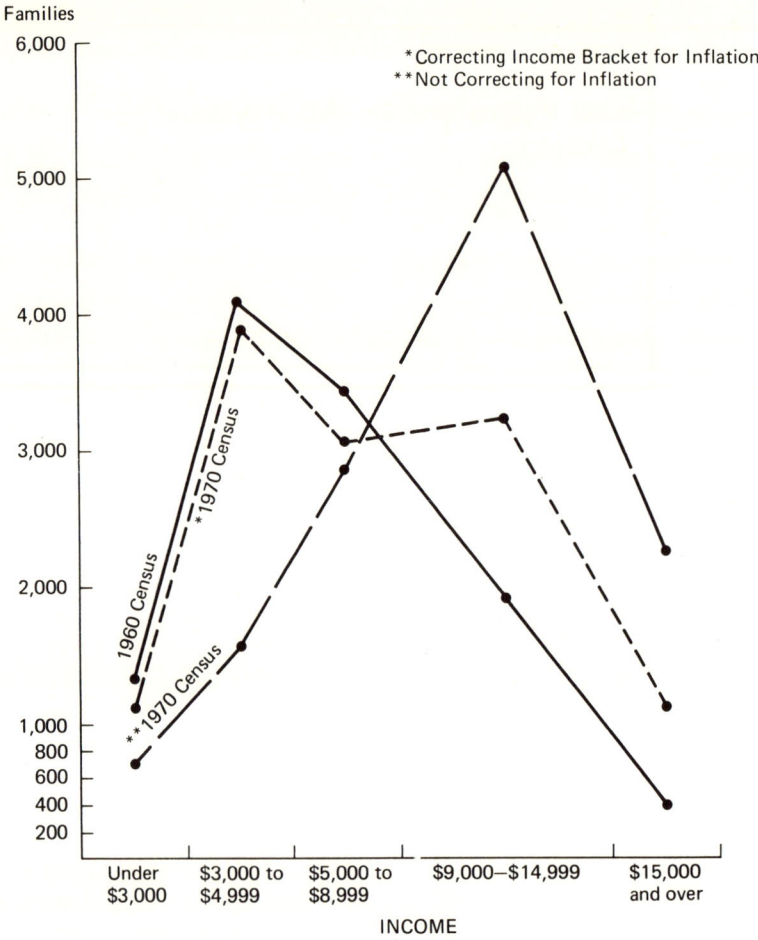

Figure East Providence 1. Income Distribution in East Providence

Compared to the other cities studied, there is a higher percentage of families below poverty level (5.8 percent; households—7.1 percent) which also exceeds that of Providence SMSA (6.9 of total households). Yet the city experienced a 2 percent decrease of families below $3,000 and a 6 percent increase of those earning more than $15,000. Its family median income of $10,179 in 1970 increased 67 percent since 1960—a smaller increase rate than the Providence SMSA's.

Table East Providence 1. Income Distribution in East Providence 1960-1970; and Poverty Indicators

1960 No. Families	%	Income Brackets in $	*	1970 No. of Families % Change	**	% Change
1,329	11	Under $3,000	1,170	− 2	750	− 6
4,118	37	$ 3 − 5,999	3,984	− 6	1,584	−25
3,434	30	6 − 8,999	3,039	− 6	2,820	− 8
1,831	16	9 − 14,999	3,235	+ 9	5,092	+36
400	3	15 and Over	1,156	+ 6	2,341	+16
11,112	100		12,584	+13	12,584	+13

*Correcting the income brackets for Inflation (CPI Index)
**Not correcting for inflation

	1960	1970	% Change
Median Family Income:	$6,082	$10,179	+67

Population in Poverty	1970
Families Below Poverty level	727 (5.8%)
Persons Below Poverty level	3,639 (7.7%)
Percent of poverty households lacking some or all plumbing	7.1%

Table East Providence 2. Population 1960-1970

	1960	1970	% Change
Population	41,955	48,151	+14.8
White	41,068	46,469	+13
Black	817	1,343	+64
Other Non-White	70	339	+384

Table East Providence 3. Selected Demographic Characteristics 1970

Count of all Males	22,877	Count of all Married Couples	10,990
Count of all Females	25,274	Yrs School Completed − None−8 Yrs	8,103
Persons Age 5 and Under	4,621	1-3 Yrs High School	6,186
Persons Age 6 to 20	13,093	High School Graduate	8,697
Persons Age 21 to 64	24,938	1-3 Yrs College	2,359
Persons Age 65 and Over	5,499	College Graduate or More	2,427

Table East Providence 4. Ethnic Composition 1970

Country of Foreign Origin	No. of Persons of Foreign or Mixed Parentage
Portugal	9436
United Kingdom	1539
Canada	1850
Italy	1763
Ireland	1225
Sweden	713

There has been a sustained rate of economic growth in the 1960s and by 1970 the city's labor force increased by 24 percent, its unemployment kept to a low 3.6 percent. East Providence's occupational structure experienced—like most cities in the area—a major percentage increase in service occupations (70 percent), professional personnel (41 percent) and operatives (35 percent), losing 41 percent of household workers.

The city's population in 1970 was slightly younger—median population age 31.5 dropping by 1.5 since 1960. Yet the 65-and-over population group increased by 29 percent—compared to 10 percent increase of persons under 18 years and 15 percent for those between 19-64 years of age.

Table East Providence 5. Labor Force Characteristics 1970—East Providence

A. General	
Total Employed (16 years old and over)	20,367
B. Occupation	
Professional, Tech.	2,529
Managers, Administrators	1,390
Clerical	3,804
Sales	1,540
Craftsmen, Foremen	2,956
Operatives	4,098
Private Household Workers	104
Service Workers	2,159
Laborers	733
C. Industrial Sector of Employment	
Agriculture and Mining	150
Construction	1,204
Manufacturing	6,845
Transportation, Comm., Utilities	1,357
Wholesale	1,107
Retail	2,926
Finance, Insurance, Real Estate	1,312
Service	4,647
Public Administration	839

Economic Base

The stability of a town's economic growth and of its guaranteed revenue are important indications of its ability to absorb the added expenses of new low income housing, and, in this respect, East Providence qualifies well. The highly integrated pattern of commercial and industrial firms, and single family residences in East Providence yielded property taxes which amounted to 78.7 percent of the city's revenue in 1969; yet the tax burden for residents is one of the lightest in the state. Only six communities with populations below 20,000 had experienced a smaller increase in property tax rates than East Providence— $3.00 during this period.

In the fiscal year 1968, East Providence's total expenditures were $10,524,388. Of this, approximately 20 percent was spent on public safety, 7 percent on public works, 5 percent on sanitation, and less than 1 percent on public health.

The main industries are manufacturing, shipping, distribution, retail trade and services.

Education

In 1968, East Providence spent $4,328,305, or 41.1 percent of its budget, on public education. This represents an expenditure per pupil of $527, which includes state and federal aid. The local contribution per pupil was $379. Of the thirty-nine communities in Rhode Island, East Providence had the third lowest per-pupil expenditure and the sixteenth lowest local contribution per pupil. By 1985, the city plans to spend approximately 20 million dollars for the modernization of its existing school structures.

In 1970, the median education level of East Providence citizens was 11.8 years. In the same year, 48.5 percent had completed high school, while only 8.7 percent had completed four or more years of college, and 7.2 percent had less than five years of formal education.

Administration

East Providence has a government consisting of a city council, mayor, and city manager. The city council, composed of five councilmen, each elected for two-year terms, is politically strong. Four councilmen are elected from wards which represent the former villages that make up the East Providence area, and the fifth is an at-large councilman. The mayor, elected by a majority vote of the council for a two-year term, has no more power or influence than the other members of the city council, since he has only one of the five votes cast and has no power of veto. The city manager is appointed by the city council for an unspecified period and may be discharged at the council's discretion.

This type of city government does not provide for continuity of policy, sustained community action, or long-term commitment since the whole council is subject to election every two years. This lack of continuity was clearly demonstrated during the period of the LMIH controversy from 1966-1971. In the 1968 and 1970 city council elections, both the candidates and populace were divided, not along party lines, but on the basis of attitude toward the low income housing project. Of the ten councilmen elected in 1968 and 1970, five campaigned as proponents of scattered site housing, four as opponents, and one as a mild, but uncommitted, proponent. However, in 1970, all four councilmen representing the wards were defeated in their bid for reelection by three anti-LMIH candidates and the noncommitted candidate; only the at-large councilman was reelected. The council was then made up of two Democrats, two Republicans, and an Independent. As a result of the election, the city council's position on low income housing shifted dramatically and resulted in its effort to defeat the proposed housing plan by means of a "no confidence" vote. From 1970-1972, the city council appears to have been an adequate reflection of the electorate's attitudes and position.

In addition to the elected city officials, the city government includes a Citizens Advisory Committee (CAC), whose function is to maintain contact with the public by dispensing information to and soliciting opinions from the community. The chairman is appointed by the city council. He has no power and only limited funds at his committee's disposal. From the beginning of the LMIH controversy, CAC, under the chairmanship of Edward Otis, failed to take adequate initiative and, thus, proved ineffective; in 1970, when Joseph Pangborn became CAC chairman, the committee began to coordinate its efforts with those in support of the city council and the Housing Authority.

The East Providence Housing Authority (EPHA), the initiator and backbone of the drive to build low income housing, is a five-member board appointed by the city council for five-year terms, one term expiring yearly. Though appointed by the city council, the Housing Authority was established and operates under state rather than city laws, and has the power to take land by eminent domain.

This became an important factor in the LMIH controversy, as Rhode Island law exempts low income housing projects constructed by the Housing Authority from the "provisions of any zoning ordinance or any building ordinance." Zoning, therefore, was not to be a major problem in the selection of public housing sites in East Providence. However, the Housing Authority has no independent source of funds and is dependent upon federal, state, and local government funds for its projects. In addition, federal law requires local government approval of public housing. At the height of the LMIH controversy in 1971, the city council refused to give its approval to the Authority's scattered site plan.

Land Uses and Housing

In 1970, the people of East Providence were spread over an elongated land area of 13.9 square miles, with a gross population density of 3,080 persons per square mile. Of the 13.9 square miles, 31 percent is presently used for residential units, 29 percent for public or recreational area, 27 percent is currently vacant, 9 percent is commercial, and only 4 percent is for manufacturing.

East Providence developed from a separated set of small, scattered, colonial farming villages founded during the late seventeenth and early eighteenth centuries. When, in the early twentieth century, immigration, industrialization, and urbanization set in, there was rapid social and economic growth. Villages merged and the number of commercial and manufacturing facilities in East Providence increased, as did resort areas for summer use. The subdivision of the land into numerous small lots, and the hasty construction of many structures built close together, led to numerous problems which are still evident—substandard housing, undersized lots, overcrowding of land, and poor street layouts. Most of the recent residential areas have developed on the periphery of industrial and commercial areas and transportation routes.

A contributing factor in this "haphazard" land use pattern is the high percentage of vehicular transportation routes. The city has 149.5 miles of streets and highways, and anticipates the construction of still more roadways. Some areas that suffer most from high housing density are shown by census tracts to be plagued also by many undesirable land characteristics such as excessive slopes and pits, inadequate drainage, and areas subject to frequent flooding and consequent erosion. It was in these census tracts that the majority of LMIH units were to be constructed.

East Providence housing stock of 15,481 is inadequate and the city has a severe housing shortage, especially for families in lower income brackets. Of its housing stock (68 percent owner-occupied, 66 percent single family dwellings, detached) 6.6 percent were subsidized units in 1973. Yet not enough, Population increase, unavailability of land, and changes in attitude on the part of the citizens regarding apartment dwelling are part of the problem. Like its urban neighbors, Providence and Pawtucket, East Providence experienced a decrease in the number of newly constructed single family dwellings from 71 percent in 1960 to 68 percent in 1970. Over the entire ten-year period, there was an increase of only 10 percent in the total number of East Providence dwelling units in new single family structures, compared to a 57.4 percent increase in dwelling units in multi-family structures. Also, availability of total housing units decreased. In 1970 the rental vacancy rate for the city was 2.3 percent, the lowest of any city in the state. The vacancy rate of single family housing for sale was much lower (.4%). Figure 2 shows the decline in one-family house construction in East Providence and the rise of apartment construction in the last twenty years.

As would be expected, the decrease in the housing supply served to bolster rents and property costs. The median rent for East Providence in 1970 was $74.00, making it the fourth highest rental rate of all Rhode Island cities. In terms of the median value of housing units, East Providence ranked third highest among the seven largest cities in the state, with a median value of $16,900.

Table East Providence 6. Selected Housing Characteristics 1970—East Providence

A. Type, Condition, Density

Total Housing Units	15,481
Housing Units Owner Occupied	10,597
Housing Units Renter Occupied	4,547
Vacant Housing Units	337
Total 1 Unit structures	10,116

Housing units with—
1.01 to 1.50 persons/room	767
1.51 or more persons per room	117
Median number of persons per unit	
Density: 3,080 persons per square mile	

Units with telephone available	14,222
Units with complete kitchen	15,345
Units with complete plumbing	15,152
Subsidized Housing Units (as of June 1973)	4,024 (6.6 percent of total)

B. Value

Median value of housing units	$16,900
Median Contract Rental	$ 74

Value of Owner-Occupied Units
Less than $5,000	55
$5,000 to $9,999	699
$10,000 to $14,999	2,505
$15,000 to $19,999	3,156
$20,000 to $24,999	1,606
$25,000 to $34,999	796
$35,000 to $49,999	210
$50,000 or More	40
Total Reporting	9,067

Rental Contracts for Renter-Occupied Units
Less than $60	1,329
$60 to $79	1,104
$80 to $99	604
$100 to $119	369
$120 to $149	528
$150 to $199	312
$200 to $299	53
$300 or more	10
No Cash Rent	218
Total Reported	4,527

C. Vacancy

Total vacant units	323
Homeowner vacant units (Sale)	39
Rental Vacant Units	109
Other type vacant	175
Homeowner Vacancy Rate .4 Percent	
Median Value Homeowner Vacancy	$15,800
Rental Vacancy Rate 2.3 Percent	
Median Value Rental Vacancy	$ 84

D. Property Assessment

Rate per $1,000 assessed val. $44.00 (1971), $44.40 (1972), change 1971-72: +$0.40

Assessed Valuation: $158,967,065

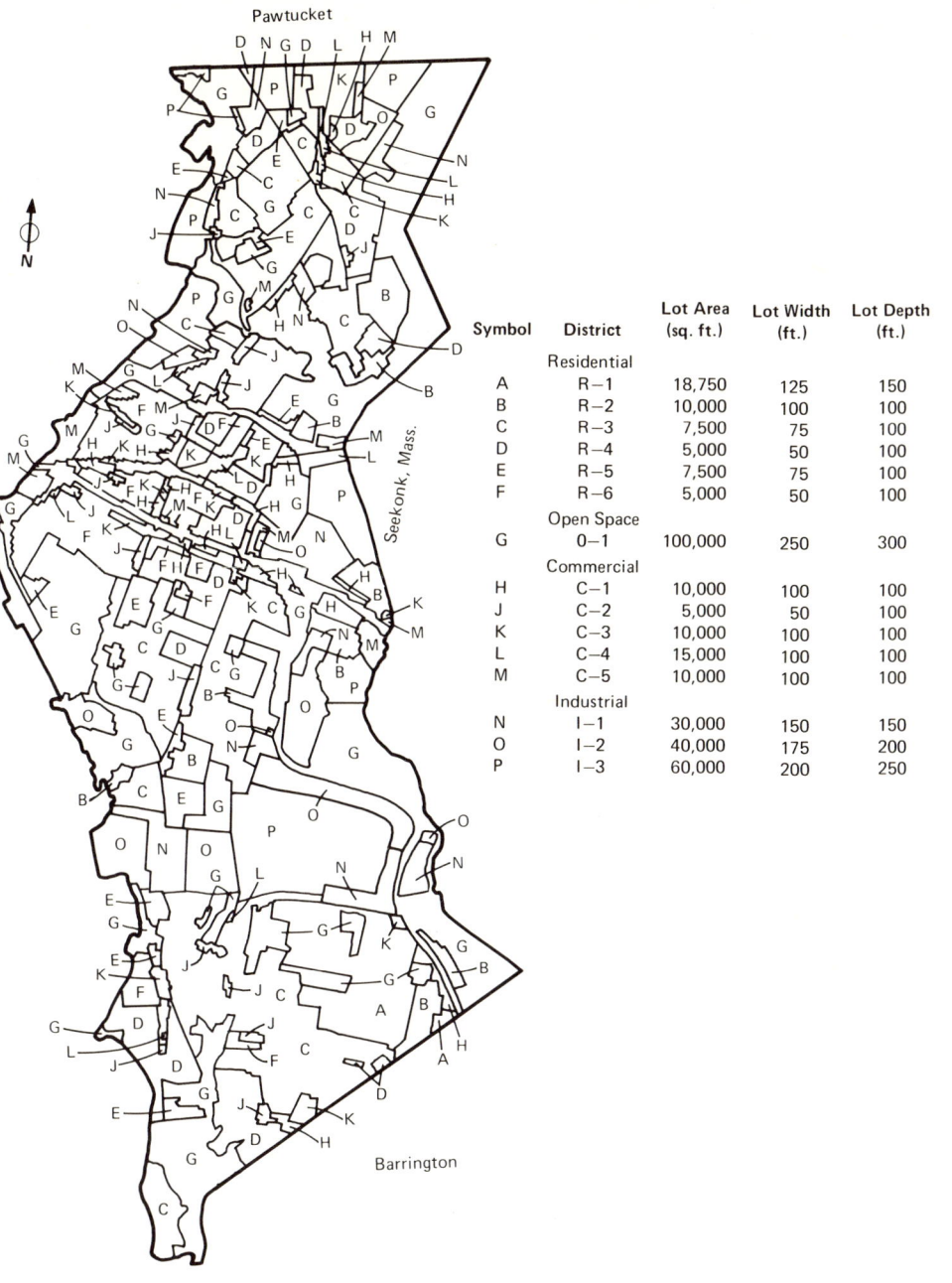

Figure East Providence 3. Land Use Map East Providence

Given the average value of single family units, many families in the $5,000-$10,000 income bracket would be unable to purchase a single family house in East Providence. Lower income families pay more for housing than an acceptable 25 percent of their income. In 1970, 24.5 percent of the 1488 rental housing occupants, earning less than $5,000 were spending 25-34 percent of their income on rent, and 49 percent were spending more than 35 percent. The city's median percentage of income spent for rent for those occupants earning less than $5,000 was 35 percent. While the median percentage of income expended on rent by those rental occupants earning $5,000-$9,999 was a more reasonable 17.6 percent, 12 percent of these persons were spending 25-34 percent of their income on rent, while 3.7 percent spent 35 percent or more.

With respect to the city's Black households, the rent of Black occupied units was $75.47, second highest among Rhode Island's cities. East Providence also ranked second in the average value of $15,221 for the 305 Black single family housing units, coming to only $238 lower than the average value of all owner occupied units. Thus, among Rhode Island's cities, East Providence has a significant middle class of Blacks, who are homeowners with housing equivalent to the white population.

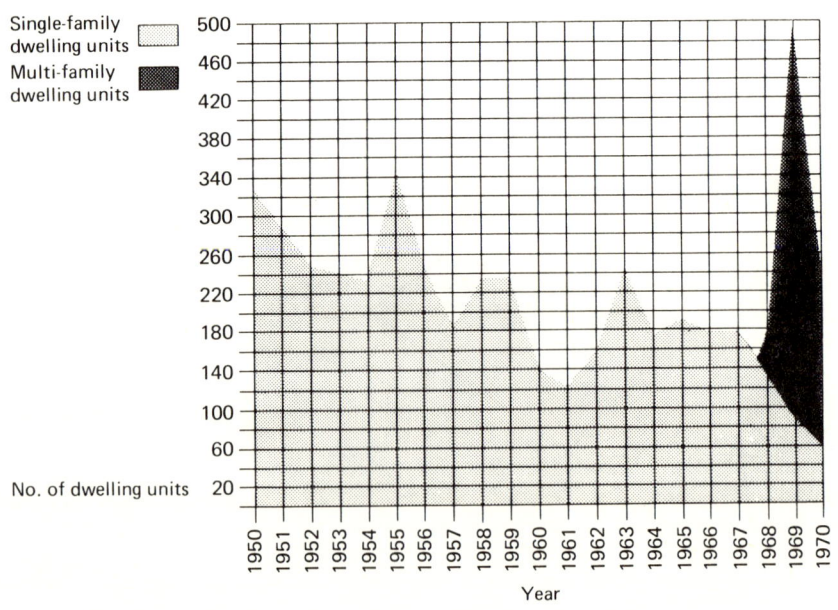

Figure East Providence 2. New Residential Construction

The reaction of the Negro Men's Civic Association and other Black community leaders to the prospect of LMIH raised interesting questions. Black opposition to locating low income housing in predominantly Black neighborhoods appears to have been based on the belief that there is no need for such housing and that such a project would make more difficult the economic development of their neighborhood.

The Housing Need

Fully 15.8 percent of the city's housing units were deficient because of lack of adequate plumbing (4.2 percent), deterioration (8.7 percent) or dilapidation (2.8 percent). Of the 2,100 households with gross incomes of less than $3,000 per year, 670 were deficient for one or more reasons.

The East Providence Planning Department estimated that 486 of these deficient households were occupied by elderly persons and 184 by nonelderly families, who would be eligible for public housing. The Department assumed that only 25 percent of those eligible would desire to live in public housing and it recommended in 1966 the construction, at a minimum, of 50 units of nonelderly family LMIH and 50 units for the elderly. These units were to be available by 1969-1970; another 100 units of LMIH (50 units for elderly and 50 for nonelderly families) were to be available in 1972-1973. These units were deemed essential as relocation resources for anticipated urban renewal projects. Furthermore, based on the 1960 census data estimates that 10 percent of all households in the city contained 6 or more persons and that an average number of persons per household for 160 families receiving public welfare was 3.8 persons, the Planning Department recommended that LMIH accommodations focus on 4-, 5- and 6-person families. Finally, the Planning Department emphasized housing design and architecture. Its intent was to provide good quality housing of interesting design. It recommended low density, scattered site apartments which would be an integral part of the community, thereby avoiding the isolation and stigma of large ghetto projects for welfare families. The recommendation did not indicate where such housing should be built.

A Community Renewal Program household analysis survey, taken in 1964, indicated that the vast majority of East Providence residents were satisfied with their housing and neighborhoods. Major areas of dissatisfaction, according to the survey, were the lack of recreational facilities and poor traffic conditions and control. This survey is an important factor when considering the LMIH controversy in East Providence. For, despite evidence presented by the Planning Board in support of the need for LMIH in the city, this need did not seem to be evident to the community. Such dichotomy of opinion is central to the controversy.

How should need be determined?

How should differences in the perception of need be treated?

Should there be limits placed on the state in its pursuit of community renewal?

THE PRESS REPORTS

The remaining story of the East Providence LMIH struggle is presented through a series of newspaper clippings spanning the period from 1966 to 1971. In this way, the controversy can be seen as unfolding over a period of time as it did to the average citizen of the community, who, we assume, knows at least "what he reads in the newspapers."

Riverside: Phase One

April 21, 1966, was the first announcement by means of a news release from HUD, Washington, D.C.:

> The Department of Housing and Urban Development announced today a $20,000 loan to the East Providence, R.I. Housing Authority.
> The funds, requested by the East Providence Housing Authority, will enable it to begin preliminary planning on its program for 100 new low rent homes at East Providence. These dwellings, to be available to low income families at rents they can afford, will have an important role in the community's efforts to eliminate conditions associated with poverty.
> Following completion of preliminary planning, the local Housing Authority will prepare and submit to HUD a program which will include a description of the proposed housing site, sketch plans, and an estimate of the total cost of the proposed housing development.
> The program will serve as a basis for an annual contributions contract. This contract will permit the Housing Authority to proceed toward construction of the proposed housing units, which will add substantially to the local economy, and to set rentals within the means of low income families.

Housing Plan Protested
in Riverside
Providence Journal, Oct. 11, 1966

> Riverside residents protested strongly last night to plans of the East Providence Housing Authority to construct a 60-unit low cost housing development at Bullocks Point Avenue and Sunset Street.
> Tentative plans for the development were announced last night by Miss Dorothy Angell, executive secretary of the housing authority at a meeting of the Narragansett Terrace Association.
> Members of the Association said they had had no prior notice of the authority's plans. "The people didn't know anything about it

until they heard through the grapevine," Kenneth Wilmot, association president, said. "The people here just don't know what's going to happen. We were never told. Now it seems that we can't do anything about it anyway."

Miss Angell said that the developers will be placed on a five and one-half-acre tract of land selected by federal authorities.

The plans were made, she said, by the housing authority and the planning board which is planning an urban renewal project for the Riverside area.

The actual cost of the project will not be known, she said, until approval from the federal government comes later this month. At that time, she said, further plans will be disclosed.

Mr. Wilmot said members of his organization questioned why the Bullocks Point site was picked from the several that were available. The housing authority announced several weeks ago that it was working on plans for the project.

Fears of "a crime ridden ghetto" sparked resistance to a proposed Riverside low income housing project last night as the East Providence Housing Authority met to answer questions from local residents.

A petition opposing the project was being circulated at the end of the meeting.

Several residents expressed the view that the 60-unit government project will create a ghetto situation for crime while others believed the project was "being forced down our throats."

William F. Fidalgo, housing authority attorney, said those who opposed the project could write to the federal housing authority in New York City.

Mrs. Bertha Phillips and Mrs. Addison Fowler, who were circulating the petition, said they will send copies to the government and to Congressional representatives.

Two members of the Housing Commission and Miss Dorothy Angell, housing authority director, were under continuous fire from more than 150 persons who crowded into a small auditorium in the old Riverside Junior High School.

Joseph Rock, housing commission chairman, answered one resident, who called the project "a crime ridden ghetto," by saying all applicants to the project would be "thoroughly screened."

He said low income housing projects in Providence and Pawtucket showed an increase in crime but that the Riverside project was a much smaller complex. The projects in Providence and Pawtucket had 700-800 apartment units while the Riverside facility will have only 60, Mr. Rock said.

Miss Angell described the project as a series of duplex houses in which either two or four apartments would be located. The complex, costing nearly a million dollars, will be located on a five and a half acre site bordered by Crescent View, Bullocks Point and Providence Avenues. The entire project will be paid for by the federal government.

Claude E. Needham of 33 Harvey Ave., Riverside, called the meeting "a farce" since none of the affected Riverside residents were ever asked if they favored it. "The government is forcing something down our throats without asking the people if they want it," Mr. Needham said.

Miss Angell said the project was open mainly to East Providence residents and that Riverside residents would be given preference. "Some applications from Riverside have already been received," she said.

Mr. Rock said the project would also provide housing for those persons forced to relocate because of a contemplated urban renewal project in the area.

Earlier in the evening Joseph L. Savick, Jr., city director of planning and urban development, said the city expects to begin an urban renewal project of the Riverside Square area within the next ten years. Forty percent of housing in the area is "deficient" and may be torn down upon further investigation, Mr. Savick said.

He said he favored the housing project regardless of whether the urban renewal project comes through.

Other complaints last night centered on the construction of the project. Mrs. Fowler, who circulated the petition, asked if it was possible to purchase separate sites for each housing unit throughout the city.

"This way the project would not be in a ghetto situation but spread out," Mrs. Fowler said. She said that New Haven had a housing project built along those lines.

Miss Angell said the cost of separate site purchases would be too prohibitive. The cost of the present site is still being negotiated with the owner, Arthur Simmons, president of Crescent Amusement Park, Miss Angell said.

John F. Conley, Independent council candidate from Ward Four (Riverside), said he could not support the project because of a bar located on the edge of the proposed site. He identified the bar as the Gold Post on the corner of Bullocks Point and Crescent View Avenues.

Mr. Conley said the bar should have been condemned for the project just as an adjoining market had been. "I could see the market," he said, "but a café is out of the question. We must be able to control these people in the project," he said.

Mr. Rock said he did not know why the bar was not purchased. "The federal authorities picked the site, we didn't," he said.

Riverside Residents Fear "Ghetto"
Providence Sunday Journal, Oct. 16, 1966

Not since the East Providence Housing Authority suffered severe personality squabbles in its embryonic stages four years ago has it faced the problems it faced last week.

The five-member board announced a plan to build a 60-unit, one-million-dollar, low cost housing development in Riverside near Crescent Park and ran smack into organized and vocal opposition. The board members are surprised.

More than 150 Riverside residents expressed fears that the development will result in a "crime-ridden ghetto" and argued that the project is being "forced down our throats."

The opposition, characterized by unusual unanimity, claims that it was not given sufficient notice about the impending project, that it was not consulted and, in general, that the local housing authority suffers from a lack of good public relations policy.

The local housing authority, on the other hand, operating in the autonomous manner created by federal and municipal law, has spearheaded more than five million dollars in construction in the city without a hitch.

With two projects for the elderly completed and one under way, the local housing authority moved into a new area of construction—housing for low income families—and that's when the trouble started.

In the simplest terms, Riverside residents feel that a 60-unit project is "too big" to be located on the five and a half acre site bordered by Crescent View, Bullocks Point and Providence Avenues. They suggest scattering the units throughout the city.

According to the opposition, the project probably would eliminate the Little League Field and infringe upon an area where open space is already at a premium.

Nobody has suggested what impact the project would have on the overcrowded public schools in the area and Riverside residents have indicated privately that they fear the influx of nonwhites. They also cite other "problems" associated with low income housing development and point to troubles in Providence and Pawtucket as examples.

Mrs. Phillips, commenting on the remark by Joseph J. Rock, chairman of the authority, that the applicants would be "thoroughly screened" asked by what authority does the housing board determine the relative character and morals of needy applicants.

To head off the project, the Narragansett Terrace Casino off Bullocks Point Avenue is being used today by the Riverside people to obtain signatures on petitions to be turned over to the state Congressional delegation, the federal Housing Authority in New York and to the city council.

Thus, the local authority is embroiled in a project with farreaching social, economic and political implications. When the dust settles, the project probably will go forward anyway because the construction is based on estimates of public needs and is totally financed by the federal government.

This is indicated by the study of the U.S. Census of 1960 which indicated that 2,057 housing units in the city are deficient (15.8 percent). The general welfare is of prime consideration.

The 2,507 units include structurally sound units lacking in basic plumbing facilities.

Planners and housing officials maintain that a deficient housing unit does not provide decent, safe, and sanitary housing for its occupants, and occupants of these units are eligible for a number of federal housing and financial aids, based primarily on the fact that they live in substandard housing.

In East Providence, according to a report to the local housing authority from Joseph L. Savick, Jr., director of planning and urban development, there are 184 nonelderly households with incomes of less than $3,000 a year who live in deficient housing units.

Officials interpret this to mean there is an immediate demand for 46 low cost housing units and suggest the construction of approximately 50 units of nonelderly public housing.

Opposing factions say this may be true, but why not scatter the 60 planned units over the city instead of concentrating them in one place. Officials say this would not be feasible because the cost would be prohibitive.

Mr. Savic emphasizes that the low cost housing is definitely needed, irrespective of any urban renewal plans. It has been suggested that nothing less than the 33-unit complex on Warren Avenue (for the elderly) could be considered.

The three cottage-type apartment buildings there were designed for elderly persons with no children and thus requirements differ greatly with those needed for whole households with children.

A spokesman for the Riverside group noted the 60 units proposed ought to be broken up into 10 units of six families each. They would not object to a six-family unit.

In a never-before released memorandum from the planning department to the local housing authority, however, official thinking on the structural aspects of the needed project is outlined as follows:

"Design considerations in the planning of public housing are crucial. For, in addition to its primary function of housing per se, every public housing project should stand with architectural distinction as evidence of pride in the community and a symbol of respect for beauty and design.

"The brick box monotony of the past must not be echoed in the future. We need more examples of imaginative thinking about design so that we really do get better and not just more housing. The respective responsibilities of the local housing authority, the architect and the Public Housing Administration must be clearly understood if a thoughtful design concept for each project is to be shaped."

The city planners said the location and size of such projects is "of extreme importance." A solid effort is required to insure that each project is truly an integral part of the community and not an area which has been isolated for the welfare of needy families.

In a city the size of East Providence, "extensive consideration should be given to the scale of public housing in light of existing private housing. The feasibility of scattered site housing with a low number of families in each structure should be studied. Great care "should be taken to avoid the creation of monuments to dullness which in themselves become ghettos of the disheartened."

Housing Agency Firm on Plans
Providence Evening Bulletin, Oct. 19, 1966

The East Providence Housing Authority officials repeated this morning that protests from local residents against the proposed 60 units of low cost housing thus far have not swayed them and the project will proceed.

"There is a positive need for this development according to data gathered by our planners and our staff and it centers here in Riverside—emphasize that," Commissioner Warren Ivers said. He is supported unanimously by the other commissioners.

The controversial housing project, slated to be erected just north of Crescent Park off Bullocks Point Avenue, was the topic of conversation by three groups simultaneously last night.

One meeting at the Neighborhood Center (old Riverside Junior High School), saw more than 100 Riverside residents who opposed the development organize into a formal group, elect officers, adopt three major proposals and ask 13 questions of the local authority.

The East Providence Housing Authority met at precisely the same time at Harbor View Apartments, went over all the objections it had heard, and decided to go ahead on the project as originally conceived.

Finally, the city council, at city hall, agreed to meet Tuesday at 7:30 p.m. with the housing authority, the city solicitor, the city manager, the antipoverty director and the city planner to discuss the Riverside problem.

City Manager Charles F. Reynolds was asked to compile a report covering the success or failure of low-income housing projects, particularly in Providence and Pawtucket.

Mayor Albert Perry and Councilman Eugene J. Amaral said no one seems to know what role the city could play in solving the problem. F. Thomas O'Halloran, city solicitor, said he'd wait for legal questions to arise, and Councilman Frederick J. Connors accused the Antipoverty Community Action Committee of actually "being against the program."

At the Riverside school, the 100 remonstrants elected Frank G. Thompson as chairman, William Miner as vice chairman, and Mrs. Norma Clauss and Mrs. Elizabeth Nadrowski as secretaries.

Mr. Thompson is a member of the East Providence Opportunity Committee.

Then they approved a motion to send a letter to the local housing authority and "the appropriate officials of the regional office of the Department of Urban Renewal" requesting "no further action on the proposed ... housing units ... until such time as residents of the affected area are satisfied that the ... project is indeed suitable ... or alternative proposals are submitted and approved by the people ..."

They further compiled a list of questions and attached these to the 1,000-name petition objecting to the development, and will send the questions to the local board for answers.

Housing authority members, meeting only a few hundred yards away in the home for the elderly, conferred with their attorney, William F. Fidalgo, and their architect, Michael Traficante, and studied the site and plans for the project.

Housing authority members immediately obtained a copy of the 13 questions compiled by the objectors and answered them at the open meeting.

They said, in answer to appropriate questions:

—There is no public copy of the proposed project at this time because the development is still being negotiated.

—Participating in the planning of the project were the city planners, the housing authority and the housing authority's staff, within guidelines set by federal regulations.

—The reason for picking the site (north of Crescent Park off Bullocks Point Avenue on a five and a half acre site) was because there was "open space, near a playground, schools, with adequate sewer and water facilities, and less people would be displaced" by its acquisition.

No price was released but the authority said the price it is negotiating is based "upon independent appraisals, that the duplex apartments blend in with the housing in the area and its details will be released upon final approval by the regional office in New York."

To the question of "what basis is used for the selection of tenants in a federal low-income housing complex," the authority answered: "need, as outlined in the definition for needy in federal government definitions." The title and identification number of the project is, R.I. 7-3.

To the question of "What action may the residents take in the event that they are strongly opposed to the proposed project," the authority answered, "Make complaints to the Public Housing Administration and to the local housing authority."

The local authority said it considered three other sites in the city, but settled on the Riverside site. Federal officials made the same survey and came to the same conclusion.

Other types of structures were considered and rejected, according to the authority because, in the opinion of experts, the duplex apartments were deemed to be more desirable.

Housing Authority is "High Handed"
East Providence Post, Oct. 27, 1966

In a statement released yesterday, John F. Conley, independent candidate for City Councilman from Ward 4, cited the East Providence Housing Authority as indulging in "high-handed actions" in the location and planning of a 60-unit low rent housing project in Riverside.

Mr. Conley listed several questions which he claims that the housing authority has not yet answered. Among these were: Didn't the Housing Authority, and not the Federal government, select the site for the project? What are the plans for the houses vacated by families moving into this housing unit? With a cafe on one corner, traffic problems at Crescent Park, and already crowded schools, how can the housing authority pick the Riverside site as an ideal location?

Claiming that the project was publicly unpopular and that public support should be a vital part of any such program, Mr. Conley suggested the following actions:

1. Withdrawal by the housing authority of their present application.
2. Reactivation of the plans only when they could be combined with the relocation of families displaced by urban renewal.
3. Submit plans for architectural competition, thereby creating a greater possibility for imaginative housing.
4. Thoroughly investigate the possibility of scattered housing.
5. The incoming City Council should name the City Planning Department as its urban renewal agent, supplemented by an advisory board of qualified citizens.

Mr. Conley stated that he is not opposed to low rental housing, but that he is opposed to the "lack of imagination" that the housing authority has exercised in the present project.

Back in City Lap
Providence Evening Bulletin, Oct. 28, 1966

A federal housing official has thrown the responsibility of deciding on a site for the proposed Riverside low-income housing project back onto the East Providence Housing Authority.

Frank H. Thomson, chairman of the East Providence Improvement Association, a group formed to oppose the development, disclosed this morning that he has received a telegram from a federal official who said that "the selection of sites is the responsibility of the local commission."

The local authority, answering criticism of the site near Crescent Park which has been chosen for the 60-unit development has maintained that the site was selected by federal officials from four sites suggested by the local authority.

The telegram from Horton H. Neilsen of the office of the acting assistant regional housing assistance administration in New York City states that "in this instance selection of the site is the responsibility of the local commission."

In reviewing the sites, Mr. Neilsen said his agency is concerned only with compliance with local laws and regulations and with certain technical criteria. Because of this, he said, the opposition group's position should be taken up with the housing authority.

"What he is saying," Mr. Thomson said this morning, "is that his people are not concerned with whether the location is good or bad for the city. All they are concerned with are the technical aspects such as whether there are good roads and water and sewer lines and whether the project complies with the zoning and building laws. This leaves the local authority and the local people to be concerned with how the project will affect the community," he said.

Mr. Thompson said that as of this morning he was not sure what steps his group would take as a result of the information received in the telegram. He said he has already received communications from Sen. John O. Pastore and Sen. Claiborne Pell, who were asked to assist the group. Both have indicated that they will look into the problem.

The EPIA has not opposed public housing but has questioned whether the Riverside site is suitable. The group has maintained that the housing would best fit into the community if it were broken down into smaller units and spread through different sections of the city.

"What we want to do," Mr. Thomson said this morning, "is integrate these low-income people into the community, not segregate them into one development."

Opponents Take New Tack
Providence Evening Bulletin, Nov. 10, 1966

Members of the East Providence Improvement Association will work through civic organizations and the local housing authority to get federal housing authorities to reconsider plans for a low income housing development in Riverside, it was decided last night.

Meeting at the old Riverside Junior High School, the organization prepared to work on an alternative plan which would be acceptable to both the organization and to federal authorities.

The improvement organization was founded last month to oppose the 60-unit Riverside project which it believes would be "an institution" for low-income families. The project is planned for a five-and-a-half-acre site at the corner of Crescent View and Bullocks Point Avenues.

The group in the past has proposed that the duplex units be located individually throughout the city.

The meeting last night was marked by confusion over the role of the local and federal housing authorities in changing plans for a project.

Frank H. Thomson, chairman of the improvement organization, said housing commission members considered themselves administrators of federal policy.

In her motion to meet with the local authority, Mrs. Berta Phillips called for a united citywide front in an effort to persuade the federal government to change its mind.

"We don't want just any low-income housing project, but the best darn project this city can get," she said. "The city housing commission is our instrument to get it done."

It was not known when the group plans to meet with the local housing authority. City Manager Charles F. Reynolds has requested a meeting with federal officials next Thursday, but that date has yet to be confirmed by the New York office of the Public Housing Authority.

Joseph Rock, housing commission chairman, and Miss Dorothy Angell, its executive director, were not adverse to individually placed housing units, Mrs. Phillips said.

Miss Angell has said the "scattered housing" plan was considered too expensive by Federal officials.

Mr. Thomson at the start of the meeting read letters of support from Sen. Claiborne Pell, Sen. John O. Pastore, and Governor Chafee. In a letter to Mrs. Phillips, Senator Pell said he had "personally discussed the matter with Miss Angell," but did not elaborate.

The group sent petitions to the state's Congressional delegation signed by 1,000 persons who opposed the project. Rep. Ferdinand St. Germain and Rep. John Fogarty did not reply, Mr. Thomson said.

Among the 30 persons attending the meeting were Councilmen-elect Samuel H. Ramsay, Jr. and John F. Conley, both independents.

Both men endorsed a search for an alternative plan.

Additional Sites Being Studied
East Providence Post, Dec. 8, 1966

Although a Riverside low-income housing unit is still being sought by the city housing authority, two additional sites are now being studied for this type housing.

At a special meeting of the authority Tuesday, it was unanimously agreed to consider sites located in an area off South Broadway and another in the Phillipsdale area.

In essence, the authority is now investigating the possibility of "scattered" low income sites. Miss Dorothy Angell, executive director of the authority, said the group is therefore, "Not ignoring the Riverside people."

The East Providence Improvement Organization, a group that favors scattered housing, has opposed the Riverside project.

Miss Angell said that if the new sites prove feasible, 20 units will be "scattered" on each of the three sites, or a total of 60 units.

The planning director, Miss Angell said, had previously suggested these two new sites as possible locations for low-income housing. Each new site is about two acres.

Miss Angell predicted that it would take about a month before any firm plans have been formulated. If these sites are agreeable, she added, federal housing officials would then have to review the sites.

Assuming that the sites are acceptable, she continued, then a revised development program would have to be made. This would determine if it is economically feasible.

At a meeting of city officials on Nov. 28 a federal housing official warned that a new plan for the proposed Riverside low-income project may cost more.

As it stands now, the authority still desires to have low-income housing units on a single five-and-a-half acre site at the corner of Crescent View and Bullocks Point Avenues.

Site for 20 Low-Income Housing Units
Providence Journal, March 1, 1967

The East Providence Housing Authority's first choice of a site for a 20-unit low income housing project is the area in Riverside originally selected for a 60-unit development which was deferred because of public protest.

Joseph J. Rock, chairman of the authority, said last night at a meeting of the group that an area off Bullocks Point Avenue near Crescent Park was the first choice of the authority for 20 units of low-income housing. A 60-unit project had been planned for the land last year, but it was set aside after residents protested, and the authority turned to investigating the "scattering" of three 20-unit projects throughout the city.

Although the authority announced one site selection, Mr. Rock declined to name others that were under consideration for the remaining two projects, and the authority met in closed session for more than an hour after the time at which Mr. Rock said the meeting had ended except for a "slight discussion."

It is believed that a site near Pawtucket Avenue and Wampanoag Trail and a site off South Broadway are among those under consideration. Mr. Rock said he did not want to mention the sites until the authority chose three, because, he asked "Why get seven different locales upset at the same time?"

In the discussion of the Riverside site, it was said that the planned expansion of the nearby Oldham School would provide classroom space for children in the project. Warren A. Ivers, an authority member, said that, based on certain studies, each 20-unit dwelling might contain from 50 to 60 children. Consequently, the sites are being measured against capacity of schools concerned.

The site is also near the "Maze" area of Riverside which has been scheduled for urban renewal, and the authority envisioned that persons moving from the renewal area could enter the low income housing suggested. Miss Dorothy Angell, executive director of the authority, said "Without public housing, there can be no urban renewal."

The Riverside site also is near an area which is likely to be developed in the Green Acres project, it was said.

The choice "doesn't eliminate one big objection," however, Mr. Ivers said, referring to a bar located near the recommended site.

Six Proposed Sites Rejected for Housing
Providence Evening Bulletin, June 24, 1967

Federal housing officials have rejected six possible sites for scattered low income housing in East Providence for a variety of reasons, Miss Dorothy Angell, executive director for the housing authority said last night.

Two inspectors for the office of Housing Assistance viewed two proposed sites in Rumford, two in the center of the city, and two in Riverside and found none suitable, Miss Angell said.

A complete report on the reasons for rejecting the sites will be written and turned over to the local authority.

The housing authority is seeking at least three sites on which to locate 60 units of housing for low-income families. A plan to erect the entire 60 units on a site in Riverside off Bullocks Point Avenue, made public a year ago, ran into solid opposition from Riverside residents and the authority agreed to try to revise its plans to erect the housing in three developments of 20 units each in different parts of the city.

Miss Angell said as the result of the rejection of the six sites by the government inspectors, the authority will begin a new search for suitable land for the scattered sites.

Inspecting the sites yesterday were Joseph V. Russo, development planner, and Frank Governali of the land section of the New York office.

Reasons given for rejecting the sites included the presence of brooks, poor soil conditions, high land costs and conflicts with the zoning ordinance.

Riverside: Phase Two

New Goal: 30-Unit Housing Project
Providence Evening Bulletin, Nov. 30, 1967

East Providence will ask the Federal Government to approve 30 units of low income housing in Riverside, or half the number in the original plan, it was revealed last night at a meeting of the city council and the East Providence Housing Authority.

The meeting was held to begin a new plan to provide housing for low income residents of the city, irrespective of urban renewal plans that are not expected to materialize for at least another year and a half.

The original plan to construct 60 units in Riverside was scrapped after vigorous opposition developed from local residents and housing authority began to consider "scattered site construction" of smaller units.

Plans were stymied after several suggested sites were found to be unacceptable to officials of the Public Housing Administration of the Housing and Urban Development Agency.

At last night's meeting there were still a division of opinion among some housing authority members and the councilmen on the merits of the larger and smaller units, but it was agreed that something should be done immediately. Thus officials settled on a goal of 30 units.

This would be about 1/3 of the low income housing considered by some officials to be the absolute minimum needed in the next couple of years.

The Federal Government is now processing a survey and planning grant application for the city's urban renewal program.

Councilman John F. Conley said the city realizes the objection of local residents to the housing but that it also "realizes the need" for the housing.

Authority chairman Joseph J. Rock emphasized that the housing would be mainly for Riverside residents displaced by urban renewal.

Throughout the meeting, Councilman Samuel H. Ramsay Jr. stressed the need for "scattered sites" for the housing rather than massive projects. He supported the plan that would give the Riverside site, located off Bullocks Point Avenue north of Crescent Park, 30 units of housing rather than the original 60.

Mr. Ramsay said his idea of the aim of low-income housing is to help to raise standards of living. He added that such an aim could not be achieved by big housing projects but by integrating small projects into neighborhoods so that the residents would be given the incentive to raise their standards.

Warren A. Ivers, an authority member, said the primary reason for having a large project was so that it could prove workable and allow others to be built. He said one large project would be more easily supervised than several smaller ones and thus could be more easily shown to be beneficial to the community.

Michael Traficante, an architect who drew up the preliminary plans for the original project, said one of the prohibitive factors in "scattered sites" is that the costs of such items as utilities would be much higher in the three 20-unit sites than in one 60-unit site.

Mayor George A. Lamb opposed the large project concept, saying it was applicable in block-tenement areas in larger cities but not in a small city like East Providence. He said a large project is "in effect, a colony."

Mayor Lamb asked whether the housing program meshed with the urban program to be conducted in the city. Mr. Ivers answered that urban renewal is the factor that set the authority to work on low-income housing.

Mr. Rock said that in 1965 the Housing Authority had questioned the city's planning agency as to how many units of housing were needed in the city. The answer came back from Joseph L. Savick Jr., planning department head, that irrespective of urban renewal, approximately 50 new units were needed.

Thus when urban renewal in the Riverside area begins another 70 to 90 low income and 100 middle income units would be needed, according to Mr. Savick.

When questioned Mr. Savick said the urban renewal program probably would begin in about two and a half years. Councilman John F. Conley said that if the housing is put up too soon before urban renewal, residents would move into it from the substandard housing in Riverside while new occupants would move into the poor housing.

Mr. Ivers asked about the possibility of boarding up the substandard housing until urban renewal comes, but Mr. Savick said that if its owner wanted to, he could fix such a house up and keep it occupied.

Councilman Raymond L. Murray Jr. asked whether the people to be displaced by urban renewal were asked if they would live in public housing. City Manager Pete A. Pakey said that such a survey would be one of the planning steps in the Community Renewal Program.

Mr. Savick said that his department expects to have the draft of the survey and planning application to be sent to the Federal Government ready by next week. It must go to the council for approval before being submitted to the Federal Government.

Regarding the residency requirement for new public housing, Councilman Daniel E. Marso asked if the residency requirement shouldn't be lengthened from six months to two years.

The possibility of nonresidents coming into the area was one of the main objections of prospective neighbors to the 60-unit project. Mr. Rock said that he had tried to explain that most of the people to be relocated into the new housing would be from Riverside but added that the people in the area were not receptive to his message.

Housing Authority Meets New Delay
Providence Journal, April 11, 1968

The confusing Riverside housing situation was plunged into chaos last night by a series of contradictory statements and behind the scenes activity attributed to federal housing officials and a private developer.

The East Providence Housing Authority met with the city council last night to ask council approval of its plan to build low-income housing.

The authority had expected that such approval would clear the way for the long delayed housing construction to begin within a week. Instead, a new meeting in New York has been requested and the authority's plans are once again stalemated.

At a meeting two weeks ago, with Franklin W. Simon, a private developer from Quincy, Mass., both the authority and Mr. Simon agreed that housing must be built in Riverside.

However, they were stymied because both claimed the right to use a 10-acre parcel of land near Crescent Park. Mr. Simon wants to put 174 units of moderate income housing there while the authority seeks to build a 100-apartment building for the elderly and 30 units of low-income housing.

Mr. Simon has offered to lease 30 of his 174 units to the authority which can then use them as its proposed low-income housing project.

The confusion began unraveling at the meeting when it was disclosed that both parties had received federal approval for their proposed projects.

Mr. Simon had the okay from the Federal Housing Administration, which agreed to provide a long-term low interest mortgage for his project. The authority had the approval of the Department of Housing and Urban Development.

Then the complications began to pile up.

About a week after its meeting with Mr. Simon, the authority was informed by Sirrouko Howard, regional coordinator for HUD, that the proposed 30 units of low-income housing was no longer favored by the federal government.

In a telephone conversation with Miss Dorothy Angell, the authority's executive director, he reportedly said he would not approve the units because of the need for more than 30 low income units in Riverside.

He also reportedly told Miss Angell that the FHA had suggested to him that the housing authority should acquire 40 additional units on a rent supplement basis from Mr. Simon for a total of 70.

With this development, Miss Angell and Warren A. Ivers, the authority vice chairman, went to New York to confer with HUD officials there.

Mr. Ivers said Charles Burns, director of development, assured them that if the authority received council approval to build 60 units of low-income housing, federal approval was guaranteed and the authority could begin building immediately.

When the authority met with the council to get this approval, Pete A. Pakey, city manager, informed the authority that HUD has requested a meeting in New York of the city manager, Miss Angell, the city's director of planning and urban development, the chairman of the citizens advisory committee and federal officials.

Mr. Pakey said Mr. Howard informed him of this development yesterday. Mr. Pakey also said he had learned that Mr. Simon was in Mr. Howard's office at the time.

Mr. Ivers reported that Mr. Howard had consulted HUD officials in New York about Riverside housing without informing authority members. Eugene Amaral, an authority member, said, "Apparently Mr. Howard has been doing a lot of work on this without informing us."

The authority also learned that federal officials have conducted several meetings on the Riverside housing situation without consulting the authority. "They've had a lot of meetings to which we have not been invited," Mr. Ivers said angrily.

"I'm confused, I don't know what is going to happen next." said Mr. Pakey. "Join the group." said Mr. Ivers.

Housing Plan Voted Council Approval
East Providence Post, Dec. 7, 1967

Approval, with qualifications, of a 30-unit low-income housing project in Riverside was voted unanimously by the City Council at Monday night's session.

The qualifications were advanced by Councilman John H. Ramsay, Jr., and Councilman John F. Conley. The former said he would favor the project, provided there will be no additional housing erected on the site.

The addition of a two-year residency requirement was advocated by Councilman Conley, recalling that the original residency proposal was put forth by Councilman Daniel E. Marso at a joint meeting last week of the council and the housing authority.

The two groups believe that the 30-unit figure would be more acceptable to its residents than the 60-unit plan. This plan was the result of the meeting of the two groups on November 29.

Warren A. Ivers, housing authority member, stated the new plan would give the city "something else to work on" while it investigates the possibilities of the "Turnkey" program.

The Turnkey program is a new one which has a number of ways of building low-income housing that meets federal specifications for urban renewal and other grants.

Chairman Joseph J. Rock of the Housing Authority stressed that the housing would be mainly for Riverside residents displaced by urban renewal.

Two Alternatives Weighed
East Providence Post, May 9, 1968

The East Providence Housing Authority last night once again met with city officials to try to settle the Riverside housing dilemma, but once again the problem remained unsolved and the only decision taken was to meet to discuss it again.

A certain amount of progress was made however, in that the once bewildering assortment of housing alternatives has effectively been reduced to the two propositions discussed last night.

On the one hand, the housing authority, which has final approval to build 30 units of low income housing in Riverside, would like to put 60 such units there.

On the other hand, Franklin W. Simon, a housing developer from Quincy, Mass., has federal approval to build 174 units of moderate income housing providing the local housing authority leases 30 of those units as low income housing and 35 more are used under the federal rent supplement program.

In a new development, it was reported last night that Mr. Simon does not have a written agreement to buy the housing site from its owner, Arthur Simmons, as previously believed.

When housing authority officials said they were unable to determine the nature of the agreement allegedly held by Mr. Simon, Councilman Raymond L. Murray Jr. called Mr. Simmons' lawyer who reportedly said there was no agreement.

The authority and Mr. Simon have been involved in a long wrangle over who held prior rights to the land.

Housing authority officials revealed last night that Mr. Simon does not, as previously believed, have a final federal commitment allowing him to build 100 moderate income apartments independently of the authority.

It was Mr. Simon's proposal to build 174 apartments upon which most of the discussion centered. The entire city council and housing authority, as well as Joseph L. Savick, director of planning and urban development, and representatives of the citizens advisory committee and the redevelopment agency were at the meeting.

Joseph J. Rock, chairman of the authority, said, "We called the meeting tonight hoping to come to some conclusion." Rather than a conclusion, however, a tentative division of opinion has appeared in the council concerning Mr. Simon's proposal.

Most vocal and explicit about their beliefs were Councilmen Daniel E. Marso and John F. Conley. "I am in favor of the housing authority building the 30 units of low income housing we have already agreed upon, stop this pussy-footing around and get the show on the road," he said.

Mr. Conley referred to the housing authority proposal to build 30 units of low income housing approved by both the federal and city governments.

Mr. Conley objected to Mr. Simon's proposal because "it is a very distinct possibility" that all 174 units will eventually be used as low income housing.

Mayor George A. Lamb and City Manager Pete A. Pakey explained that according to federal officials the maximum number of low income units permitted in a project such as Mr. Simon's was 87 or 50 per cent of the units.

Warren A. Ivers, housing authority vice chairman, warned that federal officials have made contradictory statements and that a change in regulations was possible.

Speaking for the Citizens Advisory Committee, its vice chairman, George Allen, agreed with Mr. Conley and Mr. Ivers and said, "If these apartments are rented at about $150, I feel there is a definite possibility that all 174 units will become low income housing."

The three men felt that the $141 maximum monthly rent proposed by Mr. Simons would be too high for the area near Crescent Park and that many of the apartments would remain unrented.

"Will they let half of the apartments stay empty?" Mr. Allen asked. "Perhaps in a few years the federal government will allow 75 per cent of the apartments to be used for low income housing," Mr. Ivers added.

Mr. Conley also objected to the arrangement whereby the developer would choose the tenants for the proposed 35 rent supplement units. "They can come from out of state," he said, adding "Here's where I want some insurance. I would rather see the housing authority control it."

"What we're talking about here is not my idea of scattered site housing. Just because there is one low income unit for every two moderate income units all on the same site, this is not scattered site housing." Mr. Conley said.

Mr. Marso said, "I am not enthused about the 174 units. Mr. Conley expressed my feelings very well. I would rather see 60 units of low income housing over there managed by the housing authority."

Councilman Samuel H. Ramsay Jr., in general, favored the Simon project. "I would like to see the building plans first before definitely committing myself." he said.

"Initially I opposed a large low income housing project but this proposal involves scattering low income units among the moderate income units. I think it will satisfy all concerned and the city needs housing badly."

Mr. Ivers objected because "65 low income units out of 174 is not much dispersal." He also complained that Mr. Simon could bring his rent supplement tenants "from East Oshkosh and we couldn't do anything about it."

Anthony Albanese, a housing commissioner, also opposed the Simon proposal. "I think we should have gone through our original proposal to build 60 units. There was a near rebellion when we planned 60. I'm disturbed now that an outsider is coming in."

Mayor Lamb gave tentative approval to the 175 unit project. "I lean toward this proposal but I am definitely not committed," he said.

Mr. Murray, who proposed a meeting of the full membership of all involved agencies be called, said "I really don't know enough about it to take a stand at this time."

Marathon Parley Fails to Resolve Housing
Providence Evening Bulletin, May 28, 1968

The latest installment of the Riverside housing wrangle unfolded last night with a marathon meeting of 20 officials from five agencies and departments in which little was accomplished beyond the rehashing of facts.

The meeting closed with a promise from Warren Ivers, vice chairman of the authority, that the housing authority will build 30 units of low income housing as soon as possible and will search for sites outside Riverside on which to put additional low income housing.

The housing authority called the meeting to obtain the opinions of the other city agencies on the approach it should use in building 30 units of low income housing in Riverside.

Franklin W. Simon, a Quincy, Mass., developer, plans to build a 2.8 million dollar, 174-unit moderate income housing project on an 11-1/2 acre tract near Crescent Park.

The authority has long been embroiled with Mr. Simon over the rights to the land. Mr. Simon's project and the authority's proposal to build the 30 low income apartments have both been approved by different federal agencies for construction on that land.

Since the expiration of the authority's option to the land, Mr. Simon two weeks ago announced he has negotiated to buy it from its owner Arthur Simmons.

Mr. Simon has offered to lease 30 units of his project to the authority for use as low income housing. The authority has been undecided about this proposal for the past two months.

The officials agreed that Mr. Simon apparently has rights to the land and can build independently of the housing authority and some urged the authority not to lease from the developer.

Most insistent in urging independent action upon the authority was Councilman Samuel H. Ramsay Jr. "Since Simon has a binding option, we're wasting time in even discussing this."

Mr. Ramsay said the city needs the low income housing badly. "We should be talking about other areas in which to build the housing."

Councilman John F. Conley agreed: "Forget Simon! Dickering around about this is what has held up this program. The housing authority has a job to do and it should do it on its own."

Eugene A. Amaral, a housing commissioner, was more cautious, and said the authority should wait to compare Mr. Simon's project with a 250 unit moderate income housing development planned for South Broadway.

He said it might be possible to lease the low income housing from the First Realty Co. of Boston, the Broadway developer.

An innovative note was introduced by Edward Costello of the Redevelopment Agency who proposed a program of home ownership by the poor.

"I would like to see the people in their own homes. It's the happiness of the people that is paramount. If they're not going to be happy in apartments we should build houses in the target area. If a program has to be pushed, that's it." he said.

Joseph L. Savick Jr., director of the city's department of housing and urban development, explained that federal programs to provide the poor with their own homes are available in urban renewal areas.

Mr. Costello feared that Mr. Simon's project may hurt urban renewal efforts because the substandard houses vacated by his future tenants will be reoccupied by other people, thus irritating the housing situation in Riverside.

Both he and Mr. Amaral felt that housing authority construction plans might conflict with urban renewal plans.

Mr. Savick and City Manager Pete A. Pakey said that it would do no good for the Housing Authority to wait for urban renewal, which is an estimated two years away, to begin. Both advised that the city's application for renewal planning funds would be expedited by federal officials if the city immediately begins to build low income housing.

Throughout the meeting, Mr. Simon's project and his proposal to lease 30 units to the authority was in some way the focus of discussion, with some opposed and some in favor of it.

Councilman Daniel E. Marso said, "The more meetings such as this I sit in, the more riled I get. We have never accomplished anything and nothing has been accomplished tonight. The city has procrastinated. The housing authority should take the bull by the horns and do something positive."

Federal Pressure

Complex of 250 Apartments
Providence Evening Bulletin, Nov. 26, 1968

The East Providence Planning Board last night recommended approval for the preliminary subdivision of the Broadway Village Plat, a complex of 250 apartments being developed on lower South Broadway by the First Realty Co. of Boston.

The plat will include two six-story buildings surrounded by 11 two-story garden apartment structures on a 15-acre site which adjoins the large Ferland subdivision now nearing completion.

Five new roads will be cut into the tract to service the apartments which are being built with the aid of a long term, low interest federal loan and according to federal specifications concerning facilities, apartment space, parking and recreational facilities.

The federal government also controls the rents which will range from about $115 for a one bedroom apartment to $145 for a three bedroom unit. Under federal standards, the maximum income allowed each family in the apartments will be $8,500, Joseph L. Savick Jr., the city planning director, said.

Mr. Savick said the project will "provide a relocation resource for moderate income families displaced by urban renewal in Riverside."

He told the planning board the area off South Broadway surrounding the project is one of the fastest growing in the city with 100 luxury apartments to be built immediately to the north and 32 units of low income housing planned directly behind the project.

Also due to be built nearby are an elementary school and a playground, Mr. Savick said.

The planning director said the luxury apartments will be built by Alphage Ferland and Sons. Preliminary plans call for a swimming pool, club and private streets to service the apartments that will be situated on 11½ acres of land fronting on South Broadway.

Land has been set aside for the playground directly behind or to the east of the luxury apartments with the school to be built east of the playground.

"Because of internal circulation problems" due to the rapid residential growth of the area, Mr. Savick suggested a pedestrian walkway be built between South Broadway and Pawtucket Avenue that would run along the grounds of the proposed school and along the border between the two large housing projects.

He said the walkway would provide ready access from the apartments to the school so pupils would not have to walk along streets and would also serve as a route to St. Martha's Church on Pawtucket Avenue.

Two Oppose Housing Site
Providence Evening Bulletin, Nov. 26, 1968

Two members of the East Providence Planning Board objected last night to the location of one of four proposed complexes of housing for low income families and to the effects public housing will have on the city.

Joseph Quattrucci objected to the proposed location of 20 apartments in six buildings on a two-acre site bounded by Grosvenor Avenue and Apulia and County Streets.

The federal government has recently approved the construction of 100 apartments on four different sites in a total of 26 brick-faced, two-story colonial style buildings.

"The people up near Apulia Street are really up in arms; they're circulating petitions with seven or eight hundred names" objecting to the proposed housing site, Mr. Quattrucci said.

Initially, Mr. Quattrucci complained the site is a poor one for public housing because "there are two drinking establishments in the area."

Joseph L. Savick, director of the city's planning and urban development department, argued the "drinking establishments" had no bearing and should have no influence on where the housing is located. "It's not illegal for a man to have a drink," Mr. Savick said.

When Mr. Savick asked him if he would object to the construction of apartments by a private developer on the same site, Mr. Quattrucci did not answer.

Mr. Savick explained "every piece of vacant land in the city of more than two acres, zoned residential and with utilities available" had been presented for approval to the federal department of Housing and Urban Development.

Of the 35 parcels considered, HUD approved only the Grosvenor Avenue site and three others in different sections of the city, Mr. Savick said. He said the city was "darned lucky" to get scattered site housing because "an ultimatum was practically given to us" by HUD to come up with suitable sites.

Mr. Quattrucci then complained the planning board "had no say" concerning the location of the public housing. He contended the board should have reviewed the sites because of the planning required in locating and building the apartments.

When Mr. Savick pointed out that public housing is the sole responsibility of the housing authority, Mr. Quattrucci then objected; "The poor people down there (Apulia Street) are building up a nice section with nice homes and now . . . "

Harold R. Nelson, a board member, joined with Mr. Quattrucci in complaining that the four complexes of public housing to be built in the city will result in overcrowded schools in their areas.

The two men also were worried about the possibility that some low income families would come from outside the city to live in the apartments. Mr. Nelson seemed particularly concerned about this and he told of three persons from outside the city who gained immediate admission recently to housing for the elderly "on doctors' certificates."

Mr. Savick suggested the only solution to the problem as posed by Mr. Nelson and Mr. Quattrucci would be to "prohibit all further development in the city."

Housing Project Stirs Residents
Providence Evening Bulletin, Dec. 16, 1968

A protest against a low-income housing project planned for the center of East Providence is expected at the city council meeting tonight.

The development is one of four being planned on scattered sites throughout the city by the city's housing authority in compliance with federal requirements for federal aid in the city's renewal program.

Residents have compiled a petition bearing 369 signatures that has been submitted to the city council and will be taken up at tonight's meeting.

The city council, however, has no jurisdiction over the proposal because the housing authority is an autonomous body and has the authority to select sites and erect public housing without city council guidance or approval. It is expected that Mayor Daniel E. Marso will ask the protesting citizens and the housing authority to meet with the council at public hearing to discuss the site.

The development to which residents are objecting is scheduled to be built on land bordered by Lynn, Howard and Oregon Avenues in the central area of the city.

Almost three years ago the housing authority announced plans to erect a low-income development in Riverside, but residents protested so strongly that the authority dropped its plan and began to seek scattered sites throughout the city.

Otis Pullum of 61 Dunbar Ave., a leader of the movement who collected most of the signatures, said 1,100 circulars have been disseminated in the area listing the major grievances against the proposed project and urging residents to attend the council meeting.

One of the major complaints, not listed on the circular, but made by Negroes and whites interviewed last night, is that the Oregon Avenue site and two of the other three proposed low-income housing sites are located in predominantly Negro or racially mixed neighborhoods.

The East Providence Negro Men's Civic Association and prominent blacks in the community claim the public housing has been designated for Negro areas because it would not be tolerated in white middle class neighborhoods.

All persons interviewed also claimed the project would result in overcrowded schools, lower surrounding property values and cause a hazardous traffic problem on residential streets.

No one objected to the principle of public housing for low-income families but they all complained that such housing should not be built in a middle class neighborhood of single family, owner-occupied houses such as theirs.

The site they are protesting is one of four approved last month by the federal Department of Housing and Urban Development.

For the total project the local housing authority plans to build 100 apartment units. These units will be contained in 26, two story, brick-faced colonial structures.

The project has been urged by HUD partly to provide relocation housing for families that will be displaced by the Riverside urban renewal project.

Mr. Pullum said a committee was formed to organize the opposition and three community meetings have been held to sound the opinions.

"They're placing these units in predominantly black areas. They were supposed to go into Riverside which needs them. We don't need them here," Mr. Pullum said.

He said the nearby, recently opened Orlo Avenue School, which has a capacity of about 460 pupils, now has an enrollment of 310 to 320 and will become overcrowded if the project is built as planned.

He complained that the public housing would lead to the deterioration of the character of the residential neighborhood. "The city has other areas with more land area that it can build these units on," Mr. Pullum added.

His group has requested a hearing at the city council tonight so "we can be informed of what is actually going on, so we can get the true picture," he said.

Nathan Murray of 124 Vincent Ave., vice president of the Negro men's association, said: "I believe there is no need for low-income housing for this area. If anyone can show me the need for such housing in my area, then I say 'yes,' but I believe there has to be a need.

"We do wonder why three of the four sites are to be built on the fringes of black communities and we'd like to know why. These homes range from $11,000 up to $32,000," Mr. Murray said of the local residences.

"We think there should be a black person on the redevelopment agency who could check with the people. Why didn't the councilmen check with the people? Ten sites were offered but we've received no answer on why these four were chosen and the other six were turned down," he added.

"It's time the black community finds out what's going on. We're paying high taxes like everyone else. These people are middle class, professional people. We've got to let the white community know what kind of people are living among them. This thing has got to come to a head. We should get representation," Mr. Murray continued.

He described the areas for the housing projects as "very well integrated" and he said "we live very happily with our neighbors."

Mrs. Francis Cute of 1 Lynn Ave. said: "We don't feel they're helping the people by building it here. We feel they're putting it here just to put it someplace ... to get it out of the way.

"We don't think it's fair to the people here who never had anything. The Negro people have lovely homes and they're very proud of them," Mrs. Cute added.

Joseph J. Rock, chairman of the housing authority, said the authority chose the four sites from those submitted by the planning department for consideration; the sites were then approved by HUD.

Joseph L. Savick, the city's director of planning and urban development, said his department submitted to the housing authority more than 50 undeveloped sites of more than 1½ acres which were residentially zoned, with water and sewers available, close to elementary schools, playgrounds, public transportation if available, and near a major traffic artery.

Council to Ask Housing Plans Halt
Providence Journal Bulletin, Dec. 17, 1968

Because of an uproar of protest from residents throughout East Providence against the proposed location of four low rent public housing projects, the city council last night voted to advise the housing authority to cease preliminary planning on the project.

During the meeting, attended by nearly 150 persons, and punctuated frequently by shouts of opposition to the proposed project sites from the audience, the council also agreed to arrange a public meeting at which the citizen's protests can be aired.

The meeting, to be held soon at the high school, will be attended by members of the redevelopment agency, planning department, and city council who will explain the need for low income housing to the citizens and the housing authority which will explain why the offending sites were selected.

Opposition to the proposed projects has been building since the housing authority disclosed their locations last month and that federal approval had been received for their preliminary development.

Present plans call for 16 apartments in four buildings on 1.44 acres between Roger Williams and Albert Avenues in Rumford; 32 apartments in eight buildings on 3.51 acres on a site bounded by Oregon, Howard and Lynn Avenues in the central city; 20 units in six buildings on a two-acre site bounded by Apulia Street, Grosvenor Avenue and County Street; and 32 units in eight buildings on a 3.68 acre tract at the end of Valley Brook Drive off Brown Street.

On behalf of the Negro community, the East Providence Negro Men's Civic Association has led the fight against the projects because three of the four projects have been designated for predominantly black or racially mixed neighborhoods.

All Negroes interviewed concerning the situation and those black persons at the meeting last night were indignant because they say the projects are being located in Negro areas because white middle class or affluent neighborhoods would not tolerate them.

However, the protests have not been brought solely by Negroes and both black and white have charged the projects, all of which have been proposed for middle class neighborhoods of single family dwellings, will lead to deterioration of the areas and cause property values to fall.

The protestors also claim neighborhood schools will become overcrowded and hazardous traffic conditions on residential streets will result from the projects.

The specific issue which prompted the large and lively turnout at last night's meeting was a petition bearing 369 signatures objecting to the site at Oregon, Howard and Lynn Avenues.

After Councilman Raymond L. Murray Jr. proposed the meeting, Mayor Daniel E. Marso of Ward 1 who represents the petitioners, said: "I know how my constituents feel and they are up in arms."

Mr. Marso said the citizens should be informed of the possible impact upon schools and neighborhoods and he requested the public meeting be held "as soon as possible."

When Mr. Marso asked the audience whether a separate hearing for the residents of each ward or a single mass meeting was preferable, the audience responded with a great roar in support of a single meeting.

Councilman John F. Conley said he opposed large concentrations of low income housing but that he supported the concept of scattering small housing projects throughout the city.

"I don't think there is any doubt of the need for low income housing. I'm 100 per cent in favor of scattered site low income housing. Whether they've picked the right sites, I don't know."

Mr. Conley's last statement was greeted by loud shouts of "no!" from the audience.

Edward Boisvert of 28 Lynn Ave. requested "the city council move as rapidly in setting up the public meeting as the housing authority has moved to develop the sites." He said test borings were made on the proposed sites within weeks of the announcement of their selection.

Stanley Clark, secretary of the Negro Men's Association, submitted to the council a letter from the department of housing and urban development advising that local housing authorities are responsible for project construction and maintenance.

"The location of a project is a matter for determination by local officials who represent the communities involved," the letter continued.

Low-Income Housing Action Threatens Plan
Providence Journal, Jan. 27, 1969

The action of the East Providence City Council in killing the plan to build 100 apartments for low-income families may jeopardize the proposed seven-million-dollar Riverside urban renewal project, it was learned last night.

Officials of the federal Department of Housing and Urban Development refused comment to the press yesterday on the impact of the council's decision, but one source said city officials had several telephone conferences with personnel in the New York HUD office who are reportedly deeply concerned about the situation.

Also left unanswered by the scuttling of the housing project, and apparently a problem not yet discussed by the council, is the payment of the more than $50,000 planning bill for the two low-income housing proposals that have been aborted in the last three years.

In a related issue, the council's action brought sharp criticism from the Citizens Advisory Committee on the grounds that full citizens' participation was not solicited by the council before its decision was made.

Councilman Samuel H. Ramsay Jr. made it clear that the housing project has not been permanently abandoned and that it will not be jettisoned until an alternate housing program is adopted.

The Rev. Alexander D. Stewart, chairman of the redevelopment agency, said last night, "It is highly unlikely that the federal government would look favorably on any Neighborhood Development Program project where low income housing is not under way."

The NDP is the new federal program governing urban renewal.

Father Stewart and Joseph L. Savick Jr., planning director, have said in the past that federal officials have indicated the urban renewal project might not be approved if plans to build low-income housing in the city are not being implemented.

They have also said one of the reasons for the year-long delay in federal approval of the city's application for renewal money has been the lack of low-rent housing.

The council's decision to kill the housing project was rendered under a federal law which stipulates that the city reimburse the housing authority for all money spent on the abandoned project.

Dorothy M. Angell, executive director of the housing authority, said $50,000 to $70,000 in preliminary planning funds has already been spent on the 100-unit project and the defunct plan to build 60 units in Riverside three years ago.

The money has been spent on surveys, architect's fees, test borings and appraisals and includes interest on the unpaid bills for the Riverside project.

Mr. Ramsay said the council has not yet made plans on how to reimburse the money. "It can't be reimbursed at this time. I guess we will have to put it into the budget for next year," he said.

Mr. Ramsay, who insisted the project not be abandoned until an alternate low-income housing program is adopted, said "there is a definite need for low income housing in the city. Several millions of dollars in government programs depend on the following of federal guidelines and one of the guidelines is a provision of low-income housing."

He was pessimistic about the council's directive to the housing authority that it explore the possibility of providing individual homes for low-income families: "You've got to look at the money market. Under the new administration the money will come from private institutions and why should they lend at low rates when they can make more money by lending at higher rates?"

Low-Income Housing Plan is Killed
Providence Journal, Jan. 28, 1969

The proposal to build 100 apartments for low-income families scattered on four sites in East Providence was killed last night by the city council.

The council informed the housing authority, at a private meeting in the home of City Manager Pete A. Pakey, it "is not in favor of the low-income housing project as presently proposed," Mayor Daniel E. Marso said.

The mayor said the council's decision was determined in an "informal poll" after a lengthy discussion of the housing situation by the full membership of the authority, the council, Miss Dorothy M. Angell, authority director, and Mr. Pakey.

Councilman Samuel H. Ramsay Jr. "did not agree to the abandonment of the project until an alternate plan which would satisfy low-income needs could be assured. The housing authority was requested to look into other programs available to satisfy the needs of the community," Mr. Marso said.

The housing authority's proposal to build the low-income apartments has drawn massive, organized and angry protests from residents of the neighborhoods in which the four housing developments were to be built.

At least three grass roots organizations emerged to bring identical complaints against the plan. They all contended the housing complexes would detrimentally affect the middle class residential character of their neighborhoods. They all complained the apartments would result in hazardous traffic conditions on residential streets and would overcrowd neighborhood schools.

Citizens also argued the housing, none of it planned for Riverside, should be built in that southernmost district of the city because the need for low-income family accommodations is greatest there.

However, city planning surveys show low-income housing is most urgently needed in the central city, the area in which two of the projects were to be built.

The citizens' groups gathered thousands of signatures for petitions of protest and hundreds of letters objecting to the proposed housing were sent to members of Congress.

Mayor Marso said last night the widespread protest was the major reason for his disapproval of the housing plan: "I feel I am a representative of the people and of necessity I must listen to the people of my ward who have made their objections known personally to me."

Mr. Marso said the council asked the housing authority to explore the possibility of building individual homes for low-income families: "Every avenue should be explored in that direction," he said.

"Since the city has mostly one-family houses, any complex would be the least-desirable form of low-income housing in this community. Individual homes would better fit the needs of the occupants and their neighbors," the mayor added.

A dejected housing authority chairman confirmed that work on the 100-unit project would immediately stop: "We have to stop planning, it's a directive from the council," Joseph J. Rock said.

"I'm a little disheartened," Mr. Rock said. "You work so hard on something and when it hits you like this, it's really discouraging. But I'm not a quitter. We're still the housing commissioners and we still are going to try to fulfill our responsibilities."

He emphasized, however, that the program to build housing for low-income families has not been abandoned but "what the solution is we have no idea."

U.S. Rebufs East Providence in Housing Dispute
Providence Evening Bulletin, Feb. 3, 1969

The federal government has returned East Providence's application for urban renewal planning funds because of the city's action in killing a low-income public housing project last week.

Mayor Daniel E. Marso disclosed today that the Department of Housing and Urban Development has informed the city by letter that the application for a survey and planning grant for the Riverside renewal project is being returned "inasmuch as the community cannot demonstrate that adequate relocation resources would be provided for those families and individuals displaced by the project."

The letter, signed by Charles J. Horan, assistant regional administrator for renewal assistance, continued, "Regulations of this department require that families and individuals displaced by urban renewal projects must be provided the full opportunity of occupying housing that is decent, safe, and sanitary, located in the community and within their financial means. The Riverside application will not be accepted for review by this office until such time as the city of East Providence demonstrates its willingness and ability to provide low-income public housing in sufficient quantity to meet the relocation needs of the program contemplated."

Just what steps the city will now take could not be learned immediately. The federal action returns the city's renewal plans to the status of a year ago when the application for the planning grant was submitted.

Several local officials warned last week that the abandonment of the low-income housing project could endanger the renewal program and one federal official indicated that the government would not look kindly on the renewal application unless the city shows it is ready to provide low-income housing. Thus the federal action was not entirely unexpected.

Grass-Roots Response

Duplexes for Low-Income Families
Providence Evening Bulletin, March 26, 1969

Preliminary work to determine the feasibility of building 50 duplex houses for low-income families in East Providence has been started by the housing authority and the planning department.

Joseph J. Rock, housing authority chairman, said the work will be expedited so the suspended urban renewal and housing-for-the-elderly program can be reactivated as soon as a low-income housing plan is implemented.

It is not yet known how much the duplex program will cost; it is hoped the investigations now underway will lead to a cost estimate.

This is crucial because the federal Department of Housing & Urban Development will not provide funds until it has studied and approved the proposed program budget.

Work on the program has been undertaken at the request of the city council which has suggested the duplex project as an alternative to the 100-apartment, four-site plan it killed in January.

The housing authority is not optimistic about its prospects: "As far as the housing authority is concerned, we still think the duplexes are economically unfeasible. I think they will cost too much, but then I'm no expert," Mr. Rock said.

The project tentatively calls for 28 two-bedroom apartments, 32 with three bedrooms, and 41 with four bedrooms. Miss Dorothy M. Angell, housing authority director, said, "combinations of different sizes of apartments will be used" in the duplexes.

As the first phase of work on the program, the housing authority has asked the planning department to provide a list of all available vacant lots suitable for public housing by April 7.

Joseph L. Savick Jr., director of planning and urban development, said the information developed by the 1965 land use survey has been processed by computer which indicates there were 300 lots in the city that met minimum requirements at that time.

Mr. Savick said these 300 lots will now have to be personally inspected by his staff to determine how many have been built on since 1965. Only residentially-zoned lots of 75,000 square feet or more in areas which "do not have undesirable land characteristics" are being considered, Mr. Savick added.

As soon as compilation of sites is completed, Miss Angell said the housing commissioners will inspect them and then ask for federal land experts in New York to survey the sites.

"Before the professional survey team comes into the city, we will need as many suitable sites as possible for them to review," Miss Angell said.

After the sites have been reviewed, the housing authority will obtain appraisals from which a general outline of the total program costs can be plotted. Miss Angell said HUD officials will indicate tentative approval or disapproval based on the appraisals.

As a result of the council's action in killing the scattered site low-income housing plan, HUD provisionally rejected the city's urban renewal and housing-for-the-elderly programs.

"The curtailment of the housing-for-the-elderly has really hurt us," Mr. Rock said. "We want to build low-income housing as soon as possible because we were so close to getting the last apartment for the elderly built."

U.S. Repudiates East Providence Urban Request
Providence Evening Bulletin, June 27, 1969

The federal government, for the second time in five months, has repudiated East Providence's urban renewal application because of the city's failure to provide low-income housing for those families that would be replaced by the project.

In a letter mailed to Mayor Daniel E. Marso on Wednesday Charles J. Horan, chief of renewal projects in the New York office of the Department of Housing and Urban Renewal, said "the Riverside application will not be accepted for review by this office until such time as the city of East Providence has specific commitments for the construction of low income public housing in sufficient quantity to meet the relocation needs of the project."

In the terse letter Mr. Horan said displaced families "must be provided the full opportunity of occupying housing that is decent, safe and sanitary, located in the community and within their financial means."

Although the housing authority is now exploring the possibility of building 50 duplexes for the poor on 50 different sites, the city does not now have working plans that have been submitted to the federal government for approval.

The urban renewal planning application was first submitted to HUD in February, 1968. That agency has withheld its approval of the plan for a year because of the lack of commitment to low income housing.

HUD officials first warned, at a meeting with city officials in New York a year ago, that urban renewal would be approved only if low income housing is provided.

The housing authority then drew up plans to build 100 garden apartments for the poor on four scattered sites throughout the city.

When HUD approved this proposal widespread and angry opposition from neighbors of the proposed sites resulted in the city council's veto of the project in January.

HUD reacted to this veto almost immediately by rejecting the renewal proposal until the council could demonstrate that adequate relocation housing for the poor would be provided.

The council then committed itself to the 50 duplex plan and ordered the housing authority to begin development work immediately.

When the council, two months ago, passed a formal resolution committing the city to low income housing HUD agreed to reconsider the urban renewal planning application which was resubmitted last month.

HUD's latest repudiation, in effect, tells the council it is no longer interested in verbal promises. It now wants action and has confronted the council with a clear choice.

City Manager Pete A. Pakey attributed responsibility for the current stalemate to the council and said only the council and the housing authority can resolve it.

"The administrative staff has done everything that can be done. There is nothing more the staff can do. What is needed now is positive action. The city council and the housing authority have got to make a policy decision," Mr. Pakey said.

He added, "this is the result of inaction through the failure of the city council to make a decision. The city council has assumed the responsibility to make decisions in this matter, but has not made one."

The Rev. Alexander D. Stewart, chairman of the renewal agency, said this morning that nothing will probably be resolved until his agency meets with the city council Tuesday night.

"I have to emphasize," he said, "that we were told by HUD a year ago that this was the specific reason our application was being held up. The housing authority then proceeded at full speed to do its best to resolve the problem. I can't praise them too much for the efforts they made."

The mayor denied that the council has not provided the leadership required. "The council, in its desire to make progress, is still subject to the whims of the people," he said.

"We have bowed to the wishes of the people in vetoing the four site proposal," he continued. "I think our biggest mistake was when we turned down the original proposal to build low income housing near Crescent Park."

The city's difficulties with low income housing began three years ago when the council rejected the housing authority's plan to build 60 units of housing in Riverside because of public opposition.

Warren A. Ivers, chairman of the housing authority, said his agency is no longer willing to take the initiative in developing a low income housing program that might break the impasse because of the council's repeated interference.

Father Stewart said his interpretation of specific commitment as contained in Mr. Horan's letter means that the city must at least have approved building plans ready to go out to bid.

Mayor Marso said, "when you get this type of information it doesn't make you happy. We still have high hopes that the government will favorably consider the 50 duplex plan."

Joseph L. Savick Jr., director of planning and urban development, whose department has worked for several years preparing for urban renewal, said, "I'm beginning to feel like a yo yo."

He added, "We have worked on this and worried about it and nursed it and now we can't do any more because the implementation of it is not under our control."

He predicted that because of the new setback, the actual beginning of urban renewal is now at least two years away.

Session with HUD on Housing Plan
Providence Journal, July 30, 1969

East Providence Councilman Raymond L. Murray Jr. was "very optimistic" after his trip with two other city officials to the federal Department of Housing and Urban Development in New York yesterday, according to Mayor Daniel E. Marso.

However, no details about the meeting will be released until Mr. Murray, Councilman Samuel H. Ramsay Jr. and Pete A. Pakey, city manager, report to the full council at a special meeting called for tomorrow night, Mr. Murray and Mr. Marso said last night.

The three went to New York to try and get a definite answer from HUD officials on the council's proposal to build duplex apartments on 50 scattered sites as low-income housing.

Two letters from Mr. Marso to HUD asking for such an answer have failed to provoke any response. However, HUD officials have told the housing authority and others that rejection of the proposal is likely, because the plan is "economically unfeasible" due to the cost of the sites.

Though Mr. Marso said Mr. Murray was very enthusiastic about the trip, he would not say whether Mr. Murray is enthusiastic about the chances for the 50-site proposal or some other possibility.

Warren A. Ivers, chairman of the housing authority, said last night that he talked to HUD officials by telephone yesterday. He also would not disclose what was said until tomorrow night.

The city must come up with some type of low-income housing acceptable to HUD before it can start its urban renewal program. The stalemate over low-income housing has held up urban renewal for several years.

On June 25, HUD turned back the city's urban renewal application because of the lack of a "specific commitment" to low-income housing.

When Mayor Marso disclosed last week that yesterday's trip to New York was planned, he prompted strong criticism from Mr. Murray, who said the mayor had broken a "gentleman's agreement" not to release anything until the trip was completed.

The trip evidently was planned at a secret meeting between the council and the housing authority before last week's council meeting. According to Mr. Murray, everyone there—including Mr. Marso—agreed not to say anything.

Mr. Murray, who said he headed the delegation to New York, said he did not want anything released to the press because it could be "blown up out of proportion." He also indicated that if HUD told them in New York that the duplex proposal would be rejected, the council might appear to be in a bad position.

The city council has been adamant on the 50-site duplex apartment proposal, refusing to accept anything less than a written "no" for an answer from HUD before abandoning the plan. However, it has adopted a plan to build 100 units of low-income housing on six sites if the favored plan is definitely rejected.

The four councilmen reached last night, and Mr. Pakey and Mr. Ivers declined to make any comment.

Mr. Murray said last week he preferred to make the trip public on his return, when he could describe the results. However, last night he said the whole council should have a chance to hear his report before reading about it in the newspapers.

Council Vote Dooms 35 Duplexes
Providence Evening Bulletin, April 6, 1971

Although everyone who spoke seemed to agree that their city needs a low-income housing program, the third attempt in the last several years to implement one was almost certainly killed by a three-to-two vote at a rowdy, heated East Providence council meeting last night.

A resolution, introduced by Councilman James W. Driscoll, requesting the city housing authority to drop plans for 35 duplex homes, received the support of Councilmen Martin P. Slepkow and David H. Friedman.

Mayor Samuel H. Ramsay Jr. and Councilman David A. Kenahan opposed the measure, which allows the authority to complete only the 15 duplexes already under construction.

The council took no action on a proposal to abandon the 15 duplexes as well. Although a referendum on the entire housing program was suggested several times, it never came before the council for a vote.

The Driscoll resolution begins a fourth attempt to provide housing by directing the authority to investigate rehabilitating the buildings where low-income families now live.

Duplex opponents, agreeing with supporters that East Providence needs low-income housing, were enthusiastic in their advocacy of rehabilitation. Rehabilitation, they said, would go further toward preserving neighborhoods and fostering home ownership and pride.

However, Mayor Ramsay said that yesterday afternoon, federal officials informed him that the Nixon administration has put a freeze on money for rehabilitation programs, which have been riddled with rampant "fraud, corruption" and misuse of funds.

And when Mr. Driscoll was asked how much of the city's money he would be willing to spend on renovating existing houses, he gave no answer.

Mr. Slepkow suggested that the city could possibly get federal aid for rehabilitation by offering a model program proposal.

Asked what he would do if federal officials denied such a proposal, he said "well, I'll have to take this one step at a time. I'd have to see what (Washington's) reasons are."

Technically, a shade of doubt exists that the resolution will actually kill the duplex program, since it only "requests"—and doesn't order—the authority to stop.

Warren A. Ivers, chairman of the authority, however, said he doesn't think the difference in semantics will be enough to prevent the federal office of Housing and Urban Development, which is funding the duplexes, from killing the program on its own. HUD is unwilling to build houses where elected officials don't want them, he said.

Mr. Ivers said the authority will meet Monday night to pick up the pieces of its program.

Several of the residents who spoke on the resolution during the two hours of hot debate that preceded the council vote concentrated on the relationship between the housing program and the city's application for urban renewal funds.

Those who opposed the resolution pointed out that HUD officials have told the city it will receive no aid for redevelopment unless it first provides adequate housing resources for low-income families.

Supporters countered with arguments that rehabilitation would satisfy the HUD requirement. Mr. Friedman noted that Washington has given no guarantee that East Providence will receive renewal funds even if it does implement a housing program.

Mr. Kenahan, who represents the renewal area, said he considered the resolution "ill timed." Congressman Fernand J. St. Germain has promised to answer a number of questions about redevelopment and housing within the next few weeks, and until he does, the council is acting on emotion rather than information, he said.

Mayor Ramsay, who tried unsuccessfully to table the resolution, said scuttling the housing program would breach the city's contract with HUD to construct a total of 50 duplexes, and would place the city in debt to Washington for whatever funds have already been spent.

He also said that by passing the resolution, East Providence would abdicate its responsibility to provide for its poor. At a time when leaders are needed in the fight against poverty, the council would be "leading the retreat brought about by the forces of hate, bigotry and prejudice," he said.

Reminding those at the meeting that local opposition, which he attributed to a vocal minority, had already caused the death of two low-income housing programs, he said "these opponents won't stop here. They will keep on opposing until they've stopped any attempts to help these people."

Several of the mayor's statements met with long, loud choruses of catcalls and laughter from the audience, which packed the council chamber and overflowed into the city hall corridors.

Reaction to the resolution's passage was extremely strong, from both opponents and supporters of the duplex program. Richard Botelho, secretary of the city development agency, said he was "sick" that the program had been killed.

"It's out and out bigotry, that's all it is," he said, seething. "This council has just broken faith with everyone who lives in the urban renewal area."

George A. Lamb, a former councilman, said the resolution had "just set East Providence back 10 years."

Members of the Cooperative Citizens' Committee, which has opposed the program since its introduction about two years ago, turned out in full force for the meeting and vigorously cheered each councilman announcing support of the resolution.

After the meeting, they were darting around the chamber, slapping each other on the back, saying "peace" as they raised two fingers into a V, and grasping the hands of Councilmen Driscoll, Slepkow and Friedman, thanking them for "a job well done."

The three-hour meeting was explosive right from the start.

A continual loud murmur was heard from the audience throughout the session. Before the resolution came up for discussion late in the evening, Mayor Ramsay had to interrupt several discussions of stop signs and no parking zones to call for order.

The first real eruption occurred when the council, acting on a motion from Mr. Slepkow, denied Leo J. Campbell, a citizens committee member, permission to discuss an alleged "lack of interdenominational representation concerning invocations by clergy at council meetings."

Mr. Campbell, who wanted to ask why the invocation is never delivered by a Rabbi (there is none in East Providence), stood up and shouted "why are you denying my request to speak?"

Mayor Ramsay pounded his gavel and said that unless he sat down, Mr. Campbell would be removed from the chamber. It was the first of three such warnings Mr. Campbell received last night.

After the meeting, Mr. Slepkow explained that he had moved to deny Mr. Campbell's request in the interests of saving time, and that he would be willing to discuss the matter at a future meeting.

The second major explosion came when James F. Morgan, a Riverside resident, asked to present a petition to the council calling for abandonment of the 15 duplexes under construction.

Again, Mr. Slepkow moved to deny permission to speak, and again calls of "whatever happened to freedom of speech? Whatever happened to the constitution?" arose from the audience.

This time, however, Mr. Slepkow's motion was voted down. The council did, however, limit discussion of low-income housing to five minutes a person.

The councilmen received Mr. Morgan's petition as information, listened to him for about five minutes, and took no further action on his proposal.

Discussion of the Driscoll resolution was one explosion after another.

On several occasions, Mayor Ramsay reprimanded resolution supporters for what he termed impoliteness.

When the Rev. Joseph Bracq, chairman of the city Clergymen's Association, approached the council to speak in favor of the duplex program, several persons yelled.

A number of people started shouting "time! time!" when they thought Father Bracq had exceeded the five-minute speech limit.

When Father Bracq left the platform, one woman shouted, "when was the last time you paid taxes in East Providence?"

THE PEOPLE VOTE

Before construction had a chance to begin, East Providence residents elected a new city council. Only one member of the old council, Samuel Ramsay, the at-large candidate, was reelected. This new council was overwhelmingly opposed to the housing plan which had just been approved by the previous council. It wasted no time in dealing with the housing issue in its own way. Newly elected councilman Martin Slepkow, with the avid endorsement of Anthony Perry, proposed a vote of "no confidence" for the project. Faced with the threat of a no confidence vote, Joseph Pangborn, Chairman of the Citizen's Advisory Committee, immediately proposed a truce. He suggested that the vote be postponed, that no more land be purchased, and that the appropriate city officials and agencies meet in the near future to try to come to some accord. This proposal was accepted, and the low income duplex project was granted a temporary reprieve.

The reprieve was short-lived, however, for on April 5, 1971, in an attempt to convince HUD that the Housing Authority did not have popular support for its plan, the city council passed, by a 3-2 margin, a vote of no confidence. The resolution accepted the 15 units under construction, but called for a halt on the building of any new units. This vote put the Housing Authority in an awkward position. It needed public support for its plan, yet if it abided by the resolution, it would violate its contract with the federal government. Legally, it was impossible for the Housing Authority to comply with the ruling. The dilemma seemed to elevate the controversy to the height of absurdity. Either way the Housing Authority appeared to be in trouble.

In an effort to break the stalemate, representatives of the city council and the Housing Authority met in April 1971 with the state Director of Housing of the Department of Community Affairs, Anthony Buzzetti, and other high officials of the department, including its Director. Soon thereafter the council withdrew its opposition. By the end of May 1971, the council nodded approvingly at a proposal that the Housing Authority adopt a Turnkey III housing program. Under such a program, the remaining 70 units would be built as private homes. Eligible low income families would pay a certain percentage of their income, on a monthly basis, into a down payment account; when the down payment account contained enough money to cover the costs not paid for by federal funds, the occupants would receive an ownership title. The families would be responsible for all maintenance of the home, including the cost of materials. The proposal was eventually accepted by the Housing Authority and city council and there was little community opposition or mourning.

QUESTIONS

1. Several municipal officials and elected representatives opposed some or all of the proposals. Should elected representatives go against the wishes of their constituents? Which was the constituency of low and moderate income housing in East Providence?

2. What are the appropriate functions in the division of power among the locally elected city council, the state chartered, but predominantly federally financed Public Housing Authority, the State Department of Community Affairs, and HUD?

3. How much of the subsidized housing in East Providence was in response to felt community need and how much due to federal initiatives and federal funding?

4. What are the implications for future policy of the rising opposition by segments of the Black population to locating low and moderate income housing in their neighborhood?

Chapter Eight

Stoughton

---The Success Story
---Stoughton Revisited

Stoughton is in the unique position of being the first town in Massachusetts to successfully build low-income housing. This has brought the community to national attention.

THE SUCCESS STORY

Hard-pressed financially to absorb its economic growth of the past decade, it proved more receptive to low-income residents than any other town studied. Although technical problems and slight opposition did delay final action, effective local public strategy and federal incentives convinced Stoughton of its need and desire for low- and moderate-income housing. What can other towns learn from Stoughton?

THE COMMUNITY

A Place to Live and Work

Situated outside of Route 128, Stoughton was protected for a long time from the impact of Boston's urban problems by a 19-mile buffer. However, the recent years have introduced rapid changes to the 98.2 percent white community.

From 1960-1970, Stoughton's population increased by 43.7 percent from 16,328 to 23,450. In 1970 there were 389 (1.6 percent) blacks in Stoughton, an increase of 317 percent from 1960, and 14 other non-white (.2 percent). The population growth was primarily caused by a net increase in migration, as it changed to a commuting, suburban community. Given Stoughton's accessibility to the Boston metropolitan area and the availability of developable land (over 50 percent of all land in the town is classified as undeveloped), a continued increase in its population can be expected.

Stoughton can be characterized as an industrial-residential community whose population is largely comprised of blue-collar workers. The

Table Stoughton 1. Income Distribution in Stoughton 1960-1970; and Poverty Indicators

1960 No. Families	%	Income Brackets in $	*	1970 No. of Families % Change	**	% Change
292	7	Under $3,000	348	– 1	228	– 3
1,425	36	$ 3 – 5,999	862	–21	466	–28
1,471	37	6 – 8,999	1,773	– 6	856	–22
647	16	9 – 14,999	1,916	+18	2,730	+32
167	4	15 and Over	768	+10	1,387	+20
4,002	100		5,667	+41	5,667	+41

*Correcting the income brackets for Inflation (CPI Index)
**Not correcting for Inflation

	1960	1970	% Change
Median Family Income:	$6,460	$11,699	+81

Population in Poverty	1970
Families Below Poverty level	202 (3.6%)
Persons Below Poverty level	1,001 (4.3%)
Percent of poverty households lacking some or all plumbing	2.4%

Table Stoughton 2. Population 1960-1970

	1960	1970	% Change
Population	16,328	23,459	+43.7
White	16,218	23,011	+41
Black	91	389	+317
Other Non-White	19	59	+210

Table Stoughton 3. Selected Demographic Characteristics 1970

Count of all Males	11,564	Count of all Married Couples	5,109
Count of all Females	11,895	Yrs School Completed – None–8 Yrs	2,160
Persons Age 5 and Under	3,004	1-3 Yrs High School	2,201
Persons Age 6 to 20	7,191	High School Graduate	5,190
Persons Age 21 to 64	11,582	1-3 Yrs College	1,450
Persons Age 65 and Over	1,682	College Graduate or More	1,050

median family income in 1970 was $11,699 in Stoughton—an 81 percent increase—and $11,449 in the Boston SMSA. In 1960, the comparable figures were $6,460 in Stoughton and $6,622 in the Boston SMSA.

An increase in the population of nearly 7,000 persons since 1960 has done little to alter the percentage of persons earning less than $3,000 (−1 percent) but the number of families with income over $15,000 increased by 10 percent. Yet a high percentage of the city's families (3.6) are below poverty level (5.6 percent of its households); but only 24.8 percent of its families below poverty level received public assistance in 1970 (45.6 in Boston City).

Because Stoughton's income distribution is more similar to the Boston SMSA than to other suburbs like Newton or Concord, LMIH persons were more likely to fit economically into the community.

Stoughton has traditionally been considered a Democratic town. In 1972, 45.4 percent of the voting population were registered Democrat, 16.3 percent were registered Republican; the remaining registered voters, 38.3 percent, are Independents. Although the 1960-1970 changes were more moderate than in other cities (Democrats increased by 16.1 percent, Republicans decreased by 16.3, and Independents increased by 38.3) the Democratic majority in Stoughton exceeds that of the state (42.6). Stoughton has a Board of Selectmen-Town Manager form of government. The Town Manager is the Chairman of the Board of Selectmen and is removable by the Board. He has no special veto powers and is entitled to only one vote. Stoughton also has a five-member Planning Board, whose members are appointed by the Board of Selectmen for a five-year term; while the Planning Board exercises subdivision control powers, all of its proposals must be approved by the Board of Selectmen.

The proximity of Stoughton to Route 128 gives residents of the town automobile access to other metropolitan industrial areas. Public transportation, although not as extensive as the MBTA, also provides access for low- and moderate-income families to local and outside employment. In 1968, 309 local firms employed 3,412 persons and had an annual payroll of $17,773,000. These firms are predominantly manufacturing (54.8 percent of total employees) and trade industries (employing 20.9 percent of total).

Stoughton's 1970 labor force of 9,207 increased 56 percent since 1960—a higher rate than the Boston SMSA. Although operatives constitute the largest single group of Stoughton's occupational structure (23 percent)—followed by clerical (18 percent), craftsmen-foremen (16 percent) and professional personnel (15 percent)—the occupational group with the highest 1960-1970 growth rate are managers (130 percent increase) followed by laborers (112 percent increase) and professional personnel (108 percent increase)—higher growth rates than Boston SMSA, the state, or other cities studied. Manufacturing is by far the dominant source of employment.

A relatively high percent (97.1) of Stoughton's school age children (6,876 or 29.3 percent of the city's population) were in public—rather than private—schools in 1972-73. Stoughton's school system is rather traditional, partly geared toward college and business preparatory courses. Both the percent of Stoughton's budget spent by schools (42.6 in 1972) and the amount spent per child ($711.40 in 1971) are lower than those of the other cities studied (Newton spent 45.07 percent of its budget on schools and $1,233.44 per child, and Concord 50.9 percent and $1,107.51, respectively). Stoughton's per pupil expenditure ranks 42nd in the state—being lower than Boston's $935.24. The percent of the 1971 class going on to higher education is no exception: 56.45

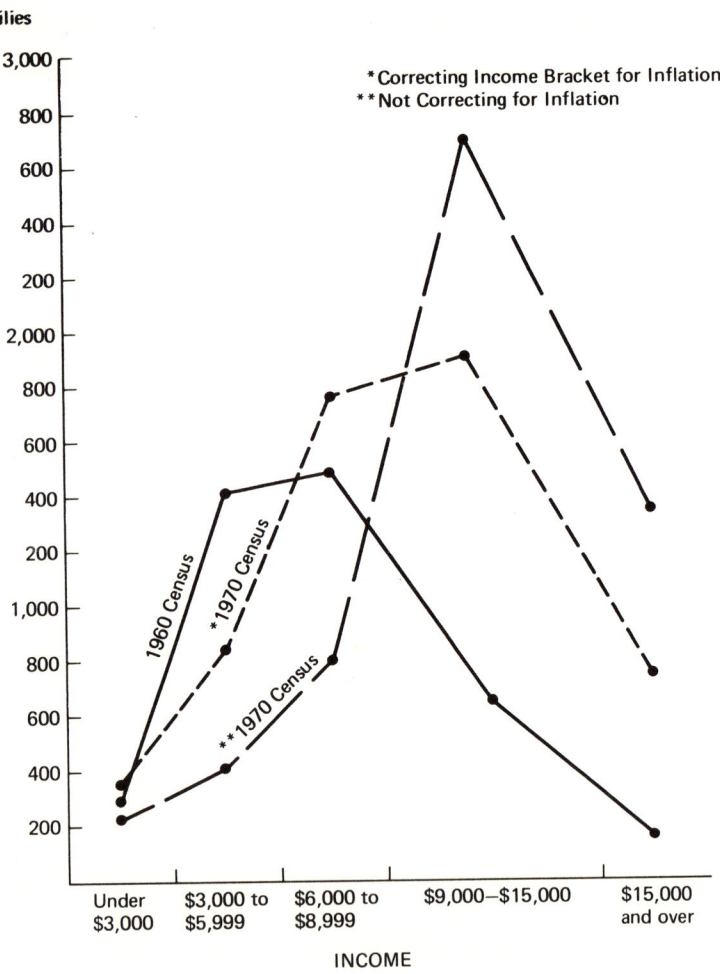

Figure Stoughton 1. Income Distribution in Stoughton

Table Stoughton 4. Firms by Industry

Industry	Number of Firms	1968 Annual Payroll	August 1968 Employees	Distribution by Employees
1. Agriculture & Mining	3	$ 32,234	8	0.2%
2. Construction	54	1,667,085	233	6.8
3. Manufacturing	48	12,286,830	1,871	54.8
4. Trans., Comm., Utilities	20	584,694	118	3.5
5. Wholesale & Retail Trade	105	3,045,505	714	20.9
6. Finance, Ins., Real Est.	10	219,836	40	1.2
7. Service Ind.	69	1,363,461	428	12.6
	309		3,412	

Table Stoughton 5. Labor Force Characteristics 1970—Stoughton

A. General

Total Employed (16 years old and over)	9,207

B. Occupation

Profess., Tech., etc.	1,342
Mgrs., Off., Prop.	767
Clerical, etc.	1,695
Sales	621
Craftsmen, foremen, etc.	1,472
Operatives	2,116
Household Wkers.	7
Service Wkers.	784
Laborers	380
Farm Workers	23

C. Industrial Sector of Employment

Agriculture and Mining	86
Construction	657
Manufacturing	3,036
Transportation, Comm., Utilities	512
Wholesale	502
Retail	1,672
Finance, Insurance, Real Estate	384
Service	1,940
Public Administration	418

percent continued to higher education compared to Newton's 73.76 and Concord's 72.0 percent. Yet the median education completed (in years) by Stoughton's men over 25 in 1972 was 12.10—almost as high as Canton's 12.30, Concord's 12.70 and Newton's 14.0.

A Place for Land Development

Stoughton's developed land consists of an urban center, surrounded by scattered areas of development that gradually extend out from the geographic, social, commercial, and governmental center. The pattern of growth, outside the concentrations in the central district, has been mainly residential, clustered according to existing roads, soils, and proximity to the use of the public water system.

According to the town's 1970 Master Plan, a considerable percent of Stoughton land was classified as undeveloped. Of its 10,410 acres of land, about 30 percent was considered developed, the principal use being single-family residential. Lot sizes vary greatly from 5,000-20,000 square feet in the center area to 7,500 square feet-2 acres in the remaining sections. The amount of developed land is expected to increase from 3,200 acres to 5,200 acres in 1980.

Stoughton has a general goal in planning future land development. Land is to be divided into suburban neighborhood areas (both residential and industrial) of varying sizes, each containing its own local center, and separated by open spaces. Existing downtown Stoughton would remain the center for the urban residential areas, as well as for the commercial business and government of the town. Future land development and uses depend upon the type of land available, water resources, sewerage, drainage systems, and zoning ordinances. The suggestions made by the Master Plan study indicate the nature of the problems in these areas.

Soil. A study of soil suitability for various uses was made by the U.S. Department of Agriculture Soil Conservation Service as a part of the 1970 Master Plan study. It was determined that much of the existing nonsewered town development is located on soil which is of limited suitability for development. This is especially evident in areas in Southeast Stoughton. Another area, Northern Stoughton, has soil with limited development capacity but, with much site preparation, could be utilized for industry. Land in Southwest Stoughton is unsuitable for building.

Water. The public water system is the key to the development of Stoughton's housing. The Master Plan study showed that, dependent upon groundwater sources, it serves about 98 percent of the town's population. The water yield is estimated at 3.05 million gallons per day (mgd), but delivered yield is only 2.8 mgd. The town's water supply could be capable of providing at least enough water for the average water use per day, which was 2.55 mgd in 1970 and is predicted to be 4.06 mgd for 1980. A more efficient system should provide enough water for maximum one-day use, which was 5.10 mgd in 1970 and is predicted to be 8.12 mgd for 1980. If no new sources are discovered, there will be water shortages; hence there is a need to develop a new groundwater source, and to connect to the Metropolitan District Commission (MDC) system as soon as possible. New water storage facilities are also needed to provide reserves for days of peak demand. Finally, an improved water distribution plan is necessary to insure that high-demand areas, such as industrial parks and high-density residential areas, receive sufficient water supplies.

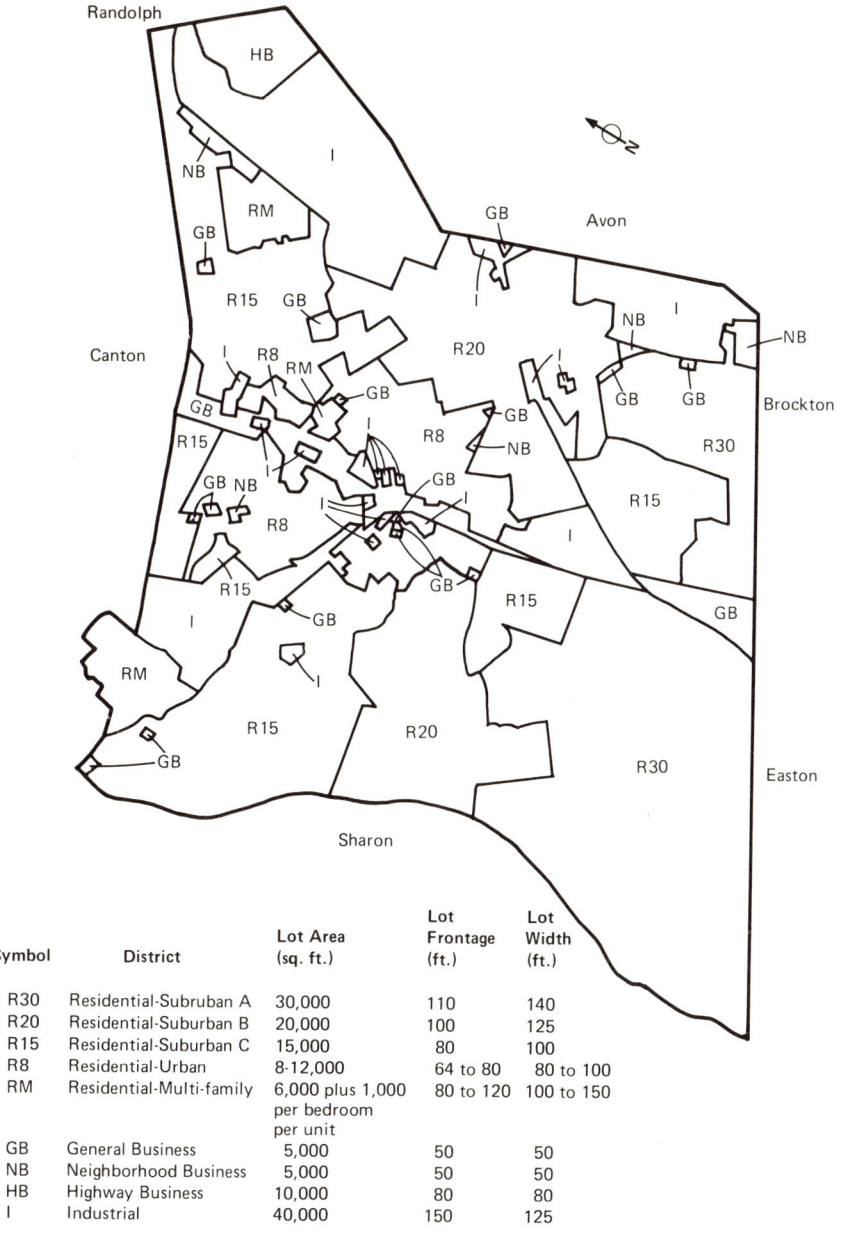

Symbol	District	Lot Area (sq. ft.)	Lot Frontage (ft.)	Lot Width (ft.)
R30	Residential-Subruban A	30,000	110	140
R20	Residential-Suburban B	20,000	100	125
R15	Residential-Suburban C	15,000	80	100
R8	Residential-Urban	8-12,000	64 to 80	80 to 100
RM	Residential-Multi-family	6,000 plus 1,000 per bedroom per unit	80 to 120	100 to 150
GB	General Business	5,000	50	50
NB	Neighborhood Business	5,000	50	50
HB	Highway Business	10,000	80	80
I	Industrial	40,000	150	125

Figure Stoughton 2. Land Use Map Stoughton

Sewerage. The Stoughton Public Works Department operates a sewerage system that connects to the MDC system. Only about 29 percent of the Town's population is connected to the public system; the rest use individual sewage disposal systems. The Master Plan study recommended the extension of the public system and additional use of the MDC system.

Drainage. Drainage is a problem in Stoughton. The Town's system consists of formal, man-made drainage facilities and natural drainage ways (ponds, streams, wetlands). Flooding problems were observed at certain sites. Drainage facilities will have to be increased in order to handle larger capacities in future years, as land development increases. To fit into the existing system and not overtax natural waterways, new developments will have to include, formal, man-made drainage facilities.

Zoning Ordinances. In Stoughton, as elsewhere, zoning laws are meant to protect the town against inappropriate development. The Master Plan study listed several main weaknesses in the zoning bylaws:

1. the zoning districts, both residential and commercial, are not sufficient in number, nor do they reflect varying use densities or the locations of public water and sewer services.
2. there are no special exception zoning uses allowed outside of the controls of the Board of Appeals, resulting in too little flexibility.
3. multi-family zoning is now only permitted in the business zone, not in residential areas.
4. there is no provision for new zoning ideas, such as cluster zoning or planned unit development.
5. Stoughton lacks underlying long-range objectives and a plan based on sound land-use concepts and community enrichment.

The Master Plan study indicated that a new zoning bylaw and map were being prepared for submission to the Stoughton Planning Board.

A Place for Apartments

Stoughton's residents are spread over a land area of 16.25 square miles, with a low population density of 1,441 persons per square mile—far less than Newton's 5,070 but higher than Canton's (900) and Concord's (626). According to the 1970 census, both the number of housing units and the percentage of renter-occupied units have been increasing. In 1960, there were 4,517 housing units in Stoughton, 1.8 percent of which were vacant. Of the occupied units, 80.8 percent were owner-occupied, and 19.2 percent were rented. By 1970, the number of housing units had increased to 6,504—a 40 percent increase. Of these, 2 percent were vacant. The percentage of owner-occupied units had increased to 81 percent, while the percentage of renter-

Table Stoughton 6. Selected Housing Characteristics —1970

A. Type, Condition, Density

Total Housing Units	6,504
Housing Units Owner Occupied	4,930
Housing Units Renter Occupied	1,442
Vacant Housing Units	132
Total 1 Unit structures	4,890

Housing units with—

1.01 to 1.50 persons/room	453
1.51 or more persons/room	56
Median number of persons per unit	3.4
Density: 1,441 persons per square mile	
Units with telephone available	6,084
Units with complete kitchen	6,472
Units with complete plumbing	6,417
Subsidized Housing Units (as of Dec. 31, 1971)	330 (5.2 percent of total)

B. Value

Median value of housing units	$19,800
Median Contract Rental	$ 107

Value of Owner-occupied units

Less than $5,000	18
$5,000 to $9,999	115
$10,000 to $14,999	671
$15,000 to $19,999	1,511
$20,000 to $24,999	1,233
$25,000 to $34,999	839
$35,000 to $49,999	100
$50,000 or more	15
Total Reporting	4,502

Rental Contracts for Renter-Occupied units:

Less than $60	143
$60 to $79	240
$80 to $99	235
$100 to $119	205
$120 to $149	176
$150 to $199	310
$200 to $299	69
$300 or more	4
Total Reported	1,432

C. Vacancy

Total vacant units	131
Homeowner vacant units (Sale)	17
Rental Vacant Units	60
Other Type Vacant	54
Home-owner Vacancy Rate	.3 Percent
Median Value Home Owner Vacancy	$21,900
Rental Vacancy Rate	4 Percent
Median Value Rental Vacancy	$169

Table Stoughton 6 (cont.)

D. *Property Assessment*

Rate per $1,000 Assessed Val.: $44.60 (1971), $44.00 (1972), change 1971-72: $0.60.

Assessed Valuation:	$37,549,400
Tax Levy:	$ 6,263,239

occupied units remained about the same—19.0 percent. Stoughton has a high percent of single-family detached dwellings (86 percent). As of December 31, 1971 the city's subsidized housing amounted to 330 units or 5.2 percent of its total housing stock—mainly for elderly persons or veterans.

In 1960, the census revealed that 87.8 percent of the town's housing units were in sound condition. The remaining units were considered unsound; 9.3 percent were classified as deteriorating, while the remaining 2.9 percent were classified as dilapidated. The 1970 census indicated that 87 (1.3 percent) of the town's units lacked some or all plumbing facilities, 26 units (less than 1 percent) were without adequate heating facilities, and 32 units (less than 1 percent) lacked complete kitchen facilities.

Despite the increase in the number of housing units in Stoughton, the rapid population growth forced the value and cost of housing to rise, as well. In 1960, the median value of a single-family house was $12,100. By the end of the decade, the median value had risen to $19,800. In 1970, the median gross contract rent was $107 per month. It is evident that any available housing is too expensive for lower-income families. Given the median value of single-family units, families in the $6,000-$10,000, approximately 20 percent of the population, cannot afford to purchase a single-family house in Stoughton. The 1970 census also revealed that approximately 15% of those renters who earned less than the median percentage of income were spending 25 to 35 percent of their income on rent—while those between $5,000-$9,999 spent approximately 20 percent of their income for rent. These figures present a strong argument for the need for LMIH. Moreover, until the opening of Presidential Courts in 1970 Stoughton had no complex for low- or middle-income families.

THE CHANGE AGENTS

The LMIH effort began in March of 1966, when a group of Stoughton residents, clergy, and local government officials met to discuss the need for low- and moderate-income housing in the town. As a result of this meeting, the Citizens Housing Corporation (CHC) was formed, with a goal of purchasing land and building a town house community.

As a local, nonprofit organization, CHC was immune from attacks that it was trying to impose an alien project on the town or that it was motivated by material gain. However, since it was aided and sponsored by the

Interfaith Housing Corporation of Boston (IHC), CHC had to avoid the appearance of control by an outside organization. The IHC was chartered as a nonprofit organization in 1965 through the work of religious leaders of the major faiths in the Boston metropolitan area. Its goal is to provide technical and legal assistance to local communities seeking to build housing for low- and moderate-income families.

Under the auspices of the IHC, the CHC developed plans for the implementation of a LMIH community in Stoughton, to be named Presidential Courts. The IHC offered criteria for selecting architects and builders, and with the CHC chose the development architect to prepare preliminary plans for the housing. The IHC provided $19,500 for the development of plans and strategy for the project, exclusive of actual land, legal, and engineering costs. Without the professional guidance of the IHC of Boston, the CHC may never have succeeded with its LMIH project; without the local cooperation of the indigenous CHC, the IHC in turn may not have realized its goal. This cooperation was the primary driving force behind the LMIH effort in Stoughton.

Initial Plan

On January 7, 1967, the CHC unveiled its plans for a 140-unit town house community for residents in the low- and moderate-income brackets. The plans called for 2-story town houses clustered around landscaped courtyards, to be built on a 10-acre site between Central and Pearl Streets. Since the plot on which they were to be built was already zoned for urban-residential use, there was no need for rezoning. A short while after the initial announcement, CHC lowered the number of proposed units to 104—a change made in part to undermine the argument that the original complex would bring in too many school-age children and overtax the school system.

Also included in the proposed complex were a community center with day-care facilities, a nursery school, hobby and meeting rooms, and recreational areas for children. The complex was to include 16 1-bedroom, 52 2-bedroom, 28 3-bedroom and 8 4-bedroom apartments. The proposed complex was planned as a "cooperative" in which each prospective resident would be an owner and shareholder, and would technically not pay rent, but a service fee instead. Each tenant would be charged a $200 down payment. The service fee would range from $114 to $156, and would entitle the resident to vote in deciding how the complex would be governed.

The eligibility requirements for residents of the project were established by the CHC, advised by the IHC. The requirements attempted to provide a fair selection opportunity for LMIH residents in Stoughton:

1. no discrimination on the basis of race, color, creed, or age;
2. income limitations of $4,000-$8,000 per year;
3. previous or present Stoughton residents and returning veterans were to be given priority;

4. persons whose primary employment was in Stoughton would also be given priority;
5. persons must meet the occupancy requirement limitations as stated by the FHA.

The total cost of the Stoughton project was placed at $2,000,000. The CHC planned to finance the complex with federal funds allocated for Section 221(d)(3) of the National Housing Act, under which the interest rate is reduced to 3 percent at the final endorsement.

However, 221(d)(3) did not provide the subsidy needed if Presidential Courts were to include apartments for low-income tenants. Therefore, in the initial financial strategy, CHC turned to Chapter 121A of the General Laws of the Commonwealth of Massachusetts. Chapter 121A provides for tax concessions to private groups who are willing to invest capital to redevelop land "if a proposed project, among other things (a) will be built in a blighted, decadent, substandard area, (b) will be consistent with an existing master plan, (c) will not in any way be detrimental to the best interests, public safety, and convenience of the town, (d) will be consistent with the most suitable development to the land, and (e) will constitute a public use and benefit." Each sponsor is allowed only one project, and it must have community and DCA approval. This method of financing Presidential Courts was made possible when, in 1965, Stoughton was certified as having a "workable program" under the National Housing Act; the certification laid the groundwork for the future development stages of the project.

Strategy and Presentation to the Community

Besides proceeding with the legal, financial, and physical aspects involved with the planning of Presidential Courts, IHC and CHC simultaneously began an intensive program to inform Stoughton residents of their activities. Over 100 meetings were held with individuals and various interest groups to communicate the proposed plans and to obtain community acceptance.

In the process of presenting its plan, CHC focused on the need for LMIH and its characteristics. The major aim was to allay racial fears, both overt and latent, among the Stoughton residents, who feared that black, welfare families from Boston would occupy a large percentage of the proposed LMIH units. The meetings were also aimed at dispelling apprehensions about increases in taxes and public school costs. Opponents who founded their position on the economic infeasibility of the project argued that, "such a project would increase the tax rate $2 to $3." CHC and IHC argued that, on the contrary, it was anticipated that Presidential Courts "could bring in an estimated $23,000 to $25,000 a year." CHC also tried to dispel fears that the added population would overburden community services and facilities. That the LMIH project was publicly proposed by leading clergymen and lay citizens in the community played an important role in CHC's strategy. Had the project been publicly proposed by an outside agency or a governmental agency, it is likely that the community's opposition would have been stronger.

Opposition on the part of Stoughton residents was weak and disorganized. The lack of any opposition groups can, in part, be explained by the fact that Presidential Courts was to be built on a plot that had no site abutters. Yet the development, as initially conceived, faced significant political obstacles. The sponsors had to petition for town approval of a plan to correct a severe drainage problem at the site. In January 1968, after a year's discussion between the Stoughton Planning Board and the CHC, a decision was made by the Planning Board to not approve the petition. Their decision was transmitted to the Board of Selectmen. The Planning Board denial was based on the fact that the financial burden to the town, in order to provide the necessary drainage facilities for Presidential Courts, would be too great. Furthermore, the Board noted that the anticipated number of school children residing in the development would place a strain on the Town's school facilities. The Board also thwarted CHC's attempt to use Chapter 121A by deciding that in their estimation the development was not in the town's best interest and would not constitute a public use or benefit.

Based upon the decision of the Planning Board to deny CHC's petition, the Board of Selectmen, in a stormy meeting on April 23, 1968, also rejected the application. The efforts of CHC and IHC to construct low- and moderate-income housing in Stoughton appeared stymied.

New Plans and Strategy

The CHC and IHC began to reexamine the plans for Presidential Courts, and to review engineering changes that might enable the project to meet specifications proposed by the Planning Board.

Meanwhile, CHC also was challenged by financial difficulties. Section 221(d)(3) had not provided an interest-rate subsidy sufficient to allow Presidential Courts to offer housing for low-income persons and families, and plans to use 121A had to be discarded when the Board of Selectmen disapproved the project. But in 1968 the Housing and Urban Development Act was passed; with it an avenue was opened for IHC to obtain the interest-rate subsidy that was needed for low-income housing in Stoughton. Therefore, IHC reapplied for an FHA mortgage commitment under Section 236. Their application was conditionally approved in March of 1969.

CHC and IHC presented their new proposal, with the change in financial arrangements and further engineering changes, to the Planning Board. The Board suggested additional engineering changes in Presidential Courts. ICH and CHC revised the plans once again to obtain the Planning Board's approval in July 1969. Plans for better drainage were introduced. Essentially, they provided for large-size drainage pipes, substituting one 60-inch pipe and a 66-inch pipe for the twin 30-inch pipes originally proposed to handle the surface water drainage through the site. The 54-inch open channel through the property was to be covered over.

THE GREAT TRADE-OFF

The circumstances leading to the agreement are not publicly documented in detail, but major events are reconstructued as follows: Water supply and storage had always been one of the most critical factors in Stoughton's very existence—overshadowing other major public issues. It had been reported, for example, that the Town Manager, Paul L. McCauley, was appointed and given the specific assignment of solving the water crisis. He had also been quoted as stating that his main concern was the water emergency and that he planned to resign after the problem was solved. If this story was true, it partly explains the Town Manager's keen interest and deep involvement in the water emergency and its relation to the Presidential Apartments. He and Sam Larsen of Interfaith played key roles in the prolonged negotiations generated when it became apparent that HUD was not likely to approve federal funds for Stoughton's water supply and storage if the town did not approve additional subsidized housing. As Sam Larsen indicated, it was this mutually advantageous relationship that made possible the working out of the trade-off.

The water storage system of Stoughton, although operating at its maximum capacity, was insufficient to meet current demands. Efforts to secure a connection with the Metropolitan District Commission water system had proven unsuccessful, and explorations for a regional solution to the problem with Randolph, Holbrook, Braintree, and Avon had been inconclusive. The Town hired Camp, Dresser, and McKee, an engineering consulting firm, which, after studying the problem, concluded that Stoughton was rapidly approaching the point when the water supply would not meet even average consumer demands. In June 1969 they recommended a long-term expenditure of $3.08 million to reclaim and expand Stoughton's water storage system and to seek out additional water sources in the area. The study of storage facilities indicated that by 1980 an additional 4-million-gallon storage capacity would be needed. Emphasis was to be placed first upon expansion of the existing water storage system, rather than on the development of new water sources; any more water, even if it were available, would build up too great pressure and actually push water back into the wells.

The water emergency was critical enough to generate deep and continuing concern among the selectmen who had been grappling with the problem since 1961. Water restrictions forbade all outside uses of water other than the watering of vegetable gardens by means of watering cans or other hand-carried vessels. No hoses were permitted. In June 1969 the selectmen called a special town meeting to approve $1.5 million for the first phase of the long-term $3.08 million program. Simultaneously, they decided to seek State permission to impose a ban on the construction of apartment complexes until

Stoughton's critical water storage problem was solved. Presidential Courts was specifically cited as an example of the type of dense-population-development which the Town could not afford from a water standpoint at that time. Selectman Woodward commented, "This may even deter the building of new schools. When it comes right down to it, we can sacrifice a little education for water."

The attempt to impose an apartment construction ban in Stoughton was unsuccessful. First, it soon became evident that the real solution to the water crisis was the improvement of Stoughton's water system. Second, the Governor signed House Bill No. 5581, which put Anti-Snob Zoning into law. Third, the State Department of Public Health did not react favorably to Stoughton's original June 24 petition. "Legally, it's a real thicket," Hyman J. Steinhurst, Associate Sanitary Engineer of the department, was reported as saying. Moreover, other Towns had attempted to institute such bans and had been stopped by the courts in Massachusetts.

At that time, and given this impasse, the Town Manager, who was committed to both the solution of the water problem and the construction of low-income housing, began to emphasize publicly that progress could be made to obtain federal funds for improving the water system. He implied that there were also hopes for reviving Stoughton's 35-acre urban renewal program, which included the Central Business District—it had been voted down at a special Town Meeting in January 1967 because of a required appropriation of $960,000 for the Town's share. He also publicly suggested that Stoughton could accommodate additional housing—including subsidized housing—provided the water system was expanded and overhauled. To this end he began to work out a collaborative solution satisfactory to HUD, the State, the Board of Selectmen, and Interfaith. In Sam Larsen he found a devoted partner. Mr. Larsen stated to the *Patriot Ledger* that his organization had ties with HUD which had originally funded Interfaith's program; "We are going to help the town in every possible way now in terms of federal funding," was a quote attributed to Mr. Larsen.

The Town Manager, in a five-page report to the Board, stated that several direct sources from the Nixon Administration had stressed that the number one federal effort in community aid would be toward providing housing. He further emphasized that "the word is very definitely out" that all public improvements supported by federal funds or state programs receiving federal monies should work towards the common goal of establishing housing throughout the nation. Finally he suggested resubmission of the Town's application for federal assistance to build a new water distribution system. In this connection he emphasized the importance to HUD officials of accepting Interfaith's Housing Plan before reapplying. HUD's attitude was reaffirmed at a meeting Mr. McCauley had with the Deputy Director for HUD, Workable Program Division, Region I, who reportedly said: "The new theme is that all roads lead to housing."

The collaboration with Interfaith included trips to HUD's offices in New York with Mr. Larsen's participation. A local newspaper reported: "Traveling to New York were Chairman of the Board Earl D. McMann, Town Manager McCauley, Consulting Engineer Rhomas Monahan. Meeting with the Town officials in the Assistant Regional Administrator's Office was Mr. Larsen of Interfaith, who testified as to the Town's cooperation in establishing low-cost housing. Town officials at this visit filed a 101 application (Federal Assistance for Public Works and Facility-Type Projects) for $2,500,000, the eligibility of which will gain $1,500,000 for Stoughton." According to reports by those who attended the meetings, the Metropolitan Development representative reacted favorably to the application. As the newspaper further reported: "Town officials are quite optimistic that the Town will be in a position to file formal application with the Metropolitan Development in no longer than four weeks, whereas in the past, formal application had been a six- to eight-month wait.

"Further, in the past it has taken from five to six months to receive grant money. The officials also seem optimistic that this waiting period can be cut drastically. The Board of Selectmen's tentative plan is to start construction on the Town's water distribution system in the Spring of 1970. . . .

"The officials were pleased to find that their representatives, Kennedy, Brooke, and Burke, have strong interest in their problem."

In October 1969 the final steps needed for a go-ahead on the project were completed. At this time a building permit was issued and FHA financing was given final approval. Construction got under way and finally, on September 20, 1970, Presidential Courts opened its 104-unit development to its new tenants.

In the major evening address at Interfaith's annual meeting, saluting persons of Stoughton, Boston, the State, and the nation for the successful efforts towards the construction of Presidential Courts, Malcolm Peabody, Deputy Assistant Secretary for Equal Opportunity in HUD stated:

> In our struggle for security, we have seriously upset national ecological balance and apparently our sociological balance as well by the unnatural separation of elderly from families and children, rich from poor and man from his work. This is the separation that must be ended if either city or suburb is to survive. Such a change will take a lot of effort, a complete redirection of our urban planning system, and the altering of our institutions at every level.
>
> At HUD, we're in the process of making those necessary changes, not only in regulations and the directions of old programs, but by instituting fresh actions under existing legislation. We at HUD have shifted the planning program from a community to a metropolitan basis; we are funding area planning agencies, such as the Metropolitan Area Planning Council of Boston, and are also requiring that each of these agencies include an analysis of housing needs and recommendation for filling such needs, particularly the need for low-income housing. . . .
>
> Indeed this is finally the way we achieved local approval of Presidential Courts in Stoughton; and this, in fact, was the first time we utilized HUD grant power in this way.

Ironically, these federal policies soon changed in the wake of President Nixon's statements against forced integration of the suburbs. Reports *The New York Times* of April 10, 1971:

> —Because of pressure by the Federal Government in 1969, this white suburb of 23,000 has a new, subsidized housing development for low-to-moderate income families. But two neighboring towns recently blocked similar projects, and the Nixon Administration's stance against "forced integration" was said to have figured in the opposition. . . .
>
> Rejection of the proposals for garden apartments came in emotionally charged town meetings even though Interfaith leaders noted that the Stoughton development did not precipitate a rush of blacks and poor from the slums of Boston, as many Stoughton residents had feared.
>
> The controversy surrounding the efforts of Interfaith in the Boston area point up what is involved in tense suburban housing struggles across the country. . . .
>
> Federal policies play an important role here. The Department of Housing and Urban Development was able, through the leverage of Federal funds, to affect the Stoughton development.
>
> In the past, the Department of Housing and Urban Development quietly withheld funds from a few communities across the country for excluding federally subsidized housing, but just as the department was preparing a stronger stance last fall, the issue was elevated to the White House. President Nixon made it clear that the Administration was opposed to using Federal funds as a leverage for bringing subsidized housing to the suburbs.
>
> A few days after Randolph rejected the Interfaith project, Representative James A. Burke, Democrat of Massachusetts, announced in Washington that the Federal housing agency had approved a $780,000 water and sewer grant for Randolph. The application had been pending since last July.

STOUGHTON REVISITED

As a general rule, most studies focus on the relatively early stages of housing controversies in suburban communities. Few suburbs, if any, have been revisited after an initial successful or unsuccessful effort to introduce low-income housing. This practice has inhibited a broader understanding of the issues involved, frustrated efforts to gain a longer time perspective, and makes it difficult to contrast predictions made during the debate of the housing proposal with the actual events which subsequently occurred. If some housing units were constructed, was the project completed according to expectations of proponents and exponents? Or were the worst fears of the opponents realized?

"Stoughton Revisited" is written with this shortcoming in mind. It aims to broaden the understanding of low-income housing controversies and to supplement extant literature. More specifically, it presents a picture of the implementation and evolution of the project. The purpose of the examination is not to indicate merely who was right or wrong in initial arguments, but rather what can be learned from the experience, three years after the construction of Presidential Courts (P.C.). More specifically, the following aspects provided the framework for the study: (1) who lives in P.C. today and why?, (2) how do P.C. residents feel about the project and life in it?, (3) what kind of leadership and social relationships developed in P.C. and how well does its co-op government work?, (4) what kind of relationships have developed between the P.C. community and Stoughton?, (5) so far, which of the major hopes and fears of both exponents and opponents have materialized?

Quantitative data were obtained mainly from a survey administered to P.C. residents and their neighbors (at different distances from the project). The survey was conducted on a Sunday afternoon, in order to gain a representative response and to reduce the usual wave-like reactions of respondents anticipating the interviewers' visits in a small community. Forty-four of the 104 households were interviewed (an additional 15 families present refused to collaborate) and an equal number of neighbors were polled.

To verify and reformulate assumptions reflected in the quantitative data, members of the research team also employed the following techniques: (1) Participatory observations over a period of time by team members who attended Board of Directors and Co-op general meetings, as inconspicuously as possible mingled informally with a number of residents, and, in general, participated in several informal activities in P.C., (2) informal, in-depth interviews with owners of stores in the vicinity of the project and with schoolmates of P.C. children, (3) informal discussions with Stoughton officials, (4) review of Co-op records and data provided by the Board of Directors of the Co-op, which approved in advance the observation team's activities in P.C. and permitted the observation of certain community functions. The Board was promised—and given—a copy of the aggregate responses to the questionnaire. Interfaith collaborated by providing some information.

It is reasonable to assume that personal values and interpretations have been inadvertently injected in "Stoughton Revisited." An effort was made to indicate the source of the material presented so that the reader could better assess the degree of the information's objectivity.

The Residents of Presidential Courts

Construction of Presidential Courts was completed in December 1970—three years after the initial proposal. The community conflict it generated stemmed from the following apprehensions: (1) the need for low-income housing is insignificant, (2) blacks will take over the town, (3) there will be an enormous strain upon the school system, (4) increased money will be needed for amenities, (5) outsiders and malcontents will immigrate into the town from the Boston region. These fears created the climate in which the new community was born.

The general location in which P.C. was constructed intensified rather than dispelled this negative, fear-producing climate. It was a wooded section of the town formerly used as a training ground for the National Guard. This area—sought by the School Superintendant for possible future school expansion—was also used by the neighborhood's younger population as their favorite playground and as a shortcut to the elementary and high schools. At other times, the site was used extensively by the teen-age population of the community as a favorite night time parking spot for "summer time activity"—having thus acquired the territorially defined name, "Paradise Field." It is therefore reasonable to accept the claim that the take-over of the site by P.C. did not reduce the prevalent negative predisposition toward the project; the concept of turf and territoriality may well have accentuated existing negative community feelings.

During the construction of P.C. there was a small fire—one whose origin was not specified—but, according to some observers, directly related to the antagonistic attitudes toward the project. With this exception P.C. was built without major mishap—a fact which did not silence some of its earlier critics. "That dump will burn down before the year is out.... The construction is shoddy, third-class workmanship," proclaimed some members of the Stoughton Housing Authority. In spite of this criticism, P.C. today looks neat, pleasant, relatively well-constructed and maintained. The 4 2-story courts—Jefferson, Jackson, Roosevelt, and Wilson—are situated so as to provide a smaller, more individualized "neighborhood" clustering in close proximity to the main community building for general activities. The Recreation Hall provides ample space for auditorium activities and large meetings. Laundry machines are also located in the Hall, rather than being dispersed within each court, and thus increase social interaction among residents.

In March 1973—when the revisiting took place—all 104 units of P.C. were occupied. Although detailed records were not made available, it was estimated that most of the original residents (approximately 70 percent) are still living in P.C. Since the establishment of P.C., only three families have been evicted for unbecoming and undesirable conduct; three families have been taken to court for not paying "carrying charge" (rent), but are still residents and Co-op members.

The racial composition is as follows:

Race	Apartments
White	88
Black	13
Other (Spanish-speaking)	3

Total: 104 units

While only 12 percent are blacks, this percentage exceeds that of blacks in the Census Tract in which P.C. is located (#4563), in the adjacent

Census Tract (#4564), or in Stoughton as a whole (6.6 percent blacks).

Elderly persons, as well as younger individuals, and families with children occupy P.C.:

Type	Apartments
Elderly (7 couples, 3 individuals, all white)	10
Nonelderly	94
Total	104

The present "carrying charge" (rent) for each type of apartment unit is as follows:

Number of Bedrooms	Number of Apts	Basic Rent*	Market Rent*
1	14	$114	$207
2	52	140	254
3	28	151	272
4	8	160	282

(Including utilities, heat, range, and refrigerator.)

*Tenants qualifying pay basic rents; those earning in excess of qualification pay 25 percent of income up to an income of $6,210 for one person, $7,620 for two persons, $7,695 for three persons, $8,100 for four persons, $8,500 for five persons. Individuals earning in excess of $6,210 pay market rates.

It was not possible to ascertain the exact number of children—records were not made available. The mean number is 2 for the families surveyed. The Stoughton Board of Education reported 99 children as residents of P.C. attending public schools in 1972-1973. Interfaith Inc. claimed that of the 96 P.C. school-age children (1970), 53 came from Stoughton and 43 from other towns.

Most of the original P.C. residents lived outside of Stoughton, prior to moving into the project. Six of the first 13 black families were prior residents of Stoughton; 14 families were public welfare recipients (9 on AFDC), of which 9 were prior residents of Stoughton. The percentage of initial residents who came from outside Stoughton is higher than the original agreement, which stipulated at least 60 percent Stoughton residents, 40 percent to come from other locations. Apparently in the beginning it was difficult to attract local applicants, but a year and a half after the project was occupied, the situation has reportedly been reversed.

The survey indicated that 11 percent of the present residents were living in Stoughton before moving to P.C., 53 percent were from Boston (11 percent from Mattapan), and 36 percent from neighboring towns. The predominant reason for which present residents chose to live in P.C. was the low-housing cost. Location and the Co-op arrangement rated second and third respectively. Fifty percent of the residents first heard about P.C. through word of mouth, rather than through Interfaith's publicity (7 percent). Twenty-five percent learned of it through newspapers.

Most of the present residents have an income between $4,000-$8,000 per year, 13 percent have incomes between $8,000-$12,000, and only 17 percent have incomes less than $4,000. It is difficult, therefore, to call P.C. a low-income housing project in the conventional sense—it is rather a moderate-income housing development. Sixty-three percent of the residents surveyed were high school graduates and 17 percent college graduates.

The concern that P.C. residents would compete with local residents for jobs was not warranted. Ninety percent of those questioned work outside Stoughton; only 10 percent in the town. Ninety-six percent of the P.C. residents commute to work by private cars; only 4 percent use public transportation.

Family and friendship ties are difficult to assess. Forty-nine percent reported that their friends are located outside Stoughton; 24 percent in Stoughton, but outside P.C.; 10 percent in P.C.; 10 percent equally in P.C. and outside the project. Sixty-seven percent do not belong to any local organization, while the remaining 33 percent do.

To the extent that immediate future plans to relocate are indicators of identification with the community or satisfaction with it, most P.C. residents plan to continue living in the project. Seventy percent reported they are not likely to relocate in the immediate future; only 24 percent are likely to move, and 3 percent do not know. In response to another question, this was reconfirmed. When asked where, ideally, they would like to live, 38 percent reported in P.C., 14 in Stoughton, but outside P.C., and 48 percent outside Stoughton. The persons in the latter category seem to be the most upwardly mobile—thus indicating less stake in the community and minimal interest in integration.

Of the residents responding to the questionnaire, the following groups were involved in the occupations indicated:

Craftsmen, foremen	40 percent
Service workers	13 percent
Retired	13 percent
Managers, officials, proprietors	7 percent
Operatives	7 percent
Housewives	7 percent
Miscellaneous	13 percent

The Cooperative Way of Life

The key to understanding P.C. as a community and assessing its level of human transactions within a broader social context is its cooperative organization and governance. For this pattern affects both the behavior of its residents and the administration of its community affairs. Fundamentally the residents of housing cooperatives like P.C. are not ordinary tenants, but partners in a social enterprise and co-owners of their immediate residential community. The effort, therefore, to review P.C. also should be placed within the special perspective of cooperative ownership and its ideological pattern.

Cooperatives and Cooperative Housing

Since their early beginnings, cooperative movements, first in England (Rochdale Society of Equitable Pioneers) and continental Europe, and later in this country, through such organizations as the United Housing Foundation, the Middle-Income Housing Corporation, and the Foundation for Cooperative Housing, have reflected two major characteristics: an ideological motivation and a distinct organizational structure. The fundamental motivating force was not to merely lower costs and meet needs, but also to consciously establish cooperative housing as a fundamental ideological principle.

The literature about cooperative housing, including Interfaith's, suggest the basic principles:

> The cooperative approach to housing instills a pride of ownership resulting in a deeper interest in maintaining the property and participating in civic affairs. A cooperative is operated on a democratic basis. It gives the residents a greater insight and appreciation of the democratic process in general. Cooperative residents normally occupy the premises with their fellow residents and learn to work together for the overall betterment of the project and the community. This working together makes for better understanding between individuals of different backgrounds and income levels.

The benefits which accrue to members of housing cooperatives also include significant economic and pragmatic considerations:

1. the absence from the monthly housing cost of owner's profit inherent in most rental projects;
2. income tax advantages:
    a) in computing the overall housing cost, the members are entitled to deduct from their gross income their proportionate share of real estate taxes and mortgage interest paid by the cooperative. At the end of each year the cooperative will advise each member of his proportionate share of the total amounts paid by the corporation for mortgage interest and real estate taxes. This will be of significance to those members whose status is such that it is in their financial interest to itemize deductions on their income tax returns. The actual amount of any tax benefit will depend upon the

income of the taxpayer, as well as his deductions and tax bracket;

b) a member of a cooperative has available to him the same basic federal income tax advantages available to a homeowner who sells his home and purchases a new one. If a person sells or exchanges his principal residence at a gain, the gain is taxable. However, if within the year before or the year after the sale, the seller buys and occupies another residence, the gain is not taxed at the time of the sale if the cost of the new residence equals or exceeds the adjusted sales price of the old residence;

3. rental schedules usually include an allocation for vacancy loss. In a cooperative, the monthly charges usually include only such income losses, if any, as have actually been incurred;
4. maintenance costs in a well-operated cooperative are minimized, since experience has shown that owners take better care of their property. Cooperative members frequently handle the redecoration of their units on a "do-it-yourself" basis, thus eliminating this as a project expense;
5. a cooperative is operated on a nonprofit basis. Thus, increases in the monthly housing cost are limited to actual increases in operating costs;
6. if a cooperative is successfully operated, a modest equity accrued upon resale may result, subject to limitations set forth in the bylaws.

In short, co-op members ("tenants") enjoy the status and economic benefits of homeownership without making the large investment usually required for acquiring a house.

In spite of this framework—and frequently because of it—cooperatives have experienced major difficulties. Vulnerable to the usual problems of regular business (poor management, high overhead, insufficient capital) they also experience special problems related to their cooperative structure, as well as conflicts inherent in any business-ideology combination. In fact, most failures are attributed first to poor management, and, second, to poor application of fundamental cooperative principles and methods.

Two fundamental sources of conflict exist: one concerns the initial leadership establishing the co-op, the other relates to conflicting interests inherent in most co-op structures.

Most cooperative housing complexes are now initiated, sponsored and developed by a nonprofit agency which has been organized, financed, and directed for this purpose. Interfaith was such an agency. They often plan and, sometimes, build the project before the residents are selected. In such cases members of the sponsoring agency act in the beginning as members of the board of directors of the co-op until the residents elect their own board. They provide technical and legal services, establish the cooperative, its leadership, the corporate structure and its bylaws, make financial arrangements, and in general, secure the beginning essentials of community life. This early stage is a delicate transitional period which may become a source of conflict between the residents and the sponsoring agency—particularly if the "outside" managing agency unduly prolongs its leadership role at the expense of local leadership.

Another source of friction is the relationship between board and management functions. First, there is potential for conflict between strictly business tasks of the board and tasks designed to enhance efficient participation of co-op members in the democratic administration of the project. The board performs the dual, and usually antithetical, role of businessmen and community resident leaders. Moreover, board members themselves (and all residents) are both tenants and landlords, expected to act equitably and in the interest of both—frequently conflicting—sides.

Second, the board of directors, determining policy and being responsible for the budget and all financial matters, must delegate managerial functions to a capable manager acceptable to the mortgagee. However, there is a delicate line of demarcation between the board's policy making and management's functions of implementation. Theoretically the board determines policy which is implemented by management—but real life activities are not neatly separated into one or the other category. Thus, the management of cooperatives has special maintenance problems attributable to complex decision-making processes which involve both the board and the residents.

Organization of Presidential Courts

The most critical management problem which P.C. faced was the episode culminating on August 31, 1972, in the dismissal of Interfaith by the residents and their Board of Directors. While all the reasons are not quite clear, the claim was made that Interfaith provided inadequate managerial-fiscal services to P.C. Perhaps this was due to Interfaith's structure and inexperience—particularly to lack of coordination between the Fiscal and Management Departments of Interfaith. A contributing factor seems also to have been the inadequate involvement of Interfaith's Director in management activities and supervision of the Fiscal Department. This was accentuated during the Director's illness and absence at a critical stage of relationship with the residents.

Interfaith suggests that the reason for the break in relationships was attempts to establish tenants' committees designed to increase residents' participation and to decrease the concentration of administrative power in a few persons. This was antithetical, suggests Interfaith, to the views of the Board of Directors, which saw the move as a threat to its power. Finally, Interfaith's man-on-the-scene and his supervisor in the Management Division of Interfaith frequently disagreed—particularly regarding the establishment of committees. Whatever the reasons, the result was an almost complete communications breakdown between P.C. residents and Interfaith. Animosity rose on both sides.

The view of the Board of Directors of P.C. is that Interfaith sought in October 1971 a management fee increase from $9,000 (5 percent of gross) to $18,000 (10 percent of gross). Interfaith denies this—typical of the conflicting information and varied interpretations encountered in the effort to reconstruct events.

An undisputable fact is that in mid-1972 the Cooperative requested HUD to release it from the management-agent contract. HUD investigated the situation and concluded that (1) a genuine dissatisfaction among the Cooperative owners existed regarding Interfaith's management, (2) in spite of HUD's efforts to resolve the conflict, the Co-op owners were reluctant to accept Interfaith, and (3) the Co-op's substitute Management Agent was acceptable to HUD. Consequently, HUD acceded to the request of the Co-op.

The Management Agent

The present Managing Agent who replaced Interfaith is Eastern Housing Cooperation Association Inc.—also paid 5 percent of the gross. The survey of residents indicated a general satisfaction with the present management and its relationship to the Board of Directors. In fact, the change of management (and the subsequent performance of the new agent), was viewed by the residents as follows:

Improvement	45 percent
Same	25 percent
Deterioration	10 percent
Don't know	20 percent

The management agency oversees much of the Co-op's work under the Board's supervision; as such, it is inevitably more involved in actual operations and in creating a climate of relationships than would be suspected. Its representatives attend all Board meetings and some meetings of residents, thereby influencing policy making.

The management frequently acted to legitimize the authority and decisions of the Board of Directors—serving also as a buffer between Board and residents.

In consideration of eviction notices to Co-op members, the Management's Representative noted:

> These people (the residents) are first and foremost human beings. They should and must be on time with their rent; but exceptions should be made. Certainly we're not here to hurt them.

The residents responding to the survey were generally satisfied with the way responsibilities between the Board and management are divided:

Positive	85 percent
Negative	15 percent

Residents are also satisfied with the manner in which maintenance work is carried out by management:

Satisfied	79 percent
Dissatisfied	21 percent

The Board and Its Dynamics

The conflict with Interfaith—and indeed the story of P.C.—is intricately related to the composition, function, and dynamics of the present Board of Directors.

The P.C. Cooperative functions as a corporation. Its Board of Directors makes policy decisions; the cooperative resident has the right to choose Directors—not unlike a stockholder in a corporation—but is supposed to participate in its administration. Each unit in the cooperative has one vote.

> The cooperative functions through its Board of Directors, which acts on behalf of the member. The Board performs important duties such as engaging a management agent acceptable to the mortgagee and to the FHA for the operation of the project; establishing eligibility standards for admission to membership; determining the degree and type of maintenance and service; promulgating rules and regulations pertaining to use and occupancy of the premises; and adopting an operating budget subject to the approval of the FHA, which must reflect carrying charges adequate to meet the costs of operation. Thus the voting right means that the member participates through his elected representatives in the management of the project's affairs. Each member should bear in mind that the management agent takes its assignments from the President of the Board of Directors, speaking for the Board, and not from individual members. A cooperative that harbors irresponsible factions which are at odds creates an undesirable image. Property values could be adversely affected in a project known for its irresponsible actions. The elected Board of Directors should receive the full support of all the members. Full support does not preclude constructive criticism. If necessary, any Board member who is not properly fulfilling his duties may be removed by a vote of the members as prescribed in the bylaws.

While in theory co-op members should be intimately involved in administering the co-op, our observers noted that this option is rarely exercised. This apparently stems from the climate generated by the board itself and the way board members exercise their leadership.

How representative is this particular board and how typical its members? It includes one secretary working for the State legislature, an accountant, a retired man, and two blacks. All seem to function above the capacity of the average resident. As one board member noted:

There isn't one board member who isn't strong on ability. You must have a board of directors which knows what it is doing and is not getting the runaround; and we have had such a board since we took over in December 1971.

Expertise and compassion are the key words of self-characterization by the board. The board president feels that board member relationships are based on an equalization of roles. This was not corroborated by some of our observers. In fact, one called attention to the fact that in both the monthly residents' and board meetings, equal participation was not the general rule.

While they are residents themselves, board members seem to act frequently as outsiders. They see themselves as the embodiment of the co-op's purpose and power. Not only do they identify with the collectivity, but they also make it a part of their own individual identity.

Board members serve without pay—a fact frequently mentioned by them. Most members see their role as a sacrifice without rewards other than the satisfaction from the co-op's success. In the president's view:

> The present board members have much responsibility and spend endless hours with no compensation. In effect we have a civic responsibility. While our decisions are unpopular, we keep most things in the strictest of confidence. As to why we all serve, that is some of the reason. But let me tell you, there is no prestige; if you want prestige from this job you might as well forget it.

One of the dominant influences of the board upon its residents stems from its power to screen applicants, determine the characteristics of future members, and to issue eviction notices. Through the tenant selection process, the board determines the image of the co-op to the external community. In so doing the board views itself as better than and different from the residents as a whole:

> We know what's right, and they (the residents) don't seem to understand. It's difficult for them to realize that in fact they are all owners and all of this property is theirs. As the board, we must educate them, and that's a hard problem. There is a lack of understanding in these people, and we must break that barrier. The possibility of educating members, though, is a slow process.

Despite the board members' relative detachment and feeling of superiority, resident reaction in the survey was generally favorable to the board:

Very satisfactory	21 percent
Satisfactory	63 percent
Unsatisfactory	7 percent
Very unsatisfactory	9 percent

Tenant Selection

Tenant selection—a crucial process determining P.C.'s population and standards—became a controversial issue even before the construction of the project. As reported in "Stoughton—A Success Story," Interfaith and the Town clashed over authority for tenant selection, determination of tenant characteristics, and general procedures. Much of the controversy centered on whether tenant selection was to be color-and-income blind or was to be designed to secure a proportion of minority families.

The original Tenant Selection Committee was immediately confronted with complex issues and misunderstandings. One resulted in the resignation of Selectman Goulston on November 20, 1970, because: "I do not wish to serve on a Selection Committee when I have no selection to make." Mr. Goulston was apparently referring to both his advisory capacity as a member of the Committee and to his understanding that Interfaith had the final word of approval.

The President of P.C. responded as follows:

> One of the statistics to bear in mind is that the total number of minority people that have applied to Presidential Courts has been less than 54, and if we were to give significant preferential treatment to Stoughton applicants, we would not be able to achieve our goal of representative integration. It was with this in mind that I said that no more than 50 percent of the applicants should be from Stoughton.
>
> As a member of the Board of Interfaith Housing, President, and a member of the Tenant Selection Committee of Presidential Courts, I was at the meeting in which Mr. Goulston was invited to become an advisory member of the Tenant Selection Committee. There was no effort to deceive Mr. Goulston or anyone else at the meeting as to the status of the advisory members. It is interesting that the other advisory member to the committee fully understood that it was an advisory position and not a voting position. Many of the statements I have read attributed to Mr. Goulston are full of half-truths, which I feel are designed to deliberately mislead. From some of Mr. Goulston's comments that I have read, it would seem that for the past four years, we of Interfaith have had nothing but smooth sailing and cooperation from the Town Fathers. Anyone remotely close to the situation knows that this was not the case and probably looks upon Mr. Goulston's current efforts as a continuation of the types of "cooperation" that we of Interfaith have received in the past.
>
> When serious thinkers try to find a rationale for Mr. Goulston's actions, they probably conclude that his actions are completely inappropriate responses to the situation. It wouldn't be surprising if the people in Stoughton have already heard enough of one individual's dissatisfaction with the situation and are probably tired of the constant fanning of the smouldering issue.

Regarding the latter accusation, Interfaith denied that any applications had been approved without the Committee's review: "There is a small group of people who have come to our office and paid the entire amount necessary to move in. We had to give them a receipt, and with that we sent a reservation agreement. In fact, these people were accepted subject to FHA approval. This violation had effects beyond the issue of tenant selection. . . . It resulted in further misunderstandings between the Board of Selectmen and Interfaith. Selectmen frequently complained of a "lack of goodwill on the part of Interfaith. . . . The Board bent over backwards to please Interfaith and made many concessions to enable the construction of the project. But everything we asked for has been denied. . . . We asked for a list of Stoughton applicants . . . we were shown a list of people allegedly from Stoughton but unknown to us."

The *Stoughton Chronicle* reported the following incident, related to the quality of the initial tenant selection:

> Mrs. Elizabeth LaFrance capped a week of controversy over tenant selection at the Presidential Courts apartments by moving into a 4-bedroom apartment on her own authority early yesterday. Sporting a "reservation agreement" from the Interfaith Housing Corporation which said she had paid rent for the period from November 16 to November 30, Mrs. LaFrance pulled up in a pickup truck and unloaded several cartons of household goods into the apartment. Explaining her move to construction men still working on neighboring apartments in the 104-unit complex, Mrs. LaFrance awaited what she thought was an inevitable attempt by IHC to have her move out.
>
> Instead Jehue N. Smith, an IHC representative, arrived an hour later to hand her the keys to the apartment and to offer her a job as IHC's temporary maintenance and security representative. Mrs. LaFrance promptly accepted the offer, which carries an unspecified salary plus temporary free rent. Mr. Smith's offer, he explained, was IHC's way of avoiding problems that could result from calling Mrs. LaFrance a tenant.
>
> Mr. Smith said no other occupants will be allowed in the development until the end of next week, when final approval of tenants' applications will have been made by IHC. Should other tenants try to move in this weekend, he said, IHC will have to take a stronger stand. He did not add, however, that he does not think any of the people now holding reservation agreements will be denied apartments at the development. Certainly this challenged any claim of the careful tenant selection process that Interfaith had promised.

In spite of these difficulties, Interfaith seemed satisfied with the initial selection, noting that "at least half of the residents selected were from Stoughton" and that "successful orientation sessions were held for new occupants as each of the four courts was filled." Jehue Smith, Interfaith's Management Director conducting the orientation sessions, claimed that the selected residents formed an integrated group racially, ethnically, economically, and in terms of age—"a group of cooperative owners who will gradually assume full responsibility for the operation of P.C."

Another complication related to selection of residents arose from Interfaith's failure to request an FHA rent subsidy when the mortgage was negotiated. As a result, Interfaith was forced to rent the apartments only to applicants who could pay the full rent. However, Interfaith did apply to the Stoughton Housing Authority for a state rent subsidy under Chapter 707, as well as to the Town selectmen for additional federal subsidies. But the position of the Stoughton Authority was that Chapter 707 was available only for tenants and not for co-op operators. Consequently, P.C. initially accepted families who could afford to pay rent without financial assistance. Jehue Smith noted: "The kind of integration we were seeking was mainly economic. We're not achieving what we wanted."

According to the results of the survey over 25 percent of the tenants were dissatisfied with the initial tenant selection; 40 percent of those responding to the question thought that the tenant selection process improved after that function was taken over by the new Board. Special attention was focused on the opinion of residents regarding the racial composition of P.C.:

Satisfied	66 percent
Not satisfied	7 percent
Indifferent	27 percent

If there was inadequate screening of applicants under Interfaith, the opposite is probably true under present selection procedures. It has been reported, for example, that the Selection Committee rejects otherwise eligible families for arbitrary, largely "other" reasons (too many children for instance) rather than the established criteria. Several aspects of present tenant selection remain unclear because of conflicting information. For example:

A Board Member: Tenant selection is a completely objective process with none of our biases operating. We have a waiting list and when a vacancy occurs we start reviewing the possible list of tenants and examine their material very objectively. Selection is done on the basis of their income. No politics enters in on the selection; we do not allow such a thing.

Interfaith: We had certain quotas to fill and thus we operated with the Board in conjunction with that. Certainly they did not want to have an overabundance of families with women head-of-household, or any other criteria which would unbalance the project. Thus certain decisions had to be made. One selectman in town had tried to get one friend of his into the project but he was refused because we were determined to stop all appointments that way. Thus his support was withdrawn and we were slandered in the paper the next couple of days.

A former Board Member: Look, of course certain things were decided and these things were not looked at objectively. This is a nice community and we wanted to keep it that way. I for one did not want certain groups of people I would call undesirable as inhabitants of the complex. Thus arguments as to the social desirability of the project residents would be made all the time.

I don't care what the Board told you of how they operate. They only tell you what you want to hear, but I know what went on; believe me, I was there.

While the Board of Directors suggested that turnover of residents is approximately 7 percent annually, the person in charge of the committee claims a 30-35 percent turnover rate for the first two years. Cooperative records were not available. However, reality, as confirmed by the survey, seems to support the 30 percent rate: over 20 percent of tenants interviewed had not been living in P.C. for more than a year—while the project had been open for over two years. Generally the turnover does not appear to have affected the Cooperative financially—there is no problem filling vacancies especially for the multiple-bedroom apartments. It has been far more difficult to fill one-bedroom units, for which a six-month period of vacancy has not been uncommon. In spite of conflicting information, whenever a vacancy occurs for any other unit and is advertised, there is adequate and prompt response, so that the selection committee has a choice of 15 to 25 applicants.

Residents' Views of the Co-op

Although the majority of residents approve the Board, there is also opposition to it. The nature of this opposition—although advocated by a minority—is fundamental in understanding life in P.C. The rather extensive analysis of criticisms follows:

While I was on the committee there was much fighting among members and the board, and many times we could not reach a decision that could please the board. The board is a prestige-seeking institution that is not really concerned with the members of the co-op and what they want. Instead they are concerned with getting members to accept what they want. If you look at the rate of participation among the co-op members you'll see that very few of them attend the general meetings. They do not seem interested with the welfare of the co-op or else they are fed up with the board. I myself was fed up with them and that's why I resigned.

Generally, ad hoc negative comments regarding the Board were:

Elect a Board of Directors which is qualified; the Board is unsatisfactory; it doesn't get much done; it doesn't like dogs; it shouldn't have anything to do with the outside; only part of the Board seems interested; get rid of the Board; everybody lives their own lives; the Board should not be residents; there is no privacy; they are a waste; there is no faith in the Board of Directors.

The dissatisfaction of residents seems to center around the way decisions are made and particularly the depersonalization in relationships with the Board. On the other hand—the Board President points out—"This is a business and must be run so; otherwise it would not function."

The fundamental explanation is, perhaps, that P.C. is not yet a cooperative in the full sense—or at least in the minds of the residents:

We own	55 percent
We do not think we own	36 percent
We do not know	9 percent

Typical of the negative comments elicited in informal discussions are the following:

It isn't a co-op, let the people have more of a voice; more people should be participating; there should be more knowledge of programs for co-op living; there is not proper knowledge of co-op living; what co-op living amounts to is questionable; I don't feel like it will be owned after a few years; people should join together with the Board; more participation; I would like to see it more of a community; we need more community spirit, more involvement; more cooperation is needed among neighbors; only about 30 percent of the members are cooperative; the whole thing depends upon whether you get the right people; there are bad people in every neighborhood.

In spite of these comments there seems to exist a certain degree of identification with P.C., as well as cohesiveness and sociability.

Positive feelings toward P.C.	80 percent
Negative feelings toward P.C.	20 percent

A typical comment:

> Generally I socialize with people from all four courts. Friendships though are, of course, by age, and the age brackets are separated because of the arrangement of the number of bedrooms in each of the courts. Each court has only so many 3- or 4-bedroom apartments, and it seems that those occupying those apartments have more kids, and therefore are generally younger. Those in the 1-bedroom and 2-bedroom apartments are generally the elderly, and most are very antisocial and very private.

A Board member noted:

> There is cooperation within age groups. There are certainly different factions, but the people do socialize to an extent. Certainly the community is still new and more relationships will be formed. The younger people seem to congregate more, however.

A helpful insight into the pattern and quality of social relationships can also be provided by the kind of behavior which resulted in evictions from P.C. and the spreading of several rumors (usually magnified out of proportion) among Stoughton residents:

> A year or so ago there was a woman who lived here whose husband was serving time in prison. At night she would always have a number of what would seem to be teen-age boys coming to her apartment, to obviously engage in sexual relationships. Heavens, she certainly made enough noise. Well, anyway, her husband finally got out of prison and they lived o.k. for a while. But it was only for a while. It seems that the teen-age boys would still come back and the husband found out about it. There was a lot of shouting and beating for every night for at least a couple of weeks. Finally they were sent up before the Board. Although they were warned, they did not stop, and the Board eventually evicted them.

> People playing cards in one of the apartments were approached by a member of the police department one night, due to a complaint from a neighbor that they were making too much noise. The wives were sitting outside and just gossiping. When the police came they could not find a disturbance but warned the people just the same. After they left they were again phoned a complaint and once again they returned to the scene to find nothing. This happened once again and finally they realized that it was an unjustified complaint. Finally it was found out who was causing the complaints. Well this same guy then started going around late at night and early in the morning banging on peoples' doors waking them up. He, too, was brought up before the Board, but this persisted. Finally he was evicted.

In spite of such episodes, most residents responding to the questionnaire believe that Stoughton families feel positive toward P.C. residents:

Positive feelings by neighbors	70 percent
Negative feelings by neighbors	5 percent
Do not know feelings by neighbors	25 percent

In general, the dissatisfaction expressed by residents of the project regarding physical and social conditions seems to be of the routine complaints associated with most living situations:

> We are too close to other people; there is no place for the children to play; it's too noisy; the buildings are not well built; people should be able to vote for what they want; we need better maintenance, plumbing, too; there is no privacy; people have nothing in common; there should be a better screening of the tenants; get rid of the roaches; we need more interdependence, community, cooperation; the recreation center and the laundry are inadequate; should be more social programs; I want to move to the uncrowded suburbs; there should be a new color for the courts ... not enough playgrounds ... it is not kept clean and orderly; it's good, it allows people to increase their standard of living; I like the village style of the courts around the co-op; I'm totally happy as far as it goes; the children should be better watched; we need a day-care center; need more cooperation among the neighbors; each person should make a better effort to maintain his apartment and get along better; we need more social activities, in the summer people sit outside and talk on the steps of their homes but not much other activity really goes on except for the kids.

The survey resulted in the following recommendations to improve conditions in P.C.:

Structural changes and physical features	57 percent
Changes in regulations	39 percent
Better safety and sanitation	30 percent
Educational, social activities	22 percent

Supplementary information regarding some of the above is provided by answers to the question regarding future projects of this type:

Better physical structure	50 percent
Lower densities	18 percent
More space in units	18 percent

Residents were asked to list their opinions of the advantages and disadvantages of projects like P.C. for themselves and for the Town:

	Town		Residents	
Advantages:	Good for Business	27%	Finances	52%
	Manpower	20%	Better Housing	
	Educational	8%	and location	31%
	Increase Housing		Better Utilities	
	Units	8%	and Facilities	13%
	Bring in more		Feeling of	
	People	8%	Ownership	18%
Disadvantages:	None	31%	None	43%
	Burden on		Social Prob-	
	Facilities	20%	lems	20%
	Social Problems	18%		

Interaction with the Community

It is reasonable to assume that integration problems stem from the earlier controversy and perceptions of Stoughton's residents even before actual construction of the P.C. For many, it did not matter which individual families were to move into P.C. as much as that the homes were for low- and moderate-income people. When construction was completed there was a transfer of these opinions to the people who joined P.C. This has probably affected social relationships between P.C. and the Stoughton community more than any other single factor.

The relationship with Stoughton was forced by the need to acquire federal help for improving the water system. This became the dominant variable in creating a "we-they" dichotomy and a distinct group consciousness in Stoughton. Incoming residents were under strain in establishing a reputation as "regular citizens" and not as malcontents or other undesirables.

That low-income residents in Stoughton were reluctant to move into P.C. is perhaps indicative of this predisposition.

The we-they dichotomy can be further accentuated when a lower-status group is interjected into a higher status community. The characteristics of the Census Tract into which P.C. was interjected are as follows:

	Tract 4563 (P.C.)	4564 (Adjacent)
Population	4,503	7,706
Blacks	1 percent	1.7 percent
Families	1,070	1,890
Median Years Schooling	12.2 yrs	12.4 yrs
Median Family Income	$11,547	$11,454
Mean Family Income	$11,526	$12,076
Persons per Household	3.41	3.77
Foreign-born	516	648
	Canada	Canada
	(276)	(399)

	Italy (176)	Italy (323)
Residence same house as 1965	2,575	4,161
All workers	1,726	2,970
In County	521	773
Outside SMSA	994	1,834
Elementary Public School Enrollment	738	1,227
High School	390	548

In both Tracts (similar to Stoughton, as a whole) there is a dominance of blue-collar workers. But 25 to 30 percent of the employed labor force consists of professionals, managers, and administrators—people with higher status than the residents of P.C.

Neighbors responding to the questionnaire were also of higher income than those responding in P.C.:

Income (in thousands)	Neighbors	P.C.
over 15	10 percent	—
12 - 15	21	—
8 - 12	32	13 percent
4 - 8	29	70
below 4	7	17

Residents of P.C. feel that Stoughton has adopted a condescending attitude towards them. This feeling is typified by the comments of one P.C. resident:

> We are looked down upon as an aggregate of malcontents. There was bitter hostility when the apartments were first proposed and this view has carried over. The Town, for instance, blames all of their troubles on us, and the kids in school are feeling the pressure. This is very unfair. They have no right to judge us personally because we are of a lower income.

Yet the President of the Board believes that acceptance and mutual feelings of a positive nature now exist between Stoughton and P.C.:

> There is total acceptance in the neighborhood, unlike before. We had our problems at first, but certainly we have been accepted by the Town now. In fact, much of it may be due to our public relations committee. A few years ago, for instance, we had what we called a "circus of arts," in which the whole Town could participate. Money was made from it and it was donated to charity—the Town liked that. It was successful to the utmost, and was even filmed for television. Certainly most of our original problems with the community are gone. We are now totally accepted.

Judging from the survey results, however, the President's view may be too optimistic. Neighbors responding to the questionnaire voiced their present feelings toward P.C. as:

Satisfied	49 percent
Dissatisfied	38 percent
Undecided	13 percent

These percentages show some difference from those representing neighbors' feeling toward P.C. in 1971, particularly regarding the undecided:

Satisfied	45 percent
Dissatisfied	18 percent
Undecided	37 percent

Although there is now a higher percent of "satisfied," two years of observation have also increased those who are dissatisfied with P.C. and such projects in general.

Of the neighbors dissatisfied with P.C., most felt that the fundamental obstacle is a difference in life-style. Location of the project, the decrease in property value, congestion and lack of need for the project in Stoughton, all ranked second as reasons for dissatisfaction. Increase of welfare recipients in town, and pressures upon schools or amenities, as well as poor design of the project, ranked third in importance.

Of the neighbors satisfied with P.C., most felt that it meets the housing needs for those already living in Stoughton. They support it because it is seen as a civil rights issue; also, it provides opportunity for low-income people. Very few felt that P.C. provides an opportunity for Stoughton to enrich its life-style or that it contributes to the solution of the problems of the Boston SMSA.

Social interaction is limited. Neighbors responding to the questionnaire rate their knowledge about P.C. as follows:

Excellent	11 percent
Fair	28 percent
Poor, nonexistent	61 percent

It is also established that the majority of neighbors have no friends in P.C.

No friends	61 percent
Few	35 percent
Many	4 percent

Even less significant ties, such as acquaintances, are limited. The response to the question "Do you know any P.C. resident by name?" is as follows:

Many	9 percent
Few	35 percent
None	56 percent

The majority of the neighbors have never even visited P.C.:

Never	52 percent
Once	32 percent
Once weekly	16 percent

An attempt was made to determine neighbors' knowledge or opinions regarding the number of blacks and welfare recipients in P.C. The results were:

	Blacks	Welfare
Do not know	60 percent	63 percent
Believe majority are	2 percent	9 percent
Half and half are	9 percent	20 percent
Minority are	29 percent	9 percent

Again, there is a striking lack of knowledge reflected. There is some evidence, however, that welfare recipients are more closely associated with P.C. than blacks.

Another picture emerges from answers to the question, "Do you think P.C. residents participate in Town affairs?"

More than other residents	4 percent
As much as other residents	20 percent
Less than other residents	18 percent
Do not know	58 percent

Informal interviews provided more material regarding feelings toward P.C. One neighbor expressed a negative attitude toward "those low-income people" and claimed that they represented a drain on the area's tax structure, school system, and water supply, while being particularly vehement toward the black segment:

> Those Goddam good-for-nothing niggers are coming into the town and ruining everything. I don't know why they should be allowed to

come here. Hell, I've lived here all my life and they come and ruin everything. My taxes are going up, a guy can't find a decent place to live; they've taken up our spaces.

Another neighbor, living in an apartment complex close to P.C., reflected a different viewpoint:

People say the Presidential Courts are filled with blacks, stabbings, and rape in the hallways. There are many rumors that are started in this regard. For instance, a year ago there was an epidemic of bugs in the children's hair in the elementary school, and the whole town blamed the new Presidential Courts for it. I know better, and these stories just aren't true. Most of the times the incidents are just blown out of proportion.

A query concerning the "other children" from the P.C. was made to a little boy who was in the 7th or 8th grade:

There is no difference made in school by where the kids come from. While the other kids know of the Courts, there is no special things that happen because of this. The school is just like my other school where I came from before we moved here.

Several respondents differentiated between the project per se and the people as such. One said:

The *project* was not needed and is bad. But as far as I'm concerned, the *people* are normal, just like the rest of us. I've lived here all of my life, practically, and will probably stay. There is nothing wrong with the town as it is. If you really want to know, however, the Portugese are taking over the town more than the people in the Courts.

As illustrated by the above examples, neighbors' comments during the informal discussions vary widely. Nevertheless, taken as a whole, our data and observations provide a realistic basis in favor of the argument that P.C. is gradually becoming a part of the community.

Initial Arguments Reviewed

During the course of the initial controversy over the project several arguments were raised by both sides in defense of their positions. Three years later and in view of subsequent developments—how reasonable are they? What conclusions can be drawn—if any—in light of factual outcomes?

The original, major arguments can be grouped into five broad categories: need, taxation, impact on Town's facilities, cooperative pattern, and tenant selection.

The need for low-and moderate-income housing.

Opponents: There is no need at present for a LMIH complex in the Town of Stoughton.

Proponents: Under the criteria established for eligibility of occupancy, a total of 3,700 persons presently living in the Town of Stoughton would be eligible for the proposed project.

Factual Results: According to Town officials, in 1972 there were more than 800 persons in the Town who received welfare assistance. Further, the 1970 U.S. census indicated that there were 800 persons with incomes below the poverty level. Of these few were given occupancy. In fact at present, only 27 percent of the total population of the complex were originally Stoughton residents prior to moving into the Presidential Apartments.

This is partially due to poor selection procedures, rather than a result of an unexpressed desire to assist inner-city poor.

Taxation.

Opponents: The site of the proposed project was not sufficiently blighted to come under Massachusetts Chapter 121 A.

Any development with an obvious impact on the Town services should not be tax exempt, but be subject to the same taxation as any other apartment complex in the Town (25 percent of gross rents paid).

Proponents: The area selected for the development of the complex was blighted and substandard; any construction would be an improvement over existing conditions.

The only demand placed upon the Town by the Presidential Courts would be incurred by the school system. No other Town supplied services would be required. In lieu of taxes, the complex would pay $28,000 to the Town for the burden of the school system.

Factual results: The Stoughton Board of Selectment refused to allow the complex to be considered under Massachusetts Chapter 121 A. As a result, the Presidential Courts paid $45,339 in 1972 in local property taxes (25 percent of gross rents).

An evaluation of these arguments is necessarily subjective; the perception of the blight in the area is likely to coincide with the viewer's overall reactions to the problems of LMIH.

Impact on Town services.

Opponents: The construction of the project on the site selected would further aggravate an already existing water supply problem in the area.

Drainage systems for the proposed complex would cost the Town $200,000 because the planned complex would greatly overload the existing system.

Because there would be a projected 300 new school-age children living in the complex, it would be necessary for the Town to construct a new elementary school in the area.

Proponents: Interfaith proposed that it would assist the Town in obtaining a federal grant for water supply.

Surface drainage problems in the area could be solved by constructing a pond and a standpipe system. Therefore the present system would not be overloaded.

Impact of the complex would not be nearly as great as opponents pictured. First, half of the residents would be Stoughton residents. Second, Interfaith projected that only fifty to seventy-five school-age children would live in the complex.

Factual Results: The Town of Stoughton did receive a $1.5 million grant from the federal government for the construction of a water supply system.

A pond and standpipe system were constructed for the complex. The only modification was the use of slightly larger pipes.

Of the first P.C. residents there were 96 school-age children. Of these, 53 were previously Stoughton residents and 43 were not. Upon full occupancy of the complex there were only 99 school-age children in the complex, and of these 67 were in the elementary grades and 32 were in the secondary grades.

Thus, it appears that the fears of the opponents of the complex were not realized. The drainage issue was resolved by compromise and the school issue has never matured.

The Cooperative Concept.

Opponents: The poor (who would necessarily be in the majority in the complex) would not have the ability or educational background to run a cooperative. As a result, the complex would be poorly administered and eventually turn into a ghetto.

The requirement that new tenants pay a certain amount towards equity would become prohibitive as both the equity and the operating cost increased.

Proponents: F.H.A. standards would be the guiding factor in the management of the complex by the residents. F.H.A. standards require adequate maintenance reserves and good management. Further, most of the residents would be responsible wage earners.

The requirement of an equity payment would give the residents a feeling of ownership, and resulting pride in maintenance.

Factual Results: The buildings and the grounds of the Presidential Courts are both sound and well-kept.

Tenants pay only two weeks rent towards the equity. Few of the tenants of Presidential Courts feel that they are owners in the true sense of the word.

Interfaith can be said to have trained the Board members so well that a year after the initiation of the project the Board felt confident enough to dismiss Interfaith; several of the administrative oversights of Interfaith were altered by the residents and their elected representatives.

Tenant Selection.

Opponents: geographic: The Town of Stoughton should take care of its own residents first. Ultimately, between 70 percent and 80 percent of the residents of the residential apartments should be from the Town of Stoughton.

Racial: There would be an influx of blacks from the Boston ghetto areas. A rumor circulated that there would be 300 black children living in the complex.

Welfare: The bulk of the residents would be large families on welfare incomes, burdening the Town in many ways.

Proponents: geographic: Not more than 50 percent of the occupants would be from Stoughton. This would allow the community to remain well balanced, and also allow various special groups to remain in the town (the young, the elderly, people with large families, and veterans).

Racial: Racial mixture and balance are good and necessary. As a result, the proponents of the project would give priority to black applications to achieve a racial balance.

Welfare: Income mixture is important and welfare applicants would therefore be accepted.

Factual Results: geographic: Of the first 200 applicants, 49 were Stoughton residents. Of the first 96 units rented, 38 were to Stoughton residents, 3 to persons originally from Stoughton, 23 to persons from adjacent towns, and only 22 to persons originally from Boston. This mix seems to indicate a defeat for the opponents of the plan.

Racial: Of the first group of applicants, only 5 percent were from minority groups. Of the first 96 units, 13 were occupied by blacks, and half of these were originally from the Stoughton area. There are 88 white families and 16 nonwhite families in the complex; while this figure is well above the overall Town percentage, it is still considerably less than the opponents of the complex feared.

Welfare: Only 14 of the first 96 occupants were receiving any form of public assistance; and, of these, 9 were previously from Stoughton.

QUESTIONS

1. In all low- moderate-income housing case studies which we have examined, there have always been elements of controversy. In no single case has the concept of LMIH been accepted by the host community without organized opposition to the proposal. Why then has the concept ultimately gained acceptance in Stoughton while it has not elsewhere? What element of the Stoughton case makes it unique from the majority of the remaining cases? Does this mean that in future cases a trade-off will have to be effected in order to establish projects like P.C. in other communities? If so, what would the impact be upon the developers? What kind of trade-off could be effected in rich suburban communities?

Consider three key conditions. First, Stoughton had a high percentage of low-income families. Second, the majority of the families in Stoughton were blue-collar workers. Finally, Stoughton was a rapidly growing suburb, both in size and affluence. This rapid growth of the Town greatly increased the demand for supportive services; the demand increased at a rate that could not be easily absorbed by the Town systems. In addition, tax increases would reduce the attractiveness of Stoughton as a place to live and the Town was thus anxious to avoid any such increases in the tax rate.

2. Is Stoughton a successful project? If so, by which of the following criteria?

       units completed;
       delivering what was promised;

physical appearance;
siting;
cooperative form of operations;
tenant selection;
community acceptance;
easing the Boston central city situation;
future development and growth of Stoughton.

3. Discuss the advantages and disadvantages of cooperatives as the organizing form for low-income housing. Would you recommend cooperative housing in your community? Why?

4. Regarding the tenant selection process:

a) Evaluate the selectman's position and the reasons for his resignation from the original tenant selection committee.

b) Compare and discuss the outcome of tenant-selection with the original understandings.

Part Three

A Discussion Framework: Policies, Programs, and Dilemmas

The odyssey of the low-income housing controversies of the five suburbs not only raises as many questions as it answers, but also casts the issue in a broader policy context. Like the tip of an iceberg, the initial perception of the problem appears deceptively limited and straightforward. How can the local community accept low- and moderate-income housing? And where, within its border, should such housing be located? This line of inquiry suggests strategies of change directed at the grass-roots level. But the dynamic network of interrelationships between housing and other basic public policy issues—the huge, submerged body of the iceberg—constitutes a far more complex policy dilemma bearing directly on national-regional urban development, residential segregation, racial and economic inequities, redistribution of income-power-status-services, and national investment policies in human resources. The complexity of these issues suggests solutions at the national and regional planes rather than at the local level alone; moreover, it raises the issue of the appropriateness of the forum, be it court or legislature, and from which level of government should it operate; again, it requires a rethinking of housing policies and of the guidance and location of urban development. Above all, who in this country, for so complicated but not atypical issues, bears the responsibility for public policymaking?

Painfully aware of these complexities and policy implications, the reader is now ready, perhaps, to consider a wider range of interlocking or alternative solutions. He can also reassess trends or formulate fresh approaches for major community functions and for all geographic levels.

The material of this part aims to provide basic information on these issues and to place the fundamental questions that trouble most of us in sharper focus for policy reformulation. The main emphasis here is, first, on housing policies in the context of urban development, civil rights, racial and economic segregation and, second, on what theories of social change are most applicable to the goal of increasing social mobility and assimilation. The part is divided into three major sections:

1. The nature of the suburb in the context of urban development and social mobility. From a peripheral part of the central city in the 1950s, suburban communities have become the fastest growing portion of the metropolitan areas in the 1970s and the key to metropolitan planning.
2. Major public policy options and dilemmas regarding housing in the context of civil rights, racial and economic integration, social assimilation, and income redistribution. Housing, like Tennyson's flower, stretches out to involve major aspects of numerous social problems.
3. Social, judicial, and institutional means for achieving national housing and urban development goals. All have been placed under increasing tension as the nature of the suburbs and their relationship to the metropolitan area has changed.

Chapter Nine

The Suburb as a Metropolitan Unit

We have, so far, looked at the five suburbs and their housing controversies essentially on an individual basis. The emphasis has also been more on the housing controversy itself and less on the community and its structural, demographic, socioeconomic, ecological characteristics—or on its relationship to the metropolitan region and its units.

In order to remove these limitations, tables of comparative data are presented on pages 292-318. Thus, the reader has the opportunity to proceed with broader analytic considerations, employing his own insights, hypotheses, or understanding of the relationship between community characteristics and the conflict-change processes described earlier.

All tables present data for each of the five communities; in addition, and for purposes of comparative analysis, data are provided for the City of Boston, the Boston Metropolitan Area (SMSA), and Massachusetts as a whole. Since Stoughton and East Providence are parts of the Brockton SMSA and the Providence SMSA, respectively, data on these two metropolitan areas are also included.

There are varied interests in or reasons for data analysis and, therefore, different ways of looking at the data presented. The reader will no doubt choose his own. But two suggestions might prove helpful.

The first concerns sketching an individual community profile of each of the five cities involved, and highlighting key questions. A more complete understanding is likely to emerge by looking at each community separately, following the variables presented by the tables.

Secondly, the reader is encouraged to make a comparison of aggregates and change rates for each community with those of the central city, the metropolitan area, the state, and the other suburban communities which experienced controversy. This is likely to enhance: a) a better understanding of the community in the context of the metropolitan area and the state; b) a more contemporary appreciation of the evolving nature of present-day suburbs, particularly when contrasted to earlier suburban studies; and c) a beginning exploration of associations between certain variables (or between certain clusters of communities) and the degree of low-income housing which has occurred.

In analyzing the data, it may be helpful to review early studies of suburban community organization and function, and to contrast them with the nature of today's suburban communities as reflected by the data presented. The general tenor of this early literature, particularly that of the 1940s and 1950s, suggested that the suburb had a "parasitic" or "symbiotic" relationship to a large, adjacent central city, which was the heart of urban growth and activity. Although administratively independent, the suburb depended culturally and economically upon the central city and provided it, mainly, with residential functions.[1] Attention focused on two major suburban characteristics: the unique geographic position of the suburb in relation to a large, adjacent central city; and, the high incidence of commuting to the city for work. Both of these ecological characteristics were said to exercise a fundamental influence upon suburban social relationships. Suburbanism as an ecological phenomenon was seen as closely linked with suburbanism as a sociopsychological phenomenon.[2] The ecological position was alleged to restrict the suburbanite's participation in social transactions within the central city, while the commuter was thought to participate less than noncommuters in voluntary associations and informal groupings in the suburb. As a result, among other things, women were believed to play an unusually important role in suburban social relationships.[3] And, in general, residential suburbs were said to have a high degree of informal, primary group contacts.

Thus, earlier studies frequently suggested that life and social relationships in new suburbs were radically different from those of the cities and towns of America, reflecting a change in American values and life patterns. These new values and life patterns included a low proportion of unrelated individuals, a preponderance of young married adults, and an abundance of young children within a middle-class, middle-income environment. The relative homogeneity of suburban dwellers in experience, stages in family cycle, income, and occupational roles was alleged to be reflected in their agreement on a distinct country landscape, mode of living, neighborhood activities, interests, and

---

1. W. Dobriner, ed., *The Suburban Community* (New York: G.P. Putnam's Sons, 1958).

2. Sylvia Fleis Fava, "Suburbanism as a Way of Life," *American Sociological Review*, vol. 21 (February 1956): pp. 34-37.

3. Martin T. Walter, "The Structuring of Social Relationships Engendered By Suburban Residence," *American Sociological Review*, vol. 21 (August 1956): pp. 446-453.

values. Some observers, like Whyte[4] in his study of Park Forest, suggested a decline of individualism, most evident in and partially created by the new suburban communities. A galaxy of publications created an image of social relationships in the suburbs, emphasizing purported increases in marital friction, divorce, drinking, and mental illness. Several of these myths were later dispelled by more perceptive research, such as Gans's "Levittowners"[5] and various other demographic analyses. The monumental Report of the President's Task Force on Suburban Problems in 1968 showed how, almost without the awareness of their residents, the social problems of the newer suburbs spawned since World War II were growing at a pace akin to those of the central city.[6]

Census demographic data analyses published in the middle 1950s presented certain distinct differences between suburbs and the large central cities. Duncan and Reiss[7] found that, compared to suburbs, central cities have more females and older people. Suburbs, on the other hand, have a considerable excess of persons 0 to 13 years, and a slight preponderance of individuals 14 to 19 and 25 to 44. They also had a higher fertility ratio; a lower percentage of single, widowed, and divorced people; larger families; a predominantly white population; a higher educational level; a larger percentage of white-collar workers; more home ownership; and a higher family median income.

How does this demographic picture compare to the following data? Have these trends changed? Has the occupational structure and the composition of the suburban labor force changed? Is the relationship between the suburbs of a metropolitan area becoming more significant than their relationship to the central city? Do you find a "parasitic" or "symbiotic" relationship of suburbs to

---

4. W.H. Whyte, *Organization Man* (New York: Simon & Schuster, Inc., 1956). W.H. Whyte, "The Outgoing Life," *Fortune*, no. 49 (July 1953): p. 86. Bennett Berger, *Working Class Suburb*, chapter 1, (Berkeley: University of California Press, 1960). Among some of the principal contributors to the myth were a novel by Charles Mergendahl, *It's Only Temporary* (Garden City: Doubleday, 1950), perhaps the first of the flood of fiction and nonfiction about the suburbs, Harry Henderson, "The Mass Produced Suburbs," *Harper's Magazine*, November 1953, pp. 25-32 and December 1953, pp. 80-86; Frederick L. Allen, "The Big Change in Suburbia," *Harper's Magazine*, June 1954, pp. 21-28 and July 1954, pp. 47-53; John Keats, *The Crack in the Picture Window* (Boston: Houghton Mifflin, 1956); and, most recently, Peter Wyden, *Suburbia's Coddled Kids* (Garden City: Doubleday, 1962).

5. H. Gans, *The Levittowners* (New York: Pantheon Books, Inc., 1967).

6. Charles M. Haar, *The End of Innocence* (Glenview, Ill.: Scott, Foresman and Co., 1972).

7. D.O. Duncan and J.A. Reiss, *Social Characteristics of Urban and Rural Communities, 1950* (New York: John Wiley & Sons, Inc., 1956).

the city? Does it differ from earlier accounts? If so, in what way and what are some of the major implications?

A word of caution on the nature of statistical correlations is in order.

Most social science thinking involves a consideration of events in terms of their relationship to other events, which seem to have been either their cause or their outcome. But, pure cause-effect relationships in human social behavior are extremely difficult (if not impossible) to establish, and cannot usually be demonstrated as can the laws of physical science. Therefore, social scientists focus mainly upon the association of things, rather than on pure cause and effect. For example, a degree of acceptance or rejection of low-income housing may be associated with a given type of suburb (i.e., one having low income, or one with a dominantly Catholic population). Even if this proves to be actually true, it does not necessarily mean that there is a cause-and-effect relationship.

Data collection and analysis have other inherent limitations. The sample may be inadequate or inaccurate; the factors might be more varied than we know; the association of one variable with another, even when "established" and "explained," does not necessarily reflect the whole or the real world. This is because there can still be several other associations—perhaps stronger ones—which have not been examined; or the association may not hold true when controlled for certain other factors; or the nonexplained relationships may be more important than those which are explained.

Limitations of multiple linear regression techniques should also be noted. The "independent" factors are rarely, if ever, truly independent of the consequences of the behavior of the variables with which they are correlated, and there are time delays between the change in value of the causal factors and the impacted variables. Hence, correlating variables with one another at one or more discrete points in time ignores the effects of the feedback and time lags. Moreover, the direction of the causality cannot be derived mathematically. Furthermore, technique can deal with linear relationships only; nonlinearities or "thresholds" effects cannot be treated adequately.

With these caveats in mind, a number of observations and questions are suggested by the tables which follow. How, for example, do we explain Canton's relatively phenomenal population increase? It increased at a faster rate than any of the other four communities (except Stoughton), more than three times the rate of the state, and almost three times the rate of the Boston SMSA. It has also one of the highest percentage increase in the $15,00-and-over annual income category. Does this fact relate in any way to the extent of opposition to low-income housing? How? What about the fact that, after Stoughton, Canton has the smallest budget percentage expenditure for schools?

Looking now at the possible clusters of the five communities in terms of similar or dissimilar characteristics, consider the following: What two clusters readily suggest themselves in relation to most of the demographic and other characteristics? Would you cluster Canton and Stoughton together? Why? For analytic purposes would you cluster those communities which produced some low-income housing (Stoughton, East Providence) and those which did not (Canton, Concord, Newton)? If so, what conclusions do you draw, based upon common and differing variables between the two clusters? How reliable are they? If more data were available and factor analysis (or other quantitative analytic techniques) were possible, what kind of generalizations would you suggest as hypotheses to be tested regarding types of suburbs associated with high degree of acceptance and rejection of low-income housing?

Figures speak and when they do, people listen. But the value system of suburbs is elusive and inadequately studied through them alone. On the other hand, attempts to psychoanalyze communities and to make a composite whole out of diversities of motivations, attitudes, and prejudices are equally suspect. Few reliable measures are at hand. Nevertheless, such sources as public-opinion polls do provide insights useful to policymakers. With all their possible biases and limitations, they do reflect preferences of individuals and social classes regarding the residential environment and its characteristics.

If politicians hover over opinion polls, should not a developer interested in working in the suburbs also be interested in them? Consider the five cases in light of the following:

Figure 1a. White Attitudes Toward Residential Integration

	Approve Residential Integration		
	Whites Nationwide	Northern Whites	Southern Whites
1942	35%	42%	12%
1956	51	58	38
1963: June	61	68	44
December	64	70	51

Paul B. Sheatsley, "White Attitudes Toward the Negro," *Daedalus* (Winter 1966): 222.

Figure 1b.

"Which of these statements would you agree with: First, white people have a right to keep Negroes out of their neighborhoods if they want to, or Second, Negroes have a right to live wherever they can afford to just like white people?"

(In Percent)

		White	
	Men	Women	Total
Whites have a right to keep Negroes out	27	32	30
Negroes have a right to live anywhere	64	59	62
Negroes have a right to live anywhere if they are the "right kind"	3	2	2
Other	3	3	3
Don't know	3	4	3
	100	100	100

Figure 1b. (cont.)

"How about laws to prevent discrimination against Negroes in buying or renting houses and apartments? Do you favor or oppose such laws?"

(In Percent)

	White		
	Men	Women	Total
Favor such laws	42	38	40
Oppose such laws	23	19	21
Undecided, don't know	8	11	9
Feel whites have a right to keep Negroes out	27	32	30
	100	100	100

Figure 1c

"If a Negro family with about the same income and education as you moved next door to you, would you mind it a lot, a little, or not at all?"

(In percent)

	White		
	Men	Women	Total
Mind a lot	17	21	19
Mind a little	25	26	25
Not at all	53	44	49
There is already a Negro family next door	3	5	4
Don't know	2	4	3
	100	100	100

"Suppose there are 100 white families living in a neighborhood. One white family moves out and a Negro family moves in. Do you think it would be a good idea to have some limit on the number of Negro families that move there, or to let as many move there as want to?"

(In percent)

	White		
	Men	Women	Total
There should be some limit	45	52	48
Let as many move there as want	44	36	40
Don't know	11	12	12
	100	100	100

Angus Campbell and Howard Shedman, *Racial Attitudes in 15 American Cities* (Ann Arbor, Michigan: Survey Research Center, 1968), pp. 32-3.

Figure 2. Attitudes and Preferences of Low- and Moderate-Income Households

Preferences for New House Location
(In Percent)

Location Preferred	White Households	Black Households
Prefer Own Neighborhood	43	61
Prefer Suburb	53	34
Indifferent to Location	4	5
Total	100	100

Sample: 214 respondents, drawn from a sample of low- and moderate-income households in Dayton, Ohio. The low-income individuals were from households that earned less than $5,000 per year—half from black households and half from white. The moderate-income individuals were from households whose income ranged from $5,000-$10,000 per year—again with an evenly divided racial mix.

Nina Jaffe Gruen and Claude Gruen, *Low and Moderate Income Housing in the Suburbs*, p. 64, New York: Praeger (1972).

Figure 3. Attitudes of Suburban Residents

Reasons for Considering Low- Moderate-Income Households Undesirable Neighbors
(In Percent)

Reasons	Very Important	Important	Unimportant	No Answer
Property values would drop.	55	29	9	7
Property taxes would increase due to need for increased services.	36	31	26	7
Neighborhood would face a drop in social status.	31	32	30	7
Neighborhood would become less stable.	40	43	9	7
Those people would not fit in with rest of community.	29	37	25	8
Housing maintenance and conditions would decrease.	59	23	9	8
Decrease in law and order.	43	30	20	7
Change in character of neighborhood with shopping facilities catering to new groups' needs.	19	34	40	7
Drop in quality of schools.	38	18	40	7
These people would be a bad influence on my family because they don't believe the same things we do.	15	23	54	8
Other:				
Race.	2			
Low-income persons would feel insecure in higher income areas.	1			
Low-income households have too many children.	1			

Sample: 288 respondents in four suburban Dayton area communities. The sample design specified three major income categories: $10,000-$15,000, $16,000-$24,000, and $25,000 and over.

Nina Jaffe Gruen and Claude Gruen, *Low and Moderate Income Housing in the Suburbs*, p. 26, New York: Praeger (1972).

QUESTIONS

1. If public support for economic and racial integration has shown a continuing advance in the past three decades, why—as all five cases demonstrate—is it still so difficult to build low- and moderate-income housing in the suburbs?

2. Consider the suburban residents' concern for schools and property taxes. Is the concern just for money, or rather for where one's children go to school and who goes to school with them? What can be done to preclude a drop in the quality of the local schools? Did the plans of proponents in the five cases respond adequately to citizens' fears about schools, taxes, and public services?

The tables in this section were constructed from data provided mainly by the U.S. Census 1960 and 1970 Publications, the County and City Data Book 1971, the Massachusetts Department of Commerce Community Profiles, and the Massachusetts Department of Education publications.

Table 1A. Population By Age—1960

Area	Under 18 Years Number	Percent	19 to 64 Years Number	Percent	65 Years and Over Number	Percent	Total Number
Canton	5,160	40	6,688	53	923	7	12,771
Concord	4,645	37	6,797	55	1,075	8	12,517
East Providence	14,206	34	23,500	56	4,249	10	41,955
Newton	32,864	32	49,656	54	9,864	11	92,384
Stoughton	6,696	41	8,395	51	1,237	8	16,328
Boston	200,172	29	411,440	59	85,585	12	697,197
Boston SMSA	840,910	32	1,466,594	54	281,797	11	2,589,301
Brockton SMSA	53,277	36	79,450	53	16,731	11	149,458
Massachusetts	1,480,833	36	3,096,136	53	571,609	11	5,148,578
Providence SMSA	282,844	34	450,667	55	87,590	11	821,101

Table 1B. Population by Age—1970

Area	Under 18 years		19 to 64 years		65 and over		Total
	Number	Percent	Number	Percent	Number	Percent	Number
Canton	6,819	40	9,024	53	1,257	7	17,100
Concord	6,205	38	8,497	53	1,398	9	16,148
East Providence	15,635	33	27,017	56	5,499	11	48,151
Newton	26,430	29	53,545	59	11,091	12	91,066
Stoughton	9,232	39	12,545	54	1,682	7	23,459
Boston	181,805	28	345,556	59	81,759	13	641,071
Boston SMSA	878,293	32	1,565,522	57	309,885	11	2,753,700
Brockton SMSA	69,929	37	102,108	54	17,783	9	189,820
State of Mass.	1,875,764	33	2,575,268	56	636,185	11	5,689,170
Providence SMSA	297,759	33	512,087	56	100,935	11	910,781

Table 1C. Changes in Population By Age Group—1960-1970

Area	Under 18 Years Rate of Change in Percent	19 to 64 Years Rate of Change in Percent	65 Years and Over Rate of Change in Percent	Total Population Rate of Change in Percent
Canton	32	35	+36	+34
Concord	33	30	+30	+29
East Providence	10	15	+29	+15
Newton	−20	8	+12	− 1
Stoughton	−32	55	36	44
Boston	− 9	−16	− 4	− 8
Boston SMSA	4	7	10	6
Brockton SMSA	31	29	9	27
Massachusetts	27	3	11	11
Providence SMSA	16	7	15	11

Table 1D. Median Population Age and Changes—1960-1970

Area	1960 Median Age	1970 Median Age	Change in Years
Canton	28.0	26.3	−1.7
Concord	29.6	27.7	−1.9
East Providence	33.0	31.5	−1.5
Newton	34.1	32.9	−1.2
Stoughton	27.3	25.9	−1.4
Boston	39.9	28.1	−2.8
Boston SMSA	32.0	29.1	−2.9
Brockton SMSA	31.0	26.8	−4.2
Massachusetts	32.1	29.0	−3.1
Providence SMSA	32.6	29.7	−2.9

Table 2A. Household Size—1960-1970

Area	Households (Total Number)			Average Household Size		
	1960	1970	Rate of Change in Percent 1960-1970	1960	1970	Size Change 1960-1970 in Percent
Canton	4,278	4,566	+ 6	−	2.43	−
Concord	928	4,339	+30	3.32	3.55	+0.23
East Providence	12,499	15,144	+21	3.31	3.13	−0.18
Newton	25,688	26,958	+ 5	3.47	3.19	− .28
Stoughton	3,358	6,372	+47	−	3.64	−
Boston	224,432	217,622	− 3	2.93	2.77	−0.16
Boston SMSA	770,215	859,701	+11	3.23	3.09	−0.14
Brockton SMSA	43,629	54,895	+26	3.31	3.34	+0.03
Massachusetts	1,534,732	1,759,692	+15	3.23	3.12	−0.11
Providence SMSA	247,822	284,375	+14	3.19	3.04	−0.15

Table 2B. Families and Families with Children Under 18—1960-1970

Area	All Families 1960	All Families 1970	Families With Own Children Under 18 1960	Percent 1960	1970	Percent 1970	Percent Change of Families With Own Children Under 18
Canton	3,165	4,088	1,964	62	2,532	62	0
Concord	2,975	3,757	1,764	59	2,368	63	4
East Providence	11,112	12,584	6,061	55	6,577	52	−3
Newton	23,076	22,694	12,798	55	11,509	50	−5
Stoughton	4,002	5,667	2,597	64	3,570	54	−10
Boston	164,215	142,019	70,361	43	70,181	49	6
Boston SMSA	542,398	661,650	349,409	64	351,605	53	−11
Brockton SMSA	37,317	45,698	20,354	62	27,265	59	−3
Massachusetts	1,292,404	1,390,982	654,603	51	752,934	54	3
Providence SMSA	185,141	231,427	108,244	58	124,060	53	−5

Table 3. Educational Indicators—1972

Area	No. of School-Age Children (1972-1973)	Ratio of School-Age Children to Total Population (1972-1973 Children to 1970 Population)	Percent of School-Age Children in Public Schools (1972-1973)	Elementary Child-Teacher Ratio (1970-1971)	Secondary Child-Teacher Ratio (1970-1971)	Percent of Budget Spent on Schools	Percent of 1971 Class On To Higher Education	Median School Years Completed (Males 25 yrs old and over)	Amount Spent per Child in Public Schools (1970-1971)
Canton	5,082	29.7	83.8	26.18	19.64	43.67	64.53	12.30	$ 912.18
Concord	4,896	30.2	91.1	25.50	16.80	50.90	72.00	12.70	1,107.51
East Providence	13,301**	27.6**	85.2	27.00	N.A.	45.00	60.00	11.50	772.00
Newton	19,401	21.3	87.0	18.69	16.16	45.07	73.76	14.00	1,233.44
Stoughton	6,876	29.3	97.7	24.26	20.14	42.65	56.45	12.10	711.40
Boston	126,692	19.8	76.4	24.01	16.45	20.8	34.45	12.1	935.24
Boston SMSA	634,336	23.0	86.3	NA	17.96	NA	58.30	12.2	1,020.87
Brockton SMSA	51,352	27.1	94.5	NA	NA	NA	NA	12.2	NA
Massachusetts	1,359,742	23.9	87.2	23.45	NA	NA	NA	11.2	NA
Providence SMSA	238,868**	26.2**	73.7**	NA	NA	NA	NA	12.4	NA

**1970

Table 4. Racial Composition 1960-1970

	White			Black			Other		Non-White Rate of Change in Percent 1960-1970	Total	
	Absolute (1970) No.	Percent	Rate of Change in Percent 1960-1970	Absolute (1970) No.	Percent	Rate of Change in Percent 1960-1970	Absolute (1970) No.	Percent		Population 1970	Rate of Change in Percent 1960-1970
Canton	16,991	99.3	33	66	.4	725	43	.3	514	17,100	33.9
Concord	15,845	98.1	27	208	1.3	188	95	.6	955	16,148	29.0
East Providence	46,469	96.6	13	1,343	2.7	64	345	.7	84	48,151	14.8
Newton	89,237	98	−2	1,092	1.2	63	737	.8	279	91,066	−1.4
Stoughton	23,011	98.2	41	389	1.6	317	59	.2	210	23,459	43.7
Boston	524,709	81.9	−17	104,707	16.3	66	11,655	1.8	−24	641,071	−8.1
Boston SMSA	2,602,741	94.5	4	127,035	4.6	6	23,924	.9	157	2,753,700	6.1
Brockton SMSA	185,864	97.7	26	3,260	2.0	81	696	.3	−82	189,820	27.0
Massachusetts	5,477,624	96.3	9	175,817	3.1	57	35,729	.6	163	5,689,170	10.5
Providence SMSA	884,994	97.2	11	21,083	2.3	46	4,704	.5	202	910,781	10.9

Table 5A. Family Income—1960

Area	$0-$2,999		$3,000-$5,999		$6,000-$8,999		$9,000-$14,999		Over $15,000		Total
	No.	Percent	No.	Percent	No.	Percent	No.	Percent	No.	Percent	No.
Canton	233	8	885	28	1,096	34	773	24	178	6	3,165
Concord	215	7	572	19	823	28	815	28	550	18	2,975
East Providence	1,329	12	4,118	37	13,434	31	1,831	16	400	4	11,112
Newton	1,391	6	4,376	19	5,759	25	6,085	26	5,465	24	23,076
Stoughton	292	7	1,425	36	1,471	37	647	16	167	4	4,002
Boston	27,359	15	60,893	33	46,520	26	24,998	14	22,316	12	182,086
Boston SMSA	70,716	11	196,719	31	197,441	31	130,149	20	45,501	7	640,526
Brockton SMSA	4,046	16	13,986	39	12,403	28	5,756	13	1,126	4	37,317
Massachusetts	160,470	13	441,788	34	397,616	31	225,214	17	67,313	5	1,292,401
Providence SMSA	32,968	11	83,597	38	60,413	33	27,123	15	7,444	3	211,545

Table 5B. Family Income—1970*

Area	$0-$2,999		$3,000-$5,999		$6,000-$8,999		$9,000-$14,999		Over $15,000		Total
	No.	Percent	No.	Percent	No.	Percent	No.	Percent	No.	Percent	No.
Canton	168	4	486	12	980	24	1,354	33	1,100	27	4,088
Concord	134	4	289	8	752	20	1,152	30	1,430	38	3,757
East Providence	1,170	9	3,984	32	3,039	24	3,235	26	1,156	9	12,583
Newton	1,032	5	2,564	12	4,247	18	6,460	29	8,392	36	22,694
Stoughton	348	6	862	15	1,773	31	1,916	34	768	14	5,667
Boston	15,622	11	68,170	48	26,984	19	19,882	14	11,361	8	142,019
Boston SMSA	40,217	6	71,512	10	110,204	16	240,578	37	199,139	31	661,650
Brockton SMSA	1,313	3	2,457	5	3,341	7	12,179	27	26,408	58	45,698
Massachusetts	89,536	6	163,548	12	257,075	19	530,523	38	350,300	25	1,390,982
Providence SMSA	20,828	9	32,399	14	48,600	21	85,628	37	43,972	19	231,427

*Corrected for inflation

Table 5C. 1960-1970 Changes in Family Income By Income Bracket

Area	0-$2,999 Percent Change	$3,000-5,999 Percent Change	$6,000-8,999 Percent Change	$9,000-14,999 Percent Change	$15,000 & Over Percent Change	Total Families Rate of Change in Percent
Canton	-4	-16	-12	10	22	34
Concord	-3	-15	8	3	23	29
East Providence	-3	-30	2	25	3	15
Newton	0	+1	-5	3	4	-1
Stoughton	-1	-22	-7	20	10	44
Boston	-4	15	-7	0	-4	-13
Boston SMSA	-5	-21	-15	17	24	14
Brockton SMSA	-8	-32	-26	12	55	22
Massachusetts	-7	-22	-18	21	20	11
Providence SMSA	-5	-26	-8	24	15	11

Table 5D. Median Family Income—1960-1970

Area	1960	1970	Change 1960-1970 in Dollars	Rate of Change 1960-1970 in Percent	1970 Income Corrected for Inflation	Change 1960-1970 in Dollars	Rate of Change 1960-1970 in Percent
Canton	$7,241	$13,752	$6,511	89	$9,489	$2,248	30
Concord	$8,538	$16,460	$7,922	92	$9,917	$1,379	16
East Providence	$6,082	$10,179	$4,097	67	$7,023	$ 941	15
Newton	$9,008	$15,381	$6,373	70	$10,312	$1,304	14
Stoughton	$6,462	$11,699	$5,239	81	$8,062	$1,600	24
Boston	$5,747	$ 9,133	$3,386	59	$6,302	$ 555	10
Boston SMSA	$6,622	$11,449	$4,827	73	$7,900	$1,278	19
Brockton SMSA	$6,117	$10,928	$4,811	77	$7,540	$1,423	23
Massachusetts	$6,272	$10,845	$4,573	73	$7,476	$1,204	19
Providence SMSA	$5,666	$ 9,767	$4,101	72	$6,733	$1,067	19

Table 5E. Income Below Poverty Level—1970

Area	Number of Families Below Poverty Level	Percent of All Families	Percent of Families Below Poverty Level Receiving Public Assistance	Number of Households Below Poverty Level	Percent of All Households	Percent of Households Below Poverty Level Lacking Some or All Plumbing Facilities
Canton	96	2.3	—	224	5.2	6.3
Concord	89	2.4	—	175	4.4	4.0
East Providence	727	5.8	12.1	1,551	9.8	7.1
Newton	636	2.8	9.1	1,287	5.4	1.2
Stoughton	202	3.6	24.8	330	5.6	2.4
Boston	16,624	11.7	45.6	32,025	17.3	8.6
Boston SMSA	40,236	6.1	30.8	77,770	10.4	6.7
Brockton SMSA	2,361	5.2	28.6	4,422	9.1	9.0
Massachusetts	86,691	6.2	27.3	163,701	10.8	7.7
Providence SMSA	18,137	7.8	26.0	32,949	13.3	6.9

Table 6A. Occupations* of Residents—1970

	Profess. & Techn.		Managers		Clerical & Kindred		Sales		Craftsmen & Foremen		Operatives		Household Workers		Service Workers		Laborers (Nonfarm)		Farm Workers		Not Reported		Total Employed (16 yrs old and over)
	No.	%	No.	%	No.	%	No.	%	No.	%	No.	%	No.	%	No.	%	No.	%	No.	%	No.	%	No.
Canton	1324	20	857	13	1466	22	508	8	826	12	752	11	37	1	684	10	238	4	7	0	—	—	6,699
Concord	1821	31	922	16	1016	17	481	8	404	7	336	6	124	2	597	10	109	2	41	1	—	—	5,851
East Providence	2529	12	1390	7	3804	19	1540	8	2956	15	5062	25	104	1	2159	11	733	4	90	0	—	—	20,365
Newton	11334	29	5798	15	7247	19	3692	9	2928	8	2765	7	580	2	3499	9	1001	3	93	0	—	—	38,937
Stoughton	1342	15	767	8	1695	18	621	7	1472	16	2116	23	7	0	784	9	380	4	23	0	—	—	9,207
Boston	44894	17	15035	6	71655	27	15073	6	27157	10	36695	14	2005	1	42683	16	11031	4	277	0	—	—	266,505
Boston SMSA	227092	20	101886	9	260400	23	87754	8	131593	11	155067	14	8231	1	135299	12	36694	3	2458	0	—	—	1,136,474
Brockton SMSA	10087	14	6277	8	13874	19	5341	7	11722	16	15117	20	340	0	8414	11	2729	4	339	1	—	—	74,240
Massachusetts	230341	17	157328	12	112943	9	94906	7	268116	20	171214	13	1058	0	128831	10	70229	5	8850	1	80733	6	1,324,599
Providence SMSA	49344	13	26485	7	65412	17	24185	6	55843	15	79919	21	1909	1	40646	11	13973	4	1233	0	—	—	371,782

*Only major occupational groups are included.

Table 6B. Change in Occupations of Residents By Occupation—1960-1970 (In Percent)

Area	Professional & Technical	Managers	Clerical & Kindred	Sales	Crafts & Foremen	Operatives	Household Workers	Service Workers	Laborers (Nonfarm)	Farm Workers	Total Work Force
Canton	57	77	66	13	25	7	−37	95	87	−85	38
Concord	60	50	26	53	−18	13	−37	70	−7	−35	26
East Providence	41	10	28	16	13	35	−41	70	24	350	24
Newton	42	−8	22	−13	−12	−17	−58	62	−4	—	5
Stoughton	108	130	80	93	19	45	−83	75	112	−54	56
Boston	34	−3	21	−18	−16	−30	−44	24	−7	−13	−8
Boston SMSA	52	8	36	7	−2	−8	−45	45	1	—	20
Brockton SMSA	75	42	67	25	36	4	−40	91	25	—	33
Massachusetts	50	13	13	−10	−3	−10	−45	31	−2	−43	8
Providence SMSA	65	12	40	18	18	−8	—	71	22	—	19

Table 7A. Employed Residents—1970 (In Percent)

Area	Civilian Labor Force Unemployed	In Manufacturing Industries	In White-Collar Occupations	Government Employees	Workers Outside County of Residence
Canton	2.3	25.0	62.0	16.9	40.7
Concord	3.3	23.0	72.5	14.4	15.2
East Providence	3.6	33.6	45.5	11.1	14.8
Newton	2.8	16.3	72.1	14.7	40.2
Stoughton	4.5	33.0	48.1	13.2	40.5
Boston	4.3	17.5	55.0	17.5	19.5
Boston SMSA	3.5	22.4	59.6	15.6	31.0
Brockton SMSA	3.7	30.7	47.9	14.5	37.8
Providence SMSA	3.9	37.8	44.6	13.9	24.7

Table 7B. Resident Labor Force Employed in County of Residence—1960-1970

	Resident Work Force Employed in County of Residence					
	1960			1970		
Area	Total Work Force	Number	Percent	Total Work Force	Number	Percent
Canton	4,842	2,399	49.5	6,538	3,582	54.8
Concord	4,653	3,646	78.4	5,882	4,452	75.7
East Providence	16,079	13,811	85.9	20,365	15,950	79.7
Newton	38,023	19,532	51.3	30,429	19,877	65.0
Stoughton	5,909	3,371	57.0	9,150	4,966	54.3
Boston	287,997	219,462	76.0	259,781	183,140	70.5
Boston SMSA	1,023,725	659,658	64.4	1,122,516	691,331	61.6
Brockton SMSA	55,878	34,805	62.3	74,240	38,862	52.3
Massachusetts	1,989,293	1,487,791	74.8	2,282,248	1,570,392	68.8
Providence SMSA	313,663	271,552	86.6	374,636	299,628	67.9

Table 7C. Persons* Employed Locally—By Industry

Area	Wholesale and Retail		Service		Construction		Manufacturing		Other		Total
	Number	Percent	Number	Percent	Number	Percent	Number	Percent	Number	Percent	Number
Canton[3]	2,325	36	675	11	415	7	2,804	44	194	3	6,413
Concord[1]	975	23	875	20	176	4	1,482	35	782	18	4,290
East Providence[2]	NA	20	NA	13	NA		NA	34	NA	21	NA
Newton[2]	7,555	47	4,367	19	2,011	10	10,023	17	1,476	10	25,432
Stoughton[2]	714	21	428	13	233	7	1,871	55	166	4	3,412
Boston[2]	117,509	32	67,228	18	17,505	5	69,324	19	101,400	27	372,966
Boston SMSA[2]	286,640	31	148,933	16	53,083	6	297,936	32	154,458	16	941,050
Brockton SMSA	NA		NA		NA		NA		NA		NA
Massachusetts	NA		NA		NA		NA		NA		NA
Providence SMSA	NA		NA		NA		NA		NA		NA

*Residents and commuters.
[1] 1968.
[2] 1970.
[3] 1971.

Table 8. Taxation

Area	Rate per $1000 Assessed Val.	Assessed Valuation	Tax Levy	Rate 1971	Rate 1972	Change 1971-1972
Canton[3]	38.00	$160,319,219	$6,092,133	38.00	40.50	+2.50
Concord[2]	39.20	$162,777,232	$6,380,867	43.30	48.00	+4.70
East Providence[2]	39.70	$158,967,065	$8,333,765	44.60	44.40	−0.20
Newton[1]	72.20	$327,798,250	$37,798,250	121.60	139.60	+18.00
Stoughton[2]	166.80	$37,549,400*	$6,263,239	44.60	44.00	−0.60
Boston	156.80	$1,617,000,000	$253,545,600	174.70	196.70	+22.00
Boston SMSA	NA	NA	NA	NA	NA	NA
Brockton SMSA	NA	NA	NA	NA	NA	NA
Massachusetts	NA	NA	NA	NA	NA	NA
Providence SMSA	NA	NA	NA	NA	NA	NA

*A 1971 Revaluation showed $148,000,000 assessed value
[1] 1967.
[2] 1970.
[3] 1971.

Table 9. Political Party Registration—1962-1972 (In Percent)

Area	Democrats			Republicans			Independents		
	1962	1972	Rate of Change	1962	1972	Rate of Change	1962	1972	Rate of Change
Canton	31.3	38.0	6.7	29.2	11.3	−17.9	39.5	50.7	+11.2
Concord	12.4	32.3	19.9	39.5	33.7	−5.8	48.0	34.0	−14.0
East Providence*	30.5	21.3	−25.1	5.6	5.6	6.2	.5	.9	74.7
Newton	21.8	42.6	20.8	32.0	22.6	−9.4	46.2	34.9	−11.3
Stoughton	29.3	45.4	16.1	23.7	16.3	−7.4	46.9	38.3	− 8.6
Boston City	64.6	71.6	7.0	9.5	8.2	−1.3	25.9	20.2	− 5.7
Boston SMSA	39.1	46.3	7.2	21.9	18.6	−3.3	39.0	35.1	− 3.9
Brockton SMSA	28.0	43.5	15.5	29.5	23.5	−6.0	42.5	33.0	− 9.5
Massachusetts	35.0	42.6	7.6	23.1	19.0	−4.1	41.9	38.3	− 3.6
Providence SMSA	NA	NA	NA	NA	NA	NA	NA	NA	NA

*1960 and 1970.

Table 10A. Housing Units—1970

Area	All Housing Units	Rate of Change 1960–1970 %	Year Round Housing Units	Total Occupied Housing Units	All Occupied Housing Units					All Year Round Units	One Unit Dwelling Detached		Subsidized Housing as of 31 December 1971	
					Owner		Renter						
					No.	%	No.	%		No.	%	No. of Units	Percent of Total
Canton	4,673	32	4,662	4,566	3,647	79.9	919	20.1	4,656	3,787	81.33	98	2.1
Concord	4,444	27	4,440	4,339	3,428	79.0	911	21.0	4,444	3,638	81.86	32	0.7
East Providence	15,481	19	15,467	15,144	10,586	68.0	4,547	32.0	15,450	10,148	65.68	1024*	6.6
Newton	27,425	5	27,422	26,958	19,101	70.9	7,883	21.1	27,424	17,035	62.11	401	1.5
Stoughton	6,504	40	6,503	6,372	4,930	77.4	1,442	22.6	6,510	4,792	73.60	330	5.2
Boston	232,448	–3	232,413	217,622	59,230	27.2	158,392	72.8	232,406	27,519	11.84	26,235	11.3
Boston SMSA	396,273	10	890,756	859,701	452,033	52.6	407,668	47.4	890,981	377,091	42.32	NA	NA
Brockton SMSA	56,669	22	56,566	54,895	37,597	68.5	17,298	31.5	56,554	34,664	61.29	NA	NA
Providence SMSA	301,510	–3	297,229	284,375	167,595	58.9	116,780	41.1	297,980	152,680	51.23	NA	NA
Massachusetts	1,890,400	12	1,836,198	1,759,692	1,012,173	57.5	747,519	42.5	1,839,028	908,120	49.38	15,038*	5.7

*As of June 1973

Table 10B. Housing Units Change—1960-1970 (In Percent)

Area	Total Units	Owner-Occupied	Renter-Occupied	Single-Family Dwellings (Detached)	Percent Units in Apartments With 5 or More Units
Canton	+32	NA	NA	NA	NA
Concord	+27	NA	NA	NA	NA
East Providence	+19	-5	+5	-4	-5
Newton	+5	+6	-6	+3	0
Stoughton	+40	NA	NA	NA	NA
Boston	-3	0	0	+5	0
Boston SMSA	+10	-2	-3	+4	-1
Massachusetts	+12	-8	-1	+4	0
Brockton SMSA	+22	+2	-1	NA	NA
Providence SMSA	-3	+2	-2	+2	NA

Table 10C. Characteristics of Housing Units—1970 (In Percent)

Area	Units in Structures Built 1960-1970	Units With 3 or More Bedrooms	Units With More Than 1 Bathroom
Canton	29.8	69.4	45.1
Concord	27.1	74.1	56.8
East Providence	18.9	47.7	22.1
Newton	7.8	52.6	14.0
Stoughton	31.5	65.2	20.2
Boston	9.1	34.4	10.8
Boston SMSA	14.1	49.0	24.8
Brockton SMSA	22.4	56.0	20.3
Massachusetts	16.3	51.3	22.7
Providence SMSA	17.0	48.0	19.5

314 Housing the Poor in Suburbia

Table 11. Value of Specified* Owner-Occupied Units—1970

Area	$0-$5,000 No.	%	$5,000-$9,000 No.	%	$10,000-$14,999 No.	%	$15,000-$19,999 No.	%	$20,000-$24,999 No.	%	$25,000-$34,999 No.	%	$35,000-$49,999 No.	%	$50,000 or More No.	%	Total Units	Median Value 1970	Median Value 1960
Canton	18	1	67	2	219	6	628	18	802	24	985	28	493	16	171	5	3383	$24,700	NA
Concord	2	—	16	1	53	2	223	7	491	16	942	30	670	21	707	23	3104	$33,100	$15,500
East Providence	55	1	699	8	2505	28	3156	35	1606	17	796	9	219	2	40	—	9067	$16,900	$11,800
Newton	5	—	112	1	321	2	1048	7	2292	14	4808	30	4281	27	2953	19	15820	$33,600	$22,300
Stoughton	18	—	115	3	671	15	1511	34	1233	27	839	19	100	2	15	—	4502	$19,800	NA
Boston	578	2	2162	8	4133	15	7656	28	7335	26	4472	16	863	3	450	2	27658	$19,600	$13,500
Boston SMSA	1483	—	7861	2	28040	8	71693	22	84164	24	86416	25	41869	12	22991	7	344517	$23,800	$15,900
Brockton SMSA	210	1	1305	4	6113	29	12431	39	6895	22	3604	12	781	2	203	1	31542	$18,300	$12,100
Massachusetts	6990	1	39867	5	20462	15	202517	25	172477	21	147013	18	64153	8	30941	4	684420	$20,600	$13,800
Providence SMSA	1317	1	899	6	30281	23	42131	32	23698	18	15799	12	6583	5	3950	3	131658	$18,100	$12,300

*Limited to one-family home on less than 10 acres and no business on property.

Table 12. Characteristics of Vacant Year-Round Units Owner-Occupied

Vacant Units For Sale 1970

Area	No.	Percent of all Occupied Units	Median Price Asked
Canton	30	.65	$38,500
Concord	35	.80	$44,000
East Providence	33	.40	$15,400
Newton	50	.18	$37,800
Stoughton	17	.26	$21,900
Boston	546	.25	$17,600
Boston SMSA	2444	.28	$28,200
Brockton SMSA	223	.40	$19,900
Massachusetts	5403	.30	$22,900
Providence SMSA	1177	.41	$20,400

Table 12a. Densities of All Occupied Units (Owner)

Persons per Room—1970

	1.00 or Less		1.01 to 1.50		1.51 or More		
	No.	Percent	No.	Percent	No.	Percent	Total
Canton	3,467	95.1	163	4.5	17	0.5	3,647
Concord	3,343	97.5	75	2.2	10	0.3	3,428
East Providence	9,980	94.2	543	5.1	74	0.7	10,597
Newton	18,708	98.0	352	1.8	41	0.2	19,101
Stoughton	4,504	91.3	387	7.8	39	0.8	4,930
Boston	55,123	93.0	3482	5.9	625	1.1	59,230
Boston SMSA	429,741	95.0	19831	4.4	2461	0.5	452,033
Brockton SMSA	956,519	94.5	49391	4.9	6263	0.6	1,012,173
Massachusetts	34,810	92.6	2504	6.7	283	0.8	37,597
Providence SMSA	157,509	94.0	9015	5.4	1071	0.6	167,595

Table 13. Characteristics of Vacant Year-Round Units Renter-Occupied—1970

	Number	Percent	Median Rent Asked* ($)
Canton	22	2.3	103
Concord	9	1.0	128
East Providence	109	2.3	84
Newton	213	2.6	176
Stoughton	60	4.0	169
Boston	10.034	6.0	87
Boston SMSA	17,913	4.2	95
Brockton SMSA	783	4.3	88
Massachusetts	37,130	4.7	86
Providence SMSA	6,959	5.6	60

*For places where all utilities are included

Table 13a. Densities of All Occupied Units (Renter)

Persons Per Room—1970

	Percent	1.00 or Less	1.01 to 1.50	1.51 or More	Total
Canton	NA	863	48	8	919
Concord	NA	875	27	9	911
East Providence	4.2	4,280	224	43	4,547
Newton	2.5	7,511	245	101	7,883
Stoughton	NA	1,359	66	17	1,442
Boston	4.0	381,322	19,902	6,444	407,668
Boston SMSA	5.0	698,467	37,993	11,059	747,519
Brockton SMSA	5.1	146,028	9,059	3,305	158,392
Massachusetts	5.4	16,094	943	261	17,298
Providence SMSA	6.4	109,371	5,936	1,473	116,780

Table 14. Gross Rents Specified Renter Occupied 1970

Area	Less Than $40		$40-59		$60-79		$80-99		$100-119		$120-$149		$150-$199		$200-$299		$300 and Over		No Cash Rents		Total	Median Rent	Percent Change 1960-1970 in Median Rent
	No.	%	No.	%	No.	%	No.	%	No.	%	No.	%	No.	%	No.	%	No.	%	No.	%	No.		
Canton	0	0	20	2	93	11	72	8	142	16	210	24	226	26	50	6	16	2	53	6	882	133	—
Concord	6	1	17	2	40	5	43	5	36	4	115	13	286	32	118	13	82	9	144	16	887	170	—
East Providence	230	5	234	5	689	15	865	19	903	20	739	16	497	11	150	3	17	0	201	4	4525	103	+51
Newton	0	—	232	3	181	2	281	4	579	7	1254	16	2392	31	1966	25	566	7	389	5	7840	175	+62
Stoughton	0	—	59	4	109	8	201	14	212	15	314	22	387	27	93	7	6	0	38	3	1419	130	—
Boston	699	0	5862	4	17816	11	18946	12	26854	17	40829	26	31369	20	10658	7	3075	2	1774	1	157972	126	+62
Boston SMSA	1538	0	14107	3	32537	8	42745	11	64768	16	101134	25	93495	23	37064	9	8712	2	9627	2	405727	133	+62
Brockton SMSA	245	1	1253	7	1721	10	3244	19	3790	22	3683	22	2143	13	443	3	23	0	561	3	17106	110	+80
Massachusetts	5483	1	41511	6	85501	12	117054	16	127968	17	155400	21	126907	17	44732	6	9389	1	27166	4	741111	117	+56
Providence SMSA	3154	3	12732	11	23831	21	26111	22	18960	16	4974	13	8374	7	2242	2	338	0	5468	5	116184	91	+34

Table 15. Zoning-Percent of Total Land by Category

		Industrial Zones (Percent)	Commercial Zones (Percent)	Total	Multi-Family	Residential Zones (Minimum Size Required in Square Feet)								
Area	Density (p/square mile)					8,000	10,000	15,000	20,000	25,000	30,000	40,000	45,000	80,000
Canton[a]	900	18	2	80	6[c]	—	10	16	16		24			
Concord[a]	626	4	3[d]	93	—		4[d]					28		45
Newton[b]	5070	4.5	2.8	92.9	.2	—	30.3[e]	37.3		25.1			24	
Stoughton[a]	1444	13	4	83	5	10		25	19		25			

[a]Percentages estimated from zoning map. Exact figure unavailable.
[b]Does not include publicly-owned land and cemeteries (3,254 acres, or 28.3 percent of city).
[c]Two-family permitted by right and apartments by special permit.
[d]Garden apartments permitted by special permit (up to 2-1/2 stories, 3,500 square feet per DU, and a maximum of 8 DU's).
[e]There are actually 4 zones here. One (equally 15.1 percent) is limited to single-family occupancy. The next two (14.8 percent combined) permit two-family occupancy by right. The final zone (.4 percent) permits apartments by special permit.

Chapter Ten

Public Policy Options

Federal Policies and Equal Opportunity

Equality of opportunity is a key to the American character. The effort to put low- and moderate-income housing in the suburbs falls squarely within this tradition. From their different perspectives, the Declaration of Independence was never far from the minds of the participants in the housing controversies of the five communities. Definitions of equality and the means necessary to achieve that goal differentiate national as well as local decision-makers. His administration's policy regarding the national goal of free access to housing opportunities was outlined by President Nixon in an 8,000-word statement concerning equal housing opportunity on June 11, 1971. The statement first espouses a passion for enforcing antidiscrimination laws and for the right of low-income workers to live in the suburbs where they work and to where industry is moving; it proceeds, nevertheless, to the declaration that his administration "will not attempt to impose federally assisted housing upon any community."

The federal government's role, asserted the President, is not to impose federally assisted housing upon municipalities that do not want it. Thus, the quality of housing, how much to build, where to build it, and who has access to it should be entrusted to local officials and to local and private initiative. Do you agree with this position? What are its advantages and disadvantages? What of the distinction the President makes between racial and economic discrimination? Is the Administration's position tantamount to a refusal to pursue national civil rights policy goals through housing and residential integration and through the provision of federal financial incentives?

In formulating answers to these questions, consider the following regarding social mobility and assimilation of minority groups.

The transition from rural, preindustrial areas to cities and low-status manual occupations has been and remains a painful, depriving, and traumatic process. Segregated housing kept European immigrants and blacks residentially separated from the mainstream of society and from decent quality human resources, services, and programs necessary for adequate socialization, assimilation, and social acceptance. The melting pot ideology, in many respects more a myth than reality, ignores the resultant widespread inequality. In fact, many of these problems are deeply embedded in the social structure of our society, and in the history of discrimination toward all newcomers, but especially toward blacks. They are reinforced by discriminations in economic power and the availability of jobs.

Residential segregation has generated the poor quality of municipal services for minority groups increasingly trapped in the inner city. Housing does not mean shelter alone—it means a collection of services and opportunities based on locations. The entire standard of living of the individual, of his capacity for self-fulfillment, and of his relationship to the community can be dependent on where he lives. Access to jobs, safety in the streets, the quality of life (reflected even in mundane matters such as reliable garbage collection or in the soaring aspirations of surrounding architecture) are examples of this synergism. Education, dependent as we are upon the neighborhood-school doctrine, is a prime example of a service, so crucial to life in an urban, interdependent society, that hinges on where the child's home is located. As the court found in Crow v. Brown, 332 F. Supp. 382 (N.D.Ga, 1971), dealing with the Atlanta metropolitan area: "One of the consequences of this racial concentration is that it has become virtually impossible to achieve meaningful school desegregation . . . a second consequence has been a swelling of the unemployment rolls in the city since job opportunities have become more scarce each year although they have increased in the suburbs." Professor Coleman's study of educational opportunities indicates that the lower the social class position of the parents, the more likely that their child's education is inadequately financed and of lower quality. Quite probably, integration of education alone, were it possible throughout the metropolitan region, would have a definite impact on the social mobility and subsequent opportunities of blacks and other minorities.

In viewing housing as more than bricks and mortar, it is prudent to underscore the great symbolic meaning a house may have to a family. Housing is an objective criterion for the image each of us has of himself and of his position in the social order.

In this context consider, now, the Presidential policy statement in fuller detail:

> It will be the firm purpose of this administration to carry out all the requirements of the law fully and fairly.
>
> Racial discrimination in housing is illegal, and will not be tolerated. In order to fulfill their responsibility for eliminating this discrimination, the Department of Housing and Urban Development

and the Justice Department have been developing and elaborating a wide-ranging program aimed at creating equal housing opportunity.

By "equal housing opportunity," I mean the achievement of a condition in which individuals of similar income levels in the same housing market area have a like range of housing choices available to them regardless of their race, color, religion, or national origin.

At the outset, we set three basic requirements for our program to achieve equal housing opportunity: It must be aimed at correcting the effects of past discrimination; it must contain safeguards to ensure against future discrimination; and it must be results-oriented so its progress toward the overall goal of increasing housing opportunities can be evaluated. . . .

We will not seek to impose economic integration upon an existing local jurisdiction; at the same time, we will not countenance any use of economic measures as a subterfuge for racial discrimination.

When such an action is called into question, we will study its effect. If the effect of the action is to exclude Americans from equal housing opportunity on the basis of their race, religion, or ethnic background, we will vigorously oppose it by whatever means are most appropriate—regardless of the rationale which may have cloaked the discriminatory act. . . .

As a major part of our national effort to meet these housing needs—an effort which is both private and governmental—federally assisted housing is being built at a rate approaching 3/4 of a million units a year. These units are needed. They are being built. And they must be built someplace. The question is where.

If all the federally assisted units are packed together in one type of community or one kind of location, we will only exacerbate the social and, in all probability, the racial isolation of our people from each other.

If we build federally assisted instant ghettos, we fail both our communities and the people we are trying to help.

If we impact or tip the balance of an established community with a flood of low-income families, we do a disservice to all concerned.

The answers to these practical considerations are not simple—but they are of great importance.

Based on a careful review of the legislative history of the 1964 and 1968 Civil Rights Acts, and also of the program context within which the law has developed, I interpret the "affirmative action" mandate of the 1968 act to mean that the administrator of a housing program should include, among the various criteria by which applications for assistance are judged, the extent to which a proposed project, or the overall development plan of which it is a part, will in fact open up new, nonsegregated housing opportunities that will contribute to decreasing the effects of past housing discrimination. This does not mean that no federally assisted low- and moderate-income housing may be built within areas of minority concentration. It does not mean that housing officials in Federal agencies should dictate local land use policies. It does mean that in choosing among the various applications for Federal aid, consideration should be given to their impact on patterns of racial concentration. . . .

This administration will not attempt to impose federally assisted housing upon any community.

We will encourage communities to discharge their responsibility for helping to provide decent housing opportunities to the Americans of low- and moderate-income who live or work within their boundaries.

We will encourage communities to seek and accept well-conceived, well-designed, well-managed housing developments—always within the community's capacity to assimilate the families who will live in them.

We will carry out our programs in a way that will be as helpful as possible to communities which are receptive to the expansion of housing opportunities for all of our people.

In these efforts we will be aided by a change that already is taking place in the way subsidized low- and moderate-income housing is planned, built, and managed. In terms of new construction, the old style, massively concentrated high-rise public housing project is largely a thing of the past; the trend now is strongly toward low-rise dwellings, many of them one-, two-, three- or four-family, on scattered sites, so that they can blend in with the community without detracting from nearby properties. Under the newer Federal programs of financial assistance to low- and moderate-income housing of other sorts, the pattern has been one of variety, enabling the community to fit the development to its own needs.

By approaching local questions of land-use planning in a creative and sophisticated manner, local authorities should in most cases be able to work out site selection problems in ways that provide adequate housing opportunities for those who need them without disrupting the community. . . .

Black Jack, Missouri, came to national attention in early 1971. What made the case so prominent was its timing; it forced the Nixon Administration to spell out a policy on low-cost housing and suburbia.

Black Jack was an almost entirely white, middle-class settlement of 3,900 people. It was unincorporated and zoned for multiple-family dwellings. Then a church-sponsored, non-profit developer in St. Louis announced it would build a federally sponsored, multi-family housing project. One of the new city's first acts after incorporating was to adopt one-acre, single-family zoning.

Two years later, the case became the first legal challenge, by the federal government itself, of a suburb's use of its zoning power to exclude federally subsidized housing. *The New York Times* (April 1, 1973) described the two-week trial as follows:

A team of Justice Department lawyers sought to prove that officials in Black Jack, a small community north of here, discriminated against blacks by approving a zoning law that barred all apartments.

At the trial's conclusion on Thursday, the chief United States district judge, James H. Meredith, gave each side 75 days to file briefs. He will then begin sifting through large piles of evidence submitted in the case—including financial reports on all federally subsidized housing projects in the St. Louis area. Judge Meredith heard the case without a jury.

Specifically at issue is a planned 220-unit complex, called Park View Heights, for families with incomes from about $5,500 to $10,000. The average income for the 1,200 who now live in Black Jack was put at $15,000.

A former Black Jack Mayor, Keith J. Barbero, conceded during the trial that racial discrimination had been a factor when residents of the formerly unincorporated area created the town of Black Jack in August, 1970, and promptly ruled out the previously approved apartment project.

The Justice Department is seeking a court ruling that Black Jack's action violated the Fair Housing Act of 1968 and that the Park View Heights project should be allowed.

Attorneys for Black Jack argued that town officials opposed the proposed project on the ground that it might fail financially and not because the nearly all-white town might be inundated with black residents.

Black Jack officials testified that they believed they were avoiding discrimination—not committing it—by deciding to rule out all new apartments in the town on the ground that Black Jack was already saturated with multi-family units.

The suit against Black Jack was filed in June, 1971, within a week after President Nixon declared himself opposed to what he calls forced economic integration of communities.

In announcing the suit, John N. Mitchell, then the Attorney General, said the Nixon Administration would continue to investigate actions by local governments "where there is the purpose and effect of racial discrimination."

A previous suit filed by the Park View Heights developers seeking damages against Black Jack for blocking the project was dismissed by another Federal judge here, but the United States Court of Appeals for the Eighth Circuit said the dismissal had been erroneous and that the Black Jack issue was "ripe for judicial consideration."

Several witnesses presented by the Justice Department said during the trial that persons who opposed the housing project had used racial slurs in fighting the plan.

Frank E. Schwelb, a Justice Department civil rights lawyer, told the court that the pattern of housing segregation in the Black Jack area "was not fortuitous, but resulted from a long and melancholy history of deliberate discrimination in housing by both public and private bodies."

Justice Department lawyers presented statistical evidence that the Black Jack area was 98 to 99 percent white and that the action of prohibiting apartments for persons with low or moderate incomes would automatically have the effect of perpetuating segregation.

Sheldon K. Stock, a Black Jack lawyer, described the evidence as a "statistical wonderland proving nothing."

The Black Jack lawyers accused the Federal Government of attempting to "achieve by judicial action what it had been unable to achieve through legislative action." They said that the Justice Department was using Black Jack to "put the nation itself on trial."

The following are excerpts from the pretrial brief for the United States, Civil Action No. 71 C 372(1), United States, Plaintiff v. City of Black Jack, Missouri, a Municipal Corporation, the Defendant:

On October 20, 1970, the newly incorporated City of Black Jack passed a zoning ordinance excluding any further apartment construction within that municipality, and thereby prohibited the construction of the proposed Park View Heights development under the FHA Section 236 program. The question in this case is whether this zoning ordinance, in the context in which it was passed, constituted racially discriminatory conduct denying persons equal housing opportunity secured by the Fair Housing Act, 42 U.S.C. 3601 et seq. The United States contends that it did, and seeks relief pursuant to 42 U.S.C. 3613, which authorizes suit by the Attorney General where denials of equal housing opportunity have a public as well as a private impact.

At the trial, the United States will endeavor to establish the following:

1. The effect of Black Jack's conduct was racially discriminatory, in that it perpetuated the virtually all-white character of Black Jack and the existing pattern of racial segregation in housing in the St. Louis metropolitan area. This pattern of segregation was not fortuitous, but resulted from a long and melancholy history of deliberate discrimination in housing by both public and private bodies. Its reinforcement by Black Jack not only impaired equal housing opportunity, but equal employment opportunity and equal educational opportunity as well.

2. Racially discriminatory impact being shown, Black Jack has the burden to establish that its action was required by a compelling state interest. The evidence will show that Black Jack cannot even approach making such a showing, and that, in fact, Black Jack's extraordinary course of conduct in this case, beginning with its remarkably-timed secession from St. Louis County, and continuing through its passage of the challenged zoning ordinance, contravened established principles of zoning and planning. Our expert testimony will establish that, far from showing a compelling nonracial necessity to do what it did, Black Jack will not be able to show that its conduct, from a nonracial standpoint, was even plausible.

3. Black Jack's officials had a duty to know, and in fact knew, that the effect of their conduct would be to perpetuate segregation. Under conventional legal principles and common experience, they were presumed to intend the natural consequences of their conduct, and in that sense, their purpose was racially discriminatory. In addition, there is extensive extrinsic evidence of racially based opposition to Park View Heights both by the architects of the secession and restrictive zoning ordinance and by the citizens to whose views the leaders were responding. The proof of racially discriminatory purpose is germane not only to bolster the proof of a violation, but also to counteract any attempt to show a "compelling state interest" to justify its action.

In the suburban central-city controversy over the location of low-income housing, the site selection policies of the executive departments—especially the Department of Housing and Urban Development—are crucial. As keepers of the national conscience, they have key roles to play in the exclusionary zoning game—not to mention a strategic use of the power of the purse. Sharply brought out in the following discussions of the location of low-income housing throughout the metropolitan area are the different perspectives brought to bear by the separate branches of government on the interplay of the Housing Acts of 1949 and 1968 with the Civil Rights Acts of 1964 and 1968. The progression in the thinking of the Congress has been variously interpreted by the executive and judicial branches. Would you agree that the courts, of all three branches, have been the most willing to discover (often, with ingenuity) a national housing policy of balanced and dispersed public and low- and moderate-income housing? How do you evaluate the following expression of administrative policy?

Consider the Department of Housing and Urban Development Project Selection Criteria, 37 Fed. Reg. 203 (1972):

**Evaluation of Rent Supplement Projects and
Low-Rent Housing Assistance Application**

The purpose of these regulations is to set forth criteria by which the Department will evaluate applications for funding of housing projects under sections 235(i) and 236 of the National Housing Act, rent supplement projects and low-rent housing assistance applications under the U.S. Housing Act of 1937.

On June 24, 1971 (36 F.R. 12032) the Department first published these criteria for public comment as a notice of proposed rule making. . . .

The Department has now considered each comment received and publishes these regulations in final form to be effective February 7,

1972. Principal changes and the Department's response to significant comments are set forth below. . . .

Some comments asserted that the project selection criteria will result in too few projects being built in the inner cities, and others asserted that the criteria will result in too many projects being built there. In the same vein, some comments suggested that the criteria emphasized and encouraged one factor too much or too little. The Department has considered such comments, but believes that the present system gives each of the criteria proper weight and achieves a proper balance of countervailing needs and interests.

It was suggested that the term "housing market area," used several times in the criteria, should be defined to coincide with boundaries of local political jurisdictions. It was also suggested that certain parts of housing market areas should be allotted housing funds irrespective of ratings on the criteria. The Department has declined to adopt these suggestions because housing market areas often are independent of arbitrary political boundaries and allotments to certain parts of those areas could result in the Department's approving projects which would be less than the best that could be created for the people of each housing market area.

Some comments misconstrued the purpose of the project selection criteria as being confined to site selection. In its decision to fund or not to fund a project, the Department believes that it should take into consideration other factors in addition to proposed location of the housing. . . .

Criterion No. 1, Need for Low(er) Income Housing. In response to suggestions for improved clarity over the June version, the instructions now specify the concept of need in terms of number of rooms and structure type. The instructions omit, as unnecessary, references in the October version to specific markets (such as large families and the elderly) because consideration of these factors is included in the broad language of the criterion. The "poor" rating of the October version has been rephrased to eliminate reference to vacancy rates and to add a reference to "comparably priced, standard unsubsidized housing." Several of the comments, such as the one received from the U.S. Civil Rights Commission, pointed out that overall vacancy rates may not be an accurate reflection of ability to satisfy lower income housing needs. As suggested by NAHRO, the "superior" rating now contains the phrase "as a relocation resource" to clarify the connection between housing need and provision of housing for displacees.

Criterion No. 2, Minority Housing Opportunities. This criterion has been rephrased to clearly distinguish between three kinds of areas: (1) Areas of minority concentration, (2) substantially racially mixed areas, and (3) areas which are outside of (1) and (2).

A phrase has been added which permits building in areas of minority concentration if there exist "sufficient, comparable opportunities . . . for housing for minority families, in the income range to be served by the proposed project, outside areas of minority concentration." This is designed to assure that building in minority areas goes forward only after there truly exist housing opportunities for minorities elsewhere. The phrase "sufficient, comparable opportunities" is designed to assure that the housing available to minorities outside areas of minority concentration is more than a token amount of so few units that there is in fact no true opportunity. At the same time, the phrase is not tied to any rigid formula.

The provision for building inside areas of minority concentration if prospective residents of the project or residents of the project area express a desire for it has been stricken and will not be used. The Department is convinced that such a provision is unworkable and would have been abused, as comments, such as that of the League of Women Voters, suggested. . . .

Housing proposed to be built in substantially racially mixed areas has been omitted from the alternatives of the "superior" rating. Although building in such areas is now permitted under "adequate" where the proposed project will not cause the proportion of minority to nonminority residents to increase significantly, the Department deems it undesirable to encourage projects in these areas by giving them "superior" ratings because such projects in the large numbers a high rating could generate might contribute to a stable racially mixed area's becoming one of minority concentration.

The alternative under "superior" in the October version which referred specifically to Urban Renewal and Model Cities areas was removed because many such areas could not be expected to serve a wide range of income levels and a racially varied population. The phrase "in or near an area of minority concentration" has been shortened throughout to "in an area of minority concentration." Avoidance of adverse impact on transitional areas is addressed elsewhere in the criterion.

An additional provision (4) was added to "adequate" to accommodate housing market areas in which there is little or no minority population. Documentation requirements have been extended to all "superior" and "adequate" ratings.

Criterion 3, Improved Location for Low(er) Income Families. The phrase "similar market value" is substituted throughout for "similar price range," used in the October version of this criterion, and the phrase "unsubsidized housing" has been clarified to "standard unsubsidized housing." These revisions are intended to make clear that in considering a proposed site, HUD will compare facilities and services in the neighborhood surrounding the site with facilities and services in other neighborhoods which are made up of standard, unsubsidized housing similar in market value to the housing in the neighborhood of the proposed project.

Other changes include redefinition of the word "section," from "the project neighborhood and surrounding neighborhoods" to "the project neighborhood and contiguous neighborhoods." . . .

Criterion 4, Relationship to Orderly Growth and Development. Although there are many areas without plans which will meet this criterion, and the Department will not itself develop such plans, as comments suggested, the Department hopes this criterion will encourage their adoption. The statement of objectives and the "superior" rating specify that acceptable planning should contain a housing element, as suggested by the U.S. Civil Rights Commission and others. . . .

To dispel some confusion the "superior" instructions add a parenthetical statement that "zoning alone does not constitute an officially approved land use or other development plan." A "superior" rating now specifically recognizes a planning policy for dispersal of subsidized housing adopted by a State housing or metropolitan areawide development agency, in addition to plans of a local agency. The provision under "adequate" concerning the absence of, or inconsistency with, metropolitan or regional plans was removed because it was contradictory to the objectives of this criterion.

Criterion 5, Relationship of Proposed Project to Physical Environment. In order to remove any ambiguity in the June version and to relate this criterion to considerations of the National Environmental Policy Act, the revised criterion focuses upon the physical aspects of project design and location and is now a required criterion, as requested by the Chairman of the Council on Environmental Quality...

Criterion 6, Ability to Perform. For clarity, this criterion is revised slightly over the October version. The most important change is use of the phrase "each of the following" which removes difficulty regarding how to rate an efficient contractor who ignores Equal Opportunity guidelines and requirements.

Some comments urged that this criterion will be too harsh on minority or nonprofit sponsors. However, the Department considers the present language is sufficiently lenient without making the criterion meaningless. To achieve national housing goals, ability to perform must be a consideration. . . .

General instructions: In evaluating proposals involving five (5) or more dwelling units (25 or more in the case of public housing acquisition or leasing), the Area or Insuring Office shall utilize the following Project Selection Criteria. Enter a brief explanation on the lines provided of the way in which the proposal satisfies each applicable consideration, so that the factual basis for the evaluation and rating assigned is clear. Attach supporting documentation and extra sheet(s), if necessary for a complete explanation. Evaluate each criterion by checking the appropriate box—Superior, Adequate, or Poor.

1. *Need for low(er) income housing* ☐ Superior   ☐ Adequate   ☐ Poor

Objective: To identify the proposed projects which will best serve the most urgent unmet needs for housing for Low(er) income households.

(A) A *superior* rating shall be given to a proposed project:

(1) Which responds well to the most urgent housing needs of low(er) income households in the market area in terms of number of bedrooms and structure type; *or,*_____

(2) As to which there is documented evidence that the housing is needed as a relocation resource to serve families displaced or to be displaced by governmental action, including families or individuals being displaced by the proposed project, and that the applicant will give preference to those so displaced_____

(B) An *adequate* rating shall be given to a proposed project which responds to housing needs of low(er) income households in the market area in terms of number of bedrooms and structure type____

(C) A *poor* rating shall be given to a proposed project which:

(1) Does not respond to housing needs of low(er) income households in the market area; *or,*_____

(2) Duplicates or competes unreasonably with other subsidized or comparably-priced, standard unsubsidized housing projects in the same locality in such a way as to overbuild the market_____

2. *Minority Housing opportunities* ☐ Superior   ☐ Adequate   ☐ Poor

Objectives:

To provide minority families with opportunities for housing in a wide range of locations.

To open up nonsegregated housing opportunities that will contribute to decreasing the effects of past housing discrimination.

(A) A *superior* rating shall be given if the proposed project will be located:

(1) So that, within the housing market area, it will provide opportunities for minorities for housing outside existing areas of minority concentration and outside areas which are already substantially racially mixed; *or,*_____

(2) In an area of minority concentration, but the area is part of an official State or local agency development plan, and sufficient, comparable opportunities exist for housing for minority families, in the income range to be served by the proposed project, outside areas of minority concentration_____

(B) An *adequate* rating shall be given if the proposed project will be located:

(1) Outside an area of minority concentration, but the area is racially mixed, and the proposed project will not cause a significant increase in the proportion of minority to nonminority residents in the area; *or*, _____

(2) In an area of minority concentration and sufficient, comparable opportunities exist for housing for minority families, in the income range to be served by the proposed project, outside areas of minority concentration; *or*, _____

(3) In an area of minority concentration, but is necessary to meet overriding housing needs which cannot otherwise feasibly be met in that housing market area. (An "overriding need" may not serve as the basis for an "adequate" rating if the only reason the need cannot otherwise feasibly be met is that discrimination on the basis of race, color or national origin renders sites outside areas of minority concentration unavailable); *or*, _____

(4) In a housing market area with few or no minority group residents _____

All "superior" and "adequate" ratings shall be accompanied by documented findings based upon relevant racial, socioeconomic, and other data and information.

(C) A *poor* rating shall be given if the proposed project does not satisfy any of the above conditions, e.g., will cause a significant increase in the proportion of minority residents in an area which is not one of minority concentration, but which is racially mixed _____

3. *Improved location for low(er) income families* ☐ Superior ☐ Adequate ☐ Poor

Objectives:

To avoid concentrating subsidized housing in any one section of a metropolitan area or town.

To provide low(er) income households with opportunities for housing in a wide range of locations.

To locate subsidized housing in sections containing facilities and services that are typical of those found in neighborhoods consisting largely of standard, unsubsidized housing of a similar market value.

To locate subsidized housing in areas reasonably accessible to job opportunities.

(A) A *superior* rating shall be given if the proposed project:

(1) Will be located in a section (consisting of the project neighborhood and contiguous neighborhoods) that contains little or no federally-subsidized housing and (a) the proposed project is, or will be by the occupancy date or very shortly thereafter, accessible to

social, recreational, educational, commercial, and health facilities and services, and other municipal services that are equivalent to or better than those typically found in neighborhoods consisting largely of standard, unsubsidized housing of a similar market value, and (b) travel time and cost via public transportation or private auto from the neighborhood to employment providing a range of jobs for low(er) income workers is considered excellent for such families in the metropolitan area or town. (While it is important that elderly housing not be totally isolated from all employment opportunities, for such projects the requirements of (b) above need not be adhered to rigidly); *or*,_____

(2) Is part of a New Community Development Plan approved under Title VII of the Housing and Urban Development Act of 1970.

(B) An *adequate* rating shall be given to a proposed project which will be located:

(1) In a section already containing federally-subsidized housing if, with the addition of the proposed housing, the resulting number of federally-subsidized units will not establish the character of the section as one of subsidized housing and the housing will provide an expanded range of housing opportunity for low(er) income families; *or*,_____

(2) In an undeveloped area, but the scale of the project will not be such that it establishes the character of the section as one of subsidized housing;_____

(3) *And,* in the event of either (1) or (2): (a) The project is, or will be by the occupancy date or very shortly thereafter, accessible to social, recreational, educational, commercial, and health facilities and services, and other municipal services that are equivalent to those typically found in neighborhoods consisting largely of unsubsidized standard housing of a similar market value, and (b) traveltime and cost via public transportation or private auto from the neighborhood to employment providing a range of jobs for low(er) income workers is reasonable for such families in the metropolitan area or town. (While it is important that elderly housing not be totally isolated from all employment opportunities, for such projects the requirements of (b) above need not be adhered to rigidly); *or*,_____

(4) In an Urban Renewal or Model Cities area and such housing is required to fulfill, respectively, the Urban Renewal Plan or the Comprehensive City Demonstration Program_____

(C) A *poor* rating shall be given if:

(1) The proposed project will be located in a section characterized as one of subsidized housing; *or*,_____

(2) The proposed project will establish the character of the section as one of subsidized housing; *or*,_____

(3) Social, recreational, educational, commercial, and health facilities and services, and other municipal services: (a) are not, or will not be by the occupancy date or very shortly thereafter, accessible to the project; *or* (b) although accessible to the project, are inferior to those generally found in neighborhoods consisting largely of standard, unsubsidized housing of a similar market value; *or*,_____

(4) Travel time and cost via public transportation or private auto from the neighborhood to employment providing a range of jobs for low(er) income workers will be appreciably greater than that usually required in the metropolitan area or town. _____

4. *Relationship to orderly growth and development* ☐ Superior ☐ Adequate ☐ Poor

Objectives:

To assure that the proposed development is consistent with principles of orderly growth and development.

To prevent urban sprawl and the premature development or overdevelopment of land before supporting facilities are available.

To develop housing consistent with officially approved State or multijurisdictional plans.

To encourage formulation of area-wide plans which include a housing element relative to needs and goals for low- and moderate-income housing as well as balanced production throughout a metropolitan area.

(a) A *superior* rating shall be given if the proposed project:

(1) Will be consistent with the housing element of a local, officially-approved land use or other development plan which is consistent with metropolitan or regional plans (zoning alone does not constitute an officially-approved land use or other development plan); *or*,_____

(2) Will be located in and be consistent with plans for a neighborhood that is undergoing improvement via Urban Renewal, Model Cities, New Communities or other similar Federal, State, or local development programs; *or*,_____

(3) Is consistent with a policy adopted by a State housing or metropolitan areawide development agency or the local governing body (especially where this policy implements a multijurisdictional approach) for providing for and dispersing housing for low- and moderate-income families. . . .

5. *Relationship of proposed project to physical environment* ☐ Superior ☐ Adequate ☐ Poor

Objectives:

To provide an attractive and well-planned physical environment.

To prevent any adverse impact on the environment resulting from construction of the proposed housing.

Public Policy Options

To avoid site locations whose environmental conditions would be detrimental to the success of an otherwise sound project.

(a) A *superior* rating shall be given if the proposed housing will:

(1) Embody outstanding land use planning and excellent architectural treatment, *and*_____

(2) Be free from adverse environmental conditions, natural or manmade, such as instability, flooding, septic tank backups, sewage hazards, or mudslide; harmful air pollution, smoke or dust; excessive noise, vibration, or vehicular traffic; unsanitary rodent or vermin infestation; or dangerous fire hazards; *and,*_____

(3) Not, considering both long-term and short-term effects, impact or impair ecologically valuable or significant natural areas, such as wildlife areas, ground water or surface water areas, and parklands, or significant historical or archeological areas. . . .

6. *Ability to perform*   ☐ Superior   ☐ Adequate   ☐ Poor

Objective: To produce housing promptly and to provide quality housing at a reasonable cost, taking into account Equal Opportunity guidelines and requirements.

7. *Project potential for creating minority employment and business opportunities*   ☐ Superior   ☐ Adequate   ☐ Poor

Objectives:

To encourage housing proposals which will generate job opportunities for minority workers.

To provide opportunities for business concerns owned in substantial part by minority persons.

(A) A *superior* rating will be given if the proposal shows good potential, based on the applicant's stated, specific goals, hiring timetables, and past performance, if any for:

(1) Providing training and/or employment for minority persons; *and*_____

(2) Utilizing business concerns (including but not limited to the prime contractor) owned, controlled or managed in substantial part by minority persons. This potential may include training, employment and business opportunities in all phases of development, including but not limited to planning, site development, building, maintenance, and management. . . .

8. *Provision for sound housing management*

Objective: To encourage the development of well-managed and well-maintained projects so as to significantly increase their potential for successful, long-term operation and to foster good relations between tenants and management and the surrounding community.

(A) A *superior* rating shall be given to a proposed project which:

(1) If submitted under the section 236 or Rent Supplement programs (a) includes a management plan (based on "Management Plan

Requirements"), which significantly exceeds present HUD requirements and guidelines in terms of the quality of management proposed and the services to be provided; *and* (b) has a sponsor and, if applicable, management agent which have demonstrated, through past performance, superior: Maintenance policies, financial stability, tenant-management relations, and overall management practices (with due consideration for past performance in regard to avoiding defaults, need for mortgage payment relief or other significant problems); . . .

Summary of Ratings

Priority group. Check only one box shown below representing the total number of ratings assigned on the form; or *disapproval*. A Superior or Adequate rating is required for all criteria.

	Section 235(1)[1]				Rent Supplement, Section 236 or Low-Rent Public Housing		
Priority Group	*Ratings*			Priority Group	*Ratings*		
	Superior	Adequate	Poor		Superior	Adequate	Poor
1. ☐	7	0	0	1. ☐	8	0	0
2. ☐	6	1	0	2. ☐	7	1	0
3. ☐	5	2	0	3. ☐	6	2	0
4. ☐	4	3	0	4. ☐	5	3	0
5. ☐	3	4	0	5. ☐	4	4	0
6. ☐	2	5	0	6. ☐	3	5	0
7. ☐	1	6	0	7. ☐	2	6	0
8. ☐	0	7	0	8. ☐	1	7	0
				9. ☐	0	8	0

☐ Disapproval. A *Poor* rating on any criterion: ☐ Disapproval. A *Poor* rating on any criterion.

[1] Criterion #8 (Management) is not applicable to Section 235.

NOTE: Proposals shall be evaluated when received and shall not be stockpiled unreasonably. After rating has been assigned above, proposals in priority group 1 shall be funded ahead of those in priority group 2, proposals in priority group 2 shall be funded ahead of those in group 3, and so on. Within each group, proposals shall be funded in order of date of receipt of applications suitable for processing.

Evaluation Prepared By

(Date)   (Name and title)

The above ratings have been assigned with my approval.

(Date)   Director, Operations Division Area Office

or   Chief Underwriter, Insuring Office

In the Gautreaux and Shannon line of cases which follow, the courts were pushed into the arena of second-guessing the site selection processes of the Executive branch. How successful were they in discharging this function?

Gautreaux v. Chicago Housing Authority, 296 F. Supp. 907 (N.D. Ill. 1969)

In 1969 the District Court for the Northern District of Illinois found that the Chicago Housing Authority had violated the fourteenth amendment rights of the plaintiffs, public housing tenants and applicants, by perpetuating racially discriminatory site selection and tenant assignment procedures. Subsequently, the court ordered the Chicago Housing Authority to use "best efforts" to select new housing sites in "general or white" areas of Chicago. Gautreaux v. Chicago Housing Authority, 304 F. Supp. 736, 741, enforcing 296 F. Supp. 907 (N.D. Ill. 1969). The order specified that the next 700 public housing units, and 75 percent of units constructed thereafter, should be located at least one mile from the outer boundary of census tracts with greater than 30 percent nonwhite population, 304 F. Supp. at 738. Except under a supplementary court order in 1970, however, the Chicago Housing Authority failed to submit any new public housing sites to the Chicago City Council for the necessary approval. The supplementary order is set out in Gautreaux v. Chicago Housing Authority, 436 F. 2d 306, 310-11 (7th Cir. 1970), cert. denied, 402 U.S. 922 (1971) (upholding the order). See Note, 83 Harv. L. Rev. 1441 (1970). In Gautreaux v. Romney, 332 F. Supp. 366 (N.D. Ill. 1971), the district court granted an injunction prohibiting the Department of Housing and Urban Development from releasing Model Cities funds until the City had approved a minimum number of new public housing units in white areas. On appeal, the Court of Appeals for the Seventh Circuit reversed, holding that it was improper for the district court to threaten termination of federal funds to a program not proven discriminatory in order to remedy discrimination in a different program. Gautreaux v. Romney, 457 F. 2d 124 (7th Cir. 1972). See Note, 86 Harv. L. Rev. 427 (1972).

Shannon v. Dept. of Housing and Urban Development, 436 F.2d 809 (3rd Cir. 1970)

The court considered a challenge to HUD's authority to approve changes in a local urban renewal plan without holding further public hearings. The original urban renewal plan envisioned a medium density, homeownership oriented neighborhood, designed to "create a more stable and racially balanced environment." It was altered to allow construction of a 221(d)(3) project with 100% rent supplements, which "from a social standpoint ... is the functional equivalent of a low-rent public housing project." Challenging this alteration were residents and businessmen of the area, both black and white, who "claim that in reliance on the original plan ... they made substantial investments, commitments, and, in some cases, home purchases." Apparently the area already had a significant concentration of low income and predominantly black residents.

Carefully tracing the development and convergence of federal housing and civil rights policy, the court concluded that "increase or maintenance of racial concentration is prima facie likely to lead to urban blight and is, thus, prima facie at variance with national housing policy." "While HUD has broad discretion to choose between alternative types of housing," the court went on, "its choice must be exercised within the framework of the national policy against discrimination in federally assisted housing ... Here the agency concentrated on land-use factors and made no investigation or determination of the social factors involved in the choice of the type of housing which it approved ... the Agency must utilize some institutionalized method whereby, in considering site selection or type selection, it has before it the relevant racial and socioeconomic information necessary for compliance with its duties under the 1964 and 1968 Civil Rights Acts. ... Without in any way attempting to limit the agency in the exercise of its own administrative expertise, we suggest that some considerations relevant to a proper determination by HUD include the following:

1. What procedures were used by the LPA in considering the effects on racial concentration when it made a choice of site or of type of housing?
2. What tenant selection methods will be employed with respect to the proposed project?
3. How has the LPA or the local governing body historically reacted to proposals for low income housing outside areas of racial concentration?
4. Where is low-income housing, both public and publicly assisted, now located in the geographic area of the LPA?
5. Where is middle-income and luxury housing, in particular middle-income and luxury housing with federal mortgage insurance guarantees, located in the geographic area of the LPA?
6. Are some low-income housing projects in the geographic area of the LPA occupied primarily by tenants of one race, and, if so, where are they located?
7. What is the projected racial composition of tenants of the proposed project?
8. Will the project house school age children and if so what schools will they attend and what is the racial balance in those schools?

9. Have the zoning and other land-use regulations of the local governing body in the geographic area of the LPA had the effect of confining low-income housing to certain areas, and, if so, how has this affected racial concentration?

10. Are there alternative available sites?

11. At the site selected by the LPA how severe is the need for restoration, and are other alternative means of restoration available which would have preferable effects on racial concentration in that area?

The foregoing considerations are confined to the geographic area served by the LPA. We do not suggest that by so confining our listing we would restrict HUD to a review of factors operating only within such geographic area. The time may come when, in order to achieve the goals of the national housing policy, HUD will have to take steps to overcome the effects of contrasts in urban and suburban land-use regulations. What those steps should be we do not here suggest.

QUESTIONS

How do the HUD site selection criteria, p. 325 supra, compare with these suggested considerations?

The Shannon court left unresolved many of the substantive issues. Site selection is one variable in integrating housing. But site selection fails if a project in a white neighborhood fills up with a majority of white tenants. What role should tenant selection play in guaranteeing maximum integration? The Shannon court put its faith in procedural reform, but it reserved the right to judicial review of agency decisions under the Administrative Procedure Act. On what grounds could the courts review a decision made under the HUD regulations? Would HUD have the evidence to defend its decisions convincingly? What problems are there in relying on judicial decisions to maintain an aggressive program of integration through public housing? (Cf. 85 Harv. L. Rev. 870, 1972.)

What is the goal of site selection underlying Shannon and the HUD regulations? What would Imamu Baraka (formerly Leroi Jones), for example, have to say about it?

Could local politics frustrate an even more active HUD? How could HUD defuse bureaucratic and neighborhood opposition if it sponsored more controversial sites in mixed neighborhoods?

How do the HUD regulations approach the problem of exclusionary zoning laws? Would the Shannon decision sanction a tougher federal approach to local zoning laws?

Professors Meyerson and Banfield, in Politics, Planning and the Public Interest 269 (1955), suggest the following. "The process by which a housing program for Chicago was formulated resembled somewhat the parlor game in which each player adds a word to a sentence which is passed around the circle of players: the player acts *as if* the words that are handed to him expressed some intention (i.e., as if the sentence that comes to him were *planned*) and he does his part to sustain the illusion. In playing this game the staff of the Authority was bound by the previous moves. The sentence was already largely formed when it was handed to it; Congress had written the first words, the Public Housing Administration had written the next several, and then the Illinois Legislature, the State Housing Board, the Mayor and City Council, and the CHA Board of Commissioners had each in turn written a few. It was up to the staff to finish the sentence in a way that would seem rational, but this may have been an impossibility." Do you agree?

The Federal Leverage

On consideration, suburban growth can be seen as very closely related to many federal policies. Federal funds of all kinds have been traditionally used to enhance suburban growth and stimulate further development—and thus singled out, they are partly responsible for present residential socioeconomic segregation. For example, residents of suburbs are helped by the FHA programs that have insured more than $130 billion in mortgages. These programs have also assisted more than 9.5 million families to become homeowners, and helped build more than 1.4 million apartments. In reviewing housing subsidy programs, economists have been quick to point out that the middle classes reap the benefit of over $5 billion of annual tax savings by way of interest and property tax deductions to homeowners. Federal funds for highways provide yet another example. Both the circumferential freeways—that surround most metropolitan areas and as part of the federal interstate system are financed 90 percent with federal funds—and the standard interstate highways have facilitated the growing economic independence of the suburbs from central cities. Five years after completion of Route 128 in 1952, there were at least 99 new commercial or industrial facilities along that road, 77 of them originally located in Boston. These plants represented a loss of 3,701 jobs to Boston and a net gain of 13,000 jobs to the suburbs. In the nine years between 1958 and 1967, the number of companies rose to 729 and the employment figures to 66,041 workers. Why would the federal government, investing billions in highways, tolerate inequities in access to the suburbs and the metropolitan problems that this generates?

A classic argument offered by opponents to low- and moderate-income housing in the suburbs is the fear of increased taxes due to additional pressures upon municipal amenities, such as schools, water, and sewage systems. Can and should such pressures be offset by federal community development aids, such as, for example, urban renewal write-downs, rehabilitation loans, water and sewerage funds, and open space grants, if made available on condition that the suburb accepts low- and moderate-income housing? The financial incentives can be considerable, as is demonstrated by the Stoughton case. On

April 19, 1973, President Nixon sent to Congress the "Better Communities Bill," a special revenue-sharing proposal, for a $2.3-billion-a-year program for five years, beginning in 1974 for locally controlled urban development. Parenthetically, the present total annual HUD spending budget is $3.5 billion. If passed by Congress, this bill will alter significantly federal-state-local relationships. Consider, for example, the "grantsmanship" procedure: current programs are now funded for each locality only after an application has been submitted and approved by the federal government; but the new proposal would substitute a single annual grant to qualifying urban areas to be spent on a broad grouping of related urban programs. Another significant change is expansion of the role of state governments by allowing them to distribute about 22 percent of the funds. The question of the extent of restrictions—the degree of federal overview in order to ensure the attainment of national objectives—is the debatable issue.

Another important variant of an affirmative program would be a new financing mechanism, such as an urban development bank, that would permit construction of public service facilities at a more moderate cost. (See the *President's Task Force on Suburban Problems Report* (1968); C.M. Haar and P.A. Lewis, "Where Will the Money Come From?," *Public Interest* (Winter 1970): pp. 101-112.)

President Nixon's policy statement reflects clearly a distinct sociopolitical viewpoint. Contrast it to the recommendation of the President's Commission on Urban Housing: *A Decent Home* 25 (1968):

> *The Committee recommends that, subject to the Governor's veto, the Secretary of HUD be granted limited powers to preempt local zoning codes and any exclusionary state codes or local ordinances from application to Federally subsidized housing projects.*
>
> The Secretary's preemptive power would be issued only after a public hearing resulted in a finding that preemption was necessary to accomplish the Federal Government's goals, and that the subject zoning ordinances had an unconstitutional discriminatory effect. The Secretary's preemption order could be subject to veto by the Governor of the state concerned.
>
> In making the above recommendation, the Committee recognizes the rights of residents of any political jurisdiction to establish zoning standards designed to assure orderly community development. Also, as a general proposition, we were extremely hesitant to recommend reduction of local powers. We were convinced, however, that widespread abuses of zoning techniques and their inherent defects as a land-use control make it necessary for local prerogatives to yield to the greater common good.
>
> Despite the existing urban renewal process, many local governments still find difficulties in acquiring sufficient land for developing subsidized housing to meet local needs. The urban renewal process requires a local plan for redevelopment of a large area; consequently,

its application for acquiring relatively small sites for subsidized housing has proved too slow. Some cities presently own large numbers of abandoned or tax delinquent land parcels in slum areas but encounter financial or other difficulties in acquiring the remaining parcels necessary for assembling large areas of contiguous sites.

In this connection, consider further the following statements quoted in *The New York Times* (December 21, 1970) by officials in Dayton, Ohio, one of the first metropolitan regions to establish a regional plan for housing the poor:

> The officials, most of whom are Republicans, are worried about how much support they will receive from Washington. They believe the plan fits the philosophy expressed repeatedly by George Romney, Secretary of Housing and Urban Development, but they are disturbed by President Nixon's news conference statement last week that "forced integration of the suburbs is not in the national interests."
>
> The Dayton plan, they say, is voluntary, not forced, but one of the factors that brought its acceptance was the belief that H.U.D. would use Federal grants in a way that would encourage open communities.
>
> "If political pressures build up so that the suburbs can continue to flout low and moderate income housing and still get their money from Washington there is little we can do," said one official.
>
> Further, the development here illustrates what is involved in the housing controversy that has been under way in the national government. Plans by the Department of Housing and Urban Development to make a strong stand for open communities in the administration of Federal grants have been questioned by Attorney General John N. Mitchell and the White House.
>
> Officials here say that in the long run a firm Federal policy for open communities is essential to the success of the Dayton plan.

(For details on the Dayton Plan, se p. 369ff, infra.)

A less dramatic but practical approach is the tying of housing to employment. As jobs have increased in suburbia, the argument waxes that provision should be made for workers' homes and that units of local government should not be permitted to skim off the tax base of industry while shunting off the housing problem onto their neighbors.

The National Commission on Urban Problems recommended that the Congress amend the Housing Act to assert, as a matter of national policy, the desirability of providing for the housing of employees of all income levels in areas reasonably close to places of employment, and that immediate executive action be taken to assure the availability of housing sites around new federal installations. (National Commission on Urban Problems, *Building the American City* 243 (1968).) The Commission also suggested that no federal contract should be entered into with a private firm for work to be undertaken at any location employing more than 100 employees in an area which does not have adequate housing for employees of the plant within a reasonable distance from the place of employment:

Proposed Government Facilities Location Act of 1970
Purposes and Findings

Sec. 201. The Congress finds that—

(a) The increasing concentration of Government facilities in suburban areas has placed many jobs beyond the reach of low- and moderate-income, inner city residents;

(b) A combination of government actions, such as zoning and housing programs, together with increasing housing costs, have effectively excluded low- and moderate-income families from most suburban areas; and

(c) A positive, affirmative program is necessary to provide decent, clean and safe housing for low- and moderate-income families within the immediate area of Government facilities.

Sec. 202. It is the purpose of this Act—

(a) To require Federal agencies, Federal contractors and state governments to assure that an adequate supply of housing for low- and moderate-income families will be available in any area in which a Government facility is to be located; and

(b) To provide financial assistance to communities to assist them in meeting the requirements of this Act . . . .

Restrictions on the Location of Federal Facilities

Sec. 401. (a) After January 1, 1971 no Government facility may be located in any community which has failed to develop an acceptable plan which provides, in the opinion of the Chairman, adequate housing in the immediate area of the facility for the prospective low- and moderate-income employees of the facility.

(b) Each Government agency or Federal contractor shall, prior to initiating location procedures, require written assurance in the form of a plan that the relevant community will conform to the requirements of Section 502.

(c) Should, after the acceptance of the plan by the Chairman, any community fail to comply with its approved plan, the Chairman shall bring suit in the United States District Court for the District of Columbia to secure an injunction to require such community to conform to its plan.

(d) Should any Federal contractor locate or expand any Federal facility in violation of the provisions of this section, the Chairman shall, after giving appropriate notice, terminate all Federal contracts held by such contractor: *Provided*, That the Secretary of a Department or Chief Executive Officer of an independent agency that holds a contract with a Federal contractor who locates a Federal facility in violation of this section may, subject to court review, veto the Chairman's termination of such contract if he finds, on the basis of facts presented, that such a termination will seriously and substantially impede the mission of the Department or agency.

(e) The Chairman shall also prohibit the granting of any future Federal contracts with a noncomplying Federal contractor.

(f) Should any State take action to locate a Government facility in violation of the provisions of this Act, the Chairman shall, after giving appropriate notice, order the suspension of all Federal assistance to the State agency that has jurisdiction over such facility until such time as the community has produced an acceptable plan. . . .

Sec. 502. Each plan shall—

(a) Be embodied in a contract between the Federal government, as represented by the Chairman, and the community in which the Government facility is to be located;

(b) Provide that at least one unit of housing be vacant or built in the community for every prospective low- and moderate-income employee of the locating Government agency or Federal contractor. Such units shall meet requirements of size, price and location as set by the Chairman; . . .

Sec. 507. Each Government agency and Federal contractor shall designate one person who shall act as liaison with the Chairman. This person shall serve as chairman of an advisory committee on housing established by the Government agency or contractor. At least one-third of the membership of this committee shall consist of low- and moderate-income employees. It shall be the function of this Committee to channel employee needs and preferences to those persons responsible for the location of the facility.

Financial Assistance

Sec. 601. (a) Each community that files a plan under this Act may also file an application for financial assistance with the Chairman.

(b) Upon application meeting the standards established by the Chairman, the Chairman shall grant to each community an amount not to exceed $100,000 to reimburse such community for the expense of developing a plan to conform to the requirements of this Act.

(c) Each year the Chairman shall pay to each community filing an acceptable plan a sum determined by multiplying the difference between the average individual tax revenue and the average low- and moderate-income individual tax revenue by the number of low- and moderate-income employees who move into the community under the plan. . . .

CONSIDERATIONS

1. Consider Section 703(a) of Title VII of the Civil Rights Act of 1964: "It shall be an unlawful employment practice for an employer to . . . limit, segregate, or classify his employees in any way which would deprive or tend to deprive any individual of employment opportunities or otherwise adversely affect his status as an employee, because of such individual's race, color, religion, sex, or national origin." 42 U.S.C. §200e-2(a)(2).

In December of 1970, the General Counsel of the U.S. Commission on Civil Rights said: We have found that a close relationship exists between the location of employment facilities in areas which are inaccessible to minorities and access to equal job opportunities. To locate corporate facilities in restricted, relatively inaccessible suburban areas, thereby making it difficult and burdensome for minority employees to continue to hold their jobs and making it difficult for minorities to learn of available jobs, and more difficult for employers to recruit minority applicants, tends to deprive an individual of employment opportunities and adversely affects his status as an employee. (Address by John H. Powell, Jr., Suburban Action Institute Conference on "Open or Closed Suburbs: Corporate Location and the Urban Crisis," December, 1970.)

2. On March 2, 1971, the RCA Corporation announced it would consolidate staff functions performed at 10 locations in New York City and New Jersey cities, and relocate to suburban New Canaan, Connecticut.

Two days later:

> The Suburban Action Institute moved yesterday to bar the RCA Corporation from moving 1,000 executives from New York City and Camden, N.J., to a proposed office in New Canaan, Conn. . . .
>
> Neil N. Gold and Paul Davidoff, directors of the Institute, said at a news conference . . . that the ground cited in the complaint was that New Canaan was guilty of de facto segregation, accomplished through the zoning law.
>
> They charged that the town is a virtually all-white, upper-income, exclusionary community.
>
> Mr. Gold and Mr. Davidoff said New Canaan's zoning laws and practices "are designed to and have the effect of preventing black and brown people, typically of low- and moderate-income from living there." They said that of 887 headquarters personnel of the 1,018 the RCA Corporation plans to shift from New York City and Camden, nearly 100 are blacks. (*N.Y. Times*, March 4, 1971, p. 39, col. 7.)

The RCA Corporation cancelled the planned relocation after Suburban Action filed a complaint with the Equal Employment Opportunity Commission. (2 Yale Rev. L. & Soc. Action 318, 1972.)

3. Executive Order No. 11246, Equal Opportunity in Federal Employment, sets forth additional requirements applicable to government contractors' agreements.

> Sec. 202. All Government contracting agencies shall include in every Government contract hereafter entered into the following provisions:
> During the performance of this contract, the contractor agrees as follows:
> (1) The contractor will not discriminate against any employee or applicant for employment because of race, color, religion, sex, or national origin. The contractor will take affirmative action to ensure that applicants are employed, and that employees are treated during employment, without regard to their race, color, religion, sex or national origin. Such action shall include, but not be limited to the following: employment, upgrading, demotion, or transfer; recruitment or recruitment advertising; layoff or termination; rates of pay or other forms of compensation; and selection for training, including apprenticeship. (Exec. Order 11246, 41 C.F.R. §60-1.4, 1972, 42 U.S.C. §2000(e), 1970.)

Additional regulations specify the required contents of affirmative action programs. "Special corrective action should be appropriate" if "lack of access to suitable housing inhibits recruitment efforts and employment of qualified minorities" or if "lack of suitable transportation (public or private) to the work place inhibits minority employment."

4. The movement of jobs in private industry from the cities to the suburbs has made it difficult for the urban poor to get to work. The trend has been a significant one: New York City lost over 4,000 manufacturing plants while its suburbs gained over 4,000; San Francisco lost over 700 plants while its suburbs gained over 850; Chicago lost over 750 while its suburbs gained over 700. The trend continues to increase. (See *The New York Times*, February 22, 1971.)

Isn't it in the corporation's best interests to ensure that there is adequate housing nearby for its workers? When the Ford Motor Company located a major factory in Mahwah, N.J., it had to organize car pools to bring in workers from center city areas often more than an hour's trip; this led to high absenteeism. Consider a news release from the company in support of a plan to build a fully integrated, new community of 19,000 people in Mahwah:

> Ford Motor Company management in New Jersey believes that all citizens are entitled to have access to housing at a reasonable price within reasonable reach of their places of employment.... We believe that such a development would be good for the community, for our employees and for Ford Motor Company. Zoning that precludes local housing opportunities for large numbers of our work force imposes hardships on them and raises the cost of doing

business. When employees are forced to travel great distances to their jobs, absenteeism and turnover go up, and morale and productivity decline. (Ford Motor Company news release, December 11, 1972.)

Consider also the following statement (*Newsweek*, January 16, 1971), and assess the possibility of a new coalition between excluded groups and private industry:

> Builders, especially, are actively supporting suits to break down zoning and other barriers. Their interest is obvious: About one-third of their housing starts are "government-assisted AAA," the classification for federally subsidized low- and middle-income housing.
>
> Big employers, which have been ignoring the issue, may be starting to side with the excluded groups. McDonnell Douglas Corp., which has a major plant near Black Jack, kicked in $30,000 in "seed money" to help the blacks get housing.
>
> That company's support reflects a critical problem confronting the many companies that have moved to the suburbs. Many moved into exclusive communities, which welcomed the plants as taxpayers but did nothing to modify barriers to housing. So the workers stayed in the cities, and turnover accelerated because of the lack of fast, cheap public transportation.

Federal Housing Policy Alternatives

The discussion of equal opportunity of location also raises the direct issue of federal options in formulating and implementing national housing goals. How do you perceive the role of the federal government in housing? Should it rely exclusively on the private sector and the market to provide adequate housing for all population groups? Would you have the federal government itself furnish housing services? If you prefer a position in between these two antithetical poles, how much federal intervention would you recommend and what avenues would you choose to implement it?

Aside from the sheer production of housing, other goals were important for the groups locked in struggle in the five communities. What type of federal assistance for housing would most easily achieve those ends? Would you, for example, provide housing allowances to individuals in need, as was stressed by Senator McGovern in his housing policy report in 1972? Or would you rather rely on aid to finance and construction establishments through mortgage guarantees, interest rate reductions, tax exemptions, or secondary financing mechanisms, such as an expanded FNMA?

Is technological research to reduce housing construction costs and to facilitate the assembly of markets a better bet? Would you recommend a variant of revenue sharing for localities, without strings attached, or would you expect the federal government to approve each project in order to ensure compliance with national goals? Should funds be allotted to the states through the mechanism of state urban development corporations rather than the regional or area offices of HUD?

These issues demand fresh attention as we continue to rethink our programs. First came former HUD Secretary Romney's suggestion, before resigning from office, to terminate any direct federal role in housing. "We would end subsidy programs, privatize the Federal Housing Administration, move to a combination housing allowance-income subsidy for the poor, and end operating subsidies for public housing. We can no longer afford $100 billion mistakes." (*The New York Times*, October 24, 1972.) Second, the President's January 8, 1973, announcement of a "temporary halt" and "moratorium" on federal housing programs for low- and moderate-income families made clear that changes were in the offing. Third are the announcements by HUD regarding the general direction these new policies are taking:

a) to limit the federal role in housing by reversing the centralization of decision-making power in Washington;
b) to provide supplementary insurance support and stimulate needed state, local, and private effort in lieu of direct subsidies.

How do you view these policies, as they would affect the course of the housing location disputes in the five communities? What are their advantages and disadvantages? What population groups and sectors of the economy benefit? How would they have affected the conflicts in the five communities? What are the implications for the redistribution of income, power, status, and services? For residential, racial, and economic segregation?

In formulating answers to these questions, consider the following:

Shelter is a basic necessity for human and social survival, on the order of—without any attempt at serial ordering—food, medical care, and schooling. As such, it becomes a fundamental concern of national policy, particularly when reliance upon the economic market alone produces inequities in meeting housing needs among population groups or geographic regions. In the postindustrial society the question is assumed to be not so much whether national housing policies are required, but, rather, which of the public policy alternatives are most appropriate and effective, given the sociopolitical orientation of the nation and the structure of the housing market.

The mechanisms of the housing economic market tend to generate income, resource, and services inequities because the market (a) tends to produce unequal patterns of economic growth and (b) being primarily sensitive to profit, is geared to meeting the needs of consumers of high rather than those of low income whose needs cannot be expected to be met through the private sector and (c) is subject to erratic behavior due to cyclical declines in demand or to credit stringencies. The nation and Congress, concerned with the protection of the housing industry—of the producers, suppliers, unions, and lending groups—have also been concerned with housing's redistributive pattern among population groups. Thus, the central role of national housing policies is an amalgam: to achieve the nation's social objectives, while at the same time using the housing industry as a stabilizer of the general economy.

Assuming that the federal government will not run housing industries or provide services directly by building or leasing housing units, there remains one of the following options:

1. Various producer subsidies, be they large write-downs, as in urban renewal, or interest rate subsidies, or underwriting the maturity period or other terms of the mortgage such as down payment or amortization, or income tax provisions such as accelerated depreciation;
2. Reduction of the cost of housing production;
3. Use of the tax system and cash transfers for general income redistribution among individuals;
4. Aid to individuals for payment of what are considered essential housing goods and services;
5. Provision of grants to states and localities, as well as to institutions (financial and construction establishments) to increase their capacity for delivering housing services to all or to specified population groups and regions; or
6. In combination with the above, government encouragement of housing objectives through the regulation or provision of financial incentives to influence behavior of individuals, communities, organizations, and institutional operations.

Federal Housing Programs: Sections 235 and 236

Federal housing policy options come to a sharper focus through an evaluation of specific programs. Two recent, major federal programs for low- and moderate-income families provide a needed fresh look. Their details were much in the minds of proponents and opponents of the various housing proposals considered in the five communities.

The federal role in low-income housing, which began seriously with the public housing programs in 1937, seems to accelerate at 10-year periods. In 1949, the public housing programs were expanded by setting a national goal of 810,000 public housing units by 1955 and by emphasizing urban renewal, the immediate neighborhood and living environment of the house. In 1959, the national housing policy began to encompass below-market interest rate loans to private developers of low- and moderate-income housing. Still later, sections were added for rentals of units in private apartments to low-income tenants who pay only public housing rates (Section 23 leasing). In 1968, the national housing goal was set at 26 million units by 1978, six million of which are to be subsidized units. The goal did not include specifications of where this housing should be placed, nor the types of units. Relying more heavily on private financing, with the government only subsidizing interest, Congress established also the two new low- and moderate-housing programs. Contrasted to public housing, which is administered by local housing authorities and requires local government approval, 235 and 236 are administered by private housing sponsors and FHA offices.

Section 235 reflects the national trend regarding homeownership and aims to expand it to include lower-income families. Most American families own their own homes. According to the 1970 census figures, about 63 percent of the nation's housing units are owned by the families who occupy them.

The benefits of homeownership have not been equally available to all groups of Americans. One of these groups is lower-income families, another is nonwhite families. Whereas 65 percent of white families in the United States are homeowners, only some 42 percent of nonwhite families own their own homes, according to a 1971 Report of the United States Commission on Civil Rights.

Section 235 of the National Housing Act provides homeownership assistance for low- and moderate-income families by allowing them to obtain private FHA-insured mortgages with down payments of only $200. The assistance takes the form of direct payments to the mortgagee, reducing interest charges to as low as 1 percent in an effort to assure that the homeowner's mortgage payments do not exceed 20 percent of his adjusted income. Eligible for assistance are new or substantially rehabilitated single-family dwellings. The mortgage has a 30-year term (35 or 40 under special circumstances), bears a maximum limit of $18,000 (or $21,000 in high-cost areas), and carries ½ percent mortgage insurance premium. The mortgagor must be a family of two or more persons related by blood, marriage, or operation of law, or a handicapped person, or a single person 62 years or older.

The family must have an adjusted family income not exceeding 135 percent of income of the same size family eligible to move into local public housing units. Thus far, the average income of participants is $6,500. Families are required to spend 20 percent of their income for mortgage payments, taxes, and insurance. (Utilities and heating are not included.) Is this formula unfair and regressive, in the sense that it requires a greater portion of the income of the poor than of the wealthy? Should poor families pay as high a proportion of their income for housing as richer families?

Assess the advantages and disadvantages of this program. See the Report of the Joint Economic Committee, Housing Subsidies and Housing Policy (March 5, 1973). More specifically, relate the objective of the program to national housing objectives. Given the unmet housing needs of the poor, how do you justify investment in homeownership and for moderate-income families? Is homeownership an appropriate objective? Is the program likely to decrease or increase residential racial and economic segregation?

In the relatively brief time since its establishment, the 235 program has provided a considerable volume of housing. During 1970, fully 30 percent of all new houses that sold for less than $25,000 were purchased by 235 buyers. The benefits of the program, however, have not been equally available in all areas. Southern and border states have accounted for nearly half of all 235 housing; by contrast, only 6 percent of the units have been provided in the northeastern region—where there is a high cost to produce housing in relation to the maximum mortgage limits permitted under the program. Moreover, as seen in the five controversies, local laws and policies concerning land use have limited the choice of sites for 235 housing.

Nearly all of the new 235 housing is located in suburban parts of metropolitan areas and is owned by white families. By contrast, most of the existing housing purchased under the program is located in ghetto areas or "changing" neighborhoods in the central city, nearly all purchased by minority families. Because minority buyers have tended to purchase housing that is older and less expensive than the housing purchased by whites, they have tended to receive less in the way of assistance payments under the program. "In some cases minority families have been rejected for 235 assistance because the price of the houses they were shown was too low to permit a subsidy." As of November 1972, 21.4 percent of the families in the program were black, most of them in central cities.

Why has the traditional pattern found in the housing market in general been repeated in the 235 program? Does the answer lie mainly in the way in which the program is administered? Each of the elements involved in the housing program has played a role in producing a segregated product: the real estate broker, the builder, the mortgage lender, interested community groups, government, and the buyer himself. How would you redraft this program to avoid these shortcomings?

Section 236 provides assitance for low- and moderate-income tenants in privately built rental and cooperative housing. The assistance takes the form of monthly federal payments to the mortgagee, reducing the cost to the occupant by paying part of the interest on the market rate project.

Eligible projects include only new structures or existing ones involving major rehabilitation, designed so that basic rent is less than 25 percent of maximum income limits; they must be insured limited-dividend projects purchased by a nonprofit organization or cooperative. Eligible sponsors and mortgagors include private, nonprofit organizations, limited-dividend mortgagors, or cooperative housing corporations. The Act provides:

> *Payment*: For the purpose of reducing rentals for lower income families, the Secretary is authorized to make, and to contract to make, periodic interest reduction payments on behalf of the owner of a rental housing project designed for occupancy by lower income families, which shall be accomplished through payments to mortgagees holding mortgages meeting the special requirements specified in this section. . . .

Interest reduction payments with respect to a project shall only be made during such time as the project is operated as a rental housing project and is subject to a mortgage which meets the requirements of, and is insured under, subsection (j) of this section: *Provided,* That the Secretary is authorized to continue making such interest reduction payments where the mortgage has been assigned to the Secretary: *Provided further,* That interest reduction payments may be made with respect to a mortgage or part thereof on a rental or cooperative housing project owned by a private nonprofit corporation or other private nonprofit entity, a limited dividend corporation or other limited dividend entity, or a cooperative housing corporation, which is financed under a State or local program providing assistance through loans, loan insurance, or tax abatements, and which may involve either new or existing construction and which is approved for receiving the benefits of this section.

The interest reduction payments to a mortgagee by the Secretary on behalf of a project owner shall be in an amount not exceeding the difference between the monthly payment for principal, interest, and mortgage insurance premium which the project owner as a mortgagor is obligated to pay under the mortgage and the monthly payment for principal and interest such project owner would be obligated to pay if the mortgage were to bear interest at the rate of 1 percent per annum. . . .

Tenants: As a condition for receiving the benefits of interest reduction payments, the project owner shall operate the project in accordance with such requirements with respect to tenant eligibility and rents as the Secretary may prescribe. Procedures shall be adopted by the Secretary for review of tenant incomes at intervals of two years (or at shorter intervals where the Secretary deems it desirable). . . .

Charges: For each dwelling unit there shall be established with the approval of the Secretary (1) a basic rental charge determined on the basis of operating the project with payments of principal and interest due under a mortgage bearing interest at the rate of 1 per centum per annum; and (2) a fair market rental charge determined on the basis of operating the project with payments of principal, interest, and mortgage insurance premium which the mortgagor is obligated to pay under the mortgage covering the project. The rental for each dwelling unit shall be at the basic rental charge or such greater amount, not exceeding the fair market rental charge, as represents 25 per centum of the tenant's income.

Not more than 20 per centum of the total amount of interest reduction payments authorized to be contracted to be made pursuant to appropriation Acts shall be contracted to be made with respect to families, occupying rental housing projects assisted under this section, whose incomes at the time of the initial renting of the projects exceed 135 per centum of the maximum income limits which can be established in the area, pursuant to the limitations prescribed in sections 1402(2) and 1415(7)(b)(ii) of Title 42, for initial occupancy in public housing dwellings, but the income of such families at the time of the initial renting of the projects shall in no case exceed 90 per centum of the limits prescribed by the Secretary for occupants of projects financed with mortgages insured under section 1715*l* (d)(3) of this title which bear interest at the below-market interest rate prescribed in the proviso of section 1715*l* (d)(5) of this title. The limitations prescribed in this paragraph shall be administered by the Secretary so as to accord a preference to those families whose incomes are within the lowest practicable limits for obtaining rental accommodations in projects assisted under this section.

(Section 236 Rental Housing Program for Lower Income Families 12 U.S.C. 17152-1 (1970).)

The average family participating in this program earned $4,831 a year, and paid one-fourth of its adjusted income for housing. Most of the units have been built in the suburbs, but a substantial number are in central cities:

Both 235 and 236 usually depend upon nonprofit or limited-dividend sponsors and emphasize newly built housing which often requires zoning changes in the suburbs. What is the role of intermediaries (sponsors) in the location of federally assisted housing? Most of the nonprofit sponsors were previously organized in the central city—like Interfaith. Does this affect their performance in suburbs?

Prominent in the thinking of proponents of low-income housing in the five communities was the availability of federal and state subsidy programs. For, the ability to reach down to the lower-income groups and to provide them with decent housing, without paralyzing their remaining income from meeting other family needs, depends upon reducing the monthly carrying costs of their shelter. If a conventional mortgage is used (say, 25-year term and 7.5 percent interest rate), the service charge on a $25,000 mortgage is $185 a month. If resort is made to state agency rates (say, 40-year term at 6 percent), the carrying costs are $138; but with operating and maintenance costs, local property taxes, and the limited profits, the rent would still come to $230 a month. Applying the usual rule-of-thumb (25 percent of gross income for housing), the lowest income groups qualifying would be households earning $11,000 a year. If, therefore, 236 subsidies are added, the monthly rent would go down to $150, making it

Location of Subsidized Rental Units and Projects in FHA Processing as of January 15, 1970

	Total (Percent)
Percent of units in:	
All areas	100.0
Blighted areas	28.4
Other inner city areas	18.9
Within city limits	40.7
Suburban areas	11.9
Percent of projects in:	
All areas	100.0
Blighted areas	31.0
Other inner city areas	20.6
Within city limits	38.4
Suburban areas	10.0

Family Characteristics of Occupants in Major Housing Subsidy Programs

	Public Housing	Rent Supplement	Sec. 236 Rental	Sec. 235 Homeownership	Rural Housing (Ownership)
1. Units assisted:					
(a) Total June 30, 1970	864,769	25,409	5,439	65,654	358,000
(b) Units added, fiscal year 1971	106,000	15,000	88,263	155,746	78,600
(c) Units added, fiscal year 1972	92,000	30,000	129,700	188,600	121,800
(d) Total, June 30, 1972	1,062,769	70,409	223,402	409,990	558,400
2. Family income (median)	$2,548	$2,185	$5,303	$5,760	$6,425
3. Monthly rents (median)	$50	$51	$115	$85	$105
4. Estimated monthly subsidy	$60	$86	$73	$71	$14
5. Implied rent as percent of income	24	28	26	18	19
6. Nonwhite occupants (percent)	51	37	40	30	20
7. Elderly occupants (percent)	36	34	7	4	(6)
8. Family size (median persons per unit)	3.6	3.2	3.3	4	(6)

possible for a family earning about $7,200 a year to live there. Still further reductions might be attained through piggy-backing supplements on top of these subsidies, thereby enabling the tenant with public housing income levels to live in the housing.

Consider the cumulative costs of these programs to the average taxpayer. A $230 per month apartment, which already receives some $45 per month subsidy from the tax-exempt bond financing, receives $80 per month through 236 subsidy and $40 per month through rent supplement. Total subsidies would be $2,000 per year. Now multiply these by 750,000 or 1,000,000 units a year! These are massive supports—federal and state—if low-income families are to be served with adequate housing.

Are the production subsidies, represented by these two programs, so valuable for housing the poor in suburbia that they should be revived, or are some new forms of housing assistance now necessary?

The Role of the State

Historically, the national government has been the moving force for regional and state programs. The President's "New Federalism" and the routes of both general and special revenue-sharing focus fresh attention upon the state and its role in housing. In Massachusetts, as elsewhere, extensive executive and legislative activity has been taken regarding state organization for urban development and planning. In fact, it is increasingly suggested that regional spillovers should be decided not by a vote of the residents of a locality (even of a metropolitan community), but by the state legislature itself—the state being increasingly propelled as the appropriate force in regionalism to deal with those land-use policies affecting all the residents of the state. This would be in addition to its traditional function of coordinating state-federal-local programs. The choices across the country are, of course, variegated: the state can organize itself as the planner and decisionmaker, or it can delegate this responsibility to autonomous district structures, which would include a wide range of possibilities—state agencies with regional functional programs, special-purpose autonomous districts, a county structure, or umbrella regional councils of governments.

The Massachusetts Anti-Snob Zoning Law, the New Jersey Land-Use Planning and Development legislation, the New York State Urban Development Corporation, the approach of Fairfax County, and the Ashley proposal are some of the more prominent models. A close examination of each sharpens the focus on state responsibility and the dilemmas inherent in it.

The "Massachusetts Anti-Snob Zoning Act"

§20. *Definitions and Construction of Terms.*

The following words, wherever used in this section and in sections twenty-one to twenty-three, inclusive, shall, unless a different meaning clearly appears from the context, have the following meanings:—

"Low or moderate income housing", any housing subsidized by the federal or state government under any program to assist the construction of low or moderate income housing as defined in the applicable federal or state statute, whether built or operated by any public agency or any nonprofit or limited dividend organization.

"Uneconomic", any condition brought about by any single factor or combination of factors to the extent that it makes it impossible for a public agency or nonprofit organization to proceed in building or operating low or moderate income housing without financial loss, or for a limited dividend organization to proceed and still realize a reasonable return in building or operating such housing within the limitations set by the subsidizing agency of government on the size or character of the development or on the amount or nature of the subsidy or on the tenants, rentals and income permissible, and without substantially changing the rent levels and units sizes proposed by the public, nonprofit or limited dividend organizations.

"Consistent with local needs", requirements and regulations shall be considered consistent with local needs if they are reasonable in view of the regional need for low and moderate income housing considered with the number of low income persons in the city or town affected and the need to protect the health or safety of the occupants of the proposed housing or of the residents of the city or town, to promote better site and building design in relation to the surroundings, or to preserve open spaces, and if such requirements and regulations are applied as equally as possible to both subsidized and unsubsidized housing. Requirements or regulations shall be consistent with local needs when imposed by a board of zoning appeals after comprehensive hearing in a city or town where (1) low or moderate income housing exists which is in excess of ten per cent of the housing units reported in the latest decennial census of the city or town or on sites comprising one and one half per cent or more of the total land area zoned for residential, commercial or industrial use or (2) the application before the board would result in the commencement of construction of such housing on sites comprising more than three tenths of one per cent of such land area or ten acres, whichever is larger, in any one calendar year; provided, however, that land area owned by the United States, the commonwealth or any political subdivision thereof, the metropolitan district commission or any public authority shall be excluded from the total land area referred to above when making such determination of consistency with local needs.

"Local Board", any town or city board of survey, board of health, board of subdivision control appeals, planning board, building inspector or the officer or board having supervision of the construction of buildings or the power of enforcing municipal building laws, or city council or board of selectmen.

§21. *Proceedings Before Board of Zoning Appeals on Comprehensive Application to Build housing, etc.*

Any public agency or limited dividend or nonprofit organization proposing to build low or moderate income housing may submit to the board of appeals, established under section fourteen of chapter forty A, a single application to build such housing in lieu of separate applications to the applicable local boards. The board of appeals shall forthwith notify each such local board, as applicable, of the filing of such application by sending a copy thereof to such local boards for their recommendations and shall, within thirty days of the receipt of such application, hold a public hearing on the same. The board of appeals shall request the appearance at said hearing of such representatives of said local boards as are deemed necessary or helpful in making its decision upon such application and shall have the same power to issue permits or approvals as any local board or official who would otherwise act with respect to such application, including but not limited to the power to attach to said permit or approval conditions and requirements with respect to height, site plan, size or shape, or building materials as are consistent with the terms of this section. The board of appeals, in making its decision on said application, shall take into consideration the recommendations of the local boards and shall have the authority to use the testimony of consultants. The provisions of section seventeen of chapter forty A shall apply to all such hearings. The board of appeals shall render a decision, based upon a majority vote of said board, within forty days after the termination of the public hearing and, if favorable to the applicant, shall forthwith issue a comprehensive permit or approval. If said hearing is not convened or a decision is not rendered within the time allowed, unless the time has been extended by mutual agreement between the board and the applicant, the application shall be deemed to have been allowed and the comprehensive permit or approval shall forthwith issue. Any person aggrieved by the issuance of a comprehensive permit or approval may appeal to the court as provided in section twenty-one of chapter forty A.

§22. *Review by Housing Appeals Committee of Denial or Conditional Grant of Application, etc.*

Whenever an application filed under the provisions of section twenty-one is denied, or is granted with such conditions and requirements as to make the building or operation of such housing uneconomic, the applicant shall have the right to appeal to the housing appeals committee in the department of community affairs for a review of the same. Such appeal shall be taken within twenty days after the date of the notice of the decision by the board of appeals by filing with said committee a statement of the prior proceedings and the reasons upon which the appeal is based. The committee shall forthwith notify the board of appeals of the filing of such petition for review and the latter shall, within ten days of the receipt of such notice, transmit a copy of its decision and the reasons therefor to the committee. Such appeal shall be heard by the committee within twenty days after receipt of the applicant's statement. A stenographic record of the proceedings shall be kept and the committee shall render a written decision, based upon a majority vote, stating its findings of fact, its conclusions and the reasons therefor within thirty days after the termination of the hearing, unless such time shall have been extended by mutual agreement between the committee and the applicant. Such decision may be reviewed in the superior court in accordance with the provisions of chapter thirty A.

§23. *Limitation on Issues Before Housing Appeals Committee; Findings; Enforcement of Orders, etc.*

The hearing by the housing appeals committee in the department of community affairs shall be limited to the issue of whether, in the case of the denial of an application, the decision of the board of appeals was reasonable and consistent with local needs and, in the case of an approval of an application with conditions and requirements imposed, whether such conditions and requirements make the construction or operation of such housing uneconomic and whether they are consistent with local needs. If the committee finds, in the case of a denial, that the decision of the board of appeals was unreasonable and not consistent with local needs, it shall vacate such decision and shall direct the board to issue a comprehensive permit or approval to the applicant. If the committee finds, in the case of an approval with conditions and requirements imposed, that the decision of the board makes the building or operation of such housing uneconomic and is not consistent with local needs, it shall order such board to modify or remove any such condition or requirement so as to make the proposal no longer uneconomic and to issue any necessary permit or approval; provided, however, that the committee shall not issue any order that would permit the building or operation of such housing in accordance with standards less safe than the applicable building and site plan requirements of the Federal Housing Administration or the Massachusetts Housing Finance Agency, whichever agency is financially assisting such housing. Decisions or conditions and requirements imposed by a board of appeals that are consistent with local needs shall not be vacated, modified or removed by the committee notwithstanding that such decisions or conditions and requirements have the effect of making the applicant's proposal uneconomic.

The housing appeals committee or the petitioner shall have the power to enforce the orders of the committee at law or in equity in the superior court. The board of appeals shall carry out the order of the hearing appeals committee within thirty days of its entry and, upon failure to do so, the order of said committee shall, for all purposes, be deemed to be the action of said board, unless the petitioner consents to a different decision or order by such board.

Mass. Gen. Laws Ch. 40B, §§ 20-23 (1969)

QUESTIONS

1. Are you satisfied with the drafting of this Act? Does it adequately define "consistent with local needs"? What does the phrase "reasonable in view of the regional need for low- and moderate-income housing" mean? Does the statute define "region"? How should the state committee weigh certain traditional local planning criteria such as the protection of health and safety, the preservation of open space, and the maintenance of uniformity in applying construction regulations? What risks of expensive and extensive litigation does a developer run when using the Act? What are the possible consequences of these risks? As a Massachusetts legislator, what changes in the Act would you propose?

2. Should the state "impose" its policy on local communities? In Massachusetts and other states the constitutional right to determine land uses belongs to the state which has delegated this responsibility to local communities. What are the advantages and disadvantages of this? The constitutionality of this Act was upheld by the Massachusetts Supreme Judicial Court in Board of Appeals of Hanover v. Housing Appeals Committee in the Department of Community Affairs, No. P-7754 (Massachusetts, March 22, 1973).

The New Jersey Land-Use Law

The proposed New Jersey Land-Use Planning and Development Law provides the comprehensive planning requirements that the Massachusetts Snob-Zoning Law lacks. It gives a framework within which local communities may promulgate zoning ordinances and subdivision regulations. Such ordinances must be based upon a land-use plan, adopted as a part of a master plan by the governing body of the municipality. The land-use plan must include a statement of the standards of population and development density recommended for the municipality, along with specific policy statements relating the plan to the master plans of adjacent municipalities and the county, as well as to the development plans of the state or relevant regional agencies.

The master plan must conform to a specific set of purposes applicable to all land-use regulations. These purposes include (1) the promotion of the public health, safety, economy and the general welfare, (2) the encouragement of the orderly development of the state and regions within the state, (3) the conservation of natural resources, and (4) the provision of standards for the elimination of wasteful, inefficient, and socially costly practices. The considerations of social cost and regional development have not generally been set up as zoning purposes in legislation following the Standard Zoning Enabling Act.

The specific purposes for which land-use planning and regulation are authorized go even further in the direction of recognizing regional need. Such ordinances may be enacted (1) to ensure that the development of individual municipalities does not conflict with the development and well-being of neighboring municipalities and the state as a whole, (2) to promote maximum choice for all economic and social groups in the state among a variety of adequate housing types, (3) to promote the establishment of population densities that provide adequate public services while preventing overcrowding, and (4) to promote the conservation of open space, the development of new communities and the avoidance of urban sprawl. In addition, the act may not be used so as to exclude any economic, racial, religious, or ethnic group from the enjoyment of residence or land ownership anywhere in the state.

These specific purposes seem to prevent new zoning ordinances that exclude particular economic classes from housing, except in the special category of low density districts established to promote the orderly growth of present rural areas and the conservation of an adequate supply of open space land. However, the Act is not retroactive and most of the land in the state is presently subject to restrictive zoning. Only in the vast area of the Meadowlands and the growing areas of the northwest and southern parts of the state would the Act likely be effective. . . .

The establishment of a State Planning Commission to develop criteria for the review of zoning and planning ordinances may forestall this possibility. The review procedure is optional, in deference to the local nature of the power. A municipality may request that the Division of State and Regional Planning in the Department of Community Affairs review proposed local master plans and ordinances to see if they conform to Planning Commission guidelines. Such a review shall certify such plans and regulations based upon the standards of residential settlement, commercial land development, industrial land development, and patterns of agricultural activity for the orderly growth and development of the state, and that sufficient land be set aside so that the municipality will provide for an equitable municipal share of the regional housing needs created by those employed within the region. The latter standard allows the establishment of a prima facie test, similar to that established under the Massachusetts Snob-Zoning Act, but with increased flexibility to determine the particular needs of a given region of the state.

Legislative Development, Snob Zoning: Developments in Massachusetts and New Jersey, 7 Harv. J. Legis. 246, 265-8, 1970

QUESTIONS

The New Jersey Land-Use Planning and Development proposal died in committee. Why? Why was the Massachusetts proposal successful in that state's legislature?

The New York Urban Development Corporation

(3) After consultation with local officials, as provided in subdivision one of this section, the New York Urban Development Corporation and any subsidiary thereof shall, in constructing, reconstructing, rehabilitating, altering or improving any project, comply with the requirements of local laws, ordinances, codes, charters or regulations applicable to such construction, reconstruction, rehabilitation, alteration or improvement, provided however, that when, in the discretion of the corporation, such compliance is not feasible or practicable, the corporation and any subsidiary thereof shall comply with the requirements of the state building construction code, formulated by the state building code council pursuant to article eighteen of the executive law, applicable to such construction, reconstruction, rehabilitation, alteration or improvement. No municipality shall have power to modify or change the drawings, plans or specifications for the construction, reconstruction, rehabilitation, alteration or improvement of any project of the corporation or of any subsidiary thereof, or the construction, plumbing, heating, lighting or other mechanical branch of work necessary to complete the work in question, nor to require that any person, firm or corporation employed on any such work shall perform any such work in any other or different manner than that provided by such plans and specifications, nor to require that any such person, firm or corporation obtain any other or additional authority, approval, permit or certificate from such municipality in relation to the work being done, and the doing of any such work by any person, firm or corporation in accordance with the terms of such drawings, plans, specifications or contracts shall not subject said person, firm or corporation to any liability or penalty, civil or criminal, other than as may be stated in such contracts or incidental to the proper enforcement thereof; nor shall any municipality have power to require the corporation or any subsidiary thereof, or lessee therefrom or successor in interest thereto, to obtain any other or additional authority, approval, permit, certificate or certificate of occupancy from such municipality as a condition of owning, using, maintaining, operating or occupying any project acquired, constructed, reconstructed, rehabilitated, altered or improved by the corporation or by any subsidiary thereof.

N.Y. Unconsol. Laws §6266(3) (McKinney Supp. 1971)

The New York Urban Development Corporation (UDC) has used its power to override local zoning regulations rarely and reluctantly during its first four years. In April of 1972, the New York State Legislature voted to take the power away, but Governor Rockefeller vetoed the bill that passed in the Legislature.

Late in May 1972, a New York trial court held that, insofar as the statute set forth above purported to exempt the UDC from zoning laws and other local regulations, the statute did not violate the home rule provisions of the New York State Constitution. Floyd v. New York State Urban Development Corporation, 70 Misc. 2d 187, 333 N.Y.S. 2d 123 (Sup. Ct. 1972). Several weeks later, the UDC announced that it was prepared to preempt local zoning regulations to build 100 units of low- and moderate-income housing in each of 9 Westchester County towns. Supervisors of several of the selected towns were in the audience at the formal announcement and took the opportunity to pass out press releases of their own denouncing the UDC and threatening to bring the agency before "the highest courts." (*The New York Times*, June 21, 1972.)

> The agency's support so far has come from rather predictable institutional sources: the Regional Plan Association, the local building industry, the League of Women Voters. (*The New York Times*, July 17, 1972.)
>
> By going into 9 of Westchester's 18 towns at once, [the UDC president] hoped to avoid putting any one local government on the spot. Instead he has found himself up against a coalition of private citizens and private officials attacking the agency on the issues of big government, local control, and home rule.
>
> United Towns for Home Rule ... was formed by several dozen residents from three of the northern Westchester towns three days before the UDC formally announced its plan. ...
>
> "What we are saying to the UDC," says Stuart Greene of New Castle, the organization's president, "is, We have not been consulted, you do not have our consent. If we want New York City to move into New Castle, we'll tell you."
>
> Governor Rockefeller and Edward J. Logue, president of the State Urban Development Corporation, have apparently decided to defer the UDC's building plans in Westchester County for four months to give the nine towns involved a chance to come up with multi-family housing plans of their own. (*The New York Times*, September 26, 1972.)
>
> The chairman of United Towns for Home Rule, the group that has led the opposition to the state Urban Development Corporation's housing plans in Westchester County, announced yesterday that he was resigning because others in the group's leadership wanted to take it off a present course he characterized as 'moderate.'
>
> In an interview last July, Chairman Greene, a Harvard-educated lawyer, had said he feared that race prejudice rather than the

philosophy of local home rule might emerge as the dominant theme in the anti-UDC protest. "The minute I lose a vote to a redneck, I quit," he said then.

Asked whether the events he feared had in fact come to pass, he said, "Yes." (*The New York Times*, October 10, 1972.)

Low-income housing in northern Westchester County had looked dead. A controversial state plan to build a total of 900 units of low- and moderate-income housing in 9 Westchester towns—100 units, or apartments, in each—had been suspended by Governor Rockefeller just as last fall's legislative election campaigns were heating up. And, as the moratorium deadline of January 15 approached, there was speculation that the plan, which had kept much of the plush suburban county in an uproar all last summer, would be allowed to expire quietly and gracefully.

But on January 16, Edward J. Logue, president of the state's Urban Development Corporation, the agency that devised the so-called "nine towns plan," announced that the state would indeed proceed. He said there could be negotiation on details, but no further compromise on basic ideas. UDC, he added, expected to break ground on some of the housing projects this spring. . . .

Mr. Logue and Governor Rockefeller will almost certainly have to decide whether to force the issue once and for all if 9 projects are ever to be built. At his news conference on January 16, Mr. Logue said that the UDC, in attempting a breakthrough in the suburbs, expected what it got: rumors, fears, lack of trust. The best way to deal with them is to demonstrate to everyone, on a modest scale, desirable results. (*The New York Times*, January 28, 1973.)

On June 7, Governor Rockefeller signed into law a bill that curbs some of the power of the State Urban Development Corporation, one of the Governor's pet agencies.

In signing the bill, Governor Rockefeller noted that, except for towns and villages, the UDC authority "to waive compliance with local zoning and other local laws and regulations will be unimpaired."

The Governor also noted that the law increased the agency's authority to increase bonds to $2 billion from $1.5 billion, and he said the added borrowing capacity is "most important" because of the withdrawal of Federal housing subsidies by President Nixon's Administration. (*The New York Times*, June 8, 1973.)

QUESTIONS

1. Considering the above, would you recommend a State Urban Development Corporation in your state? Would you establish it along the above lines? Who is likely to resist such a corporation and why? Who is likely to benefit?

2. Should the scope of a State Development Corporation's (SDC) activities include the development of middle- to upper-income housing? Low and moderate? Why? Should a SDC have the power to override local zoning controls and building codes? Is the power of eminent domain alone a sufficient grant of power? Should the scope of a SDC's activities include industrial and commercial developments or the power to develop new towns?

3. Should a SDC be a semiindependent corporation? Should it act as a general partner in development and in syndication? Would federal housing funds best be allotted to the states through the single channel of an SDC?

The Fairfax County Approach

A different approach by the state was utilized in Fairfax County, Virginia. Compare it to the other approaches and evaluate its potential effectiveness, had it been on the statute books during the low-income housing controversies described in Part Two:

> A. Amend §30-1.8.8 (Definitions) to add new subsections as follows:
>
> 30-1.8.8.3 *Dwelling unit, low income.* Any dwelling unit occupied by a person or persons subsidized directly or indirectly by the Federal, State or County government under any program to assist the construction or occupancy of housing for families of low income, namely those families who meet the eligibility standards for public housing established from time to time by the Fairfax County Redevelopment and Housing Authority under the Federal Low-Rent Public Housing Program authorized by the United States Housing Act of 1937, as amended (or the corresponding provisions of future federal housing laws); or any dwelling unit occupied by a person or persons eligible for but not receiving such a government subsidy, and paying the same rentals or mortgage payments as he or they would pay under such a subsidy program.
>
> 30-1.8.8.4 *Dwelling unit, moderate income.* Any dwelling unit occupied by a person or persons subsidized directly or indirectly by the Federal, State or County government under any program to assist the construction or occupancy of housing for families of moderate income, namely those families who meet the eligibility standards established for Fairfax County from time to time by the United States Department of Housing and Urban Development for assistance under the Federal programs for homeownership and/or rental and cooperative housing authorized in sections 221 (d) (3), 235, and 236 of the National Housing Act, as amended (or in the corresponding provisions of future federal housing laws); or any dwelling unit occupied by a person or persons eligible for but not receiving such a government subsidy, and paying the same rentals or mortgage payments as he or they would pay under such a subsidy program.

B. *The following are amendments to §30-2.2.2 (Schedule of Regulations) for the PLANNED DEVELOPMENT HOUSING (PDH) DISTRICT*

1. Amend the first two sentences of the first paragraph under Column 1 (*Intent and Purposes*) to read as follows:

The PDH district is designed to encourage innovative and creative design and facilitate use of the most advantageous construction techniques in the development of land for residential uses *of and for families of all income ranges.* At the same time, the district regulations will insure ample provision for efficient use of open space, promote high standards in the layout, design and construction of residential development, *insure the provision of dwellings within the means of families of low and moderate income*, and further the purposes and provisions of the comprehensive plan. To these ends, ...

2. Amend Column 1 by adding the following at the end thereof:

a. *Required Use: Low and Moderate Income Dwelling Units*

Except as otherwise provided herein, every planned development of a PDH district shall provide dwelling units for families of low and moderate income. An applicant for PDH zoning (hereafter the "applicant") shall provide or cause others to provide, under the development plan, low income dwelling units which shall be not less (and may be more) than six per cent (6%) of the total number of dwelling units in the development. The applicant shall also provide, or cause others to provide, the number of moderate income dwelling units which, when added to the number of low income dwelling units, shall be not less (and may be more) than fifteen per cent (15%) of the total number of dwelling units in the development.

The requisite percentages for low and moderate income dwelling units shall be applied, separately, to the total of one-family, semi-detached, and two-family dwelling units, if any, and to the total of multi-family, town house, and garden court dwelling units, if any. In addition, the average number of bedrooms proposed for the low and moderate income dwelling units shall generally reflect the average number of bedrooms per dwelling unit for the planned development as a whole. . . . [Similar amendments applicable to other residential districts are omitted.]

Fairfax Co., Va., Code ch. 30 (1961), amendments approved June 30, 1971.

QUESTIONS

1. Many local builders challenged the ordinance in the courts. (See DeGroff Enterprises, Inc. v. Bd. of Co. Supervisors of Fairfax Co., Law No. 25609 (Fairfax Co. Cir. Ct., Nov. 11, 1971), writ granted, No. 8118, Sup. Ct. Va., Oct.

24, 1972.) The challengers question whether the ordinance is: (1) authorized under the Virginia enabling act, (2) arbitrary and capricious, (3) an unconstitutional taking, either per se or in individual instances, (4) an unlawful delegation of zoning authority or statutory power to HUD or county officers that should be retained in the county board, (5) void for vagueness, and (6) unlawful "conditional zoning."

No Fairfax lawyer would defend the ordinance when it was challenged; nor would any local architect or engineer appear as an expert witness.

2. In drafting an ordinance like that for Fairfax County, how do you determine what percentage of new development must be allocated to low- and moderate-income housing? Will the quotas stay the same throughout the next ten years? What would be the extent of metropolitan housing change if only 6 percent of suburban housing went to low-income persons? Could the Fairfax County standards become part of a "fair-share" plan for the Washington metropolitan area?

3. How do you avoid the possible problem of having the ordinance become in effect a deterrent to the construction of multiple-unit housing on vacant land? Will neighbors now vigorously oppose rezoning requests on ecological or density grounds? Does the ordinance increase costs and, thus, tip the economies to favor single-family housing? Is it possible that builders will go elsewhere in the metropolitan area in order to avoid the ordinance? Might a combination of new elected board members plus public pressure on rezoning requests over time substantially reduce the total production volume of housing in Fairfax County?

The Ashley Proposal

The federal government also provides carrots and sticks to induce state action. Most recently, Representative Thomas L. Ashley's proposal, which received broad bipartisan support, promised to constitute a first step toward a national urban growth policy. His measure directed the states to create a housing agency for each metropolitan area. Among other duties, these agencies would plan the construction and location of subsidized housing units to be built by private and public interests throughout an urban area; the agencies would make incentive grants to communities to help pay for services required for low-income families. These agencies were to be representative of all the political jurisdictions in the metropolitan area. The defeat of the proposal is another indication of the political and social sensitivities to introducing lower-income housing into the suburbs, which was interpreted by many as the major thrust of the block grants.

Consider the Ashley proposal in more detail:

Sec. 501. It is the purpose of this title to provide for the establishment of State housing agencies and metropolitan housing agencies within States, to prescribe the powers and functions of State and metropolitan housing agencies, and to authorize the financial and other assistance needed to enable these agencies to develop on an areawide basis, balanced housing programs which further the achievement of the national housing goal of a decent home and a suitable living environment for every American family. Its basic objective is to stimulate a better focusing of all available local, State, private, and Federal resources upon the achievement of the national housing goal by bringing about (1) greater State and local capabilities for meeting their housing and other development needs on a national, areawide basis, (2) more equitable allocation of Federal housing subsidy funds in accordance with State and local goals and priorities, (3) greater State and local capabilities for aggregating their markets for housing resulting in increased housing production at lower cost, and (4) greater economic opportunity and improved living conditions for low- and moderate-income families that are now unable to obtain housing within reasonable proximity to their places of employment.

Definitions

Sec. 502. (a) As used in this title—

(1) The term "metropolitan area" means a standard metropolitan statistical area, as established by the Office of Management and Budget, subject, however, to such modifications or extensions as the Secretary deems to be appropriate for the purposes of this title.

(2) The term "State housing agency" includes an official State housing agency or (in a State where no such housing agency exists) an agency or instrumentality of State government designated by the Governor of the State and acceptable to the Secretary for purposes of this title.

(3) The term "metropolitan housing agency" means an official housing agency designated by the Governor (or Governors in the case of agencies with interstate jurisdiction) and acceptable to the Secretary for purposes of this title, empowered under State law or interstate compact to (A) establish housing needs and objectives throughout the metropolitan area involved, and (B) carry out all activities eligible for assistance under this title. To the greatest extent practicable, metropolitan housing agencies shall be representative of the elected officials of all of the units of general local government within the metropolitan area.

(4) The term "Secretary" means the Secretary of Housing and Urban Development.

(5) The term "unit of general local government" means any city, municipality, county, town, township, parish, village, or other general purpose political subdivision of a State, and the District of Columbia.

(6) The term "population", with respect to any area or unit, means the total resident population of such area or unit based on data compiled by the United States Bureau of the Census and referable to the same point or period in time.

(7) The term "amount of poverty" means the number of persons (or, alternatively, the number of families and unrelated individuals) whose incomes are below the poverty level multiplied by two. Poverty levels shall be determined by the Secretary pursuant to criteria provided by the Office of Management and Budget, taking into account and making appropriate adjustments for regional variations in income and cost of living, and shall be based on data referable to the same point or period in time.

(8) The term "amount of overcrowding" means the number of housing units with 1.01 or more persons per room based on data compiled by the United States Bureau of the Census and referable to the same point or period in time.

(9) The term "extent of housing deficiencies" means the number of housing units lacking some or all plumbing facilities based on data compiled by the United States Bureau of the Census and referable to the same point or period in time.

Special Program Grants

Sec. 504. (a) The Secretary is authorized to make grants to any State or metropolitan housing agency to assist such agency in facilitating the provision of housing for low- and moderate-income families throughout the State or metropolitan area over which it has jurisdiction through such means as—

(1) providing grants, loans, and technical and other assistance to public and private organizations carrying out homeownership and housing opportunity programs for low- and moderate-income families to help them fill unmet needs, initiate exceptional programs, and experiment with new approaches and programs for such families;

(2) providing grants, loans, and technical and other assistance to public and private organizations with respect to the construction, rehabilitation, and operation of housing for low- and moderate-income families, including but not limited to assistance to help cover necessary preconstruction costs incurred for architectural assistance, land options, application fees, and similar items;

(3) encouraging, by means of studies, technical assistance, and advisory and information services, the elimination of unreasonable restraints on the provision of housing for low- and moderate-income families; and

(4) carrying out, by means of studies, technical and financial assistance, and advisory and information services, programs designed to aggregate housing markets in order to achieve increased production and economies of scale.

(b) In order to be eligible for assistance under this section, the applicant seeking such assistance shall demonstrate to the satisfaction of the Secretary that the funds requested are not available upon practicable terms and conditions from other sources.

(c) There are authorized to be appropriated for grants under this section not to exceed $30,000,000 for the fiscal year ending June 30, 1973, $30,000,000 for the fiscal year ending June 30, 1974, and $40,000,000 for the fiscal year ending June 30, 1975.

Metropolitan Incentive Grants

Sec. 505. (a) The Secretary is authorized to make and contract to make grants to State and metropolitan housing agencies to assist such agencies in carrying out programs which are designed to encourage the provision in metropolitan areas of an adequate supply of housing for low- and moderate-income families within reasonable proximity to their places of employment through the provision of financial assistance to units of general local government to help cover the difference between the cost to the unit of general local government involved of providing adequate supporting community services and facilities to the housing unit occupied by the low- or moderate-income family and the amount of revenues received through property and other taxes or assessments which are attributable to the housing unit occupied by such family. Assistance under this section shall be provided with respect to particular units of federally assisted low- and moderate-income housing, and may not exceed for each such unit a total amount of $3,000, which shall be provided in installments not exceeding $500 per annum.

Allocation and Distribution of Housing Subsidy Funds

Sec. 506. (a) For the fiscal year commencing July 1, 1972, and for each succeeding fiscal year, the aggregate amount of contracts to make assistance payments under section 101 of the Housing and Urban Development Act of 1965 and section 235 of the National Housing Act, interest reduction payments under section 236 of the National Housing Act, and annual contributions under section 10(e) of the United States Housing Act of 1937 shall not exceed amounts approved in appropriation Acts. Of the amounts thus approved 80 per centum shall be allocated to metropolitan areas and made available to metropolitan housing agencies as provided in subsection (b).

(b)(1) The Secretary shall allocate for each metropolitan area an amount which bears the same ratio to the allocation for all metropolitan areas as the average of the ratios between—

(A) the population of that metropolitan area and the population of all metropolitan areas;

(B) the amount of poverty in that metropolitan area and the amount of poverty in all metropolitan areas; and

(C) the amount of overcrowding in that metropolitan area and the amount of overcrowding in all metropolitan areas.

(2) The amount allocated to each metropolitan area shall be made available to the eligible metropolitan housing agency for that area for further allocation by such agency in accordance with its approved housing program.

(c) The remainder of the amounts approved in appropriation Acts as provided in subsection (a) shall be allocated to the States and made available to State housing agencies as provided in subsection (d).

(d)(1) The Secretary shall allocate for each State an amount which bears the same ratio to the allocation for all States as the average of the ratios between—

(A) the population of that State and the population of all States;

(B) the amount of poverty in that State and the amount of poverty in all States;

(C) the amount of overcrowding in that State and the amount of overcrowding in all States; and

(D) the extent of housing deficiencies in the State and the extent of housing deficiencies in all States.

(2) The amount allocated to each State shall be made available to the eligible State housing agency for that State for further allocation by such agency in accordance with its approved housing program....

The recommendation of the President's Commission on Urban Housing to overcome local zoning restrictions (p. 339) did not become public law or administrative practice, nor did it even become a legislative proposal. The metropolitan housing agency proposal of Representative Ashley did become a legislative proposal, but its many opponents included HUD's Secretary George Romney. Why did the proposal kindle so much opposition in Washington? Would such a regional housing agency for the Boston metropolitan area have helped the construction of low- and moderate-income housing in the five communities studied? Do you see ambiguities in the drafting of the legislation that might make the regional housing agency less effective in expanding housing opportunity?

What other incentives and deterrents could the federal government use to encourage suburban LMIH development? What problems might such an expanded federal role encounter?

Regional and Metropolitan Approaches

It is increasingly evident that geographically and conceptually more inclusive approaches are required in order to provide effective housing solutions. Local government autonomy in metropolitan regions generates uneven distribution of public sector costs; some governments are forced to assume the costs of decisions and policies adopted by other government units. Furthermore, multiple autonomous governments and private institutional barriers in the metropolitan region contribute to fragmentation of the housing market which, in turn, provides a basis for racial and economic segregation. Finally, the fragmentation of local government makes planning for an entire area difficult and minimizes the opportunity for desegregation.

A recent example of a broader approach is the Dayton Plan, adopted in the fall of 1970 by the Miami Valley Regional Planning Commission (created in 1964, with 30 member municipalities as well as five counties). The Plan calls for a balanced distribution of about 14,000 additional units of low- and moderate-income housing, including a considerable amount of public housing, over a four-year period throughout the five-county Dayton, Ohio, metropolitan region. The regional housing dispersal plan is based on computing low- and moderate-income housing needs by county, then allocating shares of this housing to planning units throughout the region, each based on groupings of municipalities and/or townships. Location of such housing is coordinated through voluntary agreements and working relationships with the Regional Planning Commission, as well as through a review process. The plan urges the need to achieve public and political support, emphasizing that any housing plan dropped into an unprepared environment stands little chance of survival. Housing need was quantified, using straightforward projections, with need defined as a social concept, separate and apart from the economic concept of demand. The need figures did not take into account dwelling units in need of rehabilitation; they dealt only with new units required to eliminate dilapidation and overcrowding. The housing distribution method is described as follows:

>
> There are a number of factors upon which a distribution can be based. For example, the simplest solution is to divide the needed housing units equally among the planning units. Or, each planning unit can be assigned a number of units equal to its proportionate share of the population, thus distributing units in the same ratio as the population is distributed. The greater the number of people, the more units assigned. Again, each planning unit can be assigned dwelling units according to the number of low and moderate income households it contains. The greater its population in this category, the more moderate and low income units assigned it. This method sounds quite logical on the surface, but in fact, it would simply be placing the new units in the same areas where lower cost housing now exists. Geographic opportunity would not be enhanced through this method at all. A variation of this method that would solve that problem, however, is to assign units inversely to the proportion of low and moderate income households, so that the greater the existing proportion, the fewer the dwelling unit share.

Two other methods involve the school system. Since this is one of the most sensitive points of controversy when the question of low and moderate income housing is raised, it was deemed necessary to consider ways of building it into the distribution process quantitatively. One way of doing this is by looking at school districts' assessed valuation per pupil, and distributing units according to the relative strength or weakness of this factor. The higher the assessed valuation per pupil, the greater the number of dwelling units assigned. It is recognized that assessed valuation alone does not determine the monies that a district actually receives for its schools. However, it does represent the potential for taxation for education, and that is considered to be the relevant point here.

The other school-related factor is "pupils in excess of normal capacity," which indicates overcrowding and need for more classrooms. Here an inverse rank can be used again, with the most severely overcrowded districts receiving the fewest dwelling units. In both this method and the preceding one compensation can be made for the disparities between school district boundaries and planning units boundaries by adjusting assignments to reflect the geographic differences.

The six described in the preceding paragraphs seem to hold the greatest promise of yielding reasonable results, yet each one alone has its shortcomings. Thus evolved the idea of using a composite of the six, for this would achieve a counterbalancing of the strengths and weaknesses of each planning unit and yield a distribution of units sensitive to them. . . .

The low and moderate income housing needs include both FHA-assisted and public housing units. In working toward the goals set forth here, it is necessary that each planning unit now served by a public housing authority accept a certain number of these units, as well as FHA-assisted units. The location of these will be rather strictly limited by the criteria governing their development. Within the metropolitan area, however, suitable sites are available for such housing and the way should be paved for it by execution of cooperation agreements with the Dayton Metropolitan Housing Authority to expedite its development.

In areas not now served by a housing authority, it is highly recommended that these be established. Throughout the Region there are families for whom decent housing cannot be produced by any other means. Low-rent public housing serves a very necessary purpose in helping to house the low income segment of the population and is a program that must continue apace. It, too, however, suffers tremendously from geographic confinement that limits its full usefulness. All the planning units have the capability to accept immediately a number of units of one kind or another. Based upon all of the collected data on each planning unit, the staff attempted to go through the exercise of isolating factors that might sharply curtail an area's ability to absorb the housing units. Essentially, however, they all have the necessary basic elements such as commercial facilities, transportation, land, schools, parks, utilities, etc. Not all the potential sites in a given planning unit have all these

things, but it is most likely that sites can be found in all of them that are satisfactory. A more detailed analysis will have to be made on a project by project basis as proposals are made.
Miami Valley Regional Planning Commission, "A Housing Plan for the Miami Valley Region: A Summary."

The plan attracted national attention and *The New York Times* reported it on December 17, 1970 as a remarkable development, emphasizing that the white suburbs of Dayton agreed voluntarily to provide housing for the poor, despite strong and outspoken opposition by many residents. "Although the plan is said to be unique, the heated public controversy that accompanied its initial implementation and the conditions in Dayton that brought it about are indicative of the urban dilemma across the nation."

Do you agree with the method followed to establish the distribution formula? Consider the variables included and the way the "fair-share" formula was formulated. Would you recommend such a "fair-share" plan to your community? Would you devise a different plan? Why? What are the advantages and disadvantages of the plan? Do you think it will be implemented in the long run? How would it affect the five communities?

In formulating answers to these questions, consider the following: Most people agree that problems exist which have to be solved on a metropolitan-wide basis—housing, transportation, water and sewer, education, health, land use, environmental pollution. But everyone wants someone else to solve the problems or to sustain the cost. Whether it is the location of electric power or sewage disposal plants, a superhighway, airport, or low-income housing, the hundreds of suburban communities and the central city itself want it located somewhere else. Should the suburbs help in solving critical problems facing the central city? Shall the middle class wall themselves off from the consequences of poverty, poor education, deprivation, pollution? Shall ethnic groups isolate themselves in enclaves? Is it possible to meet effectively public service needs within a fragmented structure of local government? For example, the 1965 Racial Imbalance Law in Massachusetts—the first and only state with such a law—forbids schools with more than 50 percent nonwhite enrollment. The results so far in Boston have been disappointing. In the last eight years, the number of unbalanced schools has nearly doubled. Lawsuits have been brought against the Boston School Committee, and state and federal funds have been withheld from the city. Of Boston's 97,000 school children, 36 percent are nonwhite, but 67 schools are predominantly black. Solutions cannot be found effectively within the artificial boundaries of the city of Boston, according to Mayor White; the uneven distribution of low- and moderate-income housing throughout the metropolitan region is at the heart of the school racial-imbalance problem.

The New York Regional Planning Association's 1971 plan for the concerted growth of Westchester County provides still another approach to regionalism. This plan emphasizes a slightly different concept than the Dayton Plan: the idea of choosing several suburban cities throughout a metropolitan region to become "metropolitan centers," in order to avoid the creation of a formless, spread city of housing subdivisions and office parks. The organization's report states: "Westchester is adding to the Statue of Liberty message: 'Give me ... your poor: but only during the day to man the factories, clean the houses, and maintain the hospitals.'" (*The New York Times*, March 7, 1971.)

The Plan recommends: (1) The county work out a tax-sharing program under which densely populated towns receive more funds than sparsely populated ones. (2) In return for conforming to this county density plan, localities would be able to share the tax profits from a commercial facility, even though built someplace else. (3) Most large facilities, including corporate offices, hospitals, department stores, and cultural and educational centers that draw people from wide areas of the county, would be concentrated in White Plains (the county seat), rather than scattered haphazardly. (4) The northern Westchester cities of Mount Kisco and Peekskill should be developed as secondary centers for the county. (5) The county itself would prepare a plan for placing major facilities and a plan for housing density, with a veto power over municipal opposition. (6) Subsidized housing should be located in patterns designed to let workers live near their jobs. "The right assortment of housing will not be hard to identify if Westchester is considered a complete metropolitan community, with growing self-sufficiency in jobs and services, and a well-rounded population—rather than a refuge behind a zoning moat for escapees from the problems of the nation."

Do you approve of this plan? How does it compare to the Dayton Ohio Regional Plan? Given the arguments of the opposition and the data of the five community studies, which one of the two is likely to be accepted in the Boston metropolitan region? Why? Which of their features is most attractive and which ones less desirable? To whom?

Chapter Eleven

Social, Judicial, and Institutional Change Strategies

Social Change

Aristotle suggested that the key to understanding why men want to change their social relations is to grasp how men think that their society ought to be organized.[1] The opposite is also true. Resistance to change is also understandable in terms of men's conviction that their present society is ideal.

Theories of social change are dependent upon a theory of the social system. Thus, social change and social structure are interrelated, each representing the dynamic tensions and the "static," tenuous equilibrium of social organization. However, the dichotomy between "static" and "dynamic" is grossly exaggerated among social scientists, for, short of total revolution, they always coexist in a society.

While considerable energy has been expended in developing a comprehensive theory of the social system and of social change, there is as yet no adequate theory of change (nor a fully developed general theory of society), as Etzioni[2] and Moore,[3] among others, point out. Fundamentally, two basic schools of thought have emerged. One interprets the structure of the social system in relation to its functions, emphasizing the more permanent aspects of the system. A fundamental postulate of this approach is concern with the mechanisms of stability rather than change; society is viewed as a moral community, a collaboration of people who share certain values that legitimize the characteristics of the prevailing social organization. The other school of thought postulates that conflict, coercion, and enforced constraints—not voluntary organization and consensus—make social organization cohesive. Two general theoretical perspectives have thus emerged: functionalism or the "structure-function" approach—represented mainly by Parsons, Merton, Davis—and the conflict model, based heavily on the Hegelian and Marxian dialectics—and represented mainly by Dahrendorf.

The basic postulates of the functionalist approach are three: (1) society is an integrated system, with its parts functionally interdependent and subordinate to the interests of the total, (2) unity of the social system is maintained through consensus of its subparts, which (3) are dynamically integrated in equilibrium and stability.

Pierre L. Van Den Berghe[4] describes functionalism as follows:

1. Societies must be looked at holistically as systems of interrelated parts.
2. Hence, causation is multiple and reciprocal.
3. Although integration is never perfect, social systems are fundamentally in a state of dynamic equilibrium, i.e., adjustive responses to outside changes tend to minimize the final amount of change within the system. The dominant tendency is thus towards stability and inertia, as maintained through built-in mechanisms of adjustment and social control.
4. As a corollary of (3), dysfunctions, tensions and "deviance" do exist and can persist for a long time, but they tend to resolve themselves or to be "institutionalized" in the long run. In other words, while perfect equilibrium or integration is never reached, it is the limit towards which social systems tend.
5. Change generally occurs in a gradual, adjustive fashion, and not in a sudden, revolutionary way. Changes, which appear to be drastic, in fact affect mostly the social superstructure while leaving the core elements of the social and cultural structure largely unchanged.
6. Change comes from basically three sources: adjustment of the system to exogenous (or extra-systemic) change; growth through structural and functional differentiation; and inventions or innovations by members or groups within society.
7. The most important and basic factor making for social integration is value consensus, i.e., underlying the whole social and cultural structure, there are broad aims or principles which most members of a given social system consider desirable and agree on. Not only is the value system (or ethos) the deepest and most important source of integration, but it is also the stablest element of socio-cultural systems.

Talcott Parsons[5] accounts for change with the suggestion that the idea of differentiation in function is fundamental. Yet, equally important is the concept of patterned relations among functions. As differentiation occurs, the values of a particular unit may change and become more complex, but may not necessarily change the "pattern component." In his words:

> The structure of a system and of its environment must be distinguished from process *within* the system and in *interchange* between the system and its environment. But processes which maintain the

stability of a system, internally through both structure and process, and in interchange with its environment, *i.e.*, states of its equilibrium, must be distinguished from processes by which this balance between structure and more "elementary" process is altered in such a way as to lead to a new and different "state" of the system, a state which must be described in terms of an alteration of its previous structure....

Let us start with the question of the structure of social systems and introduce both a formal and a substantive consideration. The formal one is that the structure of any empirical system may be treated as consisting in (1) *units*, such as the particle or the cell, and (2) *patterned relations* among units, such as relative distances, "organization" into tissues and organs. For social systems the minimum unit is the *role* of the participating individual actor (or status-role, if you will), and the minimum relation is that of patterned reciprocal interactions in terms of which each participant functions as an actor in relation to (orienting to) the others and, conversely, each is object for all the others. Higher-order units of social systems are collectivities, *i.e.*, organized action systems of the role performance of pluralities of human individuals....

The concept of stable equilibrium implies that through integrative mechanisms endogenous variations are kept within limits compatible with the maintenance of the main structural patterns, and through adaptive mechanisms fluctuations in the relations between system and environment are similarly kept within limits....

It has been suggested above that a process of differentiation, with the meaning we have given that term, involves the establishment of a unit having primary functions of a higher order, seen in terms of the system in which it operates, than was the function of the unit from which it differentiates. If this is the case, then the norms governing the performance of that function, including the relations of its performers to other units in the social structure, must be of a higher order of generality than before. This is what we mean by saying that they are more universalistic; they define standards which cannot, in their relevance, be confined to the lower-order function and the units performing it....

This whole discussion has been based on the assumption that the underlying value-pattern of the system does not change as a part of the process of differentiation. It does not, however, follow that nothing changes at the level of values. It is an essential proposition of the conceptual scheme used here that every social system has a system of values as the highest-order component of its structure. Its values comprise the definition, from the point of view of its members—if it is institutionalized—of the desirable type of system at a level independent of internal structural differentiation or of particularities of situation. This "system" involves both a pattern type and an element of content, namely a definition of what kind of system the pattern applies to. In our case there are the values of households and of employing-productive units. In what I am calling "pattern" terms they may be the same, *e.g.*, both of them incorporating the general American pattern of "instrumental activism." But if these values are to be implemented in either type of system there must be specifications of the more general system to the type of function (not its particularities) and to the type of situation in which the unit operates.

Where differentiation has occurred, this means that the values of the new system, which includes both the new and the residual unit, must be different in the content component from that of the original unit, though not, under present assumptions, in the pattern component. The new values must be more extensive, in the special sense that they can legitimize the functions of both differentiated units under a single formula which permits each to do what it does and, equally essential, not to do what the other does. . . .

Dahrendorf, the major exponent of the contrary view, believes that the formulation of a theory of social change will have to be found outside the structural-functional tradition. He suggests a theory of conflict-coercion and change, a view which can be traced to Hobbes: men want more out of their environment than all of them can possibly derive. The need for coercive sanctions arises from the demand of the organization itself.

The postulates of the conflict model are fundamentally four: (1) society is a setting within which various struggles take place, (2) governmental units are dominant participants in struggles on the part of one side or another, but usually on behalf of the ruling class, (3) coercion, in the form of law or other social institutions is the major factor in maintaining and justifying the value system of society and the status quo, and (4) social class is perceived as groups with antithetical interests, therefore inevitably in conflict with one another. Dahrendorf emphasizes the following:

After an interval of almost fifty years, a theme has reappeared in sociology which has determined the origin of that discipline more than any other subject area. From Marx and Comte to Simmel and Sorel, social conflict, especially revolution, was one of the central themes in social research. The same is true of many early Anglo-Saxon sociologists (although in their work the problem of revolution has been characteristically somewhat neglected), for example, the Webbs in England and Sumner in the United States. However, when Talcott Parsons in 1937 established a certain convergence in the sociological theories of Alfred Marshall, Emile Durkheim, Vilfredo Pareto, and Max Weber, he no longer had in mind an analysis of social conflict; his was an attempt to solve the problem of integration of so-called social systems by an organon of interrelated categories. The new question was not, "What holds societies together?"—no longer, "What drives them on?" The influence of the Parsonian posing of the question on more recent sociology (and by no means only on American sociology) can hardly be overrated. Thus, it is possible that the revival of the study of social conflict in the last decades appears to many not so much a continuation of traditional research paths as a new thematic discovery—an instance of dialectic irony in the development of science.

If we extrapolate the analytical approaches of the structural-functional theory somewhat beyond their boundaries, and investigate their implicit postulates, we can construct a model of society which lies at the base of this theory and determines its perspectives. The essential elements of this societal model are these:

1. Every society is a relatively persisting configuration of elements.
2. Every society is a well-integrated configuration of elements.
3. Every element in a society contributes to its functioning.
4. Every society rests on the consensus of its members.

It should be clear that a theory based on this model does not lend itself to the explanation, not even the description, of the phenomena of social conflict and change. For this purpose, one needs a model which takes the diametrically opposite position on all the four points above:

1. Every society is subjected at every moment to change; social change is ubiquitous.
2. Every society experiences at every moment social conflict; social conflict is ubiquitous.
3. Every element in a society contributes to its change.
4. Every society rests on constraint of some of its members by others.

The dichotomy of social roles within imperatively coordinated groups, the division into positive and negative dominance roles, is a fact of social structure. If and insofar as social conflicts can be referred to this factual situation, they are structurally explained. The model of analysis of social conflict which is developed against a background of an assumption of such a dichotomy involves the following steps:

1. In every imperatively coordinated group, the carriers of positive and negative dominance roles determine two quasigroups with opposite latent interests. We call them "quasigroups" because we have to do here with mere aggregates, not organized units; we speak of "latent interests," because the opposition of outlook need not be conscious on this level; it may exist only in the form of expectations associated with certain positions. The opposition of interests has here a quite formal meaning, namely, the expectation that an interest in the preservation of the status quo is associated with the positive dominance roles and an interest in the change of the status quo is associated with the negative dominance roles.

2. The bearers of positive and negative dominance roles, that is,

the members of the opposing quasigroups, organize themselves into groups with manifest interests, unless certain empirically variable conditions (the condition of organization) intervene. Interest groups, in contrast to quasigroups, are organized entities, such as parties and trade unions; the manifest interests are formulated programs and ideologies.

3. Interest groups which originate in this manner are in constant conflict over the preservation or change of the status quo. The form and the intensity of the conflict are determined by empirically variable conditions (the conditions of conflict).

4. The conflict among interest groups in the sense of this model leads to changes in the structure of their social relations, through changes in the dominance relations. The kind, the speed, and the depth of this development depend on empirically variable conditions (the conditions of structural change).[6]

Most criticism of the conflict model centers around its Marxian postulates, but in two distinct ways: one is the theorists' acceptance of Marx's determinism; the other is Dahrendorf's substitution of Marx's definition of class (as determined by the relation to the means of production) by one relating to the unequal distribution of authority.

Which of the two schools of thought helps you understand more effectively the low- and moderate-income housing controversy in the five communities? Would your approach and policy formulation be influenced significantly if one rather than the other theory is postulated? How? What are the logical consequences if you apply each of the theories in interpreting what happened in these communities?

On the other hand, you may choose to make no assumptions regarding the nature of social change, and, instead, analyze first the controversy—on the basis of your understanding—and, then, formulate tentative generalizations about social organization and social change. In the five cases, was change viewed positively, or was it perceived as promoting no real advantage?

The Process of Change and Its Community Context

What accounts for differences among suburban communities in the degree of racial and economic segregation in their housing? What local, social, economic, and political conditions are associated with variations in the extent of housing segregation? Do rich cities act differently from poor cities?

In the 1960s, various studies were undertaken to unearth associations between various municipal policies, such as urban renewal or the level of welfare expenditures, and the sociopolitical characteristics of cities. These studies relied heavily on the demographic approach to identify factors which might be thought of as causes of policy differences. Some of their conclusions are briefly mentioned in this section—with a note of caution since most of these studies were concerned with cities in general, rather than suburbs in particular.

The same basic questions can be raised in the context of social change. The diffusion of change—new attitudes, new technology, new patterns of behavior, new legislation—does not occur at random; nor does its acceptance or rejection. Comparative community analysis in the systematic explanation of suburban segregation in housing therefore constitutes a helpful analytic approach.

Cross tabulation of demographic and policy factors shows the existence or absence of relationships. But frequently we cannot be certain how much more or less of a relationship might appear if other factors were introduced, or what results are likely to be obtained if we tried to explain the so-called "unexplained" city-by-city variation (unexplained in the sense that in a regression equation, only a certain amount of variation among cities is accounted for by a set of independent variables). Consequently it is helpful, at times, to combine the demographic approach with the analysis of the dynamic processes through which social change occurs and spreads. Parts of any social system are interrelated and interdependent, so that changes in one sector are often followed by strains which necessitate adjustments in other sectors in order for the system to maintain its viability. How these chain reactions are initiated and proceed depends upon the nature of the strains and the system's ability to respond and avoid disorganization.

At times, disorganization is unavoidable. When it does occur, it can grow to the degree that it can no longer be contained within the system; then efforts at reorganization are likely to be made, sometimes involving far-reaching structural changes—depending upon the urgency of social needs, the flexibility of the social system, and the effectiveness of its change mechanisms. Acceptance or rejection of low-income housing, for example, may be associated both with certain community variables (high educational and economic level, voting behavior, concentration of power, ethnic populations) *and* the dynamic processes of change operating through the interaction of social institutions and environmental realities (such as the existence of substandard housing).

From these viewpoints, what conclusions would you draw from the five community studies? Although one needs far more extensive data and a larger number of cases, could you begin to formulate some basic generalizations to test regarding the chances of success or failure of low- and moderate-income housing in the communities, given their characteristics? Conversely, how could a long-term housing plan which establishes a level for various types of housing in the community permit conflict to be handled constructively and facilitate workable compromises?

There is a body of literature which looks at community variables in search of deeper understanding and better prediction of community acceptance and spread of specific innovations or programs. Although far more investigation is required, and in spite of the fact that low- and moderate-income housing has not been adequately included as a variable, the tentative conclusions may prove useful.

Some interpreters of political culture suggest that those cities which have majorities advocating the welfare of the total community and the public interest usually prove more innovative with respect to policies benefiting the community as a whole than do cities dominated by groups which support private-interest values. Furthermore, whites with higher education, income, and occupational characteristics are said to be more "public regarding" than lower-middle-class and working-class whites.[7] This may suggest that desegregation in housing might be associated with higher educational, income, and occupational levels in the suburbs. Banfield and Wilson explored the hypothesis that the voting behavior of some classes tends to be more public-regarding and less private- (self- or family-) regarding than that of others. To test this hypothesis they examined voting behavior in situations where one can say that a certain vote could not have been private-regarding. Local bond and other expenditure referenda present such situations: it is sometimes possible to say that a vote in favor of a particular expenditure proposal is incompatible with a certain voter's self-interest narrowly conceived. If the voter nevertheless casts such a vote and if there is evidence that his vote was not in some sense irrational or accidental, then it must be presumed that his action was based on some conception of "the public interest."

For their investigation they concentrated on city wards that were fairly representative of distinct ethnic groups. They assumed that a voter tries to maximize his income and that he estimates in dollars the benefits and the burdens to his family if a proposed program (and ensuing public expenditure) is accepted by the community. A vote for or against the proposal depends upon an individual's own perception of the dominance of benefits or burdens. Insofar as the voter acts rationally (according to his interest), no explanation is required. If not, the "irrational" behavior is generated, the authors assert, from a sense of public interest.

Their findings suggest that in the heavily nonhomeowning districts of larger cities "the voters almost invariably support all expenditure proposals. We have examined returns on 35 expenditure proposals passed upon in 20 separate elections in seven cities and have not found a single instance in which this group failed to give a majority in favor of a proposal. Frequently the vote is 75 to 80 percent in favor; sometimes it is over 90 percent. The strength of voter support is about the same no matter what the character of the proposed expenditure."

But the idea that upper-income groups may have a more dominant preference for public expenditures than middle-income groups has been suggested also by other studies. The motivation is less clear than the behavioral pattern itself. Is it public interest or the fact that affluence permits acceptance of additional expenditures which for the affluent are relatively insignificant? Can we formulate a new rule: The richer the man the smaller the sacrifice; and the richer the community the smaller the sacrifice?

Theories regarding concentration and diffusion of power[8] suggest that the greater the concentration of power in the community, the greater the potential for innovation and change. Conversely, the greater the diffusion of power, the lower the degree of innovation. For this reason, cities with centralized administrative arrangements and a strong mayor are assumed by some theoreticians to be more innovative.[9]

Amos Hawley[10] suggests, for example, that high status cities have more difficulty than low status cities in implementing urban renewal plans because power is decentralized. Starting from the assumption that power is an attribute of a social system rather than of an individual, he examines the relationship of its concentration to urban renewal success in cities of 50,000 population or more.

His concern is with the way power is distributed in the community. "The lower the ratio of managers, proprietors, and officials to the employed labor force the greater is the concentration of power." In fact:

> the greater the concentration of power in a community the greater the probability of success in any collective action affecting the welfare of the whole. This follows, if it be granted that (1) success in a collective action requires the ability to mobilize the personnel and resources of the community and (2) that ability is greatest where power is most highly concentrated. The proposition does not say that a concentration of power assures success in any community venture. Various factors might intervene to defeat a collective project. Moreover, a concentration of power might be used to block a course of action. Power concentration, however, is not needed to defeat an action on the part of a community. That might occur as a result of power being so diffusely held that mobilization of the community cannot be accomplished.

One of the best measures of success is, of course, arrival at the implementation stage; and indeed

> [p]ower is most highly concentrated in the execution-stage cities and most diffusely distributed in the never-in-program cities.

Of course, factors other than the distribution of power are associated with the success or failure of urban renewal:

> ... the probability that urban renewal might recommend itself to a community as a course of action should be somewhat contingent on the state of its physical equipment. If the equipment, in this instance its buildings, is fairly new and in good condition, urban renewal would make little sense. But where buildings are old or dilapidated a proposal to renew or rehabilitate would appear to be appropriate.

The type of city government is also important, though Hawley treats this as one dimension of the distribution of power:

> ... In cities having a commission form of government, administrative responsibility is spread over a large number of non-elective officials. Such cities probably are unable to mobilize for action unless there is a fairly high concentration of power of the kind under study here. Administrative authority is more centralized where a mayor-council government exists. And in a city manager government administrative authority reaches its highest degree of centralization and articulation.

While Hawley concludes that the concentration of power is significantly associated with urban renewal success, there are several exceptions:

> ... The relationship is not dependable for cities with mayor-council governments, with a predominance of service industry, with small proportions of college graduates among their residents, and with locations in the Northeast and the West. Some of these exceptions appear to be contrary to the positive findings involving variables known to be closely associated with them (education and income, northeastern location, and manufacturing industry). Had it been possible to refine the controls, some of the inconsistencies doubtlessly would have disappeared.

Crain and Rosenthal[11] postulate that the socioeconomic status of the community and the percentage of its well-educated population are the critical characteristics. They suggest that the climate of opinion generated by the participation of the well-educated has the following effects on people in decision-making positions:

> 1. One main effect should be to make government officials more cautious, since they will be unable to predict how citizens will respond to anything that they do. They may often perceive the citizenry as more opposed to a particular program than it is in fact since the opposition will be more easily organized.
> 2. It is likely that many politicians subscribe to the "what have you done for us lately?" theory; that issue-oriented voters are quicker to punish than to reward; if the public is more or less evenly divided on an issue, the politician will lose votes no matter which side he takes. This leads to additional pressures to remain neutral or to prevent issues from arising.
> 3. Elected officials will wish to conform to the values of citizen participation by holding public meetings, listening attentively to petitioners, and permitting decisions to be made by referenda.
> 4. Since party loyalty is weaker, elected officials will themselves be less concerned with party loyalty; they are more likely to go to the

mass media, or to publicize their position when it wins them votes, thereby increasing public discussion and controversy.

5. If an issue does arise and become controversial, the pressures on elected officials to remain neutral will increase; hence a controversial issue is more likely to result in nothing being done.

Consequently,

> ... Middle-class cities will have a less stable government, will be less willing to embark on controversial programs, and, when they do attempt to innovate, there will be higher levels of community debate and hence higher levels of controversy and a greater possibility of stalemate. In contrast, in low-status cities, citizens are less readily able to mobilize to influence the decision-making process; this may result in either government by a traditional political machine, or in a government heavily influenced by the local economic elite; but in any case there should be less controversy, and few programs, once begun, will be sidetracked.

How does this relate to Hawley's suggestion that high-status cities have more difficulty implementing urban renewal plans because power is more decentralized?

Pinard[12] hypothesizes yet another notion. He feels that the various outcomes of community reaction to innovations can be explained by the strength of the citizen's attachments to one another and to their community leaders. His conclusions appear to substantiate, for the most part, the hypotheses posited.

> ... Different degrees and patterns of attachments of a community to its leaders do in fact influence the political support the former is ready to grant to the latter. In turn, these degrees and patterns of attachments are largely influenced by structural factors very different from the sociopsychological ones often used in voting behavior studies. The size of communities, their rates of growth, their ethnic and racial composition, their occupational and power structures, and the conditions of their labor market are all important features of the social system that influence community decisions.
>
> These results confirm the importance of political processes that have often been discussed, but rarely empirically analyzed. To the extent that elites in a political system, either democratic or totalitarian, tend to be separated from the lower segments of the system by a series of horizontal and disjointed layers, the system is bound to produce a more-or-less large collectivity of politically unattached citizens that oscillate between apathy or systematic opposition to the leadership; this is true whatever actions the elites take, or whatever party may be in power. The middle class, on the other hand, seems less likely to exhibit such a pattern of behavior. As is

suggested by these data, they are either attached as a whole to their leaders or are formed into two or more groups of equally attached citizens, each of its own political elite opposing, and eventually replacing, each other in the leadership of a community.

Supporters of the community differentiation and continuity theory suggest that older and larger cities usually have more entrenched bureaucracies and, consequently, are less receptive to policy innovations. Younger and smaller cities usually exhibit higher policy innovation.[13]

Dye, in studying school segregation, has found that

> ... among Northern cities both size and age are independently associated with segregation policy. Larger and older cities tend to have more pupil and teacher segregation than smaller and newer cities. In contrast to Northern cities, size and age are not associated with segregation in Southern cities. Apparently smaller and newer Southern cities are just as segregated as larger and older Southern cities.

Dye also turned his attention to the political variables:

> It turns out that there is a slight tendency for cities with mayor governments to be less segregated than cities with manager governments. This relationship is barely significant among Southern cities and just below our level of significance among Northern cities. Of course mayor governments do not "cause" desegregation, but we believe that the "political" environment associated with mayor government is more likely to produce desegregation than the "nonpolitical" environment associated with manager government.
>
> This interpretation is reinforced by the relationship between partisan elections and desegregation among Southern cities. Southern cities with partisan elections are less segregated than Southern cities with nonpartisan elections.
>
> These findings suggest that, in Southern cities at least, more "political" forms of government—mayor governments and partisan election—may result in increased Negro political power and more progress in school desegregation. "Nonpolitical" forms of government—managers and nonpartisan elections—may suppress effective political action on behalf of desegregation.

Concerning the size of cities, Eyestone and Eular conclude that:

The policy orientations of city councilmen are essentially unrelated to city size, growth rate, and resource capability. Councilmen more favorable to development are found disproportionately in more developed cities, even when size, growth, and resource capability are controlled. Councilmen favoring a wide scope of governmental activity are found in the intermediate phases of development rather than, as hypothesized, in the more stable stages, even when size, growth, and resource capability are controlled.[14]

Linesberry and Falb postulate that city governments which are "products of the reform movement behave differently from those which have unreformed institutions—even if the socioeconomic composition of their populations may be similar." Furthermore:

1. Cities with reformed and unreformed institutions are not markedly different in terms of demographic variables. Indeed, some variables, like income, ran counter to the popular hypothesis that reformed cities are havens of the middle class. Our data lent some support to the notion that reformed cities were more homogeneous in their ethnic and religious populations. Still, it is apparent that reformed cities are by no means free from the impact of these cleavages.

2. The more important difference between the two kinds of cities is in their behavior, rather than their demography. Using multiple correlation coefficients, we were able to predict municipal outputs more exactly in unreformed than in reformed cities. The translation of social conflicts into public policy and the responsiveness of political systems to class, racial, and religious cleavages differ markedly with the kind of political structure. Thus, political institutions seem to play an important role in the political process—a role substantially independent of a city's demography.

3. Our analysis has also demonstrated that reformism may be viewed as a continuous variable and that the political structures of the reform syndrome have an additive effect: the greater the reformism, the lower the responsiveness....

[I]t is clear that political reforms may have a significant impact in minimizing the role which social conflicts play in decisionmaking. By muting the demands of private-regarding groups, the electoral institutions of reformed governments make public policy less responsive to the demands which arise out of social conflicts in the population.

The structure of the government may serve further to modify the strength of minority groups over public policy. It is significant in this respect to note that commission governments, where social cleavages have the greatest impact on policy choices, are the most decentralized of the three governmental types and that manager governments are relatively the most centralized. From the point of view of the reformer, commission government is a failure and their number has declined markedly in recent years. This greater decentralization of commission and of mayor-council governments permits a multiplicity of access points for groups wishing to influence decisionmakers. It may also increase the possibilities for collaboration between groups and a bureaucratic agency, a relationship which has characterized administrative patterns in the federal government. As a result of this decentralization, group strength in local governments may be maximized.[15]

Which of these theories helps you to understand more effectively what transpired in the five communities studied? Is there specific evidence to suggest which of these theories is/or are most appropriately related to these controversies? On the basis of what happened in each community, formulate your own generalization regarding the kinds of suburbs likely to accept or to reject change proposals for low-income housing.

Planned Interventions

Innovation may be spontaneous and unanticipated. Yet sometimes—though less frequently than one might have thought—change agents consciously plan their conquests.

Planned change and community organization strategies comprise a wide spectrum of approaches, sometimes ill-defined or inadequately tested. They all aim to enhance social and economic well-being, but they differ significantly in both their assumptions about the nature of the social system and the appropriate means to achieve objectives.

A fundamental concern in planned social change relates to objectives: should change be directed toward societal structure or to peripheral functions? Another basic concern relates to the way social scientists view themselves and their professional role: should they become professionally involved in induced social change or remain dispassionate observers and analysts of social phenomena?

The two major views of society previously discussed, functionalism and conflict, generate two different sets of answers. Functionalists are likely to insist on amelioration and the improvement of existing institutions, while conflict-oriented social scientists envision the need for fundamental alterations to society's structure, particularly to the primary institutions of society and, especially, the economic system. Functionalists are more likely to deny that social scientists should concern themselves with efforts to change society or to prescribe solutions to social problems; some even consider involvement by their peers "unscientific." Conflict theorists, on the other hand, are likely to see planned change as a legitimate and necessary task of social scientists. They are more inclined than functionalists to admit that values influence their work.

Warren[16] differentiated three major types of change strategies: collaborative, campaign, and contest. *Collaborative* strategies are based on the assumption of a common basis of values and interests, through which substantive agreement on proposals is readily obtainable. The predominant role of the change agent is that of an *enabler*, or *catalyst*. He is not concerned with putting through his own preconceived proposal, but with helping the pertinent group reach consensus on the issue at hand. Differences are assumed to be based on misinformation or poor communication. Thus, appropriate action calls for "getting the facts," clearing up misunderstandings based on faulty or incomplete information, and reconciling different points of view on the basis of discussion while accommodating the kernel of value in all such differences. The chief obstacle is not opposition, but rather, if anything, apathy and inaction.

Campaign strategies are strategies "to accomplish consensus when the chief obstacle is either apathy or opposition. Out of apathy, they attempt to create interest. Out of opposition, they attempt to create agreement." They differ from collaborative strategies, "which attempt, through discussion or voting to create proposals based on consensus." Agreement is achieved by persuading opponents of differences. *Contest* strategies are a way to pursue one's own goal in opposition to others. They are characterized "by the abandonment, temporarily at least, of efforts at consensus, and the employment of efforts to further one's own side of an issue despite opposition from important parties to that issue. The predominant role of the change agent is therefore that of *contestant*." Warren distinguishes four specific types of contest processes: a) Attempts within accepted social norms (legislative debates, legal disputes, use of mass media or personal contact) to win over public opinion. (b) Attempts to change the distribution of power. (c) Contests involving a violation of the usual community norms (break the rules of contest). (d) Attempts to harm or remove the opponent (depose an official, physical violence).

Rothman[17] poses another kind of three-fold division of purposive community change: developmental, planning, and social action. In the development of a locality, community change is pursued through broad participation of people at the local community level in goal determination and action (democratic procedures, voluntary cooperation, self-help, development of indigenous leadership, neighborhood work programs). Its prototype form includes activities commonly termed "community development" as understood by UN agencies (a process accelerating socio-economic progress of the whole community with its active participation and its own initiative).

Social planning "emphasizes a technical process of problem-solving with regard to substantive social problems, such as delinquency, housing, and mental health. Rational, deliberatively planned, and controlled change has a central place in this model. Community participation may vary from much to little, depending on how the problem presents itself and what organizational variables are present. The approach presupposes that change in a complex industrial environment requires expert planners who, through the exercise of technical abilities, including the ability to manipulate large bureaucratic organizations, can skillfully guide complex change processes. By and large, the concern here is with establishing, arranging, and delivering goods and services to people who need them. Building community capacity or fostering radical or fundamental social change does not play a central part."

Social action "presupposes a disadvantaged segment of the population that needs to be organized, perhaps in alliance with others, in order to make adequate demands on the larger community for increased resources or treatment more in accordance with social justice or democracy. It aims at making basic changes in major institutions or community practices." It seeks redistribution of power, resources, or decision-making (civil rights and black power groups, Alinsky's Industrial Areas Foundation projects, labor unions and SDS student groups).

Morris and Binstock[18] also identify three change factors: first, those strategies geared to alter human attitudes and behavioral patterns through education, exhortation, and other methods for stimulating self-development and fulfillment; second, those designed to "alter social conditions by changing the policies of formal organizations"; third, those strategies geared to effect reforms in major legal and functional systems of a society through political agitation and a host of other instruments for coping with powerful trends and developments.

Rein[19] is yet another writer with a threefold classification: consensus of elites, rational research, and organization of the poor.

The similarities among these suggestions, more particularly the three categories each proposes for our understanding, are indeed striking. For example, Morris's political agitation type corresponds neatly to Rein's organization of the poor, Rothman's social action approach, and Warren's contest type of strategies. Although literature on the subject prefers a troica typology of change strategies, all can be advantageously reduced to these two fundamental patterns: First, stemming from the functionalism perspective, are change strategies based on consensus and collaborative community efforts. From the conflict perspective are derived change strategies based on competitive action, confrontation, and coercion.

The functionalist perspective of reality, with its dominant consensus component, conditions the means by which these objectives are pursued. As expected, participation of the various segments of the community in deliberations and decision making becomes a key precondition; it is alleged to increase communication, social interaction among interest groups and, therefore, to enhance the establishment of a consensus. Self-help, self-sufficiency, and emphasis on the public interest permeate the efforts guided by a change agent of the enabler-catalyst-coordinator type. On the other hand, the conflict perspective of the social system, with its dominant confrontation-challenge component, also conditions the means by which those objectives are pursued. It stands to reason that a direct and strong antagonism by one disadvantaged community group toward another more privileged group will form the basic approach to problem-solving—emphasizing group interest more than the "public interest." Consequently the change agent's posture is that of the activist-advocate-agitator type recognizing that conflicting interests are not always reconcilable and that norm-violating approaches are at times necessary and justifiable.

Combinations of both approaches and techniques are of course both possible and frequently desirable.

This dichotomy raises interesting issues for the city planner and how he views his professional and bureaucratic role. To begin with, planning tools and methods can and are, indeed, used by both types in community problem solving; data gathering, and analysis, as well as objective methods to reach decisions on the most rational course of action for concerted development, are characteristics of a generic planning process which can be employed by either type of strategy.

More important, there is the issue of the city planner's identification with the consensus or coercion strategies of induced change. While many urban planners belong to one or the other school, others claim a more "objective," "neutral" approach based solely on scientific considerations. But urban planning is directly related to governmental units and boards; and city planners are invariably employed by city agencies or commissions and, as such, work toward objectives determined by the existing power structure. Like the two strategies already described, urban planning's perception of reality conditions the means by which its objectives are pursued. Consequently, an idealistic conception of how things ought to be permeate the approach to problem-solving—which aims to enhance efficiency of efforts and optimization of investment (rather than enhance group or locational interests). Assumptions regarding citizen apathy and his lack of technical knowledge, combined with a recognition of never-ending conflicting interests of citizen groups, reinforce the allegedly more "objective" efficiency-optimization approach in planning. The change agent's task necessitates skills and efforts to persuade the powers-that-be that his proposals enhance their basic interests; and also involves efforts to elicit or indirectly coerce community consent—through educational-persuading techniques, use of mass media, endorsements by the elite in the power structure. In the 1960's this posture came under attack, creating several dilemmas for the planning profession in the context of social change and of serving the status quo. Urban planning is thus in a state of distinct transition regarding its change-agent role in society as well as its original and dominant emphasis on physical structure of the city rather than on social goals and development.

This situation has been analyzed as follows:

> The field of urban planning and development has emerged from professional efforts to intervene and direct change in the physical environment. However, its fundamental concepts are directly related to the quality of urban life. Its practice is shaped in response to societal needs in a rapidly changing environment....
>
> Planning as a concept is progressively reformulated by various professions as analytic and predictive tools become more effective. In its most generic sense, planning is a systematic and deliberate method of decisionmaking and implementation employed in determining and achieving goals....
>
> Applied to the growth and development of urban settlements, urban planning and its methods have several orientations....
>
> *The physical emphasis.* This oldest and still dominant variation on planning is an outgrowth of the "master builder" tradition of Central Europe. It has territorial preoccupations that define and determine, in this view, the framework of urban planning. It is primarily concerned with the building of the physical environment, with conservation of certain physical resources and the provision of physical facilities; it is secondarily concerned with community

services. It emphasizes the design of the public aspects of the settlement's physical environment, including the regulation of streets and highways, land uses, municipal lands, and public structures, as well as the regulation of private land through zoning and the control of land subdivisions....

The promotional civic (municipal) version. This definition of the planning process is associated with the organized promotion of American cities as mercantile outposts....

After World War II, more elaborate development organizations, such as industrial development corporations, were frequently established....

The civic reformers originated the planning commissions during the municipal reform era early in this century to insulate zoning from politics. They brought together leading citizens under municipal authority for planning urban growth. Despite their diverse motivations, business and civic leaders as well as architects and engineers frequently collaborated in promotional enterprises, especially those that would protect the community from undesirable change....

The human welfare emphasis. This more recent concept of urban planning and development is gaining increasing acceptance, especially because it is far more sensitive to the conditions necessary for improving the quality of human life. The human welfare approach to urban planning implies a commitment to social equity and therefore involves redistributive social policies and their effectiveness in altering social conditions. Since the middle of the nineteenth century, planners with a human welfare orientation have been concerned with overcrowded and congested cities, with their slums, epidemics, political corruption, recreational facilities, and aesthetics. Early reform movements were directed toward the provision of urban equipment and facilities, settlement houses, schools, libraries, services for effective Americanization of immigrants, eradication of crime, and the revitalization of good government....

The "comprehensive approach." Urban planning is associated with the sprawl of large urban complexes and with increased organizational complexity. It takes several forms because it applies to functions as well as to spatial relations and jurisdictional levels. The effort to fuse economic, social, and physical aspects of development is an example of the concern with functions. The metropolitan government movement, the regional planning movement, the establishment of regional commissions, and the increasing interdependence of national-state-local programs illustrate these spatial-jurisdictional concerns.[20]

QUESTIONS

1. Apply the various strategies of change to the communities studied and explore their applicability and effectiveness. Which one, if any, is more useful

and why? Is it necessary to assume that only one or the other can be used as opposed to combining elements from all? Which combination would you choose in each of the five communities? Why?

2. Consider the implications of limiting planned change only to areas or matters on which consensus can be reached. Does this mean that planned change should not be attempted in certain areas of importance? Given the absence of indigenous poor people, why should suburban residents ever consider permitting low- and moderate-income housing in their communities?

3. How relevant to the low-income problems of suburbs, with their class consciousness and deeply divided residents, are consensus methods of planned change? Can these methods, practiced and developed primarily in the inner cities of technologically advanced countries, be applied effectively in the hostile sociopolitical atmosphere of affluent suburbs, united against low-income housing? In most suburbs, there usually exists a group, or groups, of disadvantaged people whose numbers are small and dwindling. These individuals are either unorganized, apathetic, or afraid; they tend to be no serious factor in planned change. In model cities programs for the inner city, the contest approach may be realistic—but will members of a relatively homogeneous society, an affluent community, adopt such a strategy in order to introduce low-income housing?

4. Politicians and elected officials, preservers of existing norms who are sensitive to abutters' votes, are likely to protect the status quo. How, then, will the interests of the poor be represented? What sociopolitical coalitions or bargains can be used?

5. Consider now the urban planning approach. Is it and can it be free of subjective values as some planners advocate? Or is it frequently imbued with the middle-class values of the planner himself and of his employers? Does this approach introduce a generally nonpolitical set of skills to the political process? Do you think that society consists of rational men, who, when faced with facts and legitimate options, can proceed to reach an equitable, reasonable solution? Are such scientific skills more often used after a political decision has been made—to implement rather than to persuade? Employed not only to demonstrate feasibility, but also to move the controversy to a higher plane? Are rational planning strategies, which involve active collaboration with the power structure and which rely upon objective facts, rather than subjective community values, more relevant in the suburbs than the consensus approaches?

6. How do you view the existence of what appear to be two antithetical assumptions regarding planning: the need to plan and, therefore, restrict individual autonomy, and the need for freedom? The optimal degree of social planning is highly controversial. It involves questions concerning social freedom,

public versus free enterprise, local autonomy versus public policies on a state and national level. Yet, it may be that democracy will only be secured by planning, which in the long run can assure freedom from lack of resources or options. Combining freedom and planning is a central dilemma in public policies in general and for housing, in particular. "It is no wonder," Mannheim wrote, "that the most disturbing effect of changing society is experienced in the uncertainty of values." Still other significant motives for residential exclusion persist. Would you suggest strategies which in effect constrain the freedom of the suburb to act as it sees fit, so that regional and national social policies can be implemented?

7. Does the situation suggest a need for alternative ways of blending the art of rational planning with the irrational political dynamics of decision making? Can long-range, collective, metropolitan elements be combined with short-range, individually-oriented, local interests and values? Can the community development of urban planning processes be combined with those of social action?

8. Underlying all this is uncertainty. We are unsure of the predictability of what will happen to the suburban community if low-income housing is introduced; we do not know what the effect will be on those who come to such housing and begin the traditional American activity of social and economic ladder-climbing. The goals themselves might be deficient. Are housing policies headed in the right direction? Does this type of planned social change arouse more antagonism than 110 or 250 units of low-income housing are worth? Does an incremental increase of this minor magnitude begin to affect seriously metropolitan housing problems when and if 25 or 40 suburban communities build low-income housing? Are the seeds of a change of the suburban structure—its environment and its values— sown from such small efforts? Is such a fundamental, longer-lasting, far-reaching metamorphosis either necessary or desirable?

4. Judges as Change Agents

Many of the concrete problems of housing the poor in suburbia are dumped willy-nilly into the laps of the courts. Can or should the judge become a change agent?

As early as *Euclid v. Ambler Realty Company*, the very first Supreme Court opinion upholding the zoning concept, the court stated:

> It is not meant by this, however, to exclude the possibility of cases where the general public interest would so far outweigh the interest of the municipality that the municipality would not be allowed to stand in the way.

But this flag, once hoisted by the Supreme Court, rallied few supporters in the judiciary.

In state court opinions throughout the 1960's, the trend was to brush away the question whether the maintenance of property values was an appropriate exercise of the zoning power, to avoid any review of intended (or unintended but inevitable) consequences of regulations that excluded selected groups or classes of people, and also to shy away from evaluating the overspill effects of local regulations on neighboring communities and the state. Despite growing sophistication about metropolitan networks, social cost-benefit accounting among local units of government, postures of presidential national commissions, exhortations by federal departments that suburbs should bear their "fair share" of the housing and welfare burdens, and the restlessness of minority groups and of central city mayors, few judges would grasp the thistle. Some *dicta* about the unreasonableness of large acreage zoning did appear. But, by and large, the quandry over the pattern of American settlements was left to other Alexander the Greats.

As students of a realistic jurisprudence, then, we can only applaud the willingness of recent decisions to isolate underlying factors. But as one attempts to grapple with the metropolitan zoning dilemma, at least two puzzles emerge, and in the curious way that paradoxes operate, they blunt initial reactions.

First, who are the true parties to the conflict? For behind the plaintiff, a man striving earnestly to earn a profit by putting a proposed use on his acreage, there march all the *amici*—the central cities which want to provide homes for their workers; federal officials, who believe that the housing, welfare, and education burdens are too heavy in the central cores; liberals, who wish to integrate suburban areas; mobile home manufacturers, seeking a mass market; and the poor—white and black—who find themselves locked into the central city. Quite an array, and seemingly all groups warranting protection by the judiciary. Yet, one must ask, how do these marchers get into the act? Or, as lawyers so picturesquely phrase it, where is their standing to sue? And, assuming their admittance, who speaks for them, asserts their interests, makes the reasoned elaboration of the case, presents testimony, provides the starting point for the judicial reasonings and conclusion, settles the terms of the final disposition? The courts, even though they provide the only local forum that does not depend upon the crisis constituency of political zones, cannot cope because they do not have before them all the parties who have a legitimate stake in the resolution. So, one difficulty with them as change agents is that the courts, under the present system, never get a chance to deal with all the interests that should intelligently be taken into account.

Second, even though he might be alerted to the inter-community struggle, how ably can a law school graduate—even donning judical robes—cope with it? Where could the judge learn of the existence and contents of a physical plan for the entire region? How would he learn whether the burden (and who would define it?) of low-cost housing was being cast unfairly on one unit of the metropolitan area, and how could he measure and assess such unfairness or disproportion? How could he perceive, and then go on to weigh, the reasonableness of a process of coordination among municipalities which was intended to provide suitable sites for houses to meet the needs of various levels of society, measured in terms of income, age, or size of family? If no published comprehensive plan exists for the entire metropolitan area, one that has been democratically participated in, voted on, and adopted, from where could he assemble one? Where, with only two parties before him, could a judge acquire the relevant information about the metropolitan trends in population, housing, transportation, and land development?

The court may be cast in a novel role of drafting, in effect, a regional plan for the contending municipalities. It also requires re-examination of various governmental decisions in order to ascertain whether or not local enactments accord with a comprehensive trend. Hardly was this difficulty foreshadowed in the easier job the court undertook of validating an ordinance on regional grounds, involving a relatively simple decision as to whether there is territory available for a particular use within a region.

Above all, the court may find, as it becomes interjected into the troubling and difficult aspects of metropolitan relations, that it is the eye of the storm swirling over the central city—suburban conflict. The least democratic branch, yet it has a roving mandate to cover the whole state territory, and, as change agent, has a constitutional imperative to act when its jurisdiction is invoked.

Despite traditional avoidance of political questions, the freezing of the political process on the metropolitan level has forced the courts to intervene. The independent state judiciary can be said to be there precisely for that job: it cannot long tolerate provisions designed to permit as new residents only certain kinds of people or only those who can afford to live in certain types of preferred housing. The judiciary reminds us of another fundamental: unlike the philosopher, we cannot, once deciding that equities are about evenly balanced, silently steal away; the question demands resolutions; one side must win, the other lose.

Some of the most revealing cases of the judge as change agent have occurred in the past few years. Oakwood at Madison represents a broad-ranging view of the courts as loosening up the arteries of the federal system. The Mt. Laurel case discusses the jurisprudential aspects of such an approach necessitated by the need for the dispersal of low-income housing. Shaw and its progeny should be related by you to the discussions dealing with municipal infrastructure, and the essential services for making urban living possible; if the equal-opportunity doctrine is extended from housing itself, the wide-ranging impact on suburbs and the metropolitan area could become one of the more engrossing issues of the 1970's.

**Oakwood at Madison, Inc. v. Township of Madison
117 N.J. Super. 11, 283 A.2d 353 (Law Div. 1971)**

Furman, J.S.C.

This prerogative writ action challenges the constitutionality of the Zoning Act, N.J.S.A. 40:55-30 et seq., and the validity under that act of the Madison Township zoning ordinance adopted on September 25, 1970. Plaintiffs are two developers, who own vacant and developable land in Madison Township, and six individuals, all with low income, representing as a class those who reside outside the township and have sought housing there unsuccessfully because of the newly adopted zoning restrictions, including one- and two-acre minimum lot sizes.

Madison Township is 42 square miles in the southeast corner of Middlesex County, extending from Raritan Bay westward. In two decades of explosive growth from 1950 to 1970, paralleling the trend in the county and region, its population mounted from 7,366 to 48,715. Most of the new housing was single-family in developments on 15,000 square foot or smaller lots, and since 1965 multi-family in garden apartments. Reflecting school construction and other expanded costs of government, the real property tax rate increased from one of the lowest in 1950 to the highest in 1970 in the county.

Despite this population surge much of the township, approximately 30 percent of its land area, excluding Cheesequake State Park, is vacant and developable. A member of the planning firm which submitted a new master plan in May 1970 testified that the township could hold a population of 200,000 without overcrowding.

A new township administration in 1970 determined to curb population growth significantly and thus to stabilize the tax rate. The township was to "catch its breath," a phrase recurrent in the testimony. Because of exigencies of time arising from a court order in other litigation, the planning firm which was retained early in 1970 was given only two months within which to submit its proposal for a master plan. The deadline was met. The master plan proposal relied in part upon the studies of the township's previous planning consultant. It purported to represent a shift in approach, from explosive growth on a patchwork basis to orderly growth in densely developed areas and the preservation of open areas. The new planning firm's recommendations were followed, with three important exceptions discussed *infra*, in the ensuing zoning ordinance ...

The Pennsylvania Supreme Court commented in *National Land:*

... Four-acre zoning represents Easttown's position that it does not desire to accommodate those who are pressing for admittance to the township unless such admittance will not create any additional burdens upon governmental functions and services. The question posed is whether the township can stand in the way of the natural forces which send our growing population into hitherto undeveloped areas in search of a comfortable place to live. We have concluded not. A zoning ordinance whose primary purpose is to prevent the entrance of newcomers in order to avoid future burdens, economic and otherwise, upon the administration of public services and facilities can not be held valid. [215 A.2d at 612.]

Minimum floor spaces by zoning were ruled valid in Lionshead Lake, Inc., v. Wayne Tp., 10 N.J. 165,89 A.2d 693 (1952), an authority which is controlling if, in context with the entire challenged zoning ordinance, the minimum floor spaces of 1500 square feet in R40 and 1600 square feet in R80 serve the valid zoning purpose of a balanced community. See Nolan and Horack, "How Small A House?–Zoning for Minimum Space Requirements," 67 Harv. L. Rev. 967 (1954), and Haar, "Zoning for Minimum Standards: The Wayne Township Case," 66 Harv. L. Rev. 1051 (1953).

In Madison Township's approach to the objective of balance, its attempted cure is a worse malady than whatever imbalance existed. About 8000 acres of land, apparently prime for low- or moderate-income housing development, have been taken out of the reach of 90 percent of the population, prohibitive in land and construction costs. The acreage available for multi-family apartments units is minuscule. Families with more than one child are barred from multi-family apartments because of the one- and two-bedroom restrictions, restrictions without any guise of a health or safety purpose.

The exclusionary approach in the ordinance under attack coincides in time with desperate housing needs in the county and region and expanding programs, federal and state, for subsidized housing for low income families.

Regional needs are a proper consideration in local zoning.

In pursuing the valid zoning purpose of a balanced community, a municipality must not ignore housing needs, that is, its fair proportion of the obligation to meet the housing needs of its own population and of the region. Housing needs are encompassed within the general welfare. The general welfare does not stop at each municipal boundary. Large areas of vacant and developable land should not be zoned, as Madison Township has, into such minimum lot sizes and with such other restrictions that regional as well as local housing needs are shunted aside. Vickers v. Tp. Com., Gloucester Tp., 37 N.J. 232, 181 A.2d 129 (1962), upholding a prohibition against trailer camps anywhere within a municipality, is not to the contrary. . . .

For all the foregoing reasons the Madison Township zoning ordinance of September 25, 1970 is held to be invalid in its entirety.

[P]laintiffs contend that the township zoning ordinance is invalid because it fails to promote reasonably the legislative purposes of the Zoning Act in several provisions dealing with single and multi-family housing which are so essential that the entire ordinance should be struck down.

About 55 percent of the land area of the township is zoned R40 or R80. The R80 zone is new, the R40 zone expanded. Minimum lot size is one acre in R40 and two acres in R80. Minimum floor space is 1500 square feet in R40 and 1600 square feet in R80. According to the former township engineer, 80 percent of R40 (or about 5500 acres) and 30 percent of R80 (or about 2500 acres) is vacant and developable. Minimal acreage is vacant and developable in the R7, R10 and R20 zones. Since the 1930s there has not been a development on two-acre lots within the township. Since 1964 only one subdivision plan for one-acre lots has been proposed. Land and construction costs are such that the minimum purchase price in R40 would be $45,000 and in R80 $50,000. Only those with incomes in the top 10 percent of the nation and county could finance new housing in R40; an even smaller percentage in R80.

The multi-family zones, which are scattered through the township, are so restricted in land area that no more than 500 to 700 additional units can be built in all. Three or more bedroom units are not permitted. Two bedroom units must be limited to 20 percent of the total units in any apartment development. New units must not exceed 200 in any year.

Madison Township, among other municipalities, is encouraging new industry. Industry is moving into the county and region from the central cities. Population continues to expand rapidly. New housing is in short supply. Congestion is worsening under deplorable living conditions in the central cities, both of the county and nearby. The ghetto population to an increasing extent is trapped, unable to find or afford adequate housing in the suburbs because of restrictive zoning. See N.J.S.A. 55:16-2 (L. 1967, c. 112): "It is hereby declared that there is a severe housing shortage in the State. . . . "

The township concedes the invalidity of the limitation to 200 new multi-family units per year but defends all other provisions of the zoning ordinance which are challenged. Its contentions are that it is seeking a balanced community, encouraging high income and moderate income housing to balance its predominant low income housing, and protecting drainage systems where high density residential development might result in floods and surface drainage problems and interfere with and imperil underground water resources.

As recently stated by the Supreme Court in Harvard Enterprises, Inc., v. Bd. of Adj., Madison Tp., 56 N.J. 362, 266 A.2d 588 (1970), litigation arising out of prior zoning provisions in Madison Township:

> . . . it should be noted that the judicial role in reviewing a zoning ordinance is tightly circumscribed. There is a strong presumption in favor of its validity, and the court cannot invalidate it, or any provision thereof, unless this presumption is overcome by a clear showing that it is arbitrary or unreasonable. [at 368, 266 A.2d at 592.]

The underlying objective of the ordinance under attack was fiscal zoning, zoning as a device to avoid school construction and other governmental costs incident to population expansion. Housing needs of the region were not taken into consideration in its enactment, according to several members of the township council and planning board.

The three recommendations in the proposed master plan which were rejected by the township council and planning board all would have tended towards increased population and governmental services. The planning consultant advised no limitation on the number of bedrooms in multi-family apartment units, minimum floor spaces of 1100 square feet in the R40 zone and 1200 square feet in the R80 zone, and "floating zones" of high population density on less than half-acre minimum lots in any zone within the township but separated from each other, up to 100 houses in each floating zone.

Fiscal zoning *per se* is irrelevant to the statutory purposes of zoning. But the Supreme Court in Gruber v. Mayor, etc., Raritan Tp., 39 N.J. 1, 9, 186 A.2d 489 (1962) recognized that "alleviating the tax burden and the harmful school congestion" was a permissible zoning purpose if done reasonably and in furtherance of a comprehensive zoning plan. *Gruber* and the antecedent Newark, etc., Cream Co. v. Parsippany-Troy Hills Tp., 47 N.J. Super. 306, 135 A.2d 682 (Law Div. 1957), may be distinguished because they dealt with the pursuit of tax revenues through zoning for new industry, not the stabilization of the tax rate through zoning to exclude new low and moderate income housing.

In any event, the Madison Township zoning ordinance must stand or fall not as fiscal zoning. The test must be whether it promotes reasonably a balanced and well-ordered plan for the entire municipality.

Several decisions have recognized balance within a municipality, which is in part undeveloped, as a valid zoning purpose. . . .

Fischer v. Bedminster Tp., *supra* is the leading New Jersey decision sustaining a large minimum lot size, five acres over 85 percent of the municipality. Its rationale does not apply. Chief Justice Vanderbilt rested his holding on "preserving the character of the community, maintaining the value of property therein and devoting the land throughout the township for its most appropriate use." The Madison Township zoning ordinance under attack has provided for one-acre and two-acre minimum lot sizes on largely vacant land, which as such has no established residential character or residential property values.

Other New Jersey decisions in favor of minimum lot requirements concern relatively small lot sizes in built-up communities. . . .

On the other hand, the highest courts of Pennsylvania and Virginia have struck down two-, three-, and four-acre minimum lot requirements in undeveloped areas as invalid zoning, without reasonable relation to the general welfare. (Citations omitted.)

QUESTIONS

1. *Enforcement and remedies*—The governing body or board of public works may provide by ordinance for the enforcement of the zoning article and

of any ordinance or regulation made thereunder. In case any building or structure is erected, constructed, altered, repaired, converted, or maintained, or any building, structure or land is used in violation of this article or of any ordinance or other regulation made under authority conferred hereby, the proper local authorities of the municipality or any other interested party, in addition to other remedies, may institute any appropriate action or proceedings to prevent such unlawful erection, construction, reconstruction, alteration, repair, conversion, maintenance or use, to restrain, correct or abate such violation, to prevent the occupancy of said building, structure or land, or to prevent any illegal act, conduct, business or use in or about such premises.

"Other interested party" persons included—For purposes of the article to which this act is a supplement, the term "other interested party" in a criminal or quasicriminal proceeding shall include: (a) any citizen of the State of New Jersey: and (b) in the case of a civil proceeding in any court or in an administrative proceeding before a municipal agency, any person, whether residing within or without the municipality, whose right to use, acquire, or enjoy property is or may be affected by any action taken under the act to which this act is a supplement, or whose rights to use, acquire, or enjoy property under the act to which this act is a supplement, or under any other law of this State or of the United States have been denied, violated or infringed by an action or a failure to act under the act to which this act is a supplement.

N.J. Stat. Ann. 40:55-47, 47.1 (Supp. 1970)—(See also Comment, Standing to Challenge Exclusionary Zoning Decisions, 22 Syracuse L. Rev. 598, 1971.)

2. What is the proper role of the courts in land-use planning policy questions that require the acquisition of special expertise and the balancing of complex societal interests? If the legislature, for example, is the more appropriate actor, what should a court do when the legislature refuses to act? Consider the Oakwood case in light of the failure of the New Jersey legislature in 1969 to enact the proposed Land-Use Planning and Development Law, supra, p. 357.

3. Precisely five months after the Oakwood decision, New Jersey Governor William T. Cahill delivered a special message to the legislature, saying in part:
> It must be apparent to members of this Legislature that the courts already have acted decisively in this area. Unless we act together to help open the way for needed housing, the courts will do it for us and will continue to move strongly in the direction of bypassing home rule by judicial process.

The Governor pointed out the decision in Oakwood and mentioned no fewer than seven significant challenges to local exclusionary zoning ordinances pending in the New Jersey Courts. (Special Message from Governor William T. Cahill to the New Jersey Legislature, New Horizons in Housing, March 27, 1972.)

Hawkins v. Town of Shaw
303 F. Supp. 1162 (N.D. Miss. 1969)

Keady, D.J. In this suit plaintiffs, who bring a class action for Negro citizens of the Town of Shaw, Mississippi, seek injunctive relief against defendants, the Town's Mayor, Clerk and five Aldermen, under 42 U.S.C. §1983, to restrain defendants from discriminating because of race and poverty in providing the inhabitants with certain municipal services, namely: street paving and street lighting, sanitary sewers, water mains and fire hydrants, and surface water drainage. Defendants entered a denial to the charge that disparity of municipal services afforded to the town's inhabitants was the result of racial or economic discrimination. Following the adoption of a pre-trial order, a three-day evidentiary hearing was conducted.

Incorporated in 1886, the Town of Shaw consisted originally of one square mile located in Bolivar County, Mississippi. Its territorial limits were not changed until 1965 when new subdivisions were added to the south and east of the original town extending into Sunflower County. The municipality is largely surrounded by Delta farms and plantations and its economy is almost wholly oriented to agriculture. The town's present population is estimated to be approximately 2500 persons, of which 1500 are Negroes and 1000 whites. There are approximately as many Negro citizens who are qualified to vote as there are white voters. The town's population was for years relatively static, showing little gain for the twenty year period 1940-1960. . . .

There are various patterns of residential neighborhoods in the town. In some instances white and Negro residents live on the same streets, yet in other instances, particularly in the oldest and newest subdivisions, there are separate white and Negro neighborhoods. A significant portion of the Negro population resides in the town's peripheral or outer area, with substantial numbers of white people residing near the town's business or commercial center. Prior to 1965, many years had elapsed since the dedication of any new residential subdivisions for either race. Some of the older Negro neighborhoods were in subdivisions laid out many years ago, without zoning regulations, which resulted in houses being erected on exceedingly small lots abutting upon dedicated streets and alleys of inadequate narrow width. To some extent, the older white neighborhoods suffer from the same planning deficiency.

The town has sought to provide its inhabitants certain services, such as street paving and street lighting, a system of surface water drainage, water mains with fire hydrant protection, and since 1963 a sanitary sewerage system. The town's services and facilities are paid from revenues derived by imposition of ad valorem taxes and the sale of water and electricity to its citizens. There are no bonds outstanding, and the town has a $145,000 operating surplus. . . .

None of the plaintiffs, or other Negro citizens of the community, ever requested the town's governing authority to provide additional municipal services in their neighborhoods. However, plaintiffs' counsel contend that the court should require defendants to complete by a specific date, namely, September 30, 1971, the construction of specific facilities "to equalize the black neighborhoods with their white counterparts" at an estimated cost of $250,000, as below detailed,* by directing the use of $145,000 presently in the town treasury and by devoting two year's general revenues, and proceeds from a bond issue, if necessary, to complete the work.

We begin with the familiar rule that the "exercise of the powers of the municipality with respect to the making of public improvements, the establishment of public utilities, and the furnishing of public services, rests in the discretion of the governing municipal authorities, insofar as the matter is not controlled by positive law, and the courts will not undertake to control or interfere with the exercise of such discretion in the absence of bad faith or abuse." 38 Am. Jur. Municipal Corporations, §560. p. 248. Nor is it a valid objection that a public improvement by a municipal corporation "incidentally benefits some individuals more than others, or that from the place of residence, or for other reasons, every inhabitant of the municipality cannot use it if every inhabitant who is so situated that he can use it has the same right to use it as the other inhabitants." Ibid. Thus, it would seem that determination of the necessity and character of public improvements, the matter of their construction and the priority of accomplishment, ordinarily, are questions to be resolved by officials, usually elected, who constitute the governing authority of the municipality. "Normally, the widest discretion is allowed the legislative judgment in determining whether to attack some rather than all of the manifestations of the evil aimed at; and normally that judgment is given the benefit of every conceivable circumstance which might suffice to characterize the classification as reasonable rather than arbitrary and invidious." (McLaughlin v. Florida, 379 U.S. 184, 191, 85 S. Ct. 283, 288, 13 L. Ed. 2d 222, 228, 2d 1964.)

Furthermore, a presumption exists that public officials will discharge their official duties in accordance with law, exercising an honest judgment, and this presumption will be given effect in the absence of clear evidence to the contrary. [Citations omitted.]

---

*Plaintiffs' counsel suggest the following definite improvements:

(1) Street paving costs of $146,000 for asphalting 8,000 feet of 50-foot wide streets and 11,000 feet of 30-foot wide streets.

(2) Sanitary sewer costs of $10,000 for laying 4,000 additional feet of line in Reeder Addition and along Elm and Canal Streets.

(3) Street light costs of $3,100 for replacing every existing street light in the black neighborhoods with mercury vapor fixtures.

(4) Water main costs of $50,000 (in excess of the 50 percent local contribution, $55,000, for the HUD project) to install new water mains and new fire hydrants in certain Negro neighborhoods.

Plaintiffs would avoid the application of these well settled legal principles by claiming that they have been denied the equal protection of the laws as guaranteed by the Fourteenth Amendment, that they have made out a prima facie case of racial and economic discrimination by showing long-continued statistical disparities between white and black neighborhoods in the services provided by the town, and that defendants have failed to explain such disparities upon rational grounds unrelated to race or poverty. While plaintiffs cite no case making that formula generally applicable to all municipal services, yet it is not to be doubted that "[t]he Equal Protection Clause reaches the exercise of state power *however manifested*, whether exercised directly or through subdivisions of the State." (Emphasis added.) Avery v. Midland County, 390 U.S. 474, 479, 88 S. Ct. 1114, 1117, 20 L. Ed. 2d 45, 51.

It is equally true that, since the central purpose of the Fourteenth Amendment was to eliminate racial discrimination emanating from a state's official sources, "racial classifications are constitutionally suspect," subject to the "most rigid scrutiny," and they are "in most circumstances irrelevant to any constitutionally acceptable legislative purpose." McLaughlin v. Florida, supra, 379 U.S. at 192, 85 S. Ct. at 288. Where racial classifications are involved, the Equal Protection and Due Process Clauses of the Fourteenth Amendment "command a more stringent standard" in reviewing discretionary acts of state or local officers. Jackson v. Godwin, 400 F.2d 529, 537 (5 Cir. 1968).

Plaintiffs have compiled certain statistics which they claim support a charge that defendants and their predecessors in office have racially classified the black and white neighborhoods by providing better or more complete facilities to the latter neighborhoods, but they would ignore all legitimate deductions to be made from the evidence running counter to statistical racial disparity. But we do not understand that a court may adopt that manner of reasoning. If actions of public officials are shown to have rested upon rational considerations, irrespective of race or poverty, they are not within the condemnation of the Fourteenth Amendment, and may not be properly condemned upon judicial review. Persons or groups who are treated differently must be shown to be similarly situated and their unequal treatment demonstrated to be without any rational basis or based upon an invidious factor such as race. Davis v. Georgia State Board of Education, 408 F.2d 1014 (5 Cir. 1969).

In this case, the fundamental fact emerging from the evidence is that, historically, the town's municipal officers, whether due to an almost static population, limited finances, or adverse economic factors, have long followed a policy of slowly providing basic municipal services to the town's inhabitants. Until the recent past, the municipal policy might be characterized by some as conservative and unprogressive, with no more than $50,000 public improvement bonds having ever been issued. The town, operating on a pay-as-you-go management, has simply not made improvements of the size and character that might be expected under more liberal minded government. That was, apparently, the kind of local government preferred by Shaw's citizens. In any case, cautious fiscal policy dominated the town until recent times, beginning not earlier than 1955. Consequently, some needed facilities were not enjoyed by anyone; they simply did not exist. For example, not until a recent date were any of the residential streets in white or black neighborhoods asphalted except those forming a state highway, or fronting upon commercial or industrial enterprises, or serving school or other public buildings. Resurfacing of these streets at periodic intervals is a maintenance necessity; the use of these streets is of basic importance to the great majority of the town's inhabitants; and their reworking and resurfacing cannot be rationally delayed until all residential streets are paved with asphalt. The streets selected for asphalt paving, in the programs initiated in the past 15 years, have been usually based upon general usage, traffic needs, adequate rights of way and other objective criteria. Also, lack of zoning regulations and haphazard subdivision dedications have hampered the town in its ability to pave all streets; the necessity for acquiring rights of way and easements in order first to properly lay sewers and then adequate street surfacing has accounted for some delay in project fulfillment. Modern sanitary sewers, by any standard certainly considered a necessity, were not installed in any part of the town until 1963. While the complaint about less than 100 percent sanitary sewerage for all residences is certainly a real one, that condition arises basically from the fact that local law does not yet require indoor plumbing. The lack of sanitary sewers in certain areas of the town is not the result of racial discrimination in withholding a vital service; rather it is a consequence of not requiring, through a proper housing code, certain minimal conditions for inhabited housing. Assuredly, a federal court is not called upon to order the adoption of a housing code by a municipality for the forcing of usage by all of a central sewerage system, and yet the lack of precisely that is a fundamental problem confronting plaintiffs.

By like token, poor drainage is a problem affecting all, both white and Negro alike, that is related to need for major dredging and channel work in Porters Bayou, and may be solved only by major corrective program. Defendants' assertions that they have not discriminated because of race or poverty are supported by substantial, rational considerations explaining the quality and quantity of presently available town's services. These facts negative plaintiffs' assertions of racial and economic discrimination. Marshall v. Mayor and Board of Selectmen of McComb, Mississippi, 251 Miss. 750, 171 So. 2d 347 (1965).

Finally, the nature of the relief sought by plaintiffs in their class action directly involves the exercise of administrative judgment in diverse areas of local government. This is a field in which courts should be reluctant to enter because of their incompetence, generally, to bring about a better result than officials chosen by the local inhabitants. This observation is particularly appropriate as to the Town of Shaw, where Negro citizens have voting power approximately equal to that of white citizens. Such problems as plaintiffs have disclosed by the evidence, and which, in our opinion, do not constitute an abridgement of their constitutional rights, are to be resolved at the ballot box. It is that remedy and not injunctive relief which plaintiffs must seek.

An order dismissing the complaint will be entered.

QUESTIONS

See Willoughby, The Quiet Alliance, 30 S. Calif. L. Rev. 72 (1965). The index to the brief amicus curiae, Joint Center for Urban Studies of M.I.T. and Harvard University, in appealing the case to the Fifth Circuit, reads as follows:

"Argument. I. The Plaintiff-Appellants in This Municipal Services Equalization Suit Having Made Out a Prima Facie Case of Racial Discrimination Through the Introduction of Uncontroverted Statistical Evidence of Substantial Racial Disparity in the Provision of Existing Designated Services, the Trial Court Erred in Failing to Require of the Defendants Positive Evidence of a Rationale of These Statistics Which Would Overcome the Established Inference of Constitutionally Forbidden Discrimination.

"A. In The Presence Of A Prima Facie Case of Racial Discrimination, A Trial Court Engaged In The Task Of Selecting The Judicial Standard For Equal Protection Review Cannot Indulge Presumptions Of Regularity Concerning The Defendants' Official Discharge Of Their Local Governmental Offices; Propound Speculative Deductions Of Alternative Rationale; Or, Rely Upon The Defendants' Professions Of An Absence Of Discriminatory Intent Or Purpose So As To Defeat The Plaintiffs' Bid For The Rigorous Standard Of Equal Protection Scrutiny.

"Any question as to the Defendants' motive is irrelevant.

"Since motive was immaterial, the Court was precluded from according any weight to Defendants' protestations that they intended no discrimination.

"The trial court was debarred from indulging either speculative deductions or presumptions in order to assist the Defendants in the discharge of their burden to refute the Plaintiffs' prima facie case by direct evidence which would explain the unchallenged statistical disparity under a rationale other than racial discrimination.

"B. When The Plaintiffs' Statistical Evidence Of Racial Disparity Was Accompanied By An Allegation That The Entire Existing Pattern Was Typical Of A History of Unequal Provision, The Trial Court Erred In Failing To Recognize An Independent Ground For Judicial Concern Which Ought To Intensify The Defendants' Affirmative Obligation To Adduce Positive Evidence In Support Of A Persuasive Alternative Rationale.

"II. Since the Plaintiffs' Case Below Rested Explicitly Upon a Charge of a Denial of Equal Protection as Guaranteed by the Fourteenth Amendment, it is the Responsibility of this Court to Independently Appraise the Evidence As It Relates to the Alleged Constitutional Right."

Is there a common law duty to provide equal (and adequate) municipal services? Would such a doctrine be preferable to equal protection litigation? See Crownhill Homes, Inc. v. City of San Antonio, 433 S.W.2d 448, 462 (Tex. Civ. App. 1968) (Sharpe, J., dissenting); Veach v. City of Phoenix, 102 Ariz. 195, 427 P.2d 335 (1967); Reid Development Corp. v. Parsippany-Troy Hills Township, 10 N.J. 229, 89 A.2d 667 (1952).

See Fessler and Haar, "Beyond the Wrong Side of the Tracks; Municipal Services in the Interstices of Procedure." 6 Harvard Civil Rights—Civil Liberties Law Review 441, 1972.

Hawkins v. Town of Shaw, Mississippi
464 F. 2d 1171 (5th Cir. 1972)

Per Curiam:

The court, having been convened En Banc and having heard additional oral argument and considered additional briefs, reaffirms the judgment entered by the original panel of this court, 5 Cir. 1971, 437 F.2d 1286. The court, however, makes the following statements dealing with some of the issues raised either originally or by Petition for Rehearing. . . .

I

In order to prevail in a case of this type it is not necessary to prove intent, motive or purpose to discriminate on the part of city officials. We feel that the law on this point is clear, for " 'equal protection of the laws' means more than merely the absence of governmental action designed to discriminate. . . .

'we now firmly recognize that the *arbitrary quality of thoughtlessness* can be as disastrous and unfair to private rights and to public interest as the perversity of a willful scheme'." (Emphasis supplied.)

Moreover, in our judgment the facts before us squarely and certainly support the reasonable and logical inference that there was here neglect involving clear overtones of racial discrimination in the administration of governmental affairs of the town of Shaw resulting in the same evils which characterize an intentional and purposeful disregard of the principle of equal protection of the laws.

Federal Courts are reluctant to enter the field of local government operations. The conduct of municipal affairs is "an extremely awkward vehicle to manage." It is apparent from our original opinion, and we repeat here, that we do not imply or suggest that every disparity of services between citizens of a town or city creates a right of access to the federal courts for redress. We deal only with the town of Shaw, Mississippi, and the facts as developed in this record.

II

We have carefully reviewed the record here, and it appears that various persons in the class of plaintiffs sought relief as to some of the services in question from the municipal government prior to filing suit. Although the district court found to the contrary, we do not think that finding can stand as to all of the services in view of the evidence on this point in the record. There can, therefore, be no question about the claim here being ripe for presentation to the United States Courts under the provisions of 42 U.S.C. § 1983 and 28 U.S.C. § 1343. . . .

Applying the foregoing standards, it is our opinion that the case under consideration is the type of case in which federal jurisdiction should be exercised. Having reached that conclusion all that remains is to choose an appropriate remedy and to frame the appropriate relief.

III

Here the original panel directed defendants to submit a plan to eliminate the disparities to the district court. This was a sound approach under the facts of this case. This is not to say, of course, that in another case involving deprivation of rights under Section 1983 requirement of the submission of a plan by the defendant governmental authority would be the most appropriate remedy. In some situations, presenting a simple issue, the case may be finally disposed of on appeal. In others the case may well be remanded to the district court, after a determination of the rights of the parties, for the purpose of permitting the trial court to exercise its full equitable discretion in the first instance. Here, however, the matter had received extended attention in the district court. All possible facts were available to the court. Also, according to statements at the time of oral argument, a bi-racial committee has been appointed by the municipal governing authorities to advise with the mayor and counsel regarding city services. A black citizen had been elected to the city council. These facts, taken together, would seem to indicate the feasibility of a remedy whereunder the municipal authorities will formulate a plan to eliminate the disparities. Once formulated, the plan will, of course, be subject to approval by the district court.

The judgment is reversed and remanded for further proceedings not inconsistent herewith.

QUESTIONS

1. In James v. Valtierra, 402 U.S. 137 (1971), the constitutional article under attack provided that no low-rent housing project should be developed unless approved by a majority of those voting at a community election. The majority (per Black, J.) upheld it as a "procedure for democratic decision making". The

dissent argued that "singling out the poor to bear a burden not placed on any other class of citizens tramples the values that the Fourteenth Amendment was designed to protect."

2. In San Antonio Independent School District v. Rodriguez, 41 U.S.L.W. 4407 (Mar. 21, 1973), the court upheld the Texas system of public school finance based on the local property tax. It held that this is not a proper case in which to examine a state's laws under standards of strict judicial scrutiny. The court reasoned, first, that the Texas system does not disadvantage any suspect class. It has not been shown to discriminate against any definable class of "poor" people or to occasion discriminations depending on the relative wealth of the families in any district. The court further reasoned that insofar as the financing system disadvantages those who, disregarding their individual income characteristics, reside in comparatively poor taxable property districts, the resulting class cannot be said to be suspect. For an earlier opposing view, see Serrano v. Priest, 5 Cal. 3d 601 (1971). For a later one, see Robinson v. Cahill, N.J. Supreme Ct., A-58 September Term, 1972.

3. In Dandridge v. Williams, 397 U.S. 471 (1970), the Supreme Court upheld the constitutionality of a Maryland statute which placed a maximum limit on the amount of welfare aid a family could collect regardless of the number of children in the family. The court stated that while "[t]he administration of public welfare assistance ... involves the most basic economic needs of impoverished human beings ... the Fourteenth Amendment gives the federal courts no power to impose upon the states their views of wise economic or social policy."

4. Must the decisions in Dandridge and Valtierra be considered serious barriers to challenges to exclusionary zoning under the equal protection clause? If so, how can you argue in a law forum that the holdings should be read narrowly along with the facts of the cases. See generally Lefcoe, The Public Housing Referendum Case, Zoning, and the Supreme Court, 59 Calif. L. Rev. 1384 (1971); The Supreme Court, 1970 Term, 85 Harv. L. Rev. 3, 122-34 (1971); Comment, James v. Valtierra: Housing Discrimination by Referendum?, 39 U. Chi. L. Rev. 115 (1971); Note, The Equal Protection Clause and Exclusionary Zoning After Valtierra and Dandridge, 67 Yale L. J. 61, 72-83 (1972).

5. In Lindsey v. Normet, 405 U.S. 56 (1972), the Court rejected the argument that strict scrutiny should be applied in judging Oregon's judicial procedure for eviction of tenants after nonpayment of rent. The tenants contended "that the 'need for decent shelter' and the 'right to retain peaceful possession of one's home' are fundamental interests which are particularly important to the poor and which may be touched upon only after the state demonstrates some superior interest." Justice White replied: "We do not denigrate the importance of decent,

safe and sanitary housing. But the Constitution does not provide judicial remedies for every social and economic ill. We are unable to perceive in that document any constitutional guarantee of access to dwellings of a particular quality or any recognition of the right of a tenant to occupy the real property of his landlord beyond the term of his lease, without the payment of rent.... Absent constitutional mandate, the assurance of adequate housing and the definition of landlord-tenant relationships is a legislative not a judicial function."

Justice Douglas dissented in part, on due process grounds. He stated that "where the right is so fundamental as the tenant's claim to his home, the requirements of due process should be more embracing than in the ordinary case."

6. The National Association of Building Manufacturers and the National Association of Home Builders joined the National Tenants Organization and the National Committee Against Discrimination in Housing in asking the Supreme Court to allow an amicus curiae brief in Valtierra. (The Court denied leave to file the amicus brief.) Babcock, The Courts Enter the Land Development Marketplace, 5 City 58, at 60.

National corporations with considerable capital are diversifying their market ambitions and moving into the housing field. What kind of coincidence of goals is there when the Suburban Action Institute wants to put housing in New Jersey suburbs, and Alcoa, Boise Cascade, ITT, and Westinghouse would like to see it there as well?

Not all home builders support efforts to build suburban low- and moderate-income housing. Many smaller builders joined in the challenge to the Fairfax County Zoning Ordinance noted above at p. 362. Are small, local suburban builders who are used to building luxury housing generally opposed to changes in exclusionary land-use laws? Why do local builders choose to side with their localities? Because they live there? Because they do not want competition from outside builders who would invade their territory, once high-density building becomes possible? Because they have close ties with the power structure in the communities where they work? Might they be unaware of the potential profitability of high-density building?

Southern Burlington Co. NAACP v. Twp. of Mt. Laurel
119 N.J. Super. 164, 290 A. 2d 465 (1972)

....It must be conceded that there is a general principle against judicial inquiry into the exercise by a legislative body of its police powers. Courts have always had the power to scrutinize the issue of discrimination. The pleadings, the evidence and the issues framed in this action evoke judicial review beyond that posed by a generalized exercise of police power. The inquiry here was not limited to the terms of the ordinance; the court received evidence of the ordinance's purpose, its ultimate objective and all the circumstances attending its adoption and enforcement.

The problems which zoning has raised were nurtured by the decision of our United States Supreme Court in Village of Euclid v. Ambler Realty Co., 272 U.S. 365, 47 S. Ct. 114, 71 L. Ed. 303 (1926). Those who oppose multi-family dwelling units find solace in the words of the late Justice Sutherland, who described multiple-family dwellings as very often a mere parasite whose presence utterly destroys the residential character of the neighborhood and its desirability as a place of residence. While the *Euclid* decision may have in effect condoned legislative zoning discretion, it did warn that:

> It is not meant by this, however, to exclude the possibility of cases where the general public interest would so far outweigh the interest of the municipality that the municipality would not be allowed to stand in the way. [272 U.S. at 390, 47 S. Ct. at 119, 71 L. Ed. at 311] . . .

Today, when municipalities give reasons for the exclusion of certain uses, although they gloss them with high-meaning phrases, they lack sincerity. It is not low-cost housing which ferments crime; it is the lower economic strata of society which moves in, yet no ordinance would dare to raise that objection to prohibit them and expect to succeed. Local legislative bodies know better than to state that more low-income producing structures will mean a higher tax rate. This is what the courts have abhorred as fiscal zoning. What local governing body would raise an objection to bringing a factory into a neighborhood because it would increase the population of the economically poor? While it may be an argument that it would affect property values, and while it is proper to zone in certain instances against factories, it is improper to build a wall against the poor-income people. In Gomillion v. Lightfoot, 364 U.S. 339, 81 S. Ct. 125, 5 L. Ed. 2d 110 (1960), the court made it clear that the Constitution nullifies sophisticated as well as simple-minded modes of discrimination. . . .

The judiciary cannot be expected to alleviate a condition that definitely calls for legislative action from either the national or state governments. The courts can only meet each specific situation as it is presented, and while one community may have facts which justify court intervention, the relief will not necessarily be the same in all areas unless the factual content justifies intervention, as this court believes in the case at hand. The Federal Government has left zoning problems to the states, and the states have largely, but not entirely, left them to the local governments. Housing, to be adequate for the poor, must be left primarily in the hands of a governmental body other than a local unit. The judiciary can only expect to give relief on a piecemeal basis, and "legislation" by the courts is often less than satisfactory.

Ever mindful of the admonitions set forth in the Constitutional mandate of the New Jersey Constitution, Art. IV, § VII, par. 11, enjoining liberal construction of provisions in that document and of laws concerning local government, I would parrot the words of Justice Hall in his dissent in *Vickers, supra*, 37 N.J. at 257, 181 A.2d at 143, when he said, "Analysis demonstrates that the mandate has no true application in this situation."

There has been too much conservatism in the definition of the words which refer to one of the purposes of zoning, *i.e.*, "to promote the general welfare." Some definitions would better apply to private welfare.

Our present State Supreme Court, in a different setting, said:

> We specifically hold, as matter of law in the light of public policy and the law of the land, that public or, as here, semi-public housing accommodations to provide safe, sanitary and decent housing, to relieve and replace substandard living conditions or to furnish housing for minority or underprivileged segments of the population outside of ghetto areas is a special reason adequate to meet that requirement of N.J.S.A. 40:55-39(d) and to ground a use variance. [DeSimone v. Greater Englewood Housing Corp. No. 1, 56 N.J. 428, 442, 267 A.2d 31, 38-39 (1970)]

The patterns and practice clearly indicate that defendant municipality through its zoning ordinances has exhibited economic discrimination in that the poor have been deprived of adequate housing and the opportunity to secure the construction of subsidized housing, and has used federal, state, county and local finances and resources solely for the betterment of middle- and upper-income persons. The zoning ordinance is, therefore, declared invalid.

Plaintiffs, in seeking declaratory and injunctive relief, argue that even if the zoning ordinance were declared invalid, the injury they suffer will not afford a remedy. They argue there is a desperate need for affirmative municipal action within parameters established by the court.

In Hawkins v. Shaw, 437 F.2d 1286, 1293 (5 Cir. 1971), the Court declared that a municipality cannot discriminate in the use of municipal services and said that a town could be required to submit a plan for the equitable distribution of such services. See also, Crow v. Brown, 332 F. Supp. 382 (N.D.Ga. 1971), aff'd 457 F.2d 788 (5 Cir. 1972).

This court agrees with plaintiffs and, therefore, orders that defendant municipality shall, upon the entry of a judgment to conform with these findings and conclusions of law, immediately undertake a study to identify:

a. The existing substandard dwelling units in the township and the number of individuals and families, by income and size, who would be displaced by an effective code-enforcement program;

b. The housing needs for persons of low and moderate income:
  1. Residing in the township;
  2. Presently employed by the municipality or in commercial and industrial uses in the township;
  3. Expected or projected to be employed by the municipality or in commercial and industrial uses, the development of which can reasonably be anticipated in the township.

Defendant shall, upon completion of the investigation referred to in the preceding paragraph, establish, to the extent possible, an estimated number of both low- and moderate-income units which should be constructed in the township each year to provide for the needs as identified in the preceding paragraph.

Defendant shall, upon completion of the analysis set forth in the preceding paragraphs, develop a plan of implementation, that is, an affirmative program, to enable and encourage the satisfaction of the needs as previously set forth. That plan shall include an analysis of the ways in which the township can act affirmatively to enable and encourage the satisfaction of the indicated needs and shall include a plan of action which the township has chosen for the purposes of implementing this program. The adopted plan shall encompass the most effective and thorough means by which municipal action can be utilized to accomplish the goals set forth above.

If for any reason the township shall find that circumstances exist which in any way interfere with or bar the implementation of the plan chosen, it shall set forth in explicit detail:

a. Each and every factor;
b. The way in which each factor interferes with or bars implementation of the plan;
c. Possible alternative plans or municipal action which temporarily or permanently, wholly or in part, eliminate the indicated factor or factors, and
d. The reason why the alternative plans have not been adopted.

To the extent possible, the aforementioned analysis, studies and plans shall be undertaken with the cooperation and participation of plaintiffs and their representatives.

The aforementioned analyses, studies, development of plans and other action shall be completed within 90 days from the date of judgment. The township shall serve copies of the analyses, studies and plans on plaintiffs' attorney and this court within 90 days. The parties shall appear before this court no later than ten days, or on a date set by this court, after service of said papers for a determination of whether defendants have complied with the order of this court and whether further action is necessary.

The judgment entered in this matter as to the invalidity of the zoning ordinance shall not become effective until this court shall decide that sufficient time has elapsed to enable the municipality to enact new and proper regulations for the municipality. Morris County Land, etc. v. Parsippany-Troy Hills, 40 N.J. 539, 193 A.2d 232 (1963).

This court retains jurisdiction until a final order issues requiring implementation of the plan as agreed upon.

QUESTIONS

1. In Bradley v. Milliken, Nos. 72-1809 and 1814, (6th Cir., December 8, 1972) the Sixth Circuit upheld a district court's conclusion that relief of segregation in the public schools of the City of Detroit could not be accomplished within the corporate geographical limits of the city. The Sixth Circuit declined to follow the recent conflicting precedent of the Fourth Circuit in Bradley v. School Bd. of City of Richmond, Va., 472 F.2d 318 (4th Cir. 1972).

What are the implications of this line of reasoning for metropolitan housing? When a state has undertaken to create local public housing authorities and has permitted them to operate in a discriminatory fashion, might an order contemplating metropolitan relief be permissible, desirable, or necessary? What if there is no other "feasible way" to correct the effects of past housing discrimination?

The opinion in Bradley v. Milliken emphasizes the facts that public education is a responsibility of the State of Michigan and that local school districts are state instrumentalities created "for administrative convenience." Does this limit the application of the theory only to certain forms of housing? Is all privately sponsored housing unrelated to the state? Although the provision of privately sponsored housing is not a function of the state, the number of state housing finance agencies assisting such housing development has grown rapidly over the last few years. Might Bradley v. Milliken reasoning call into question a system of delegation of zoning power to localities which could be shown inevitably to confine minorities to the central city?

2. The remarkable extent of potential judicial intervention and the virtues and vices of this method of fashioning institutions on the metropolitan level is revealed in Mahaley v. Cuyahoga Metropolitan Housing Authority, (N.D. Ohio 1973). The court found that the failure of defendant Cleveland suburbs to work with the city's metropolitan housing authority had "the clear effect of discriminating against Negroes by excluding them from residing in these suburban municipalities and perpetuating existing racial concentration and segregation within the individual suburbs and throughout the metropolitan area." The defendant suburbs had refused to sign cooperation agreements necessary for the housing authority in providing low-income housing in these communities. The court offered the following solution:

A second solution has been proposed. CMHA is ordered to prepare a plan setting forth the number of scattered site units it intends to place in each of the defendant suburbs. The plan should reflect the needs of each suburban city for low-income and elderly housing, and should indicate the number of units which would be used to house those residents of the City of Cleveland who wish to move into that community. In preparing the plan CMHA should examine the needs of each suburban community in Cuyahoga County, recognizing that it can only be effectuated as to the defendant suburban cities. It should not include specific locations in each suburb, but should rather reflect a numerical need. The plan is to be submitted within 90 days. Objections and any counterproposals are to be submitted 90 days thereafter by the plaintiffs and the defendants. Included in the objections should be an analysis of the reasons why the defendant suburbs can not absorb the number of houses which CMHA desires to build there. This court recognizes that it is the responsibility of the defendant suburbs to accept their constitutional obligation in this matter. Therefore it encourages that during the next 180 days negotiations be begun with CMHA in order that an amicable resolution be attained. Should negotiations prove fruitless, a hearing will be held soon after the receipt of the objections. It is anticipated that the cities may offer some reasons in opposition to CMHA's plan. Unless the reasons presented at the subsequent hearing are constitutionally permissible and meet the compelling interest test, there will be no alternative but to conclude that the suburbs' failure to sign a Cooperation Agreement is for a constitutionally impermissible reason, to wit: racial discrimination and appropriate judicial action will be undertaken.

Regional considerations—the interest of the larger community, a community found and defined despite the absence of formal territorial definition or physical demarcation—are eloquently explored in the majority and dissenting opinions of the New York Court of Appeals in the following case. Here all the general talk about interrelationships and coordination come to a crunch when the parties present specific issues to the decision maker. The case involves a rapidly growing suburb of New York City.

Golden v. Planning Board of Town of Ramapo, 30 N.Y. 2d 359, 285 N.E. 2d 291 (1972)

SCILEPPI, Judge

... Experiencing the pressures of an increase in population and the ancillary problem of providing municipal facilities and services, the Town of Ramapo, as early as 1964, made application for grant under section 801 of the Housing Act of 1964 (78 U.S. Stat. 769) to develop a master plan. The plan's preparation included a four-volume study of the existing land uses, public facilities, transportation, industry and commerce, housing needs and projected population trends. The master plan was followed by the adoption of a comprehensive zoning ordinance. Additional sewage district and drainage studies were undertaken which culminated in the adoption of a capital budget, providing for the development of the improvements specified in the master plan within the next six years. Pursuant to section 271 of the Town Law, authorizing comprehensive planning, and as a supplement to the capital budget, the Town Board adopted a capital program which provides for the location and sequence of additional capital improvements for the 12 years following the life of the capital budget. The two plans, covering a period of 18 years, detail the capital improvements projected for maximum development and conform to the specifications set forth in the master plan, the official map and drainage plan.

Based upon these criteria, the Town subsequently adopted the subject [zoning] amendments for the alleged purpose of eliminating premature subdivision and urban sprawl. Residential development is to proceed according to the provision of adequate municipal facilities and services, with the assurance that any concomitant restraint upon property use is to be of a "temporary" nature and that other private uses, including the construction of individual housing, are authorized.

The amendments did not rezone or reclassify any land into different residential or use districts, but, for the purposes of implementing the proposals appearing in the comprehensive plan, consist, in the main, of additions to the definitional sections of the ordinance, section 46-3, and the adoption of a new class of "Special Permit Uses", designated "Residential Development Use." "Residential Development Use" is defined as "The erection or construction of dwellings on any vacant plots, lots or parcels of land," and, any person who acts so as to come within that definition, "shall be deemed to be engaged in residential development which shall be a separate use classification under this ordinance and subject to the requirement of obtaining a special permit from the Town Board."

The standards for the issuance of special permits are framed in terms of the availability to the proposed subdivision plat of five essential facilities or services: specifically (1) public sanitary sewers or approved substitutes; (2) drainage facilities; (3) improved public parks or recreation facilities, including public schools; (4) State, county or town roads—major, secondary or collector; and, (5) firehouses. No special permit shall issue unless the proposed residential development has accumulated 15 development points, to be computed on a sliding scale of values assigned to the specified improvements under the statute. Subdivision is thus a function of immediate availability to the proposed plat of certain municipal improvements; the avowed purpose of the amendments being to phase residential development to the Town's ability to provide the above facilities or services.

Certain savings and remedial provisions are designed to relieve of potentially unreasonable restrictions. Thus, the board may issue special permits vesting a present right to proceed with residential development in such year as the development meets the required point minimum, but in no event later than the final year of the 18-year capital plan. The approved special use permit is fully assignable, and improvements scheduled for completion within one year from the date of an application are to be credited as though existing on the date of the application. A prospective developer may advance the date of subdivision approval by agreeing to provide those improvements which will bring the proposed plat within the number of development points required by the amendments. And applications are authorized to the "Development Easement Acquisition Commission" for a reduction of the assessed valuation. Finally, upon application to the Town Board, the development point requirements may be varied should the board determine that such a variance or modification is consistent with the on-going development plan.

The undisputed effect of these integrated efforts in land use planning and development is to provide an over-all program of orderly growth and adequate facilities through a sequential development policy commensurate with progressing availability and capacity of public facilities. While its goals are clear and its purposes undisputably laudatory, serious questions are raised as to the manner in which these ends are to be effected, not the least of which relates to their legal viability under present zoning enabling legislation, particularly sections 261 and 263 of the Town Law. The owners of the subject premises argue, and the Appellate Division has sustained the proposition, that the primary purpose of the amending ordinance is to control or regulate population growth within the Town and as such is not within the authorized objectives of the zoning enabling legislation. We disagree.

In enacting the challenged amendments, the Town Board has sought to control subdivision in all residential districts, pending the provision (public or private) at some future date of various services and facilities. A reading of the relevant statutory provisions reveals that there is no specific authorization for the "sequential" and "timing" controls adopted here. That, of course, cannot be said to end the matter, for the additional inquiry remains as to whether the challenged amendments find their basis within the perimeters of the devices authorized and purposes sanctioned under current enabling legislation. Our concern is, as it should be, with the effects of the statutory scheme taken as a whole and its role in the propagation of a viable policy of land use and planning.

Towns, cities and villages lack the power to enact and enforce zoning or other land use regulations. The exercise of that power, to the extent that it is lawful, must be founded upon a legislative delegation to so proceed, and in the absence of such a grant will be held *ultra vires* and void.... That delegation, set forth in section

261 of the Town Law, is not, however, coterminous with stated police power objectives and has been considered less inclusive traditionally. Hence, although the power to zone must be exercised under the aegis of the police power, indeed must inevitably find justification for its exercise in some aspect of the same, the recital of police power purposes in the grant attests more to the drafters' attempts to specify a valid constitutional predicate than to detail authorized zoning purposes. The latter, "legitimate zoning purposes," are incorporated in accompanying section 263 and are designed to secure safety from various calamities, to avoid undue concentration of population and to facilitate "adequate provision of transportation, water, sewerage, schools, parks and other public requirements." In the end, zoning properly effects, and only in the manner prescribed, those purposes detailed under section 263 of the Town Law. It may not be invoked to further the general police powers of a municipality. . . .

Even so, considering the activities enumerated by section 261 of the Town Law, and relating those powers to the authorized purposes detailed in section 263, the challenged amendments are proper zoning techniques, exercised for legitimate zoning purposes. The power to restrict and regulate conferred under section 261 includes within its grant, by way of necessary implication, the authority to direct the growth of population for the purposes indicated, within the confines of the township. It is the matrix of land use restrictions, common to each of the enumerated powers and sanctioned goals, a necessary concomitant to the municipalities' recognized authority to determine the lines along which local development shall proceed, though it may divert it from its natural course.

Of course, zoning historically has assumed the development of individual plats and has proven characteristically ineffective in treating with the problems attending subdivision and development of larger parcels, involving as it invariably does, the provision of adequate public services and facilities. To this end, subdivision control purports to guide community development in the directions outlined here, while at the same time encouraging the provision of adequate facilities for the housing, distribution, comfort and convenience of local residents. It reflects in essence, a legislative judgment that the development of unimproved areas be accompanied by provision of essential facilities. (Citations omitted.) And though it may not, in a definitional or conceptual sense be identified with the power to zone, it is designed to complement other land use restrictions, which, taken together, seek to implement a broader, comprehensive plan for community development (see Haar, The Master Plan: An Impermanent Constitution, 20 Law & Contemp. Probs. 353).

It is argued, nevertheless, that the timing controls currently in issue are not legislatively authorized since their effect is to prohibit subdivision absent precedent or concurrent action of the Town, and hence constitutes an unauthorized blanket interdiction against subdivision.

It is, indeed, true that the Planning Board is not in an absolute sense statutorily authorized to deny the right to subdivide. That is not, however, what is sought to be accomplished here. The Planning Board has the right to refuse approval of subdivision plats in the absence of those improvements specified in section 277, and the fact that it is the Town and not the subdividing owner or land developer who is required to make those improvements before the plat will be approved cannot be said to transform the scheme into an absolute prohibition any more than it would be so where it was the developer who refused to provide the facilities required for plat approval. Denial of subdivision plat approval invariably amounts to a prohibition against subdivision, albeit a conditional one; and to say that the Planning Board lacks the authority to deny subdivision rights is to mistake the nature of our inquiry which is essentially whether development may be conditioned pending the provision by the municipality of specified services and facilities. Whether it is the municipality or the developer who is to provide the improvements, the objective is the same—to provide adequate facilities, off-site and on-site; and in either case subdivision rights are conditioned, not denied.

Undoubtedly, current zoning enabling legislation is burdened by the largely antiquated notion which deigns that the regulation of land use and development is uniquely a function of local government—that the public interest of the State is exhausted once its political subdivisions have been delegated the authority to zone. While such jurisdictional allocations may well have been consistent with formerly prevailing conditions and assumptions, questions of broader public interest have commonly been ignored [Citations omitted.]

Experience, over the last quarter century, however, with greater technological integration and drastic shifts in population distribution has pointed up serious defects and community autonomy in land use controls has come under increasing attack by legal commentators, and students of urban problems alike, because of its pronounced insularism and its correlative role in producing distortions in metropolitan growth patterns, and perhaps more importantly, in crippling efforts toward regional and State-wide problem solving, be it pollution, decent housing, or public transportation. [Citations omitted.]

Recognition of communal and regional interdependence, in turn, has resulted in proposals for schemes of regional and State-wide planning, in the hope that decisions would then correspond roughly to their level of impact. Yet, as salutary as such proposals may be, the power to zone under current law is vested in local municipalities, and we are constrained to resolve the issues accordingly. What does become more apparent in treating with the problem, however, is that though the issues are framed in terms of the developer's due process rights, those rights cannot, realistically speaking, be viewed separately and apart from the rights of others "in search of a [more] comfortable place to live."

There is, then, something inherently suspect in a scheme which, apart from its professed purposes, effects a restriction upon the free mobility of a people until sometime in the future when projected facilities are available to meet increased demands. Although zoning must include schemes designed to allow municipalities to more effectively contend with the increased demands of evolving and growing communities, under its guise, townships have been wont to try their hand at an array of exclusionary devices in the hope of avoiding the very burden which growth must inevitably bring. Though the conflict engendered by such tactics is certainly real, and its implications vast, accumulated evidence, scientific and social, points circumspectly at the hazards of undirected growth and the naive, somewhat nostalgic imperative that egalitarianism is a function of growth.

Of course, these problems cannot be solved by Ramapo or any single municipality, but depend upon the accommodation of widely disparate interests for their ultimate resolution. To that end, State-wide or regional control of planning would insure that interests broader than that of the municipality underlie various land use policies. Nevertheless, that should not be the only context in which growth devices such as these, aimed at population assimilation, not exclusion, will be sustained; especially where, as here, we would have no alternative but to strike the provision down in the wistful hope that the efforts of the State Office of Planning Coordination and the American Law Institute will soon bear fruit.

Hence, unless we are to ignore the plain meaning of the statutory delegation, this much is clear: phased growth is well within the ambit of existing enabling legislation. And, of course, it is no answer to point to emergent problems to buttress the conclusion that such innovative schemes are beyond the perimeters of statutory authorization. These considerations, admittedly real, to the extent which they are relevant, bear solely upon the continued viability of "localism" in land use regulation; obviously, they can neither add nor detract from the initial grant of authority, obsolescent though it may be. The answer which Ramapo has posed can by no means be termed definitive; it is, however, a first practical step toward controlled growth achieved without forsaking broader social purposes. . .

The subject ordinance is said to advance legitimate zoning purposes as it assures that each new home built in the township will have at least a minimum of public services in the categories regulated by the ordinance. The Town argues that various public facilities are presently being constructed but that for want of time and money it has been unable to provide such services and facilities at a pace commensurate with increased public need. It is urged that although the zoning power includes reasonable restrictions upon the private use of property, exacted in the hope of development according to well-laid plans, calculated to advance the public welfare of the community in the future, the subject regulations go further and seek to avoid the increased responsibilities and economic burdens which time and growth must ultimately bring.

It is the nature of all land use and development regulations to circumscribe the course of growth within a particular town or district and to that extent such restrictions invariably impede the forces of natural growth. Where those restrictions upon the beneficial use and enjoyment of land are necessary to promote the ultimate good of the community and are within the bounds of reason, they have been sustained. Its exercise assumes that development shall not stop at the community's threshold, but only that whatever growth there may be shall proceed along a predetermined course. It is inextricably bound to the dynamics of community life and its function is to guide, not to isolate or facilitate efforts at avoiding the ordinary incidents of growth. What segregates permissible from impermissible restrictions, depends in the final analysis upon the purpose of the restrictions and their impact in terms of both the community and general public interest. The line of delineation between the two is not a constant, but will be found to vary with prevailing circumstances and conditions.

What we will not countenance, then, under any guise, is community efforts at immunization or exclusion. But, far from being exclusionary, the present amendments merely seek, by the implementation of sequential development and timed growth, to provide a balanced cohesive community dedicated to the efficient utilization of land. The restrictions conform to the community's considered land use policies as expressed in its comprehensive plan and represent a bona fide effort to maximize population density consistent with orderly growth. True, other alternatives, such as requiring off-site improvements as a prerequisite to subdivision, may be available, but the choice as how best to proceed, in view of the difficulties attending such exactions, cannot be faulted.

Perhaps even more importantly, timed growth, unlike the minimum lot requirements recently struck down by the Pennsylvania Supreme Court as exclusionary, does not impose permanent restrictions upon land use. Its obvious purpose is to prevent premature subdivision absent essential municipal facilities and to insure continuous development commensurate with the Town's obligation to provide such facilities. They seek, not to freeze population at present levels but to maximize growth by the efficient use of land, and in so doing testify to this community's continuing role in population assimilation. In sum, Ramapo asks not that it be left alone, but only that it be allowed to prevent the kind of deterioration that has transformed well-ordered and thriving residential communities into blighted ghettos with attendant hazards to health, security and social stability—a danger not without substantial basis in fact.

We only require that communities confront the challenge of

population growth with open doors. Where in grappling with that problem, the community undertakes, by imposing temporary restrictions upon development, to provide required municipal services in a rational manner, courts are rightfully reluctant to strike down such schemes. The timing controls challenged here parallel recent proposals put forth by various study groups and have their genesis in certain of the pronouncements of this and the courts of sister States. While these controls are typically proposed as an adjunct of regional planning the preeminent protection against their abuse resides in the mandatory on-going planning and development requirement, present here, which attends their implementation and use.

We may assume, therefore, that the present amendments are the product of foresighted planning calculated to promote the welfare of the township. The Town has imposed temporary restrictions upon land use in residential areas while committing itself to a program of development. It has utilized its comprehensive plan to implement its timing controls and has coupled with these restrictions provisions for low and moderate income housing on a large scale. Considered as a whole, it represents both in its inception and implementation a reasonable attempt to provide for the sequential, orderly development of land in conjunction with the needs of the community, as well as individual parcels of land, while simultaneously obviating the blighted aftermath which the initial failure to provide needed facilities so often brings. . . .

We are reminded, however, that these restrictions threaten to burden individual parcels for as long as a full generation and that such a restriction cannot, in any context, be viewed as a temporary expedient. The Town, on the other hand, contends that the landowner is not deprived of either the best use of his land or of numerous other appropriate uses, still permitted within various residential districts, including the construction of a single-family residence, and consequently, it cannot be deemed confiscatory. Although no proof has been submitted on reduction of value, the landowners point to obvious disparity between the value of the property, if limited in use by the subject amendments and its value for residential development purposes, and argue that the diminution is so considerable that for all intents and purposes the land cannot presently or in the near future be put to profitable or beneficial use, without violation of the restrictions.

Every restriction on the use of property entails hardships for some individual owners. Those difficulties are invariably the product of police regulation and the pecuniary profits of the individual must in the long run be subordinated to the needs of the community. [Citations omitted.]

The fact that the ordinance limits the use of, and may depreciate the value of the property will not render it unconstitutional, however, unless it can be shown that the measure is either unreasonable in terms of necessity or the diminution in value is such as to be tantamount to a confiscation.

Without a doubt restrictions upon the property in the present case are substantial in nature and duration. They are not, however, absolute. The amendments contemplate a definite term, as the development points are designed to operate for a maximum period of 18 years and during that period, the Town is committed to the construction and installation of capital improvements. The net result of the on-going development provision is that individual parcels may be committed to a residential development use prior to the expiration of the maximum period. Similarly, property owners under the terms of the amendments may elect to accelerate the date of development by installing, at their own expense, the necessary public services to bring the parcel within the required number of development points. While even the best of plans may not always be realized, in the absence of proof to the contrary, we must assume the Town will put its best effort forward in implementing the physical and fiscal timetable outlined under the plan. Should subsequent events prove this assumption unwarranted, or should the Town because of some unforeseen event fail in its primary obligation to these landowners, there will be ample opportunity to undo the restrictions upon default. For the present, at least, we are constrained to proceed upon the assumption that the program will be fully and timely implemented.

In sum, where it is clear that the existing physical and financial resources of the community are inadequate to furnish the essential services and facilities which a substantial increase in population requires, there is a rational basis for "phased growth" and hence, the challenged ordinance is not violative of the Federal and State Constitutions. Accordingly, the order appealed from should be reversed and the actions remitted to Special Term for entry of a judgment declaring section 46-13.1 of the Town Ordinance constitutional.

BREITEL, Judge (dissenting)

The limited powers of district zoning and subdivision regulation delegated to a municipality do not include the power to impose a moratorium on land development. Such conclusion is dictated by settled doctrine that a municipality has only those powers, and especially land use powers, delegated or necessarily implied.

But there is more involved in these cases than the arrogation of undelegated powers. Raised are vital constitutional issues, and, most important, policy issues trenching on grave domestic problems of our time, without the benefit of a legislative determination which would reflect the interests of the entire State. The policy issues relate to needed housing, planned land development under government control, and the exclusion in effect or by motive, of walled-in urban populations of the middle class and the poor. The issues are raised by a town ordinance, which, as one of the Appellate Division Justices noted below, reflect a parochial stance without regard to its impact on the region or the State, especially if it becomes a valid model for many other towns similarly situated. . . .

It is important to note how radically the Ramapo scheme differs from those used and adopted under existing enabling acts. The zoning acts, starting from 50 years ago, based on national models, provided simply for district zoning to control population density and some planning to protect preferred uses of land, such as single-family dwellings, from other uses considered less desirable or even harmful to residential living or environmental balance. Since the beginning, in this State and elsewhere, by amendment to the enabling acts by the Legislature, provision has been made for subdivision planning and, in some instances, planned unit development, to prevent large-scale developers from dumping homes wholesale in raw land areas without private and, to some extent, public facilities essential to the use of the homes. In more recent years, since World War II, the need for a much enlarged kind of land planning has become critical. The evils of uncontrolled urban sprawl on the one hand, and the suburban and exurban pressure to exclude urban population on the other hand, have created a massive conflict, with social and economic implications of the gravest character. Throughout the nation the conflict has risen or threatened and solutions are being sought in careful, intensive examination of the problem affecting those within and those without the localities to be regulated.

The President's National Commission on Urban Problems has made relevant recommendations, the American Law Institute is engaged in drafting a model land development code, and, in this State, the Office of Planning Coordination is working on a planning code. The conflict has surfaced in other States in efforts by municipalities to cut their own swaths in solving their difficulties, and, in every instance uncovered, the courts have struck down the efforts as unconstitutional or as invalid under enabling acts much like those in this State. Generally, there is the view that the conflict requires solution at a regional or State level, usually with local administration, and not by compounding the conflict with idiosyncratic municipal action. The Ramapo ordinance flies in the face of and would frustrate these well-directed efforts.

Decisive of the present appeals, however, is the absence in the town of legislative authorization to postpone growth, let alone to establish unilaterally phased population levels, through the expedient of barring residential development for scheduled periods of up to 18 years. It has always been the rule that a municipality has only those land use powers delegated or necessarily implied. Existing enabling legislation does not grant the power upon which the Ramapo ordinance rests. And for policy reasons, one should not strain the reading of the enabling acts, even if straining would avail, to distort them, beyond any meaning ever attributed to them, except by the ingenious draftsmen of the Ramapo ordinance.

The enabling acts for the several classes of municipalities in the State are substantially alike. They followed the model acts drafted by the U.S. Department of Commerce in the 1920's, after an earlier zoning effort by New York City in 1916. Since then they have been amended, usually in identical fashion, as the need for broader powers was envisaged and accepted. Article 16 of the Town Law is the enabling act for towns. Section 261 in pertinent part provides: "For the purpose of promoting the health, safety, morals, or the general welfare of the community, the town board is hereby empowered by ordinance to regulate and restrict the height, number of stories and size of buildings and other structures, the percentage of lot that may be occupied, the size of yards, courts, and other open spaces, the density of population, and the location and use of buildings, structures and land for trade, industry, residence or other purposes;". This is a typical district zoning provision. It grants power to define permissible physical characteristics of land and structure; and says nothing about exercising control in time. The town would stretch the reference to "density of population" to give the town the powers it purports to exercise by the ordinance. Section 263, defining the purposes of district zoning, by any standard of statutory construction provides no help. The section reads: "Such regulations shall be made in accordance with a comprehensive plan and designed to lessen congestion in the streets, to secure safety from fire, flood, panic and other dangers; to promote health and general welfare; to provide adequate light and air; to prevent the overcrowding of land; to avoid undue concentration of population; to facilitate the adequate provision of transportation, water, sewerage, schools, parks and other public requirements. Such regulations shall be made with reasonable consideration, among other things, as to the character of the district and its peculiar suitability for particular uses, and with a view to conserving the value of buildings and encouraging the most appropriate use of land throughout such municipality." It does not broaden powers granted. Instead it is intended to be restrictive in two ways: first, by making certain that zoning regulations conform to a master plan; and second, by relating them directly to specified public purposes. In short, district zoning is permitted if, and only if, it is pursuant to a comprehensive plan and it serves the purposes listed.

Going beyond district zoning, the statute provides for subdivision platting. It does not provide support for the procedures essayed in the Ramapo ordinance. But what is important is that even intensive subdivision regulation was required to be authorized by statute before towns could control subdivision developers. Statutory authorization was all the more important because the then drastic regulation required the developers to provide private and public facilities for the wholesale distribution of homes and to provide moneys and bonds to make sure that they performed as promised. Notably, no developer is forbidden to develop for a period of years.

The urgent need to control the tempo and sequence of land development has been recognized by courts, government commissions, and commentators. Techniques to control the rate, nature and sequence of community development are plentiful although not all are presently authorized or comport with constitutional limitations. Thus, in Albrecht Realty Co. v. Town of New Castle, 8 Misc.2d 255, 167 N.Y.S.2d 843, the Town of New Castle in Westchester County sought to control growth by placing a moratorium on the issuance of building permits for unspecified periods and with no apparent object other than controlling growth. The measure was voided because the enabling act did not authorize "a direct regulation of the rate of growth" (at p. 256, 167 N.Y.S.2d at p. 844). For another technique, in California the purchase of "development rights" or a time-limited easement by the local government reportedly has been employed. The community is saved the expense of purchasing the fee simple of the owner. It obtains flexibility by the power to release land for development while landowners are compensated. The method is also said to justify assessing or taxing the owner at a lower rate.

A common technique is minimum area zoning. If it does not amount to prohibitory zoning, minimum lot requirements may be used to regulate the tempo and sequence of land development. Unfortunately, however, the method is often used as an exclusionary or prohibitory device.

Finally, there is the technique sought to be exercised by Ramapo— a technique partaking somewhat of the motivation for and methods used in holding zones.

Holding zones, that is, areas reserved for future development, if legislatively authorized and carefully circumscribed, can validly and effectively implement land planning. Both the interests of localities and the broader interests of the State and its large metropolitan areas can be reconciled. Indeed, it has been suggested by the National Commission on Urban Problems that enabling legislation grant communities such power. The devising and authorization of new powers, one of which is to create holding or delayed development zones, is a chief concern of the State Office of Planning Coordination. Indeed, it plays a prominent role in its proposed legislation. Notably, in delayed development schemes limitations are invariably suggested, limitations absent in the Ramapo ordinance (e.g., 3- to 5-year limits, regional and State agency review, provision for compensation). Such limitations may be essential if the delegation is to be valid constitutionally. Aside from considerations of unlimited delegation, without the standards which universally circumscribe the conduct of administrative agencies, the limitations reflect basic doctrine that even the State's zoning power is not unlimited.

Either by legislation limited by decisional rule, or by decisional rule alone a limited amount of restraint in time has been held valid in controlling development, even without compensation.... Significantly, the time limitations should be brief, or reasonably fixed, and justified by emergency or statutory authorization.

It is not necessary now, as observed later, to confront the serious constitutional issues raised by mandatory delayed development. The crux of the matter in these cases is that before wrestling with the constitutional issues the Ramapo ordinance is destroyed at the threshold. It lacks statutory authorization, and this despite the fact that its reach is more ambitious than any before essayed even with enabling legislation. . . .

There are, to be sure, the constitutional issues in the case. Some relate to the power of government to deprive the landowner of any reasonable use of his land for a period of years, up to 18 years, without compensation. These are knotty problems confronting the draftsmen of a land development code. The problems are not insuperable. The initial, principal land zoning case, Euclid v. Ambler Co., 272 U.S. 365, 47 S.Ct. 114, 71 L.Ed.303, held rather flatly, as far back as 1926, that an owner can be made to suffer a substantial loss in the economic potential of his land without compensation. But it has always been made clear that an owner could not be deprived of all reasonable use nor could his use be postponed for more than a short time, even if only to prevent an overloading of municipal facilities. [Citations omitted.] Be that as it may, for many reasons these constitutional issues are better reserved for future consideration. . . .

[A]lthough the town had no power under the enabling act to adopt the ordinance in question, this does not mean that the town is not faced with a grave problem. It is. So are the many towns and villages in the State, and elsewhere in the country. But there is no doubt that the Ramapos, in isolation, cannot solve their problems alone, legally, under existing laws, or socially, politically, or economically. For the time being, the Ramapos must do what they can with district zoning and subdivision platting control. They may not declare moratoria on growth and development for as much as a generation. They may not separately or in concert impair the freedom of movement or residence of those outside their borders, even by ingenious schemes. Nor is it important whether their intention is to exclude, if that is the effect of their arrogated powers. . . .

As said earlier, when the problem arose outside the State the judicial response has been the same, frustrating communities, intent on walling themselves from the mainstream of development, namely, that the effort was invalid under existing enabling acts or unconstitutional. [Citations omitted.] The response may not be charged to judicial conservatism or self-restraint. In short, it has not been illiberal. It has indeed reflected the larger understanding that American society is at a critical crossroads in the accommodation of urbanization and suburban living, with effects that are no longer confined, bad as they are, to ethnic exclusion or "snob" zoning. . . . Ramapo would preserve its nature, delightful as that may be, but the supervening question is whether it alone may decide this or whether it must be decided by the larger community represented by the Legislature. Legally, politically, economically, and sociologically, the base for determination must be larger than that provided by the town fathers.

Accordingly, I dissent and vote to affirm the orders in both cases.

NOTES

1. The attorney for the Town of Ramapo has written that *Golden* was "not an 'exclusionary' zoning case." He noted the history of Ramapo's acceptance of low-income housing, and emphasized a positive role for zoning:

> ... Ramapo was the first suburban town in New York State to voluntarily develop integrated public housing for low-income families as part of its planning process, despite the objection of thousands of its citizens. The town and the public housing authority were successful in developing two public housing areas with several hundred units of public housing for low-income families. Planning for additional units is now taking place. One public housing area involves industrialized housing and both are located in landscaped, forested areas of incredible beauty, with integrated public schools and neighborhoods. In the process of establishing the public housing under our zoning ordinance, we had to bring and fight several law suits. The supervisor of the town, John F. McAlevey, stood by the public housing and won a sweet victory in the November 1971 election in which public housing was the key issue.
>
> The confusion of many attorneys in the battle against exclusionary zoning is unfortunate. There is a tendency to view all zoning as intrinsically evil simply because some communities utilize these tools in an exclusionary manner. This problem has been around for a long time. Should we go back to no zoning at all, to unlimited urban sprawl and development chaos in suburban areas merely because some of the tools are essentially neutral? They can be used correctly or incorrectly, depending upon the motivation of the regulators. Our efforts must be to eliminate the abuses, while simultaneously developing stronger efforts to preserve the quality of our communities and of the environment. We must assure economic and racial equality *in* planning, not *without* planning. (Frelich, Ramapo Township. Comments of attorney who drafted the Ordinance, 24 Zoning Dig. 72, 73-74 (1972). Cf. Note, Time Controls on Land Use; Prophylactic Law for Planners, 57 Cornell L. Rev. 827 (1972); Note, A Zoning Program for Planned Growth: Ramapo Township's Time Controls on Residential Development, 47 N.Y.U. L.Rev. 723 (1972).)

2. Do you agree that the Ramapo case is not an exclusionary case? What are the social and economic ramifications of Ramapo's decision for the region, metropolitan area, and state? How can you prevent communities from using the case to erect a stronger legal barrier against people who want to move to the suburbs?

Exclusion, purposeful or otherwise, of low-income housing raises central questions regarding the courts and their interpretation of local autonomy to legislate land uses and therefore determine patterns of community life. With the advent of the poverty lawyer and the public interest law firm, there emerge new interpretations of the ancient common law and of the constitutional doctrines applicable to land-use controls. Fresh perspectives on the role of the judiciary and of the separation of powers are in order.

Recognition of the problem of exclusionary zoning has brought about changes on the legislative front in many states, with profound impact on intergovernmental relations. It also has brought the individual into court, and has raised novel issues of standing to sue and of the scope of judicial intervention and of the breadth of court decrees.

Uncertainty as to approval, plus the American belief that all problems are susceptible to some type of rational solution, have led to a bewildering blend of methods for dealing with the central city—suburban split and for implementing the national policy of "a decent home and a suitable living environment for every American family." They are being tested by traditional property and judicial concepts. Part of our job is to analyze the compromise point at which contending forces come to rest, and also to determine which of the many offerings holds the potentials of a fruitful settlement. John Rawls has concluded, "It would appear that we are bound to perform actions which bring about a greater good for others, whatever the cost to ourselves, provided that the sum of advantages altogether exceeds that of other acts open to us." Have the courts, at least, adopted this as a governing principle?

Bibliographic References For Chapter Eleven

1. Aristotle, *Politics*, trans. Benjamin Jowett, reprinted in William Ebestein, *Great Political Thinkers* (New York: Rinehart and Co., 1951).
2. A. Etzioni, ed., *Social Change* (New York, Best Books, 1964), p. 75.
3. W. Moore, "A Reconsideration of Theories of Social Change," *American Sociological Review* 25 (1960): p. 818.
4. Pierre L. van den Berghe, "Dialectic and Functionalism: Toward a Theoretical Synthesis," *American Sociological Review*, vol. 28, no. 5 (October 1963): pp. 695-705.
5. T. Parsons, "Some considerations on the theory of Social Change," *Rural Sociology* 26, no. 3, 1961: pp. 219-239.
6. Ralf Dahrendorf, "Toward a Theory of Social Conflict," *The Journal of Conflict Resolutions*, vol. 11, no. 2 (1958): pp. 170-183.
7. James Q. Wilson and Edward Banfield, "Public Regardingness as a Value Premise in Voting Behavior," *The American Political Science Review*, vol. 58, no. 4 (December 1964): pp. 876-887. See also their *City Politics*, (Cambridge: Harvard University Press, 1963).
· 8. Amos M. Hawley, "Community Power and Urban Renewal Success," *The American Journal of Sociology*, vol. 68, no. 4 (January 1963): pp. 422-431.
Robert L. Crain and Donald B. Rosenthal, "Community Status as a Dimension of Local Decision Making," *The American Sociological Review* vol. 32, no. 6 (December 1967).
Terry N. Clark, ed., "Community Structure and Decision Making," *Community Structure and Decision Making, Comparative Analysis* Chandler 1968, and "Community Structure, Decision Making, Budget Expenditures and Urban Renewal in 51 American Communities," *American Sociological Review* vol. 33, no. 4 (August 1968): pp. 576-593.
9. J.D. Greenstone and P.E. Peterson, "Reformers, Machines, and the War on Poverty" in J. Wilson, ed., *City Politics and Public Policy* (New York: John Wiley & Sons, Inc., 1968): pp. 267-292.

10. Hawley, ibid.
11. Crain and Rosenthal, ibid.
12. Maurice Pinard, "Structural Attachments and Political Support in Urban Politics: The Case of Fluoridation Referenda," *The American Journal of Sociology*, vol. 68, no. 5 (March 1963): pp. 513-526.
13. Thomas R. Dye, "Urban School Segregation: A Comparative Analysis," *Urban Affairs Quarterly*, vol. 55, no. 2 (December 1968): pp. 141-184.
14. Robert Eyestone and Henry Eular, "City Councils and Policy Outcomes: Development People," in *City Politics and Public Policy*, op. cit. pp. 37-65.
15. Robert L. Linesberry and Edmund P. Folb, "Reformism and Public Policies in American Cities," in *City Politics and Public Policy*, op. cit. pp. 97-123.
16. Roland Warren, *Truth, Love and Social Change* (Chicago, Rand McNally, 1971), pp. 12-25.
17. Jack Rothman, "Three Models of Community Organization Practice," in Cox et al., eds., *Strategies of Community Organization* (Itasca, Ill: F.E. Peacock Publishers, Inc., 1970), pp. 20-36.
18. Robert Morris and Robert Binstock, *Feasible Planning for Social Change*, (New York, Columbia University Press, 1966).
19. Martin Rein, "Strategies of Planned Change, *American Orthopsychiatric Association*, 1965.
20. Demetrius S. Iatridis, "Environment: Urban Planning and Development" *Encyclopedia of Social Work*, (New York, National Association of Social Workers, 1971), pp. 310-323.

About the Authors

Charles M. Haar is the Louis D. Brandeis Professor of Law at Harvard University. From 1966 to 1968 he served as Assistant Secretary for Metropolitan Development in the newly formed Department of Housing and Urban Development. Before his appointment of President Johnson's Task Force on Urban Affairs and Housing (1965 and 1966), he was a long-time adviser to President John Kennedy on urban and suburban problems. He was one of the key draftsmen in the development of three of the most significant pieces of legislation of the Johnson administration: The Demonstration and Model Cities Act of 1966; The Safe Streets and Crime Control Act of 1968; and Title IV of the Housing and Urban Development Act of 1968 (New Communities). Mr. Haar has been a regular contributor to legal and planning periodicals. His most recent books are the *Golden Age of American Law* and *The End of Innocence*.

Demetrius S. Iatridis is Research Professor and Professor of Social Policies at Boston College. He holds a concurrent appointment as adjunct Professor of Ekistics and Urban Planning, School of City Planning at the University of Rhode Island. He is a former Director of the Social Welfare Regional Research Institute of HEW for Region I, a former Director of the Graduate School of Ekistics in Athens, and a former Vice President of the Athens Center of Ekistics. He has been Visiting Professor at several universities including Brandeis, Bryn Mawr, and the London School of Architecture. Currently, he is conducting research on suburban housing, social policies for child day care, and a national study on attitudes of lower income groups in Greece. He is the author of *Methods of Interventions for Organizing and Planning the Human Environment*, and has written numerous articles.